Women in the Age
of Shakespeare

WOMEN IN THE AGE
OF SHAKESPEARE

Theresa D. Kemp

THE AGE OF SHAKESPEARE

GREENWOOD PRESS

An Imprint of ABC-CLIO, LLC

A B C ⬥ C L I O

Santa Barbara, California • Denver, Colorado • Oxford, England

Library of Congress Cataloging-in-Publication Data
Kemp, Theresa D.
  Women in the age of Shakespeare / Theresa D. Kemp.
    p. cm. — (The age of Shakespeare)
  Includes bibliographical references and index.
  ISBN 978-0-313-34304-9 (acid-free paper) 1. Shakespeare, William, 1564-1616—
Characters—Women. 2. Women—England—History—Renaissance, 1450-1600.
3. Women—England—History—17th century. 4. Women—England—Social
conditions. 5. Women in literature. I. Title.
  PR2991.K46 2009
  822.3'3—dc22   2009033626

14 13 12 11 10   1 2 3 4 5

This book is also available on the World Wide Web as an eBook.
Visit www.abc-clio.com for details.

ABC-CLIO, LLC
130 Cremona Drive, P.O. Box 1911
Santa Barbara, California 93116-1911

This book is printed on acid-free paper ∞
Manufactured in the United States of America

For Sherpa One and Sherpa Zero
(who really does carry more than "nothing")

CONTENTS

ACKNOWLEDGMENTS

While writing this book, I have incurred many debts to a number of good friends and benefactors. It is with great pleasure and gratitude that I acknowledge their encouragement and support of this project.

As the 2007 Duyfhuizen Professor in English, I thank Duffy and Tricia Duyfhuizen for their generosity. As the recipient of the 2007 Morris Library Outreach Award, I would like to thank the children of John and Elizabeth Morris for funding my library discussion series on "Shakespeare's Women: Bawdy, Wicked, Winsome, and Wise"; thanks, also, to Bess Arneson and the staff of the L.E. Phillips Public Library, as well as to the library patrons who shared with me their wonderful ideas about the women in the plays. I am also grateful to the University of Wisconsin—Eau Claire's Office for Research and Sponsored Programs for a 2007 University Research and Creative Activity (URCA) grant; my department chairs, Marty Wood and Jack Bushnell, kindly endorsed my request for a course release.

I couldn't have written this book without the assistance of the librarians at UWEC's McIntyre Library, who helped obtain many of the books I needed. A special thank-you goes to the Newberry Library and Jim Grossman for providing a lovely and welcoming place to work during the summer of 2007; Jill Gage at the Newberry was especially generous with her time and her knowledge of what high-school kids find interesting at the Newberry. Thanks to Krista Hebel and Patty Greiner for their research assistance and for reading drafts. Over the years, I have been very fortunate to study Shakespeare in the company of hundreds of wonderful students in my regular classes and with high-school students and their teachers through Shakespeare in the Schools. I am especially grateful to them for their many insights, their joy, and their enthusiasm in working with Shakespeare.

If not for the support and encouragement of my friends and loved ones, I'm certain I never would have finished this project. Among them, I especially want to thank John and Rose Battalio; Becky Krug and Brian Goldberg; and Deb Barker for their inspiration, patience, and sense of humor. Most of all, I would need an entire book of its own—actually, a library filled with volumes of pages and words—to properly thank Mike and Taylor Kemp for all the ways in which they sustain me; this book is for them.

ILLUSTRATIONS

CHAPTER 3

Emma Thompson as Princess Katherine and Kenneth Branagh as Henry V (1989). Photofest.

CHAPTER 4

Charlotte Cushman as Romeo and Susan Cushman as Juliet. Lithograph, 1846. Houghton Library, Harvard Theatre Collection.

Peggy Ashcroft as Desdemona and Paul Robeson as Othello (1930). Bettmann/Corbis (U237503AP-A).

Peggy Ashcroft as Desdemona, Paul Robeson as Othello, and Maurice Brown as Iago (1930). Bettmann/Corbis (U237503P-A).

Emil Jannings as Othello and Ica von Lenkeffy as Desdemona in Dimitri Buchowetzki's silent film version (Germany 1922). Photofest.

Claire Danes as Maria and Billy Crudup as Edward "Ned" Kynaston in Stage Beauty (2004). Photofest.

Sarah Bernhardt as Hamlet (ca. 1885–1900). Library of Congress (LOT 3120 (F) [P&P].

Julia Stiles as Ophelia (2000). Photofest.

Claire Danes as Juliet (1996). Photofest.

Olivia Hussey as Juliet and Leonard Whiting as Romeo (1968). Photofest.

Elizabeth Taylor as Katherine Minola and Richard Burton as Petruchio (1967). Photofest.

Elizabeth Taylor as Katherine Minola and Richard Burton as Petruchio (1967). Photofest.

Heath Ledger as Patrick "Pat" Verona and Julia Stiles as Katarina "Kat" Stratford (1999). Photofest.

PREFACE

Weird Sisters
(weird < Old English *wyrd*, fate)
That Macbeth fellow and his biographers got it
all wrong. They saw old women with a taste
for exotic stews and an uncanny eye for character
and turned them into messengers from hell.
Still, we remember which one killed the king.
How easy it is, though, to forget
that we are also Cleopatra wielding
the power of the queen's X, Portia
dispensing justice in a cloudburst. Even
Ophelia, in a different life, might have grown
grey and wrinkled. Fierce with experience,
she might have dreamt of flowers.

Nadine S. St. Louis, *Weird Sisters*

Since their first appearances under the auspices of boy performers, Shakespeare's "women" (and his plays) have been adapted by every succeeding era. Praised as "well-developed"—even "realistic"—his female characters have both shaped and been reshaped in relation to changing ideas about women. Succeeding generations of readers and viewers of the plays have posed the question of how—and even whether—Shakespeare's women do in fact speak to the experiences and cultural expectations set for women, both in Shakespeare's own time and in later ages and places.

This book introduces students and general readers to some of the issues related to the study of women in the Elizabethan and Jacobean eras in general and Shakespeare's works in particular. Central questions will include the following: What sorts of women are represented in the plays (and what kinds of women seem missing)? What rules seem to govern the actions of female characters? In what ways does early modern patriarchy constrict or restrict them? In what ways do they resist patriarchy? In what ways do Shakespeare's female characters seem to collude with patriarchal power? What—and whom—do we mean by "Shakespeare's women"? In pursuit of these questions, we will look at some of the sources for ideas about women in Shakespeare's time and in his plays. We will also trace the responses of critics, readers, performers, and viewers of Shakespeare's women throughout the ages.

The first chapters provide background information and historical contexts for considering Shakespeare's women. Chapter 1 provides an overview of the role of women in society from the period of classical antiquity through the medieval period. This chapter also surveys some of the influential ideas about women derived from ancient and medieval sources, and it examines Shakespeare's specific use of stories, characters, and genres drawn from classical antiquity and medieval sources insofar as they involve women. Chapter 2 focuses on the history of women in Shakespeare's world, surveying their status in theory and practice and gesturing toward the extreme range of standards of living experienced by women during this period. This chapter also considers writings by women contemporary with Shakespeare, especially their representation of women and their engagement with key ideas and debates about women.

Chapters 3 through 5 turn more specifically to images of women in Shakespeare's texts, as well as the subsequent theatrical, critical, scholarly, and artistic responses to these images. Chapter 3 examines the representation of women in Shakespeare's plays and poems. Chapter 4 considers how different productions and adaptations have treated women in Shakespeare's plays from the early modern period to the present. Chapter 5 surveys the range of scholarship and criticism on Shakespeare and women from the earliest critical responses to the present time.

The final section of the book provides a selection of primary documents to be read in context with Shakespearean women, as well as a selected, general bibliography of materials useful to the study of women in the age of Shakespeare and in the works themselves. Readers will also find a brief glossary of terms used in this book.

Unless otherwise noted, all quotations of Shakespeare's works are taken from *The Norton Shakespeare*, ed. Stephen Greenblatt, et al. New York: Norton, 1997.

WORK CITED

St. Louis, Nadine S. "Weird Sisters." *Weird Sisters*. Sturtevant, WI: Wolfsong
    Publications, 2000, 5.

1

WOMEN IN CLASSICAL ANTIQUITY AND THE MIDDLE AGES

In the context of our consideration of women in the age of Shakespeare, classical antiquity and the Middle Ages served early modern English thinkers and writers in several basic ways. Ancient and medieval folk traditions—such as charivari and skymmingtons; festivals of misrule and other holiday festivities; and mummers' plays and other public social theatricals—continued through to Shakespeare's time. We see them, for example, in the Herne the Hunter episode of *Merry Wives* and the May rites in *A Midsummer Night's Dream*. Early modern people held a number of general ideas about women inherited from these earlier traditions, including both ideas that had been filtered from antiquity through the Middle Ages and those relearned during the Renaissance.

Classical types and archetypes of women also find their way into Shakespeare's plays: courtesans, such as Nell in *A Comedy of Errors*; perhaps Bianca in *Othello* (she is certainly a sexual woman not under the official control of a man); Mistress Quickly in *II Henry IV*; and a variety of abbesses in charge of convents and widows living without the protection or control of a man (as in *A Comedy of Errors*, *Measure for Measure*, and *All's Well*). Indeed, Latin language and its literatures stood at the heart of the early modern English schoolboy's studies, and writers of the period, including Shakespeare, were often strongly influenced by classical traditions of government, education, philosophy, and art. The bulk of what we find about women, however, is not positive.

Ancient mythologies (Greek, Roman, Jewish, and early Christian) all identified women as the source of all the world's troubles. From Hesiod, we get the Greek's version of the first woman, Pandora, who was sent by Zeus to punish man for Prometheus's theft of fire. Endowed with insatiable curiosity and given a box (or jar) as a wedding gift—but told she must not to open it—Pandora was unable to resist. Opening the box, Pandora unleashed upon the world death, plagues, old age, sickness, and all the miseries of human life. Similarly, the Old Testament located the cause of death and the world's sorrows in the first woman, Eve. Likewise linked to insatiability (of appetite, of curiosity), Eve's inability to obey is presented as the introduction of death to humanity. Both Greek and Semitic mythologies present the creation of women as an evil necessary to reproduction, men being incapable of it on their own. The ancients also handed down tales of wicked wives like Phyllis, who allegedly rode her husband Aristotle like a beast, and Xanthippe, who reputedly dumped a full chamber pot on her husband Socrates's head. Such stories continued to be popularly repeated and even depicted in visual form throughout Shakespeare's time.

Especially significant are the Renaissance appropriations of the ideal woman, which in the Greco-Roman tradition was the obedient, chaste, and modest wife. Such a wife's experiences were limited to the domestic and private. Shakespeare's Lucrece has thus been properly isolated from the world beyond her domestic walls. Never having "coped with stranger eyes," Lucrece found Tarquin's lustful glances incomprehensible (*The Rape of Lucrece* 99). In *Antony and Cleopatra*, Enobarbus describes Octavia as being of a "holy, cold and still conversation," to which Menas replies, "Who would not have his wife so?" (*Antony and Cleopatra* 2.6.122–124). Female chastity, however, entails not simple sexual control but a stoic constancy and patience of mind. The Roman historian Plutarch, for example, writing of Brutus's wife, Portia, in his *Lives of the Noble Grecians and Romans*, claims she "always showed a constant and patient state of mind," even when separated from her husband (124). The question of how women are able to maintain their chastity—defined as unwavering mental constancy—in the face of great external turbulence is central to the few Roman female characters who figure in Shakespeare's plays—for example, Octavia in *Antony and Cleopatra*, Portia in *Julius Caesar*, and Lavinia in *Titus Andronicus*.

In his dramatic and poetic depictions of women, Shakespeare resembled his literary contemporaries by explicitly and implicitly drawing upon antiquity's conventional ideas about women. Such ideas are woven, sometimes seamlessly, into the fabric of his plays, as when Hamlet exclaims "Woman, thy name is frailty" (*Hamlet* 1.2.146); or in *The Winter's Tale* where Leontes imagines himself a cuckold simply because he believes that many other men are; or in *Othello*, where Iago, Brabanzio, and finally Othello give voice to dark suspicion and ugly innuendos, exposing the misogynist underbelly of the world in which these plays were written. At other times, these anciently derived, misogynist ideas of women are given a more full exposition, as in the case of Posthumous, whose mistaken belief that his wife has betrayed him sexually incites his diatribe in which he lays the root of all evil at the foot of woman. Lamenting the fact that procreation cannot take place without women and claiming "there's no motion / That tends to vice in man but I affirm / It is the woman's part," Posthumous concludes that he will plague them by writing the "truth" about them (2.5.1–35). While still misogynist at heart, such ideas are also given humorous vent in several plays, perhaps most notably when Touchstone claims that the cuckold's horns brought about by marriage are unfortunately necessary (*As You Like It* 3.3.45–49).

Moreover, Shakespeare reworked specific classical and medieval stories, some of which involved women (either incidentally or as key figures). Writers from the classical and medieval past provided early modern writers like Shakespeare with source materials for narratives, character types, and literary genres. Lovesickness as a literary trope is found in many of Shakespeare's sonnets and plays. Ovid's *Ars*

Amandi and *Metamorphoses* both associate love with melancholia and an imbalance of temperaments. Ibn Hazm's eleventh-century Arabic treatise *The Dove's Neck Ring* and Andreas Capellanus's twelfth-century Latin treatise *De Amore* both similarly present a pathological image of love as a malady, as do the twelfth-century poems and romances of Chrétien de Troyes. In the fourteenth century, Boccaccio and Chaucer continue to present love as a physiological imbalance. Although the medieval period witnessed a developing shift from a magical explanation for love to a more medical one, plays like Shakespeare's *A Midsummer Night's Dream* suggest that traces of the former view lingered for centuries (and, indeed, can still be found popularly to this day). English writers of Shakespeare's time were heavily influenced by medieval continental sonnets, including Petrarch's fourteenth-century poems and sonnets about Laura. Medieval reception of Ovid, as seen in Chrétien de Troyes, Marie de France, and Chaucer, also provided early modern writers like Shakespeare with access to classical and medieval writings simultaneously.

Literary genres of note include the dawn song, or alba, drawn from continental traditions of courtly love (in which clandestine lovers must part with the coming of the day), which we see in the famous scene in *Romeo and Juliet* in which the lovers resist acknowledging that daybreak has come. Shakespeare's age retained and transformed a number of medieval conventions of courtly love. The lady of courtly lyrics (e.g., Dante's Beatrice and Petrarch's Laura) and the elevation of her as Platonic ideal and figure of beauty or the divine appears in both straightforward and mocked presentations. The modes and genre of courtly love, however, rarely imagine an inner life or subjectivity for the lady; she is merely the object of the speaker's desire. As we shall see, early modern writers did not expand the imaginative subjectivity of female characters much more than their predecessors had. Perhaps most interesting, however, is the way in which the ideology of courtly love—which viewed true love as necessarily adulterous (marriages being made by arrangement)—is transformed as emerging notions of romantic love within companionate marriage come into conflict with conventional standards that continue to retain patriarchal control over marriages. The negotiation of the tension between older views of marriage as a social enterprise and emerging ideas of marriage as a private relationship between husband and wife make up the central drama for a number of Shakespeare's comedies and tragedies.

Classical and medieval scientific and pseudoscientific ideas about birthing and gynecology also continued to resonate in the early modern period. Medieval texts like the thirteenth-century *The Secrets of Women*, for example, continued to be reissued during Shakespeare's time. In *Macbeth*, Macduff claims to have been "not of woman" born, indicating his arrival by caesarean section, and by the late twelfth and early thirteenth centuries, church officials had begun recommending the procedure as a means of saving the unborn child's life when the mother had died during childbirth. That caesarian section continued to be linked to maternal death, however, kept the procedure shrouded in mystery and the potential for the supernatural. Medieval ideas about prenatal events also carried over into the early modern period, in spite of a supposedly increasingly scientific approach to physiology. The Duchess of Gloucester in Shakespeare's *Richard III* links the wicked nature of her son to his deformed birth. The impact of visual representations on pregnant women, including the belief that they have a physiological impact, for example, can be seen in stories from Shakespeare's time of pregnant women giving birth to deformed babies after seeing chimeras (terrifying images of monstrous creatures).

Shakespeare is remarkable for his brilliance in revising, transforming, and revitalizing earlier works, and some of these reimagined tales included important female figures. On occasion he worked specifically from certain writers and texts, drawing most heavily from the following three: Ovid's *Metamorphoses* (available in Arthur Golding's 1567 English translation), Plutarch's *Lives of the Noble Grecians and Romans* (available in Thomas North's 1579 translation from the French), and Raphael Holinshed's 1587 revised second edition of *The Chronicles of England, Scotland, and Ireland*. Ten of Shakespeare's English history plays, as well as *King Lear*, *Cymbeline*, and *Macbeth*—roughly one third of his oeuvre— derive from Holinshed's work.

Greco-Roman stories provided Shakespeare not only with a good deal of his material, including basic plots, but also lengthy passages translated and sometimes even lifted whole. The story of *Pyramus and Thisbe* (produced in the rude mechanical's play-within-the-play), for example, is drawn from Ovid. He also drew upon a number of classical habits of metaphor, figures of speech, and themes, which he adapted to early modern tastes. Additionally, he incorporated the theme of transformation as developed in Ovid's *Metamorphoses*; this theme appears most notably in *A Midsummer Night's Dream* (especially Bottom's transformation into an ass, and Titania's love for him; but also the magical transformations of the lovers as well). The theme of transformation can also be seen in cross-dressing plots, the radical reversals of fortunes, and mistaken identities running through such plays as *A Winter's Tale* (with its reworking of the Pygmalion myth in Hermione's statuesque restoration), *Twelfth Night*, *Cymbeline*, and others. Shakespeare's *Troilus and Cressida* clearly draws on both classical and medieval sources, including the recent translations of Homer's *Iliad* by Chapman (1598); Chaucer's *Troilus and Criseyde* (which appeared in a new edition in 1598); and Caxton's *Recueil of the Histories* (which also appeared in a new edition in 1596).

In addition to specific plotlines, these earlier works also provided Shakespeare with conventions such as archetypes and stock characters, as well as conventions of genre (such as Senecan revenge tragedy and blasons), such themes and motifs as transformation (drawing especially from Ovid), and questions of liberty and sovereignty. While much early criticism examining Shakespeare in relation to ancient and medieval history focused on the question of the accuracy of Shakespeare's depictions of the ancient world (for example, pointing out such infamous anachronisms as the reference to clocks in *Julius Caesar* and billiards in *Antony and Cleopatra*), little attention was given to the accuracy of his gendered representations or his depiction of women from historical periods. Shakespeare, however, was a playwright and poet, not a historian. Insofar as this chapter looks at Shakespeare's use of history, I will focus primarily on his thematic and dramatic uses of history, rather than on his historical accuracy.

GREEK WOMEN

The histories of classical Rome and Greece, as Shakespeare would have inherited them, were predominantly male-centered. Moreover, even now, after several decades of feminist scholarship have lent progress to the recovery of the history of women, most of what we do know concerns an elite minority. Traditional studies of the classical period have focused on wives, relegating them to the domestic or household realm. Such studies view women as solely ruled by, rather than ever ruling over, other women and men of lower classes. The lives of most women have gone unrecorded, and it is likely that the brevity and brutality of the majority of women's lives would stand in stark contrast to even the most restrictive details of the elite minority. Shakespeare would have had access to knowledge about only a select few women from the ancient world.

Most writings about women from this period are written from male perspectives, and very little survives that is known with certainty to have been actually composed by women. The sixth-century BCE poet Sappho of Lesbos, for example, is said by ancient sources to have produced nine volumes, but only a handful of poems and other fragments of her work have survived the neglect—and sometimes blatant hostility—typically faced by women's work. Nonetheless, Sappho was praised in her own time as among the best, if not the best, lyric poet of the day; and her work was translated into Latin by Catullus and later cited positively by such revered authors as Horace, Ovid, and Martial. In addition to Sappho's works, a few scraps of poetry and letters purportedly written by women also exist (though in many cases the gendered authorship of these anonymous pieces is contested or otherwise not definitively ascertainable). The names of some of these third- and fourth-century authors include Erinna, Anyte, Nossis, and Moero—but again Shakespeare is not likely to have known them (e.g., fifty of the fifty-four extant lines of Erinna's poem "The Distaff" were not discovered until 1928).

Laws provide some insight into the lives of ancient women, but again these are generated from a male-dominant position, focusing on areas of most concern to men. When the laws do address women specifically, they usually concern elite women. Additionally, laws must be carefully used in terms of what they reveal about actual practices. Sometimes rules and laws are not always enforced with regularity (even in our own time, for example, we have laws on the books that are not upheld). With regard to prohibitive laws in particular, these often indicate the presence rather than the absence of the behaviors the authorities were attempting to eliminate (otherwise, there would be no need for a law against it).

While some differences among the various groups seem to have occurred, the dominant view of women in classical antiquity was one of inferiority, posited within a worldview based in binary oppositions (e.g., male/female; active/passive; strong/weak, and so on). At best, women were seen as deformed and defective versions of males. This was an enduringly powerful idea, one traceable from *Genesis* through Aristotle and on to Aquinas and through to Shakespeare's time.

Aristotle analyzes women in terms of two primary categories, physiological and political, and concludes that women are innately inferior to men in both categories. According to Aristotle, sexual difference is entirely biological, thus naturalizing all differences he sees between men and women, including those potentially attributable to social factors. In his works on natural science, for example, Aristotle argues that women are by nature passive while men are naturally active. In his *The Generation of Animals*, he claims that a relative lack of innate heat on women's part compared to the heat of males accounts for a number of defective attributes. For example, blood in both men and women has the potential to be transformed into semen, but whereas men possess sufficient heat to finish the process (which Aristotle likens to ripening), women's blood remains untransformed and thus must be discharged as menses, lest it rot or otherwise putrefy. Thus, according to Aristotle, "a woman is as it were an infertile male" (Lefkowitz and Fant 227). In the process of human conception, Aristotle continues, men and women "are distinguished by a certain ability and inability" as the male seed transforms and shapes the otherwise inert matter provided by the female into a living being (Lefkowitz and Fant 228).

The legal status of women in ancient Greece was similarly based on the premise of inferiority, and women were considered minors throughout their lives (whereas once their fathers died, males of the same class reached an age of majority in their mid-twenties). Women's extremely restricted access to education and economic resources, combined with their culture's view of them as innately imbecilic, extremely limited the experiences of women during this period.

Additionally, ancient Greek culture valued male homosocial bonds and homosexual friendships as being of a nobler and more spiritual nature than relations between men and women—including between spouses—ever could be. It is hardly surprising, therefore, that Aristotle claimed that marriage was always and inherently a relationship between unequal partners. Athenian women could lay claim to and use certain kinds of property (for example, they had the use of slaves, furniture, and so forth), but they could not control it—that is, they could not sell or give away what they owned without their guardian's permission. While they held certain claims to land as well, they could not use this particular form of property as they could other kinds of property without guardianship. Spartan women, on the other hand, seem to have been able to own and inherit property, and roughly one third of Athenian property seems to have been owned by women. Nonetheless, even Spartan women were explicitly expected to be obedient to their husbands.

The primary role for women was that of mother, producing sons for the family or the state. The ancient Greeks (as well as the Romans) all followed patrilocal marriage patterns. In a patrilocal marriage, the wife leaves her family and is subsumed into the husband's family line. Consequently, marriages among the elite were often used to consolidate, and even expand, the range of political power. For example, during the Hellenistic period of Alexander the Great (the Greek ruler who conquered most of the world known to his people), women were seen as conquests of war and as an important means of weaving together the interests of conquered nations with those of Greece. Alexander married two foreign women: Roxana, a noblewoman from Bactria (in what is now northern Afghanistan), and Stateira, a Persian princess; he also encouraged his soldiers to intermarry with conquered women, further consolidating the power of his empire.

As an isolated, self-sufficient, and heavily armed society, Sparta evoked many rumors, and most of what we know about Sparta comes from writers such as Plutarch, who wrote from the perspective of an outsider. The primary purpose of Spartan social institutions was to protect the state by producing the most powerfully trained soldiers in the world. Unlike Athenian and Roman culture, the state—not the father or the family—was the ultimate authority, and both Spartan men and women were expected to fulfill their duty to the state. Sons were raised by their mothers until the age of seven, and then the state took over to begin military training. Although males and females were separated, Spartan girls were trained well in both the arts and athletics, because they needed to maintain the home fires while the men were away at war and to fulfill their obligations as soldiers when necessary. In order to ensure stronger infants (rather than higher numbers), Spartan women typically married in their late teens, and there was less discrepancy in age between husbands and wives than there tended to between Athenian and Roman couples. Because men spent most of their time in military compounds rather than at home (even during times of relative peace), women lived outside the daily control of men. In general, the consensus of outsiders writing about Spartan women depicted them as ruthless warriors, less restrained by male authority than their Athenian counterparts, and consequently prone to licentiousness.

Whereas Spartan women were granted access to education, Athenian culture linked women's education to their sexuality—or rather, it linked sexual respectability for women to the absence of education and worldly knowledge. Here, the ultimate authority was the patriarch of the family, and the elite woman's primary role was to produce legitimate heirs. To maintain their social status, ancient Athenian women of the noble class had to remain cloistered sexually and intellectually. Such women rarely mixed company with men outside their families, and they were forbidden to participate in the making of public policy.

The idea that women ought to be educated was not entirely unthinkable during this period, however, and the question was on occasion debated. In his *Laws* and *Republic*, the fourth-century-BCE philosopher Plato proposed similar educations for both males and females of the guardian class, but these ideas were not particularly popular. The ideas of Plato's protégé, Aristotle, tended to be more influential—especially his views of women as defective, less fully formed versions of male humanity.

However, a certain class of women in ancient Athens, often ex-slaves or foreigners, were able to obtain a greater degree of freedom and access to education than the vast majority of women in ancient Greece. These women, known as hetaerae (similar to a courtesan), were required to wear distinctive clothing and were taxed based on their status. Ironically, a hetaera was freed by her lack of chaste reputation to engage in more wide-ranging intellectual pursuits. Those with education could dine with men and even debate philosophy in the symposia. Indeed, their opinions were often valued and even sought. Nevertheless, the freedoms enjoyed by the hetaerae depended on their perceived sexual availability, and like their more chaste peers, they were also denied the more formal means of participating in government granted to male citizens.

If the ideal, respectable Greek woman was to be cloistered from the public and devoted to the domestic sphere, the Greek dramatists provided alternative visions of powerful women who strongly affected the politics and the world around them—with both comedic and tragic results. Comedic viragos—played by male actors (as were the women's roles played in Shakespeare's time)—inhabited plays like Aristophanes' *Lysistrata*, in which the women of the warring nations unite to bring an end to the Peloponnesian War by refusing to make more soldiers (in other words, they withhold sex from the men). However, powerful and ambitious women were more likely to be portrayed as the instigators of tragedy, as in Euripides's *Medea*, which dramatizes the story of Medea's revenge after her betrayal by her husband, Jason, who abandons her for a more prosperous marriage to a Theban princess. Medea first murders Jason's new bride by sending her a beautiful, but poisoned gown (Jason's father-in-law is also killed as he tries to save his daughter), then murders her children by Jason as the harshest way to cause him grief. Classical writers could also on occasion envision tender moments between husbands and wives, as in the parting scene between Hector and Andromache near the end of Book 6 in Homer's *Iliad*.

A particularly intriguing group of women were the Amazons, a supposedly all-female tribe of warriors located throughout North Africa and Turkey near the Black Sea and who inspired the ancient imagination. According to accounts presented by such writers as Suetonius, Virgil, and other writers through the Middle Ages and the Renaissance, the Amazons were so thoroughly lacking in maternal nature that they refused to breastfeed their children, and even sacrificed their right breasts, cutting or burning them off in order to more readily accommodate their bows for war. Amazons, who were sometimes called "moon women," were perceived as strong equestrians and associated as worshippers of Artemis, the goddess of the hunt. Warriors and fierce hunters, they were everything contrary to the domestic. Numerous accounts of fights and other encounters between Amazons and famous Greek male figures and warriors exist, including the tale of Penthesilea, who was loved and killed by Achilles; Hippolyta, from whom Hercules stole her "Girdle of Ares" and whom Theseus defeated and married; and Thalestris, who reputedly captured three hundred Amazon women for Alexander the Great in hopes of breeding a generation of super children. The figure of the Amazon was an important one in early modern literature, but while Elizabeth I and courtiers writing about her often linked the virgin queen to this myth, Shakespeare did not engage the idea of the Amazon at any great length. Although Hippolyta appears among the four pairs of lovers forming the key plots in Shakespeare's *A Midsummer Night's Dream*, she is already from the opening moments of the play Theseus's defeated bride; few, if any, traces of the ancient warrior hero remain in Shakespeare's version of the character.

ROMAN WOMEN

Under Roman paterfamilias (households headed by a male with no authority above him), living fathers had an absolute authority over everyone in the household (an authority not seen under either the Greeks or the Etruscans who lived in what is now Tuscany). Not only were wives, daughters, and slaves subject to his rule, but sons also answered to him. Citizen fathers held a particularly extreme form of paternal power ("patria potestas") over the members of their household. Sons of the free class were not fully emancipated until the death of their father, but women never were fully emancipated. As it was until only a few generations ago in our culture, domestic violence was legally permitted, even when not explicitly endorsed.

Although not as strictly confined as Greek women, women during the time of the Roman Republic were nonetheless limited in their options. The funerary items buried with women typically included such domestic items as spindles; wool-making and other textile equipment; jewelry; mirrors; toiletry boxes; and cooking equipment, representing a gendered ideal for the lives of women (if not necessarily a reflection of daily practice). A woman's primary duty was to produce children (especially sons), and she could be divorced for being unable to have children. Women of the ruling classes were expected to bear sons who would become the warriors and leaders of the growing Roman Empire, while even women of the lower classes were expected to provide their share of the empire's manpower. Those who belonged to the social group known as the proletarii (from the word "proles" meaning "offspring" and from which we get the term "proletariat," which refers to a member of the working class) provided children for the workforce in lieu of taxes and other property.

While most women's lives centered on one or more forms of labor (including the bearing of children), a small and extremely privileged group drawn from elite families was able to bypass the conventional restraints of legal guardianship and obtain a degree of freedom unusual in most respects. These women were known as Vestal Virgins, and according to Plutarch, six virgins were appointed to thirty-year terms to tend the sacred fires in the Temple of Vesta, the goddess of the hearth (Lefkowitz and Fant 289–290). This station provided the only female analog to the priesthood available to women during this period. Typically, Vestal Virgins began their service before puberty and spent ten years as students, ten years as practitioners of their learning, and ten years as teachers before being released from their vows. They lived privileged lives with few restrictions, aside from two that carried lethal consequences if broken: the penalty for being unchaste or for letting the sacred fire go out was death by live burial. After finishing their term of service, Vestal Virgins were free to marry (though few seem to have done so). The Vestal Virgins were outlawed in 393 CE, less than two decades before the fall of Rome in 409 CE.

Despite this exception, the majority of elite Roman women spent their lives legally defined as existing under perpetual guardianship ("tutela mulierum"), which did not end at an age of majority, unlike the guardianship of male children. Women who had wealth, property, or slaves needed the approval of a male guardian to make legal contracts or other transfers of property. Roman law was based upon *The Twelve Tables of Law* (ca. 451–450 BCE), which deemed women the weaker sex ("infirmitas sexus") and therefore recommended that, with the exception of Vestal Virgins, women remain under full guardianship throughout their lives, in order to protect them from their own trivial natures and the weakness of their minds ("levitas animi"). If a woman were unmarried at the time of her father's death, her guardianship passed to the nearest male paternal relative (or to whomever the father designated in his will).

Upon a woman's marriage, guardianship typically was either retained by her father or passed to her husband's family, depending on the type of marriage entered into. For a woman who married "into the hand of her husband" ("manus mariti"), her guardianship went to her husband (or her father-in-law, if he was still living and the patria potestas). According to the *Twelve Tables*, however, a woman could avoid subjection to her husband's marital control by absenting herself from home for three consecutive nights, thus retaining her membership in her birth family after marriage, even though she resided with her husband and their children still fell under her husband's paterfamilias (Lefkowitz and Fant 96). Women married in this way were not technically without a guardian, but the guardian was often at a remove (certainly not in her husband's household). As a result, some women seem to have found a sort of liminal space where, although not entirely autonomous, they were not quite under full control of an immediately present male authority.

The more restrictive marriages of "manus mariti" were more common during the earlier years of the Roman Republic. By the time of the late Republic and the Empire, the comparatively more lenient mode of marriage was more common, and most women remained under their natal paterfamilias even after marriage. Although many of Rome's restrictive laws remained on the books until the third century BCE, they seem to have been enforced with increasing leniency, and women could find loopholes around the strictures confining them. Elite women of the late Roman Republic were increasingly literate and less cloistered than Greek or earlier Roman women. Although they needed to carefully guard their reputations, and they needed chaperones, these women seem to have traveled more frequently outside the confines of their households.

By the time of the late Republic, elite women were increasingly demanding access to higher education, inspiring misogynist backlash from such writers as Juvenal, the second century CE satirist who responded in his *Satire VI* that "there ought to be some things women don't understand"—a sentiment echoed through the Middle Ages and beyond (Dinshaw 19).

But attitudes and laws are not always analogous to practice. As in nearly all times, when men left to fight in wars and oversee other extended business in distant lands, women were left behind to manage households and estates usually controlled by male relatives. Eve D'Ambra notes several examples of women overseeing farms and other businesses while their husbands are away at war or working in Alexandria (78–80). Fulvia, whose husbands included Marc Antony, was famed for her political ambition and aggression (she reputedly stuck hairpins in the tongue of Cicero's severed head in revenge for his condemnations of her while he was alive). Other women, like Octavia (Augustus's sister) and Livia (Augustus's wife), were reputedly more demure, and this demureness is retained in Shakespeare's brief sketches of them over a thousand years later.

Among the native tribes the Romans came upon when they began to build city-states on the Italian Peninsula were the Etruscans, who seemed to have controlled the region. Etruscan ways apparently exerted a strong influence on Roman culture until the time of the Roman Republic, which developed after the expulsion of Tarquin the Proud and most of the royal family following the rape of Lucretia. In juxtaposition to their narrow view of women, the Romans perpetuated stories of the earlier Etruscans' shockingly free conduct. Archeological evidence provides a more neutral confirmation that some elite Etruscan women were literate and that relationships between men and women, including those between husbands and wives, were valued. Genealogical records of famous people made by the Etruscans record both male and female lines (whereas female lines are rarely recorded during the later Greek period). Later the Romans similarly juxtaposed the stories of strong, sexually and intellectually freer Etruscan women against the more cloistered and idealized chastity of figures such as Lucretia and Virginia, as told by the Roman historian Livy.

The Romans also provide our major source of information concerning the last and perhaps most powerful monarch of the Ptolemy dynasty in Egypt, Kleopatra VII. As pharaoh, she reigned for twenty years, preserving and even increasing her empire before finally facing defeat at the hands of Augustus Caesar (formerly called Octavian) in 30 BCE. Amid the civil wars in Rome, Kleopatra VII demonstrated a keen diplomacy, first developing an alliance with Julius Caesar, who aided her in her coup against her brother. Following Caesar's murder in 44 BCE, she sided with Marc Antony in the conflict among the Roman triumvirate, or political regime headed by three powerful men (the other two members being Octavian and Pompey). In addition to negotiating long-standing alliances with powerful Roman figures, Kleopatra also waged a successful public-relations campaign at home in Egypt to promote the image of herself as beloved by her people and loyal to Egypt (among her titles was that of Philopater, or lover of the fatherland). Kleopatra's self-promotion as quintessentially Egyptian was particularly significant given the fact that her ancestry was in actuality Macedonian.

The political significance of Kleopatra's giving birth to a son by Julius Caesar and later two sons and a daughter to Marc Antony has typically been overlooked. Later writers have presented her actions as purely a matter of love or seduction, rather than a dynastically motivated strategy. However, the cunning behind the production of these children in order to expand Kleopatra's empire can be seen in the fact that Octavian (later called Augustus Caesar) perceived her son by Julius Caesar as holding sufficient claim to Roman rule to be worthy of execution.

Her sons by Marc Antony disappeared (possibly murdered as well), and her daughter was married off to the king of Mauretania, a small country on the Mediterranean coast of North Africa (not to be confused with present-day Mauritania, on the west coast), which was at the time under Roman control. Finally, after more than a decade of fighting and strategizing, Kleopatra was defeated by Octavian's forces, who looted her treasury and her kingdom. Her remaining three children by Marc Antony were brought back to Italy, where they were paraded through the streets as a sign of Octavian's victory over their parents.

The main source of information about Kleopatra comes from Plutarch, who wrote 130 years after the fact. Most Roman accounts provide the victor's point of view and vilify her as an exotic but incompetent ruler. Writers ranging from Horace, Lucan, and Plutarch to later writers like Boccaccio tend to see her powers as purely sexual—and at times even supernatural—rather than as strategically political, downplaying the length of her rule. In the Middle Ages and the Renaissance, however, some writers followed the example set by Chaucer, who transformed her into a figure of heroic love, confining her earlier supernatural powers to the realm of love, not politics. All of these views disregard the significance of her twenty-year reign as Egypt's pharaoh.

ANGLO-SAXON AND ANGLO-NORMAN WOMEN

From the Anglo-Saxon period through the Middle Ages (roughly the sixth century through the fifteenth century), as Roman colonizers gained a stronghold in the British Isles, Christian religion was increasingly central to the routines of women's daily lives and to the ways in which their culture viewed women as a group.

Early Christian writers who viewed women as inferior to men continued to have a strong influence on the perception of women in later centuries. Such views, however, were complex in negotiating between the perceived imperfections of women and God's perfect creation. As perhaps the most influential figure, for example, Augustine argues that women are created human and in the image of God, but ultimately sexual difference stands at the foundation of his theology. Although Augustine describes an equality of souls between men and women, he concludes that women's particular material embodiment renders them subordinate to men.

Like the Greeks under Alexander the Great, the Germanic tribes that invaded England in the early fifth century probably intermarried with conquered native women as part of their military strategy for dominating English territories previously occupied by Roman armies. Again, information about women during the Anglo-Saxon and Anglo-Norman periods is scant and primarily concerns elite women. The history of the period is one of warfare, conquest, and the rise of the Christian church in England. Most of the information we have, gleaned from laws and other written texts as well as archaeological materials, illuminates the lives of queens and nuns. Again, we must read carefully and with attention to both what the makers of history deemed significant and worthy of recording—and what they failed to see as significant. Administrative records dealing with property and fines and fees for certain crafts tell us about women of wealth and women who earned livings in closely regulated industries such as brewing, but they do not tell us about the majority of women who own little or nothing, or who eked out livings by means of less closely scrutinized labors.

Anglo-Saxon literature, such as *Beowulf* and the elegiac poems of the period, presents either idealized or grossly vilified images of women. Women are praised according to their success at performing their roles as consort to the ring-giver, hostess in the mead hall, and as peace-weaver among tribes; in the antithesis, they are demonized and rendered literal monsters, such as Grendel's mother in *Beowulf*.

In the image of the good woman, however, we are given the story of Hildeburgh, the Danish woman who married an enemy Frisian in an effort to build peace between the warring nations. As is often the case in such tales, this effort to weave peace by joining the families fails, and Hildeburgh loses both her husband and son, as well as her brother, in the continued warfare. In depictions of the scenes at Heorot, King Hrothgar's mead hall in *Beowulf*, Queen Wealtheow passes the mead cup to the soldiers and at one point pleads with Beowulf for his kind treatment of her young sons (the poem, however, hints that her sons will be usurped by their kinsman). Two anonymous poems, "The Wife's Lament" and "Wulf and Eadwacer," similarly provide a view of the role of women caught between tribes. Written from the perspective of females, these anonymous poems were penned either by women or by men taking on a female persona.

Every person in Anglo-Saxon society had a specific monetary value, called "wergild," which was determined as much by social class (whether one was free or "villein"—a peasant, in other words) as it was by gender. Another factor of worth for women was their status as virgin, wife, or widow. If someone was deemed responsible for the death of another, wergild was paid to the victim's family (or to the person's lord or master, if a servant or slave). If an injury occurred, then the wergild was paid to the victim. In cases of rape, however, it is not clear whether payment was ever made to the victim or whether it went to the victim's husband or lord (suggesting a view of women as property). In the case of a freeman whose servant was raped, the wergild went to the servant's lord rather than to the woman herself. Interestingly, the wergild for raping an earl's servant was substantially higher than that for the servant of a ceorl or low-ranking freeman.

Marriage among freemen also involved a monetary exchange, called "morgengifu" ("morning gift"), which the husband delivered to the wife on the morning after the consummation of the marriage. This payment could include money, goods, and lands (in amounts varying according to the social standing of the couple). In the case of particularly wealthy people, the morgengifu might include entire estates, which were then named after the property's function (and some have suggested that the naming of the property was a way of creating a public memory of the gift, so a husband could not revoke it after the romance of the honeymoon period waned). Morgengifu seems to have been remanded directly to the wife, rather than to her male relatives or family. Women were apparently able to use, sell, or bequeath the morgengifu without the husband's involvement, thus providing wives with a degree of financial security in marriage.

Although early Anglo-Saxon culture was a highly military society, its women were not trained as warriors. Women did not lead troops or engage in battles, but they did defend castles and manors in the absence of their menfolk. Ordinary Anglo-Saxon women probably focused their energy on work that benefited the household: preparing food, making clothing, and so on. Burial items often include spinning and weaving equipment, suggesting that textile labor was viewed as a valued aspect of women's lives. Women also seem to have worked in harvesting crops and performing other farm tasks, as well as in such trades as baking and brewing. In some regions, women were specifically barred from membership in the trade and craft guilds (which were more like employer monopolies, small business associations, or cartels aimed at controlling labor than modern unions aimed at protecting workers). In other areas, daughters and sisters seem to have been able to inherit guild memberships (although they commonly transferred these inheritances to a son or husband).

Many women were probably slaves, although the numbers are not recorded as clearly as they are for men. Among the population recorded for the 1086 Domesday Survey ordered by William the Conqueror in order to collect taxes, 33,000 men were listed as slaves (roughly 12% of the population), along with 706 single women. It is possible that some of the 33,000 men may have had wives who were subsumed under their head counts.

Among the elite minority of women, queens could wield much power, although it was almost always dependent on the cooperation of their royal spouses—or temporary, as when a queen served as the protector for a monarchial son in his minority. Beginning in 973 with Aelfthryth (the wife of King Edgar), English queens began to be consecrated as an anointed person. Some queens held strong influence in running the country, and by the eleventh century, queens were given their own households and estates to control. Among the tenants on their lands often were great lords, thus putting individual queens in authority over certain powerful men. By the time of Henry I in the twelfth century, however, much of the queen's power was becoming the purview of increasingly influential government administrators.

For elite women who did not become queens, religion, especially during the early period of the Christianization of Anglo-Saxon England, provided noble women with an important life option. In the seventh century, a number of double monasteries were built to house both women and men who were charged with spreading the Christian religion to the surrounding countryside. These double monasteries were under the control of an abbess, who as the superior of the house often wielded a great deal of power over not only the men and women in the monastery but in the community beyond the convent walls as well. Additionally, these monasteries served as important seats of learning and theology, where both men and women participated in theological debates and other church activities. The Abbess Hilda of Whitby, for example, oversaw the great synod of 664, during which debate over the timing of Easter was resolved and the official date calculated. Hilda also provided counsel to not only local ordinary people, but to kings and princes, and she is credited with encouraging the poet Caedmon, who allegedly composed the first Anglo-Saxon poem. The nuns of the convent at Barking were especially known in the ninth century for their learning, and their convent housed an important scriptorium (or room where the nuns stored, read, and copied numerous manuscripts). Additionally, the nuns of Barking commissioned Aldhelm's treatise *On Virginity*, which presumes the reader knows not only scripture but scriptural commentaries and exegesis (critical explanation and interpretation of biblical text) as well.

Some nuns took a second step in their devotions by becoming anchoresses (the female term for an anchorite). Anchoresses were a type of religious hermit, although they did not go out into the wilderness. Rather, they withdrew from daily life by immuring themselves in a small cell (called an anchorhold), usually attached to a church, where they led lives of intensely prayer-based routines following the seven canonical hours (beginning with dawn "matins" and ending with "compline" at bedtime). The anchoress underwent a walling-in ceremony, which was symbolic of taking on a death to the world. The ceremony included a bishop performing the Office for the Dead and literally bricking up the anchoress in her cell. The anchoress's cell, however, included at least a window facing into the church that allowed for her to hear the daily mass and to take communion; she would also receive food and other necessities. Some anchorholds actually contained more than one room, so as to allow for a servant, and other anchorholds also included a window on the street side where the anchoress would dispense advice. A number of texts were written in the twelfth and thirteenth centuries specifically to guide women who chose to live the life of an anchoress, including Aelred of Rievaulx's *A Rule of Life for Recluses* (1160); the twelfth-century *Life of Christina Markyate*, detailing the life of a famous recluse in order to provide a model for others; and the thirteenth-century *Ancrene Riwle* (*Rule for Anchors*), written for three sisters contemplating the more austere life of the recluse.

Nevertheless, in spite of the range of opportunities available to elite women who chose the life of a religious, they ultimately remained barred from the priesthood and administering the sacraments. In the tenth century, some women began to forgo taking holy orders as nuns, living instead as independent lay-sisters, either under the affiliation of a nearby male monastery or with a small group of other like-minded women.

Nuns faced resistance and even hostility, both from the home front and from invaders—especially Vikings, who began a series of invasions in 793. In 870 they burned convents at Coldingham in Scotland and at Barking, and they burned the convent at Ely in 871. Following the Viking invasions, female religious houses came increasingly under the control of male ecclesiastical authorities who were not always inclined to provide equal or even sufficient funding for the sister houses. By the 970s, responsibility for the protection and patronage of the English nunneries fell to the queens, some of whom took up the charge to the convents' benefit and others of whom were more inclined to use the charge and resources to their own advantage.

In 1066 William of Normandy was crowned King of England, and for two centuries, the country was officially controlled by the Anglo-Norman aristocracy and French feudal institutions. Under the Normans, several changes in religious options took place for women seeking alternatives to marriage. While the number of convents increased, they also drastically changed in quality. In 1130 England was home to approximately twenty convents, housing mostly nuns from elite backgrounds. By 1165, the number of convents had increased to more than one hundred (mostly in the north), and they included members from a broader spectrum of England's social strata, including not only noblewomen but women from the merchant class as well.

With this increase, however, also came diminished educational opportunities for women affiliated with life in the convent. Whereas all Anglo-Saxon nunneries had been headed by abbesses, many of whom wielded substantial local power and wealth, all but three of the Cistercian and Benedictine convents founded during the Anglo-Norman period were priories—sister houses subject to the authority of a larger and typically better endowed monastery. Indeed, many of the English convents were actually subject to male authority located in monasteries in France. The rise of cathedral schools, beginning with the first built in Canterbury in 669, marked the end of the double monasteries as seats of learning for women. As the Christian church became more established and powerful in England, it became increasingly a male-dominated enterprise relegating women to unofficial or low-ranking roles within the hierarchy.

Intermarriage between Anglo-Norman invaders and conquered Anglo-Saxon aristocratic women furthered the invaders' conquest of the country. Additionally, the Anglo-Normans brought with them a change in the transmission of inheritances in aristocratic families. Under the Anglo-Saxons, inheritances had been distributed laterally across children, including both sons and daughters. Anglo-Norman aristocratic families increasingly came to attach themselves to particular pieces of land or specific estates that they wished to entail whole upon a single heir. Lineages were calculated as descending vertically (from a single male ancestor to a single male heir) rather than horizontally (across multiple heirs). By the twelfth century, primogeniture, the system by which all major properties are inherited by the eldest male child, had become the most common means of determining inheritances, especially those with land.

MEDIEVAL ENGLISH WOMEN

Misogyny remained rife throughout medieval England, which saw both the creation of new versions and the perpetuation of classical traditions of oppression under the Christian expansion into English culture. Aristotle's works, written in the fourth century BCE, gained increasing influence on western Christian writers, beginning in the thirteenth century with the rise of scholasticism. Continuing along the lines of thinking initiated by Aristotle, women were seen as the negative half of a whole host of binary oppositions (e.g., body/mind, passive/active, evil/good, and passion/reason). Many of these ideas trace to Aristotle and later

Galen, both of whom had varying teleological perspectives on women, seeing them as designed for purposes and uses aside from their own being but nevertheless categorically and essentially further from perfection than men. Christian writers perpetuated the misogyny, using sex as the basis for excluding women from teaching and preaching, as well as from the clergy. At the heart of debates about marriage was a deep-seated misogyny and distrust of women, ranging from serious theological texts to the farcical tales told by Chaucer's pilgrims on the way to Canterbury.

Counterversions of female depravity existed, including Boccaccio's *On Famous Women*, Chaucer's *The Legend of Good Women*, and Osbern Bokenham's *Legend of Holy Women*. Often, however, these portraits comprised half of what was ultimately a rhetorical exercise in debate, with a figure like Chaucer's Clerk's story of patient Griselda providing the counterargument to the Wife of Bath's exuberantly erotic joy of life.

Additionally, these comparatively positive depictions of women were beyond the reasonable imitation of ordinary women. The opposite of both Eve and the whore was, of course, the Madonna or the Blessed Virgin Mary. Conceived without the stain of original sin, Mary presented a figure of female purity. While her spotless purity was probably unattainable by most women, Mary nonetheless provided an important model of women as intercessor.

In addition to other biblical good women, folklore also offered even more popular images of good women, such as the character of Griselda, whose patient suffering and obedience was recounted by Boccaccio in *The Decameron*, Petrarch, and Chaucer in his *Clerk's Tale*. In this story, Griselda patiently submits to sadistic test after test of her obedience to her husband. After first passively complying with her husband's supposed decision to murder both her young children (they are in fact being raised safely elsewhere), she then acquiesces to her husband's divorce of her, and she returns without protest to her father's home. After enduring several years of this shame in absolute humility, she then ungrudgingly agrees to help prepare her husband's newly-chosen bride for her marriage. This young woman, however, is not a new bride but in fact the daughter Griselda has long believed to be dead. Having proven her unwavering obedience in this final test, Griselda is rewarded by being happily reunited not only with her long lost children but with her husband as well. While Shakespeare does not retell this tale wholesale, as his literary precursors did, he nevertheless makes ample use of the tropes of the sadistic testing of wives and the reward or idealization of their masochistic patience in such plays as *The Merry Wives*, *The Winter's Tale*, and even *Othello*.

An important female voice of opposition came from Christine de Pisan, a fourteenth-century French writer who composed several works in defense of women. In 1401, she also initiated what became an international debate about the merits of Jean de Meun's thirteenth-century poem, *La Roman de la Rose*. A satire on courtly love and women, *Roman* was an influential poem (Geoffrey Chaucer translated it before his death in 1400, and it had a lasting impact on English literature). De Pisan argued that de Meun's depiction was inaccurate and slanderous to women. Soon after (by 1405), de Pisan completed *The Book of the City of Ladies*, an allegory (extended narrative form of metaphor in which the story has both a literal meaning and a symbolic one) in which she builds a defense of women on the foundation of good women from the pagan, Christian, and recent past. In *City of Ladies*, de Pisan is particularly critical of Aristotle and his traditions (see, for example, *Book of the City of Ladies* 1.38.5). Her works also participate in the genre of the *querelle des femmes* ("debate about women"), which debated the worth and merits of women as a group.

Although she never came to England (her son was in the courts of both Richard II and Henry IV), de Pisan's works were well known across the channel, where they were frequently translated and printed throughout the fifteenth and early sixteenth centuries. According to de Pisan, Henry IV invited her to move to his court after he usurped the throne from Richard II, but it was an invitation she diplomatically declined: "Seeing how things were there, I was not tempted by this in any way, and I concealed my feelings until I might have my son, thanking the King profusely and saying that I was fully at his command . . . [but] I could not believe a traitor would come to a good end" (*Christine's Vision* 121). Significantly, among de Pisan's last works is a song honoring the accomplishments of Joan of Arc (1412–1431), which she composed in 1429—the year in which Joan was captured and handed over to the English, who executed the future saint in 1431. De Pisan's patriotic eulogy of Joan of Arc contrasts interestingly with Shakespeare's more typically English rendition of her as a heretic (one who rejects official and authorized religious views), a liar, and a whore in *I Henry VI*.

Even those writers who seemed less hostile to women nevertheless saw them on some level as unequal and inferior to men. The two versions of the creation found in Genesis were particularly important in determining the position of women. Aquinas and Bonaventure, for example, accepted Augustine's explanation of the creation that split between souls and bodies. Thus, the simultaneous creation of man and woman in Genesis 1:27 was interpreted to mean that first their souls were created in the image of God, then given bodily manifestation, with Adam being formed first and Eve deriving her creation from Adam, as depicted in Genesis 2:22. Other writers, however, were more inclined to see women's souls and bodies as imperfect—and even dangerous—compared to those of men. According to the early Christian writer Tertullian, for example, women "were the devil's gateway." Jerome's *Against Jovinian* linked misogamy (hatred of marriage) and misogyny (hatred of women), further urging men to forgo the company of women. Tertullian's admonitions against women's use of cosmetics in *De Cultu Feminarum* linked the female sex to duplicity, and such ideas carried forward into the early modern period in the form of sumptuary laws regulating what sorts of clothing people could and could not wear, as well as injunctions against crossdressing against gender and social status.

By the thirteenth century, the entirety of a landholder's estate typically passed to his eldest male child, and only in the event of there being no sons might daughters inherit (in which case they would divide the estate). By the fourteenth century, however, even greater effort was made throughout England to restrict entailments or the inheritance of lands and titles to the male line, with estates often passing to uncles and male cousins before going to daughters who in earlier times would have inherited in the absence of brothers. Among the consequences of the shift to primogeniture (inheritance by the eldest male descendent) was a surplus of marriageable aristocratic daughters and too many younger sons who could not expect the resources necessary to make a marriage unless they found a wealthy heiress with no male contestants to the estate. Indeed, the wealth of the rising merchant and trading classes in the thirteenth and fourteenth centuries provided some families with a way to evade the problems posed by primogeniture. Families with ancient title but insufficient land and those with newly made wealth but no claim to lineage could find it mutually beneficial to join their sons and daughters in marriage. Resistance to this solution of mixing of social groups, however, could also flare from both sides, with the aristocracy characterizing the nouveau riche as base and the wealthy merchants viewing the aristocracy as debauched and lacking industry. And a number of matches were made with blatant disregard for the opinions of the children involved. As we shall see in a later chapter, primogeniture's pressures on the daughters and younger sons of the wealthy continued to reverberate in England well past the time of Shakespeare.

As it continued to be in Shakespeare's time, key determiners in medieval women's lives involved their social class, marital status, and age at marriage (if married), as well as their occupation. Although the majority of women married, it is important to remember that, as Maryanne Kowaleski has shown, in major cities and many rural areas during the late medieval period, more than 30% of women remained unmarried throughout their lives (45–46, 50–51). Many of these, of course, were poor and indentured women, many of whom may have been too poor to marry. It is also important to remember that to be unmarried is not the same as being not sexually active, and many women are recorded (especially in criminal records and reports on poverty) as having children out of wedlock. Nonetheless, the dominant ideology framed virginity in two basic ways: as a particular life stage on the trajectory to marriage and as a profession for those who would become nuns.

The medieval household underwent a transition, in some part related to changes in architecture and the development of the chimney, which enabled the enclosure (and heating) of separate rooms within a house. It also increased the possibility of privacy for the wealthy. Typically, households of more than modest means contained not only members of the immediate family, but also various servants. In especially well-off aristocratic and gentry households, the members might include attendants, ladies-in-waiting, maids, and servants in addition to servants responsible for the menial labor. It is also important to remember that nearly everyone—both men and women, and wealthy and poor—during the medieval and early modern periods spent at least some portion of their lives under terms of service. While large numbers of people spent their entire lives in a condition of servitude, for many it was a temporary occupation, a phase in adolescent development during which young people learned skills, earned money (for women, this money often was for a dowry, while for men the money was often used to establish themselves in a business or trade). Noble and gentry daughters, as well as those of wealthy merchants, were likewise often placed in service to families just above their own social class as a means of learning social skills and making connections that would enable them to contract profitable marriages.

The process leading to marriage was determined by a combination of local customs and church prescription. In 1215 the Fourth Lateran Council determined that free will on the part of the couple was among the necessary criteria for legal marriage, thus opening the door to the opinions of daughters. An especially important consequence of the requirement for consent was its tendency to be perceived as involving choice, laying the foundation for the later view of marriage as based on individual love.

The actual age at marriage varied depending on the social class. While the legal age of majority was twenty-five, children could marry with permission of their parent or guardian at the age of twelve for girls and fourteen for boys. As Cordelia Beattie sums it, the general trend from the late fourteenth century onward was for people to marry "late (in their mid-to-late twenties) someone of their own age; they set up their own household on marriage; before marriage they often circulate between households as life-cycle servants, and a significant proportion never marry" (33–34). The majority of the population needed to secure sufficient resources to maintain a household, either by finishing a term of apprenticeship or indenture, or by outliving a father and obtaining an inheritance. Because they were older at the age of marriage, and therefore more likely to have an income and more life experiences than children, ordinary people often had somewhat more to say about the choice of their marriage partner. But even here, families expected children to pay some consideration to what the marriage partner would bring to the new household, and people who were serfs or otherwise unfree needed their lord's permission before marrying if they were able to marry at all.

Marrying at a younger age was more common among the wealthy, whose parents sought to secure economic or political advantages by linking their children in lucrative alliances with other families. In the case of families who held money, property, or power, medieval marriage was a sociopolitical alliance between families (and sometimes, in the case of the nobility, nations). Among the elite, parents or guardians arranged the marriage, sometimes determining the alliance at an early age with couples betrothed in their youth or infancy and married as adolescents. Members of the wealthy merchant class also followed this pattern, arranging marriages for their children that included concerns over money and titles and enabled social and economic mobility. But while the legal and economic features of marriage as a social contract were highlighted during the Middle Ages by the attention paid to negotiating the dowry, jointure, and other property exchanged upon a marriage, marriages often involved matters of love alongside those of money. In 1477 John Paston married Margery Brews for both love and economics. And, despite horror stories of youths being matched with wealthy geriatrics, most fathers were inclined to consider their children's affections and their overall well-being.

In the Middle Ages, a distinction was made between the promise to marry in the future, *verba de future* ("words concerning the future"), and the promise to begin the state of marriage starting in the present moment, *verba de presenti* ("words concerning the present"). By the thirteenth century, marriage was considered among the sacraments, and ceremonies in the church (or at the door of the church) were required. By the sixteenth century, however, the Council of Trent had outlawed clandestine (secret) marriages as legitimate or valid, and communities increasingly enforced the rule of the public reading of the banns for three Sundays in a row to inform the community and to provide opportunities for objection to the proposed union.

Objections often aimed at protecting one luckless partner from the other's deceit. Objections could protect partners from the dangers of disinheritance or parental refusal of dowry or jointure. For women, especially, the banns protected women from the dangers of marriages made without witnesses—especially crucial if a marriage was ultimately deemed invalid or if the reputed husband later claimed there was in fact no *verba de future*, or promise of future marriage, but just casual sex. Three weeks also provided time for ferreting out possible bigamists with families already secretly ensconced in other towns or villages. Nevertheless, clandestine marriages still occurred, and many were ultimately rendered valid in spite of the more complicated circumstances.

The period between 1200 and 1600 offered little change for free women under English common law, which had its roots in earlier feudal society. Under English common law during this period, once women reached the age of majority, they held either the legal status of *femme sole* ("woman alone") or that of *femme covert* ("covered woman"). As a *femme sole*, a woman could hold land and property, and she could sue and be sued in her own person. As a *femme covert*, a married woman's legal identity was subsumed (literally "covered") under that of her husband's. Restricted by coverture, a woman's land and property fell under the husband's control (including such things as a wife's clothing, household items, and what we would today consider to be personal items). Husbands could not alienate or sell "real property" such as land and buildings, and these items were to be returned to the wife in the event of her widowhood. Personal property, however, did not revert back to the wife except by will. Consequently, lawsuits involving real property involved both the husband and wife as claimant or defendant, while lawsuits involving personal property involved the husband only.

Femme sole, however, does not simply indicate an unmarried rather than married woman. While many women who were *femme sole* were previously unmarried or presently widowed, some married women took on the legal status of *femme sole* for a variety of reasons. For example, according to a fourteenth-century act of the City of London:

> Where a woman *couverte de baron* [i.e., married] follows any craft within the city by herself apart, with which the husband in no way intermeddles, such a woman should be bound as a single woman as to all that concerns her said craft. And if the husband and wife are impleaded [i.e., brought to court to respond to charges], in

such case the wife shall plead as a single woman in a Court of Record, and shall have her law and other advantages by way of plea just as a single woman. And if she is condemned, she shall be committed to prison until she shall have made satisfaction; and neither the husband nor his goods shall in such case be charged or interfered with. (Lacey 43)

This legal maneuver seems to have been available in other areas of England as well. Margery Kempe, the late-fifteenth-century visionary from Lynn who wrote a memoir of her religious conversion and activities, apparently undertook failed ventures in brewing and milling that were separate from her husband's finances. She also seems to have accumulated wealth (perhaps through inheritances) that was not under her husband's control, for she relates bargaining with her husband in order to abstain from sex for religious reasons. She agrees to pay off his debts, indicating her access to material wealth not under his control, while he agrees to live chastely with her, indicating his control over her physical person in spite of her finances. Indeed, the willingness of Margery Kempe's husband to negotiate is particularly striking given that in many respects he was not required to do so.

Domestic abuse and violence in medieval England (and later) was strongly related to the male-dominated and commonly misogynistic culture of the times. As wives, even women who followed a profession as *femme sole* were nevertheless still legally positioned *sub virga et potestate* ("under the rod and power") of their husbands. Medieval literature reflects the nonchalance of domestic violence as well, as seen in the tumultuous marriage between Chaucer's Wife of Bath, who has been rendered deaf by a blow to the ear by her latest husband. That the literal translation of the legal term for their subjection alludes specifically to a stick to be potentially wielded is illustrative of how deeply the idea of corporal punishment for wives (as well as children and servants) was embedded in the culture. While male children and servants of a certain class might grow out of the age at which they might be beaten, women were perceived in many respects as in a perpetual state of childhood.

Technically, both males and females could be apprenticed once they had reached the age of majority—at the age of twelve for girls and at fourteen for boys. Practically speaking, however, women did not move on from being apprentices to becoming journeymen or masters of their craft, and corporations tended to exclude women even more thoroughly than the guilds. Yet women engaged in a wide range of occupations, both in the home and beyond it. As keepers of the household, women performed a great deal of what feminist historians have termed "invisible work." Medieval women were often responsible for maintaining (or overseeing the maintenance of) gardens and the production of items needed for the household. In addition to producing vegetables and other food items, women's household duties included cooking and baking, brewing, and the growing of herbs and medicinal plants. Occupations for women included food preparation, brewing trades, textile trades, and service work.

Women participated in England's burgeoning textile industry at the lowest levels of the work, including wool-beating and fiber separation; scouring, washing, greasing, and combing the wool; and spinning, warping, and weaving. Men were more likely to be occupied in shearing, felting, and dyeing the wool. While women could be found working in small-scale sales and as petty traders, from the thirteenth century onward, male-dominated guilds increasingly excluded them from larger-scale market and trade endeavors, including the wool trade.

Like Margery Kempe, some women worked at brewing for income. Brewing was a particularly important domestic skill because of the minimal availability of safe drinking water, and alewives were among the most visible female workers in the Middle Ages. In the fifteenth century, however, the craft became increasingly commercial, and the business of brewing increasingly dominated by married women, with households (especially urban ones) purchasing rather than brewing their own ales. Single women were more likely to be sellers than brewers by the time of Shakespeare.

Indeed, regulations increasingly discouraged female independence. For example, in 1492, Coventry issued a law forbidding single women under the age of forty to set up their own households, creating an additional pressure toward marriage and preventing women from earning their own livings. With few exceptions, women who lacked the protection of a husband or other male relative lived precarious lives. Women were often compelled to take on a husband in order to continue their businesses or to have a more solidly dependable source of income. Many occupations available to women might be suitable for supplementing a primary income, but they were not sufficient for survival alone. While there were during the Middle Ages "common women"—prostitutes who made their living by residing in brothels—a number of women, both married and unmarried, also turned to prostitution, engaging in occasional sex for hire as a means of supplementing other, but inadequate, sources of income.

For some women, the convent continued to be a respectable profession and important alternative to marriage for both those never married and those widowed. Although scholasticism increasingly located education within the all-male preserve of the university rather than the home or the monastery, convent life continued to provide a few women with the ability to pursue certain forms of education. As David Bell's comprehensive list of known books and manuscripts associated with houses of female religious in England suggests, the learning in many convents was quite extensive, and the nuns owned considerable libraries of texts in Latin, French, and English. Ian Doyle has suggested that a number of manuscripts may have been copied, illuminated, and bound by some of the more well-endowed convents, such as those at Barking, Syon, and Shaftesbury (15). The interaction between aristocratic women who sponsored religious houses and the nuns in the convents was also particularly important in the late Middle Ages.

Elite women in aristocratic households also sometimes learned Latin from chaplains or tutors. Chief among the kinds of books owned by such women included lives of saints, works by mystics, and other devotional texts, such as service books, psalters (collections of Psalms), and books of hours (which prescribed prayers and readings from scripture to times of the day), as well as Arthurian romances. In particular, however, females were deprived of more formal means of schooling by being categorically excluded from the educational opportunities of the grammar schools and universities. They typically did not own books on politics, theology, philosophy, and science. Sporadic information suggests the existence of "dame schools" for girls, and that these schools were often taught by women. The languages taught seem to be English and French—languages more suited than Latin to the domestic and social duties of elite and merchant-class women.

Nevertheless, it is important to remember that definitions of literacy for use in considering the medieval period have greater fluidity than we typically use today. Because Latin was the international *lingua franca*, as well as the language of the law courts, the church, and the university, Latin literacy had an extended significance. Thus, in some medieval contexts, claims of literacy refer specifically to literacy in Latin. However, more people were likely to have knowledge of vernacular languages. While education in our own time typically links reading and writing, medieval people ranged from those we would consider completely illiterate, to those who were able to read but not write, to those who could both read and write. As Henrietta Leyser notes, "even before the arrival of printing in the 1470s, women's piety in the fifteenth century was . . . bookish" (233). It is therefore important to realize the extent to which some people were well-versed in biblical and other literatures that had been read to them. Such people included not only commoners who regularly attended sermons or might other-wise have biblical stories read to them by local priests, but also the very wealthy, who sometimes retained servants in their households specifically for the tasks of reading and writing for their masters.

Moreover, as Rebecca Krug has shown, it is more useful to engage questions of women's "literate practice"—their specific engagements with reading, memo-rization, recitation, writing, dictation, and patronage—rather than the more abstract concept of literacy. Among the explanations for why women did not produce original works of imaginative literature, Krug argues that "the familial context, construed very broadly, was the means by which women encountered literate modes and written texts. . . . Even if they might have imagined that literary writing would be useful, they were already busy with literate activities that seemed, to them, more obviously beneficial" (212).

Female patrons commissioned manuscript works by Osbern Bokenham and John Lydgate, as well as anonymous devotional treatises and books of hours. A number of noblewomen are particularly significant for their acts of literary patronage, commissioning not only manuscripts but also printed books once the printing press came to England at the end of the fifteenth century. Much of William Caxton's early work on the printing press, for example, was supported by Edward IV's sister, Margaret of York, and his wife, Elizabeth Woodville; Margaret Beaufort, mother of Henry VII, was also a key supporter of Caxton's work.

In addition to reading and sponsoring texts, a handful of women also wrote in genres more conventionally seen as literary. Marie de France, an abbess who may have been Henry II's half-sister, composed a number of works in Anglo-Norman French around the end of the twelfth century, including *The Lais of Marie de*

France (a collection of short narrative poems similar to romances, some of which are Arthurian), a collection of Aesop's fables, a version of the legend in which an Irish knight travels to St. Patrick's Purgatory to atone for his sins, and a life of the Anglo-Saxon Saint Audrey. Nuns at Barking during the Anglo-Norman period also composed lives of Saint Catherine and of Edward the Confessor.

At the end of the fourteenth century, the anchoress Julian of Norwich composed two versions of her near-death mystical visionary experience which began on May 8, 1373. Over the course of seven days and nights, during which it was believed she would die (she was administered the last rites), Julian received fifteen visions, or "shewings," concerning a variety of issues relating to her faith, including the passion of Christ and the state of sinners in the eyes of a god who is never angry. The first version of her experiences was composed in 1373, and is for the most part a direct description of her visions (some of which are nonetheless highly allegorical). The second version, written nearly twenty years later, is substantially longer and attempts to explicate the meaning of her visions for the reader.

Margery Kempe was a slightly younger visionary living in East Anglia about forty miles from Julian of Norwich, with whom she records visiting for advice. Composed in the 1430s with the help of an amanuensis (or scribe), Kempe's book records the details of her life following her religious conversion in her early twenties after the birth of her first child. Unlike Julian, Kempe was a married woman and was not cloistered in either a convent or anchoress's cell (much to the frustration of many religious and secular authorities who dealt with her). Although she bore fourteen children, she eventually secured permission from both ecclesiastical authorities and her husband to live chastely. Kempe had numerous visions, often in public places (including on pilgrimage abroad in Europe and the Middle East) and in churches. Her visions often involved loud weeping and roaring, and opinions were mixed as to whether she was possessed or divinely inspired. Although Wynken de Worde printed a substantially truncated version of her text—so extremely edited that it gave the impression that she was an anchoress—the full version of her work was not discovered until 1948 (much to the shock of those who had built their vision of the mystic on de Worde's text).

In the mid-fifteenth century, Juliana Berners, the prioress of Sopwell Nunnery, composed *The Book of Hawking, Hunting, and Fishing* (aka *The Book of St. Albans*) which Wynken de Worde published in 1496 (Richard Tottel printed it again in 1561). In addition to this text, which was popular with several centuries of courtiers, we also have a substantial numbers of letters written between 1422 and 1509 by the women of the Paston family (a prominent Norfolk gentry family). Of the more than 900 letters in the collection, 174 are by women, and more than one hundred of them are by Margaret Paston. Finally, Margaret Beaufort also deserves mentioning here, for in addition to her patronage of the early printers, she also wrote numerous letters and produced two translations: the fourth book of Thomas à Kempis' *De Imitatione Christi* (*The Imitation of Christ*), which was published in 1504, and *Speculum Aureum* (*The Mirror of Gold*), which appeared two years later. Her translation work set a precedent that was imitated by royal and aristocratic ladies educated during the humanist movement of the next generation.

The close of the fifteenth century may seem to have promised advances for women as they headed into the sixteenth century: the importation of the printing press brought greater potential for their absorption of literature and humanist ideas, for example. Nevertheless, in surveying the history of women from the classical period, through the Middle Ages, and into the early modern period that Shakespeare would have known it is not possible to write a conventional teleology of progress for women. In answer to the question posed by Joan Kelly-Gadol in the late 1970s, "Did women have a renaissance?" scholars continue to be compelled to agree that the unequivocal answer is "no." As we will see in the following chapter, in many respects the status of women continued to decline and, despite a few brilliant exceptions to the rule, the age of Shakespeare was not an age of progress for most women. While we continue to learn more details about the lives of women, and while we continue to see how certain women wielded greater power than others by virtue of their class, religion, or national identity, we will see that overall, women continued to fare poorly in comparison with men of comparable resources and social standing. And while Shakespeare's plays provide an entertaining and sometimes thought-provoking view of certain types of women (or, more specifically, give us the range of a specific male playwright's view of a certain type of women), they are not likely to give us a realistic portrait of all women. A great many of women's experiences were never noted for presentation on the early modern stage.

WORKS CITED

D'Ambra, Eve. *Roman Women*. Cambridge: Cambridge UP, 2006.

Beattie, Cordelia. *Medieval Single Women: The Politics of Social Classification in Late Medieval England*. Oxford: Oxford UP, 2007.

Bell, David N. *What Nuns Read: Books and Libraries in Medieval English Nunneries*. Collegeville, MN: Cistercian Publications, 1995.

Dinshaw, Carolyn. *Chaucer's Sexual Poetics*. Madison: U of Wisconsin P, 1989.

Doyle, A.I. "Book Production by Monastic Orders in England (c. 1375–1530): Assessing the Evidence." *Medieval Book Production: Assessing the Evidence*. Ed. Linda L. Brownrigg. Los Altos Hills, CA: Anderson Lovelace, 1990. 1–19.

Lacey, Kay E. "Women and Work in Fourteenth and Fifteenth Century London." Eds. Lindsey Charles and Loran Duffin. *Women and Work in Pre-Industrial England*. Beckenham: Croom Helm, 1985. 24–82.

Kowaleski, Maryanne. "Singlewomen in Medieval and Early Modern Europe: The Demographic Perspective." Eds. Judith M. Bennett and Any M. Froide. *Singlewomen in the European Past, 1250–1800*. Philadelphia: U of Pennsylvania P, 1999. 38–81.

Krug, Rebecca. *Reading Families: Women's Literate Practice in Late Medieval England*. Ithaca: Cornell UP, 2002.

Lefkowitz, Mary R., and Maureen B. Fant. *Women's Life in Greece and Rome: A Sourcebook in Translation*. 2nd ed. Baltimore: Johns Hopkins UP, 1992.

de Pisan, Christine. *The Book of the City of Ladies*. Trans. Earl Jeffrey Richards. New York: Persea Books, 1982.

———. *Christine's Vision*. Trans. Glenda K. McLeod. New York: Garland, 1993.

Plutarch. *Shakespeare's Plutarch; Being a Selection from the Lives in North's Plutarch which Illustrate Shakespeare's Plays*. Trans. Thomas North. Ed. Walter W. Skeat. London: MacMillan, 1875.

2

WOMEN IN SHAKESPEARE'S WORLD

According to Jacques in *As You Like It*, "All the world's a stage, / And all the men and women merely players" (2.7.138–139), but as he proceeds to enumerate "the seven ages of man," the roles played by women are omitted from the stage without comment or notice. While both males and females in Shakespeare's time may have started off as infants, "Mewling and puking in the nurse's arms" (2.7.143), the parts they played in life quickly diverged at an early age, perhaps only merging again at the end of life, with both men and women exiting the world's stage in a state of "second childishness."

The roles of early modern women included daughters and wives, sisters and mothers; they learned and worked and played. But for the most part, they were not expected to be schoolgirls (whining or otherwise). As women, they were expected to be the silently beautiful beloved and not the balladeer (who gazes upon her eyebrow rather than engaging her intellect). Women were not seen as fit to play the soldier or the judge. And as keepers of homes and households, as in our own time, women enjoyed no retirement equivalent to that of the "slippered pantaloon's" withdrawal from "a world too wide" (2.7.157–159). Then, as now, social and economic class as much as sex determined the range of roles available to a woman during the sixteenth and seventeenth centuries.

STANDARDS OF LIVING AND ECONOMIC STATUS

Elizabethan and Jacobean England was an extremely hierarchical society for both men and women, and life for the majority of English people was harsh by modern middle class standards. Early modern households were often quite violent. The laws allowed for husbands to beat their wives; at the same time, mothers as well as fathers were also allowed to use corporal punishments on their children and servants. Incidents in which someone of a superior rank strikes someone of a lower rank are recorded commonly and often as unremarkable in a range of texts, including drama (e.g., Petruchio's abuse of his servants) but also diaries, letters, and pamphlet literature. There was a strong sentiment that to spare the rod was to spoil the child, and mothers known for being resistant to whipping their children were often considered too "tender" and ultimately not having the child's best interest at heart (Mendelson and Crawford 161). At the same time, however, many educators, such as Roger Ascham and Richard Mulcaster, advocated that teachers stop caning or beating their students and instead use gentler means of teaching their young aristocratic pupils. The absence of corporal punishment in Ascham's curriculum also provided an implicit critique of parental abuse. According to Roger Ascham, his more gentle tutelage offered Lady Jane Gray with a respite from the blows routinely administered by her parents. And, as we shall see, wife-beating was a particularly debated—though far from resolved—topic in Elizabethan and Jacobean England.

One's social standing—referred to as "estate" or "degree"—was as important a factor as gender. Commoners included everyone from the poor and destitute through the wealthier bubbles of untitled merchants and skilled artisans and craftsmen. The relatively more affluent of this latter group of the "common sort" were also sometimes referred to as the "middling sort." Shakespeare and those like him would have been considered part of the middling sort. The majority of the population was untitled and considered "common," while those few people with titles ranged from the lower ranks of knights and members of the gentry ("gentlemen") through the aristocracy and the nobility. As is the case in our own time, the majority of early modern English people labored to earn the wealth they used to sustain themselves during their lifetimes, but the majority of the culture's wealth was inherited; in other words, a small minority of the population controlled the majority of land and other available wealth, and they did so by inheritance. Significantly, marriage provided a primary means of social mobility during this time for both men and women (Wayne 11). Throughout this period, as they had during the Middle Ages, women continued to be defined primarily in terms of their social standing and in terms of their gendered relationships to men as maids (daughters to be married), wives, and widows. Thus, it is crucial to consider a woman's social class and her marital status in imagining what women and their lives were like in Elizabethan and Jacobean England.

For women the standard of living was consistently and disproportionately lower than for men of similar class status. Between one-half to two-thirds of all early modern English women lived lives of relative poverty, diligently maintaining themselves and their families at or slightly above subsistence. Many, however, lived in absolute poverty, perhaps receiving poor relief or other charity, scavenging, begging, stealing, or trading in prostitution to feed and clothe themselves and their families (Mendelson and Crawford 261). While we may be shocked by these disparities, we may be even more surprised if we consider women's status as a group in our own time with that of women in Shakespeare's. As Amy Louise Erickson points out:

> In the twentieth century all overt legal restrictions have been removed, and yet women as a group remain at a profound economic, social and political disadvantage. Women today predominate among those receiving income support or welfare from the state—at the identical rate that they predominated in the seventeenth

century among those in receipt of parish poor relief. And an equivalent proportion of the poor then and now are single mothers, although the causes of their singleness have shifted. Women today earn only two thirds of what men earn. But women have earned approximately two thirds of men's wages for the last seven centuries. How is it that such severe economic disparity between women and men persists when the laws have changed so dramatically? (3)

Women's negotiations of not only law but cultural custom and expectations have a significant impact on their actual and individual lived experiences. Moreover, early modern ideas about women are often quite contradictory—both among the various writings on the subject of women and in relation to how people actually seem to have behaved in the world. On the one hand, theoretical discussions on the nature of women present a figure that needs to be contained, viewing women as inherently inferior, uncontrollable, and prone to a wide range of vices and disabilities. Prescriptive writings likewise argue for the containment of women. Nevertheless, while nearly all sixteenth- and seventeenth-century Englishmen probably believed to some degree in the general prescription of female subjection, this ideology was not always consistent with or foremost in the actual practices of these Englishmen's personal relationships with their mothers, wives, daughters, and sisters. Moreover, while many women likewise probably viewed women as categorically inferior to men, a good number seem to have viewed themselves (and a select group of others) as exceptions to the general rule.

Elizabeth I is a striking example. As one of England's most powerfully successful monarchs by conventional political standards, ruling forty-five years (in more than 200 years, only two others ruled nearly that long), she is not known for having directly advanced the cause of women's equality. Indeed, Elizabeth ruled by shrewdly deploying the concept of the king's two bodies, a theory that saw the monarchy, as God's representative on earth, as an enduring and eternal power (the "body politic") that transferred from monarch to successive monarch. The body politic was thus housed within the individual body of each rightful heir to the throne. In her speech to rouse the troops before the battle at Tilbury, for example, Elizabeth claimed the following: "I know I have the body of a weak and feeble woman, but I have the heart and stomach of a king" (Tudor 77). Elsewhere, she defended her right and authority to rule not on her personal merits or attributes of her female body, but rather on the masculinity of her body politic. Her refusal to marry (which would have subordinated her as a wife to her husband and diminished the confidence of her people in her as the nation's highest authority, under God alone) and the image of herself as the Virgin Queen further enhanced her ability to distance herself from the weakness attributed to her sex. Like the Virgin Mary, the Virgin Queen was alone of all her sex. Although the queen was not a promoter of women's rights, as we shall see, some early modern women—as well as a few men—vehemently opposed the majority view of women's subjection, arguing in favor of overall equality between the sexes.

The majority of women during this time, however, probably never had time to engage in such debates about equality. For many women (and men, too), subsistence would have taken all their energies. For extremely poor women during this time, the lines between legitimate and criminal means of eking out a living were especially precarious—and often dependent on the goodwill and interpretation of those with more power, who determined whether a poor woman's scavenging was gleaning or stealing and whether she was of the "deserving" poor or not. As William Rowley, Thomas Dekker, and John Ford's *The Witch of Edmonton* (1621) exemplifies, a great deal depended on a woman's reputation and the opinion of those above her as to whether she was a deserving poor. In the play, Old Banks attacks Mother Sawyer as a witch for gathering rotten sticks from his land to warm herself, and Mother Sawyer's community shapes her identity as witch:

> And why on me? why should the envious world
> Throw all their scandalous malice upon me?
> 'Cause I am poor, deformed, and ignorant,
> And like a bow buckled and bent together
> By some more strong in mischiefs than myself,
> Must I for that be made a common sink
> For all the filth and rubbish of men's tongues
> To fall and run into? Some call me witch,
> And being ignorant of myself, they go
> About to teach me how to be one; urging
> That my bad tongue—by their bad usage made so—
> Forspeaks their cattle, doth bewitch their corn,
> Themselves, their servants, and their babes at nurse.
> This they enforce upon me, and in part
> Make me to credit it (Rowley 2.1.1–15)

Indeed, not all women were patient in their poverty, but when they protested, they usually did so in terms of class issues rather than gender issues.

On occasion, their protests against untenable living conditions could be received as a legitimate complaint by authorities, who would then determine their need as deserving of charity; when too strenuously voiced, however, their demanding protests could be deemed insurrection. A number of women over the centuries, for example, participated in riots against food shortages and the poor quality of grains and corn; inhumane working conditions for laborers; and the enclosure of public grazing lands.

In the summer of 1607 in Newton, over a thousand people, including many women and children, gathered to tear down the fences and fill in ditches after what had once been public arable and grazing lands were enclosed for the private use of the Treshams, a local gentry family, depriving local peasants and yeomen of a crucial means of producing a living (McNeill 165; Wrightson 185–187). Women also participated in large numbers in the riots at Maldon, Dorchester, Kent, and elsewhere, and the records often indicate a history of women breaking rules in response to poverty. For many of these women, authorities seem initially to have responded with relative leniency and an understanding of the protesters' constrained circumstances, but then brought increasing harshness in situations where protests against unrelenting conditions of poverty continued. For a woman like Ann Carter, who took on the title of captain and the role of leader, the punishment was hanging alongside two fellow rioters (Walter 47–84).

EDUCATION AND VOCATIONS FOR WOMEN

Throughout the early modern period and beyond, women continued to be excluded categorically from universities. Significantly, women (along with economic, racial, and ethnic demographic groups that include men) continued to be excluded from certain prestigious universities up until the mid-twentieth century. Nonetheless, women were educated both informally and formally throughout the early modern period.

Poor girls began their training around the age of seven, and they might be apprenticed to learn lace-making, spinning, knitting, and housewifery, or they might be settled as servants in more economically stable households to assist with baking, brewing, and dairying. None of these professions were usually lucrative enough to sustain a living wage alone. Many women worked in such licensed crafts as ale-making and midwifery, but often could not afford the license, thus leaving themselves open to the whims of local officials, who might or might not enforce the laws pertaining to them.

It was assumed that marriage would be the path taken by all women, regardless of other occupations needed to earn a living. For women of the gentry and above, marriage was typically seen as the only path to be taken. "Vocation" is commonly used to refer to the role of marriage for women in numerous volumes of conduct literature, including Juan Luis Vives's *Instruction of a Christian Woman* (1523), William Whatley's *A Bride-Bush* (1617), and William Gouge's *Of Domestical Duties* (1622).

Although women of the middling sort were excluded from craft and trade guilds even more drastically than they had been during the medieval period, some examples of women learning trades as apprentices nonetheless existed during Shakespeare's lifetime. Most women who had training in such skills as leatherwork, dyeing, printing, and so forth, however, were likely to be the daughters or wives of guildsmen (members of artisan organizations). Occasionally in urban areas, as in the medieval past, some married women were granted permission by their husbands to trade or conduct business as *femme sole* (legally, as single women). Such women could proceed as if unmarried for business purposes, able to buy and sell goods or enter into contracts without needing to obtain their husband's consent each time. A woman who was *femme sole* could also sue and be sued in relation to her business activities. Women bearing that designation, however, were fewer than they had been in the Middle Ages, and early modern married women more commonly worked invisibly under the auspices of their husband's business or trade. As Sara Mendelson and Patricia Crawford have shown, "aristocratic and middling wives actually performed a significant proportion of the labour for which their husbands were paid," but the historical records often obscure such work done by wives married to men in such urban civic positions as warden, beadle, fishmonger, grocer, and company officer (341–342).

Informal evidence from Philip Henslowe and Edward Alleyn, two principal shareholders in the Rose Theater (the rival stage to Shakespeare's Globe) gives us a picture of the ordinariness of this work. Letters written by Edward Alleyn, on tour in the countryside during the summer and fall of 1593 when the Rose playhouse was closed, to his wife, Joan, and to his father-in-law, Philip Henslowe (both of whom remained in London), can provide us with some insight into how one married theater couple managed their domestic and business affairs. Joan played a significant role in the maintenance of the household, both on a day-to-day basis and while Alleyn was away, but she also figured into the day-to-day business affairs as well. Shakespeare's wife probably performed similar duties.

While for the most part, laws prohibited single women from practicing a guild craft or occupation, a few widows here and there continued as *femme sole* the trades of their dead husbands. By the late sixteenth century, however, this custom was diminishing as part of a general trend toward women's increasing exclusion from the more lucrative opportunities of the burgeoning early modern market economy. As Marjorie McIntosh's research documents, female workers met with increasing hostility from their male peers and legal measures aimed at excluding them from various trades and occupations. Women's economic roles were increasingly limited to the realm of providing lodging and food on a small scale, low-end lending, and unskilled labor; most occupations for women were not particularly advantageous in terms of either income or social advancement (116). A number of women—some single, but mostly married—also made their livings as victuallers (one who provides food), innkeepers, brewers, alewives, jail keepers, and overseers of workhouses and almshouses (houses for the poor). The bawdy Mistress Quickly, who appears in the plays about Henry IV and Henry V as well as in *The Merry Wives of Windsor*, exemplifies certain popular attitudes toward women (especially single women) who kept lodgers.

Nearly all women, regardless of their marital status, would have typically learned household tasks that include what many in our culture continue to consider "women's work." The designation of "housewife" in the early modern period was not necessarily indicative of marital status, but rather was considered an occupation. In an age before department and grocery stores existed to offer mass produced goods and materials, a great deal of labor was necessary to provide food and clothing for the members of the household.

We get a sense of the range of a housewife's everyday duties, for example, in the aforementioned letters between the actor Edward Alleyn and his wife, Joan. Edward reminds her to plant spinach, sends home stockings for her to dye a tawny orange, and inquires about her distilled waters, while she receives rents and loan payments as she tends to some of the business details in his absence. Aristocratic women associated with large estates, like Margaret Hoby, Grace Mildmay, and Anne Clifford performed (or oversaw the performance of) many of these duties on a larger, more complex manorial scale, as well as serving local politics, either as widows or in the absence of husbands who were away on business. Many of the household tasks performed by women include those that feminist historians have identified as the invisible (often unpaid) labor that is foundational to most cultures, including our own.

The education of nearly all women thus would have included training in housewifery, which they would have learned firsthand through observing their mothers or mistresses. Girls learned by doing tasks directly—cleaning the rooms, building and tending fires, fetching water, preparing and preserving food, obtaining and organizing supplies, planting and harvesting gardens, tending livestock, and so forth—or by overseeing servants in this work. In addition to experiential learning, some women also studied the numerous cookbooks and manuals on a variety of household skills that proliferated during this period. Women who were literate and could afford books of paper also kept miscellanies, or individual recipe books.

Interestingly, included in early modern notions of "recipes" were formulas for medicinal concoctions, reminding us that women were often the first (and sometimes the only) resource for healthcare, and they tended to the health of the household, which might include not only the immediate family but any servants as well. Margaret Hoby and Grace Mildmay, for example, record recipes and instructions along with entries about their attendance at numerous births as well as general instances of providing healthcare—including surgery—for tenants on their estates. Women typically held the primary duties of tending to those being born and those dying.

Among the most common feature of people's lives in the Renaissance was service, regardless of sex or rank, from the lowliest of peasants to those in the highest ranks of the aristocracy. For women without family or male protectors, however, the power dynamics of service brought a number of risks. *The Witch of Edmonton*, by Rowley, Dekker, and Ford, for example, depicts the plight of Winnifrede, who is made pregnant by her wealthy master and then abandoned by her bigamous and murderous husband, giving insight into the dangers faced by single women who found employment in wealthy households. As Sara Mendelson points out, while service in a household might bring security, it could also bring dangers posed by masters and other male members of the household, including other servants. "Having lost her reputation for 'honesty,' a pregnant maidservant was rendered virtually unemployable, and often found her only option for survival was a life of vagrancy and prostitution" (Mendelson 62). Winnifrede is fortunate in that the play's community defines her as a victim to be protected rather than a whore to be shunned.

While the poor and middling sort served masters in homes or shops, members of the aristocracy and gentry were often fostered into more prestigious households, where they were expected to learn the ways appropriate to their social standing, to find suitable marriage partners, and to make social connections advantageous for the patronage of family members. Unlike poor girls, who would be sent to serve as soon as possible, elite girls typically did not leave until their preteens or early teen years. Depending on degree, elite women would be expected to learn manners, music, dancing, needlework, and good housewifery (either to enable them to perform such tasks as wives or to oversee servants who would perform these tasks). Margaret Dakins, later Lady Margaret Hoby, met her first husband, Walter Devereaux (the brother of Elizabeth I's favorite, Robert Devereaux, the Earl of Essex) while both were in service to the Earl and Countess of Huntingdon. In her diary, Lady Margaret Hoby reflected back on the various skills in housewifery she learned from the countess, which later enabled her to efficiently run her own country estates.

Daughters from the most elite families (and high-ranking families with even higher ambitions) were placed at around the age of ten to fourteen in the royal courts as attendants for female members of the royal family. Shakespeare's plays include a number of female characters in service to royal or aristocratic households, including Nerissa in *The Merchant of Venice* and Helena in *All's Well.* While Rosalind's usurping uncle in *As You Like It* has retained her as a companion to her cousin Celia, ambitious parents often worked hard to secure spots as ladies-in-waiting and maids of honor to queens and princesses. Such girls and women would have been tutored in languages, literature, dancing, music, and other entertainments suited to court life. Mary Sidney, who was a lady-in-waiting to Elizabeth I, and later her niece, Mary Wroth, who was an attendant in the court of Queen Anne, were both known for their skills in music and dancing in addition to their literary talents. While some female courtiers held specific offices that entailed stipends, most courtiers attended members of the royal family at their own cost with an aim for benefiting through the system of patronage by receiving royal gifts, preferment to posts for relatives, and other lucrative connections.

SINGLE LIFE, MARRIED LIFE, AND
THE EARLY MODERN HOUSEHOLD

With the dissolution of the monasteries under Henry VIII, the convent as a life option for women was eliminated, and the pressure toward marriage increased for women on a variety of fronts, both legislative and cultural. In spite of the legal and customary imperatives to marry, however, large numbers of women were at any one point in their lives not married, and a significant number—perhaps as many as 20% between 1575 and 1700—never married at all (Froide 2). A few women who had sufficient means to maintain their livelihood (though not so much as to make them overly attractive as lucrative marriage matches) on occasion found support from families to remain unmarried if they desired, but most women were expected to marry. While it may seem obvious that aristocratic daughters and heiresses would be directed to marry, the pressure was equally strong at the lower end of the social spectrum, where parish officials saw marriage for poor women as a means of reducing the numbers on poor relief.

The 1563 Statute of Artificers set a minimum age at which someone might leave an apprenticeship to marry: twenty-one for women and twenty-four for men. At the same time, the part of the statute specifically relating to women provided local officials the right to compel all unmarried women between the ages of twelve and forty to "live in service," regardless of whether they were able to earn a sustainable living wage independently. As Sara Mendelson and Patricia Crawford point out, the statute concerns "those years when a woman was susceptible to pregnancy. Service was thus intended as a sexual as well as a physical and economic constraint on young women's liberty. Yet, ironically, the typical unmarried mother who was brought before the secular courts was the maidservant who had been impregnated by her master or fellow servant" (Mendelson and Crawford 97–98). At the same time, a surprisingly large number of brides arrived at the altar pregnant—anywhere from the urban low of 16% to over 20% in more rural areas. That Anne Hathaway was pregnant when she married William Shakespeare is not the anomaly that some scholars have suggested. Nor, as some of these same scholars have suggested, did her being twenty-six put her beyond the average age at marriage for women of her social class (William, however, was eighteen and thus slightly younger than typical). Indeed, a popular misconception has involved the acceptance of Juliet, who is thirteen in *Romeo and Juliet*, as representative of the average Englishwoman at marriage. Juliet's age, however, is more likely a reflection of either (or perhaps a combination of) her status as a member of the aristocracy or the fact that she is an English playwright's vision of what an Italian character would be like. In England "between 1550 and 1700, the mean age at marriage for men fluctuated between 27.6 and 29.3, while that for women was between 26 and 26.8" (Ben-Amos 32).

Although a handful of pregnant characters appear onstage in Shakespeare's plays (e.g., Hermione in *The Winter's Tale*, Juliet in *Measure for Measure*, and Helena in *All's Well*), the more particular details of this aspect of women's lives were not typically represented on stage, nor were they seen as centrally human experiences. However, pregnancy and the rituals of giving birth were central to many women's lives.

In the days leading up to a woman's labor, if she had sufficient resources, she would go into a period called "lying in," during which time the woman's close female friends and female family members gathered around her to help her deliver her baby. Although midwives were licensed by male authorities, it would not be until the early eighteenth century that male doctors would begin to dominate the delivery of babies. Usually a woman gave birth in the company of other women, surrounded by her "gossips" (from the phrase "God's siblings"). While typically a time of joy, pregnancy and childbirth were also fraught with fear (and, as we shall see, this fear prompted some educated women to leave written legacies to their children, born and unborn).

After approximately a month's period of resting following the delivery (for women of sufficient means), many women participated in the ritual of "churching," an ideologically complicated ceremony involving both the purification of the woman from the stain of childbirth, thanksgiving for the safe delivery, and an honoring of her motherhood. There is no way to know whether these important events were not represented onstage because they remained mysterious to the men who did not partake in them, because the all-male acting profession would have made staging such scenes logistically difficult, or because such events were not seen as particularly important or worth staging.

Particularly important during this time were debates about breastfeeding. On one front, early modern fashion and "science" dictated that only women of the poorer classes nursed their own children, and the wet nurses employed by women of the gentry and aristocracy uniformly came from the poorer classes. Class reasons included the need to return to sexual reproduction as soon as possible (lactation can have the effect of suppressing fertility), but upper-class men also wanted to preserve the aesthetics of their wives' breasts from sagging. On the medical front, some theories suggested that mother's milk was not healthy in the early days postpartum, and that colostrum in particular was toxic (exactly contrary to twenty-first century notions that urge women to breastfeed at least during the first days to impart colostrum's immune-system boosting properties to the newborn). Consequently, advocates in favor of wet-nursing argued that the already-matured milk of the wet nurse was healthier.

Attempting to counter the class stigma attached to nursing, however, sixteenth- and seventeenth-century proponents of maternal breast-feeding drew upon biblical images of queens and other important mothers to lend respectability, even prestige, to maternal nurture. Sarah's nursing of Isaac in Genesis 21:7 was particularly important to efforts to improve the status of maternal breast-feeding among the more socially powerful. The example of Sarah was endorsed by Robert Cleaver and John Dod in their A Godly Form of Household Government: For the Ordering of Private Families, According to the Direction of God's Word (1621) and by William Gouge in his Of Domesticall Duties (1622). Elizabeth Clinton, the Countess of Lincoln, felt strongly enough about the subject that she was compelled to write The Countess of Lincoln's Nursery (1622), an endorsement of maternal breast-feeding. Lamenting the fact that she was persuaded by her husband and others to put her eighteen children out to nurse, she urges others to nurse their own children, arguing that breast-feeding is ordained by God and that wet-nursing is ultimately exploitive of poor women who endanger their own infants by their occupation.

Anne Hathaway Shakespeare seems to have been an early subscriber to the new trend, nursing her own children several decades before these pamphlets urged the practice. In the grief-filled Latin epigraph written on Anne's memorial, her daughter Susannah praises her mother for the gifts of her breast, milk and life, in return for which she can only give stones (i.e., the stone monument on which the lines are engraved).

Although marriage in post-reformation England was no longer considered a sacrament as it was among Catholics, it continued to be viewed as a sacred and indissolvable union lasting until the death of one or both of the couple. Marriages took place with a variety of level of formalities, with the basic being a "hand-fasting"—or an exchange of consent between the bride and groom—the bestowal of the bride's dowry, and the witnesses' acknowledgment of the union (usually in a feast or toast).

In extreme cases of distress, couples could seek what were known as annulments or divorces, but the latter did not mean what it does today. While we typically see divorce as a procedure by which a marriage is ended and the separating parties are then free to enter into new marriages with new partners, early modern divorce was closer to what we might consider to be a legal separation of the parties, rather than a dissolution of the marriage. Under a divorce *a mensa et thoro* ("from bed and board"), the couple typically lived in separate households, but with a rare few exceptions, the parties were not free to remarry. This type of divorce was particularly important if there were legitimate children, as their status would not be affected by their parents' divorce. In such cases, however, because legitimate offspring were considered a type of property controlled by the father, children would be given over to the custody of the father, who would then determine whether the mother would have access to her children. Indeed, even in situations of strife when couples did not legally separate, husbands had absolute control over their children. When Anne Clifford and her first husband, Richard Dorset, were engaged in a heated disagreement concerning the lands of her inheritance, they were not legally separated (though frequently refusing each other's bed, according to Clifford's diary), but Clifford reports in her diary that Dorset determined "the Child should live at Horsely, & not come hither any more, so as this was a very grievous and sorrowful day to me" (Clifford 32).

Only if the marriage had been annulled—that is, rendered as if it never happened—could the parties enter into new marriages with new partners. Any children born from an annulled marriage, however, were likely to be rendered bastards and bypassed in their inheritances, and a wife would be barred from dower rights. The ability to separate from a spouse was additionally impeded by societal norms and legislation that was anti-singlewoman, and by many women's lesser capacity to earn a living wage on their own. Although divorce reform was advocated by some, including the sixteenth-century Bishop Thomas Cranmer, English divorce law remained limited until the Divorce Act of 1857. The permanency of marriage obviously had an impact on both parties, but it was particularly significant to wives, who were expected to endure what might turn out to be intolerable but inescapable lives of submission to their husbands.

Valerie Wayne has described early modern views of marriage in terms of residual, dominant, and emergent ideologies, noting the importance of realizing that contradictions run throughout the various ways of thinking about marriage. Deriving from ancient and medieval discourses but still active in the early modern present, the residual views of misogamy (hatred of marriage) argued against marriage for two basic reasons. Working from the long tradition of misogyny and addressing their arguments primarily to male readers, one side claimed that all women make bad wives and that a life of celibacy was to be preferred as a higher form of existence. In early modern England, after the dissolution of the monasteries, however, such an alternative was no longer viable, but the notion that all women make bad wives continued to find voice in such ideas as the cuckold, the (often ignorant) husband of an unfaithful wife.

In *As You Like It*, for example, we see the idea that marriage equates cuckoldry presented humorously by both Touchstone, who claims that "as horns are odious, they are necessary" (3.3.42), while Rosalind (disguised as Ganymede pretending to be Rosalind) informs Orlando that men's destiny is to be "beholden to [their] wives" for horns (4.1.52–53). More tragically, we see the deadly results of such distrust of wives in plays like *Othello*. The second residual version of the misogamist ideology argued against the misogynist views of women but attributed equally negative qualities to all men. Love was not compatible with this view of marriage, which was too filled with loss of freedom and tribulation. In spite of the dominance of pro-marriage ideology in early modern England, misogynist and misogamist ideas continued to readily abound, especially those highlighting misogynist reasons against marriage.

The dominant early modern ideologies of marriage endorsed the institution as a social and spiritual union based in divine law. Marriage was seen as accomplishing three primary purposes: companionship, legitimate procreation, and the avoidance of fornication. Numerous writers, including William Gouge, Edmund Tilney, John Dod, Robert Cleaver, and William Whatley, broached the subject of marriage in various manuals and sermons. Although seen as having potential value within the Christian scheme of things, marriage was presented as a responsibility, one often depicted in terms of sacrifice to the inconveniences of cohabiting with another person and to the obedience to the biblical injunction to multiply.

Early modern writers continued to build upon the medieval Catholic humanist tradition of seeing companionship as central to marriage's purpose. Following the thought process of the earlier writers who had worked from the biblical account of woman's creation as a helper for man, early modern notions of companionate marriage tended to focus predominantly on the duties of wives in relation to husbands, rather than reciprocally. Proponents of the dominant ideology in favor of marriage also frequently invoke the language of "equality in marriage," but we must be careful to understand that by "equality" they usually are referring to similarities in age, social standing, and intelligence, not an equality of power after marriage. Although marriage was seen as companionate, it was nonetheless hierarchical, with husbands as dominant and wives as submissive. Indeed, the idea of companionate marriage did not preclude the notion of wives as property—as seen, for example, in Thomas Overbury's literary character sketch of "A Good Wife," in which he described her as "a man's best moveable" (i.e., a piece of portable property).

Further complicating matters was an increased attention to the idea of companionate marriage as involving reciprocal and freely granted love, a concept that developed through medieval Catholic humanism and was further taken up by Protestant reformers (especially in relation to notions of free will). This emergent ideology promotes "unambiguously egalitarian relations between husbands and wives" (Wayne 4). Such ideas are seen in the increasing attention given to the idea that, when arranging marriages, parents or guardians should take into consideration the opinions and feelings of those to be married. While medieval courtly conventions imagined love as necessarily adulterous—a relationship taking place outside of a marriage that had been arranged for economic or political reasons rather than for romantic love—the early modern era saw the beginnings of a conflation between romantic love and marriage. That such a view occurs simultaneously with deeply entrenched misogyny, along with ideologies of hierarchies between parents and children, and husbands and wives, creates interesting tensions between the various perspectives as represented in Shakespeare's plays. Some plays present the fantasy of happily matched couples who seemingly marry purely for love (as in A Midsummer Night's Dream and As You Like It), while other plays depict with nightmarish tragedy the doom that befalls couples who transgress parental blessing (as in Othello and Romeo and Juliet).

Additionally, the juxtaposition between the womanly ideal of passivity and obedience to patriarchal authority on the one hand, and the ability to actively choose in matters of love and desire on the other hand, likewise created serious anxiety about the truth of woman's love and her fidelity in marriage. If women have wills and desires of their own—and act on them by taking lovers of their own choosing—then what is to keep a woman from changing her mind (and the culture sees women as by nature fickle and changeable) and choosing another? If women are obligated by duty to love their husbands, then how can a husband ever know if his wife truly loves him or is merely submitting to duty? Interestingly, the same dilemma of surety is faced by parents in relation to their children—as in King Lear, where Lear is anxious over the love of his daughters. We see these anxieties and tensions played out both comically and tragically in Shakespeare's plays, as well as in literature produced by his contemporaries.

Another point of deep anxiety concerned the question of domestic violence, which was a hotly debated topic during this period, both in sermons and in popular literature. The hierarchy put men at an advantage in terms of worth and prestige—and the penalties for murdering a husband were considerably different than those for murdering a wife. A husband convicted of killing his wife was judged for murder, and the typical penalty was death by hanging; a wife who killed her husband was guilty of petty treason, and the penalty could be death by burning, the same fate met by traitors (a servant who killed his or her master or a child who killed his or her parent was also convicted of petty treason). Although the pamphlets, plays, and other imaginative literature of the period suggest that pugnacious and even murderous wives posed a severe threat to the safety and well-being of early modern men, in fact women then as now were more likely to be victims of violence at the hands of their spouses and lovers, rather than perpetrators.

Throughout the centuries, a husband's physical "correction" of his wife continued to be viewed as a private matter of household government and, with rare exception, a matter too trivial for a court of law. It would not be until the nineteenth century that England and some of the United States would begin to rescind a husband's right to beat his wife, and it would take at least another century before such violence would be viewed as assault.

Nevertheless, during Shakespeare's time, wife-beating was in many respects a contested issue, similar to today's corporal punishment of children. While it was legally permissible for husbands to use corporal punishments to control the behavior of their wives—as well as children and servants—beatings did not mesh quite well with the emergent ideologies that viewed marriage as a partnership and wives as spiritual equals and domestic helpmates. This emerging concept of partnership was not one of equality but was variously imagined to be akin to the dynamic between a general and his lieutenant, or a governor and his steward; the analogy also likened the relationship between husband and wife to that between Christ and the Church. In all cases, the relationship was clearly hierarchical. As Frances Dolan notes, "Wife beating had an ambiguous status precisely because of the wife's double position as joint governor (and thus the corrector of children and servants) and subordinate (and thus subject to her husband's correction)" (219). In serious works, such as religious writings and sermons, including the *Homily on Marriage*, as well as in books of advice on marital conduct, the general consensus urged husbands to use physical violence as a last resort—and noted that to do so reflected negatively on the husband's competence at governing. Ballads and other theatrical texts, such as "The Cucking of a Scold" and "Punch and Judy" (some of these are included in Frances Dolan's excellent edition of *The Taming of the Shrew*), often presented the physical battle between the sexes as comedic entertainment (in both senses of the term: eliciting laughter and ending "happily"). An extreme case can be found in the ballad *A Merry Jest of a Shrewd and Curst Wife Lapped [Wrapped] in Morel's Skin*, in which the spoiled, boisterous, lazy wife is forced into submission by being beaten and thrown down stairs until her blood runs, then enclosed in the salted hide of a horse named Morel.

LAW AND PROPERTY

Working in conjunction with a legal system that categorized women along with children and servants was coverture, the legal fiction by which a married couple were viewed as having a "unity of person"—were seen as being of one flesh, in other words. Under coverture, early modern marriage continued the ancient and medieval tradition of transferring a woman's legal rights and identity from father or guardian to husband. As *femme covert* ("covered woman"), wives were prohibited from owning property or entering into legal agreements; with few exceptions, a married woman had no legal existence apart from her husband. Unless determined otherwise by premarital legal documents, a woman's personal property (her clothing, jewels, and so on) became her husband's property upon marriage. If a woman owned land, or real property, the use and profits of it came into the husband's control, although usually he could not sell or alienate its use without her consent.

Anne Clifford records two generations of lengthy and brutal struggles between spouses over control of the inalienable part of a wife's property—first between her mother and father, and then later between herself and her husbands, who wanted her to sell away her interests in the disputed lands of her inheritance. Because of the potential for coercion in such cases, courts often held a separate examination with the wife outside her husband's presence. In Clifford's case, she outlived not only her two husbands, but also the male relatives who had staked claims against the estates, finally inheriting them after many decades of litigation.

Women who had knowledge of the law could make use of equitable devices such as "use" and "trust," by which they could separate legal ownership from beneficial ownership. By using such laws, women could transfer the legal title of real property (i.e., land) to a third party while retaining the property's use and income (although this, of course, belonged by law to the husband during the marriage). Such legal maneuvers, which presumed the wife would outlive her spouse, aimed at preventing husbands from alienating property from wives during the marriage. Upon the husband's death, the woman would regain the legal title of the property. Such arrangements were sometimes made in secret (for example, with the assistance of parents or guardians who feared the prodigality of future son-in-laws), but often were made as part of the marriage negotiations (much like a prenuptial agreement). Also, during the reign of Henry VIII, legislation was passed specifically allowing married women to make wills, provided they had their husbands' permission. Women began to leave wills in greater (though still disproportionate) numbers. In the sixteenth century, 12% to 17% of wills were made by women, while during the seventeenth century, 20% were by women— although, across both centuries, the majority of women who left wills were widows or single women (80%). According to Mary Prior, the growing numbers of women who did produce wills in the sixteenth and seventeenth centuries indicate women's increasing assertiveness (208).

Among the wealthiest group of people, especially those with land, primogeniture was the general mode of transmitting inheritances. Under primogeniture, which prevailed in England until it was abolished in 1925, all of the real wealth goes to the eldest male heir (often with stipulations that he care for younger siblings). However, the practice and experience of people during this time did not always exactly match theory and law. As many as 20% to 25% of marriages produced daughters but no sons, meaning daughters often inherited for a generation. As Amy Erickson's study of property in early modern England demonstrates, "It is certainly true that land pulled inexorably toward males, but it spent a good deal of time in female hands along the way" (5). Mothers frequently controlled the inheritances of minor sons, and in cases where there was no male heir, the eldest daughter might inherit, or the wealth might be equally distributed among the children (coparceny). Increasingly during the sixteenth century, however, extremely wealthy heiresses who were only children found that estates that had once been entailed upon the next heir regardless of sex were being diverted to paternal uncles and cousins, as in the case of Anne Clifford.

A dowry was the portion of wealth (goods, land, money, and so forth) that the bride brought to the marriage to pay the cost of her living. In addition, the groom's side negotiated forms of settlement for the wife's maintenance, should she outlive her husband. A jointure was the amount the groom or his family promised in support of the bride should she be left a widow (typically worth one-fifth of the amount of the dowry), to be made in annual payments for the widow's maintenance. Often, such payments ceased upon remarriage, but not always. The right to dower was a third interest in lands, while chattels or other movable goods were considered personal property and could be distributed as the will maker saw fit. For those who died intestate (without a will), the standard practice was to award one-third of the income from real property (i.e., land) along with one-third of the personal property to the widow, with the rest to be divided evenly among the children, if there were any. Interestingly, the widower's version of a jointure or dower was "curtesy," which gave all, rather than a third, of the income from the dead wife's real property (i.e., land) to the husband's use during his lifetime.

The complexity of early modern property laws is demonstrated in the case of Edmund Tilney and his wife, Lady Mary Bray, the wealthy widow of Sir Edward Bray. Upon his marriage to Mary, Tilney acquired the use of her jointure received as Bray's widow, which was a substantial income from lands in Surrey. Because Mary had been childless in both her marriages, however, the lands reverted back to Sir Edward's descendants when Mary died before Edmund. When his litigation against Bray's heirs failed, Tilney found himself in strained financial circumstances upon the loss of income (Wayne 10–11).

For widows whose husbands may not have owned land but held leases (or "copyholds"), they might be granted "freebench," which was a part or whole interest in copyhold lands during the period of widowhood. This arrangement required the widow to avoid remarriage and maintain a chaste reputation. During the period of freebench, a widow was also required to make payments and undertake any obligations required of the copyhold. That widows were typically granted only a portion of the copyhold suggests several things—among them, that the wife's contribution to her husband's business or working of lands was "invisible" and that women were perceived as requiring fewer material resources than men for survival. As Tim Stretton observes, "In principle the custom of widow's estate was a simple right. . . . In practice, the custom could be the subject of bitter disagreement and conflict," comprising a substantial amount of litigation during the Elizabethan period (159).

Although some women found themselves financially secure—even wealthy— upon the death of their spouse, a significant number of women endured substantial reductions in their finances and standard of living. As the research of Amy Erickson shows, one quarter of all widows were left in debt upon the death of their husbands. Additionally, many other women were left with only 20% to 50% of their husband's inventories after all the debts had been paid, substantially reducing the amount of income available from the jointure or dower that had been promised at the inception of the marriage. The impact on lower-class women who may not have had substantial alternative resources is hard to fully realize, as their stories exist primarily in the archives of law courts and records of parish poor relief. For a number of highly publicized cases involving women of the aristocracy, however, we have more details. Mary Wroth, for example, was left a widow with a one-month-old son and debts nearly twenty times the amount of her £1,200 jointure; when her son died two years later, her control of his estate ended, and the inheritance (though not the debt) reverted back to her deceased husband's family. The limits of female education and the gendered constraints on employment meant that widows left without sufficient provision faced dire futures. Much of this, of course, is related to women's limited access to education and occupational training.

LITERACY AND ELITE INTELLECTUAL LEARNING

The majority of early modern English people (with higher percentages of women than men) would be defined as illiterate by modern standards, with slightly higher levels of literacy occurring in the urban areas. Between 1580 and 1640 in East Anglia, for example, 95% of female witnesses in the courts could not write their names, while in London the rate was approximately 90% (Cressy 147–148). By the 1690s, however, literacy rates in London had risen to about 48% (Cressy 146). Again, it is important for us to remember that not all cultures link reading and writing as ours does, and as was the case during the Middle Ages, reading literacy during this period was probably considerably more common than the ability to write (Hull 1–10).

Although Elizabethan and Jacobean England continued to be predominantly an aural/oral culture, a number of factors contributed to the rise in print literacy among English people during this time. The printing press, which had been imported into England in the late fifteenth century, made reading materials more and more widely—and relatively cheaply—available compared to manuscript books. The growing middle class of merchants and tradespeople, who had increasing amounts of expendable wealth, provided a substantial market for printed books.

Additionally, the Protestant emphasis on scripture created a need for all Christians, including women, to be able to read English, so as to have personal and direct access to the Bible. Henry VIII's 1543 law forbidding the reading of the Bible by merchants, artificers, journeymen, yeomen, laborers, and all women except noblewomen was repealed as English translations proliferated in the later sixteenth and seventeenth centuries. Women from middling and elite families were typically expected to oversee the religious instruction of small children and servants in the household. Some "poor schools" were endowed by the charity of wealthy people to teach reading in English, and many of these schools enrolled both boys and girls. Thomas Becon's *Catechism* (1564), for example, argued for the establishment of schools for lower- and middle-class children, both girls and boys, in order to promote Christian piety through the reading of scripture (Becon 175–177). Thus, the primary goal of such schools was to promote religion and foster a devout population. Schools that enrolled girls were likely to curtail their attendance beyond the age of nine.

While most educational theorists of the day focused on programs of study for male aristocrats and gentry—men who would become the religious and political leaders of the nation—a number of prominent humanists beginning in the late Middle Ages and continuing through the sixteenth century advocated educating (aristocratic) girls, a small handful of them even promoting the same or similar curriculum as for boys. While the dissolution of monastic life under English Protestantism deprived women of what had once been an important opportunity for lives of intellectual rigor, Catholic humanists in particular advocated the education of aristocratic women and noblewomen, including those who had not chosen the life of a nun. Thomas More provided his daughters with the same education as for his son, and his eldest daughter, Margaret Roper, was renowned for her learning—especially for producing an important translation of the treatise on the *Pater Noster* ("Our Father" prayer) by the Catholic humanist Desiderius Erasmus. The five daughters of Anthony Cooke (who was Edward VI's tutor), Mildred, Anne, Elizabeth, Katherine, and Margaret, were similarly highly educated, having learned Latin, Greek, and Hebrew, as well as the various subjects central to humanist education. Anne Cooke Bacon is particularly significant as the English translator of Bishop John Jewel's *Apology for the Church of England*, a key document in the Elizabethan promotion of English Protestantism. Anne also supervised the early education of her son Francis Bacon, who became a pioneer in scientific thinking and one of the most influential thinkers of his time.

Among the most influential of the early Renaissance works promoting education for women is that of Juan Luis Vives, a Spanish student of Erasmus who was brought to Henry VIII's court specifically to serve as Princess Mary's tutor. In 1523 he presented the Latin text of his *Instruction of a Christian Woman* (1523) to Henry VIII's first queen, Catherine of Aragon, as an educational model for her daughter. Originally composed in Latin for its royal female readers, the book's popularity grew exponentially after it was translated in 1529 into English by Richard Hyrde, who was the tutor to Thomas More's children. Hyrde's translation went through five editions between 1540 and 1600, as well as thirty-five editions translating it into other languages. Although the book is pro-education for women, and Vives was on the vanguard of those advocating that both men and women learn Latin and Greek, he is definitive in his caution that women not be educated to rule or take their place in the public worlds of politics and theology inhabited by men. Religion is the sole reason underlying his argument in favor of female education. The work's focus on religious and nonpolitical learning and its promotion of chastity as women's highest virtue makes it seem highly conservative by modern standards. In answer to the question of "what learning a woman should be set unto, and what she shall study?" Vives answers that the primary purpose for women's education is "the study of wisdom, which doth instruct their manners and inform their living, and teacheth them the way of good and holy life" (Vives 169).

Vives recommended moral philosophers Plato, Cicero, Seneca, Plutarch, and Aristotle, as well as the Bible, the church fathers, and Christian poetry. Although he allowed for some rhetoric, he saw no need for women to learn history, grammar, or logic—the subjects needed for governing. Women's access to higher learning, according to Vives, was unrelated to their potential for leadership in law, religion, or political diplomacy. Moreover, he explicitly forbade the reading of romances, which represented fantasy and adultery, and the licentious Greek and Latin poetry—most notably Ovid.

The vast differences between the education received by Mary Tudor and that experienced by her sister Elizabeth Tudor seems manifest in the differing successes of their rules. Vives's educational theories were aimed more at the type of domestic training Mary Tudor would have needed as a queen consort and mother to heirs, rather than the public and political acumen she needed as a ruling monarch. In contrast to her sister, Elizabeth I was without a doubt the most highly and fully educated woman of her day. Indeed, she could arguably be counted among the most educated of all sixteenth-century English people, male or female. Elizabeth's education, along with that of her brother Edward VI, was overseen by Henry VIII's final queen, Catherine Parr, a woman who had herself received an impressive humanist education. Under the tutelage of Roger Ascham, Elizabeth studied Greek and Latin, as well as the European languages. She also studied philosophy, classical orations, and the political theories of both ancient and contemporary writers, including Machiavelli's *The Prince*. As monarch, Elizabeth's patronage of the literary and scientific arts demonstrates the vast reaches of her learning and interests.

The scope and public nature of Elizabeth's learning, however, was extremely unusual in light of what most educational reformists prescribed for women during this time. A number of writers, Vives included, theorized about both men's and women's education. While educational treatises for both men and for women typically focus on the development of virtue and preparation for the vocations of life, the kinds of professions envisioned differ significantly by gender. Vocational directions for men typically entail careers in law, religion, or political diplomacy, whereas a woman's life profession is restricted to marriage. Thus a woman's education was seen as preparing her to be a suitable companion for her husband and an industrious housewife, careful of the household goods and capable of instructing young children and servants in Christian piety. Instructional manuals following Vives continued to emphasize the role of women's education in relation to the ideal of companionate marriage.

While women were not necessarily encouraged to write their own texts, they were targeted as an important market for books and as patrons of the literary arts. Vives, for example, feared the enticements of romances aimed specifically at female readers. As women's literacy rates rose, books published in the sixteenth and seventeenth centuries were increasingly addressed to female audiences, sometimes with dedications to a specifically-named woman or women and sometimes dedicated to various groups of unnamed women in general (and sometimes to both specific women and general audiences of "ladies," as in the case of works such as Edmund Spenser's *The Faerie Queene* or Aemilia Lanyer's *Salve Deus*).

In addition to publishers who sought to increase sales by targeting female readers in general, some authors sought individual patronage for both their manuscript and printed works. As Katherine Duncan-Jones observes, Shakespeare apparently did not actively seek female patronage; however, a number of other male authors did benefit from the patronage of certain wealthy, especially aristocratic and noble, women (106–109). The now-familiar system of royalties or profits from sales by which authors now make money through the publication of their works was not yet in place during the time of Shakespeare's career (indeed, we might remember that Shakespeare made his money as a shareholder in the business of theater, rather than directly from his poems and plays).

If authors expected to profit financially from their compositions, they typically did so by means of the system of patronage, through which a wealthy patron would bestow a gift, reward, or appointment in exchange. While an author might receive a one-time payment for a work dedicated or given to a wealthy or powerful patron, the amount usually was not enough to generate a comfortable, or even livable, income. Typically, authors hoped for comparatively more profitable and enduring rewards, such as a position in the patron's or another aristocrat's household, or preferment to a court, church, or government job.

Although women were most likely to have religious or devotional texts, conduct books, and sermons dedicated to them, a number of women encouraged what we might consider to be more literary endeavors. As David Bergeron, Barbara Lewalski, Margaret Hannay, and others have shown, certain women were important patrons of literature in early modern England. Margaret Beaufort was a particularly influential patron of the early printing press in late medieval England, commissioning both devotional works and romances. Later, Mary Sidney figured prominently as a patron and innovator of literary form. In addition to being a talented poet in her own right, she opened her estate at Wilton to a number of writers, including Edmund Spenser, Samuel Daniel, Thomas Nashe, Gabriel Harvey, John Donne, and Ben Jonson, providing them with an extensive library and one of the most important intellectual communities of the day. Mary Sidney's patronage activities furthered the careers of the writers who flocked to her home in Wilton, as well as those of her sons, whose careers were enhanced by the atmosphere and reputation for erudition and nobility surrounding them. Lucy, Countess of Bedford, likewise provided important patronage to such writers as Ben Jonson, John Donne, Samuel Daniel, Michael Drayton, and others.

As Theresa D. Kemp has shown, like their male counterparts, female authors such as Aemilia Lanyer, Mary Wroth, and Esther Inglis also sought the benefits of literary patronage, both directly for themselves and for family members as well. Not all efforts to obtain patronage were successful, however: for example, while Queen Elizabeth I had over 200 works dedicated to her, she was not a particularly generous patron.

Following the curriculum outlined by educational theorists, wealthy households often employed tutors to privately instruct their daughters. In *The Taming of the Shrew*, Baptista's wealth (and the dowry likely to accompany his beautiful younger daughter), for example, is implicit in Bianca's suitors' offering of tutors to instruct his daughters in languages and music. Anne Clifford, the daughter of the Earl and Countess of Cumberland, for example, was trained in the domestic arts by Anne Taylor, her governess, and in the more intellectual pursuits by Samuel Daniel, who had previously been the tutor to William Herbert, Earl of Pembroke and one of Shakespeare's patrons. Although Clifford was forbidden by her father to study languages, the range of her education was apparently impressive enough, as John Donne admiringly commented that she could "discourse of all things, from Predestination to Slea Silk" (Clifford 60 nt.).

Parents who were wealthy but nevertheless of more modest means resorted to sending their daughters to boarding schools, where they learned reading, writing,

French, music, dancing, and needlework—skills aimed at increasing their value on the marriage market. By the seventeenth century, such schools had proliferated in certain areas of London to the extent that the neighborhood of Hackney was known as the "Ladies' University of Female Arts." It is also probable that a number of women were to some degree self-taught. Others may have continued on their own beyond the point at which their parents felt they had reached a level of instruction appropriate for females and discontinued the services of a tutor. According the biography written by her daughter, Elizabeth Cary was for the most part self-taught, mastering several languages—including French, Spanish, Italian, Latin, and Transylvanian. When Cary's mother restricted her reading, she began to pay servants to smuggle candles so she could read at night. By the age of twelve, she owed her servants about £100 for more than 800 candles, and by the time she married at the age of fifteen, her debt had risen to £300 (Cary 186–188).

WOMEN AS WRITERS

While a few aristocratic exceptions exist (as we shall see, most notably Mary Sidney, Elizabeth Cary, and Mary Wroth), early modern women tended not to write in genres requiring extensive education in rhetoric and classical languages, nor did they compose in genres that might overly detract from women's typical household duties. Although we do not find numerous examples of early modern women writing epic poetry, tragedy, or history, they nonetheless composed in a vast range of genres, many of them related to the situations of their lives. They wrote letters (both private and those meant for more public audiences); prayers; anagrams and acrostics (which are pieces written usually for specific occasions); recipes for food and medicines; and other books of household information. While they produced religious and devotional works, they tended with few exceptions to avoid theology, which was seen as a masculine domain. And while many of the books women wrote circulated only in manuscript, a good number made their way into print editions as well.

In considering women's writings from this time, it is especially important to avoid anachronistic thinking. While female writers of the late eighteenth and nineteenth centuries often wrote under male pseudonyms, for example, most early modern female writers published under their own names; when they wrote anonymously, they did so in ways comparable to those of contemporary male authors. Additionally, we must resist devaluing the literary productions of women who did not write professionally or whose works circulated only in manuscript—especially when, as Margaret Ezell points out, we do not similarly devalue the work of men like Philip Sidney or John Donne, neither of whom wrote for money or print (585–586). A widened view of literary history thus enables us to consider more seriously the implications of alternative literary activities such as patronage that provided women with an opportunity to shape literary production.

As more women received, to various degrees, the curriculum we typically envision when we think of education, it is not surprising to find more women writing (though, of course, never in equal proportion to the increasing number of male authors). A common genre of writing by women was translation, partly because it was deemed a suitable genre for women, but also because translation work often developed somewhat naturally out of educational modes that used translation as a means of learning. Translation of devotional works was especially seen as suitable for women, but as Debra K. Rienstra reminds us in relation to Mary Sidney's influential translations of the Psalms,

> It is true that translating religious works was considered a safer activity for a woman than writing love lyrics, for instance, because the nature of the material was thought to keep her "undisciplined" mind from ranging freely into improper territory. But in fact translation is a freeing-enough enterprise to be full of dangers, especially when the original is a text considered divinely inspired. One of the most difficult things for modern readers to register about the *Psalmes* is the complexity and seriousness, for these writers, of manipulating biblical texts. What does it mean to manipulate an inspired text and still call it a psalm? Does artistic variation represent an assertion of the self before the text, a transposition of the relationship of authority from text-over-reader to reader-over-text? These questions might not occur immediately to the modern reader, but they were primary questions for these poets. (Rienstra 114)

The art of translation in particular played an important role in the relation to the influx of ideas from the contemporary Continent and from the classical past, and it provided women with an important way to enter into the discourses of both religion and art. A key example is Anne Cooke Bacon's 1564 translation of Bishop John Jewel's 1562 Latin *Apologie or Answer in Defence of the Churche of England*, which was officially approved for publication in 1589 by Jewel and the Archbishop of Canterbury. That Bishop Jewel used this English translation in his ongoing debate with anti-Anglicans attests to the significance of Bacon's work.

Anne Lock's writings are significant to both the history of English Protestantism and to the genre of the sonnet. After meeting John Knox in 1552, Lock zealously converted to Protestantism, and in 1557, in order to escape the persecutions under Mary I, she fled with her infant son and daughter to Geneva, where she remained until 1559. While in Geneva, she translated into English a French translation of *The Sermons of John Calvin, Upon the Song that Ezechias Made*. Included with the 1560 publication of her translation work was also her *Meditation of a Penitent Sinner, Upon the 51 Psalm*, which she dedicated to Katherine Bertie, the duchess of Suffolk. The first English sonnet sequence to be published (predating those by Philip Sidney or Shakespeare by more than thirty years), Lock's collection consists of twenty-one sonnets, each paraphrasing a verse from the 51st Psalm. In 1590, in an effort to comfort Protestants facing persecution in the Netherlands, she published her translation of John Taffin's *Of the Markes of the Children of God*. Interestingly, of the thirteen letters surviving from the extensive correspondence carried out between Lock and Knox during the mid-to-late sixteenth century, all are by Knox, suggesting perhaps a less significant value placed on Lock's words, either by Knox himself or later archivists who did not think them worth preserving.

Women translated secular works as well. In 1578 Margaret Tyler published her translation of Diego Ortúñez De Calahor's Spanish romance, making *The Mirrour of Princely Deedes and Knighthood* the first complete translation of a Spanish romance into English. Romances were a particularly popular genre, and one especially marketed to women. At the same time, women's appetite for them generated anxiety across several decades. In his *Instruction of a Christian Woman*, for example, Vives specifically forbade romances, because many of the stories involve adultery and other illicit activities. The extraordinariness of her venture did not escape Tyler, who argued that if women are fit audiences for this type of work, then they ought to be able to legitimately undertake its translation as well. As she wrote in her preface to the work:

> [M]any have dedicated their labours, some stories, some of warre, some phisick, . . . unto divers ladies & gentlewomen. And if men may & do bestow such of their travailes upon gentlewomen, then may we women read such of their works as they dedicate unto us, and if we may read them, why not farther wade in then to the serch of a truth . . . my perswasion hath bene thus, that it is all one for a woman to pen a story, as for a man to addresse his story to a woman. (Travitsky 11–12)

Interestingly, in the seventeenth century, Thomas Overbury included among his literary portraits one of "The Chambermaid" (1614) who is so infatuated with *The Mirrour of Knighthood* that she yearns to become a "Ladie Errant Knight" (43). Additionally, the fact that women could be readers of texts of course opened little by little the idea that women could be not only translators of men's texts, but also creators of their own compositions. And if they could be translators of male-authored fictional texts, then they might also compose imaginative works of their own.

Writing in the late 1560s and early 1570s, Isabella Whitney is the first known Englishwoman to publish original secular poetry. Although as far as we know, Whitney never wrote dramatic texts, she is perhaps the closest figure we have to the imaginary Judith Shakespeare conjured by Virginia Woolf in her 1928 essay, "A Room of One's Own." Whitney's work is witty and secular (though not without being "moral"), unusual in a time when (if they were to write at all) women were most likely to work on devotional subjects and translation. In 1567 she published *A Copy of the Letter, Lately Written in Meter, by a Young Gentlewoman: to her Unconstant Lover*. In 1573 she published *A Sweet Nosegay, or Pleasant Posye*, a collection of short aphoristic poems versifying in redacted form the prose aphorisms in Hugh Plat's *Floures of Philosophie*, which had been published the year before. Included in *A Sweet Nosegay* are a number of verse epistles to members of her family, most especially her brothers, Geoffrey and Brooke, and her married sister, Anne Baron. She also provides advice and guidance to her two younger, unmarried sisters who are working in service in London. Whitney's comments about her own writing are especially significant in relation to our understanding the conditions less privileged women faced in their pursuit of writing in the early modern period.

Neither a courtier nor an aristocrat, Whitney seems to have come from the ranks of the lower gentry and, like nearly all people during this time, went into service. According to her poetry, however, she was dismissed from service, perhaps because of some sort of slander or because her health was not good. The lack of employment nevertheless opened up an opportunity for her to pursue the occupation of writing. She claims that because she was ill and could not go out, her illness gave her a kind of "leisure" which enabled her to turn her attention to reading and studying. Moreover, as she writes to her sister Anne, her lack of employment gives her leave to write:

> Had I a husband, or a house,
> and all that longes thereto
> My selfe could frame about to rouse
> as other women doo:
> But til some household cares mee tye,
> My bookes and Pen I wyll apply. (Travitsky 124)

Whitney's second work is especially intriguing for its moral and social critique of English society. Her "Wyll and Testament" begins with a review of the city's wealth, but ultimately turns her attention to a satiric tour of London's failures. As it maps London's geographic and social topography, the poem demonstrates Whitney's intimate knowledge of London, including its seamier sides. As Patricia Brace observes, however, Whitney's social critique is evident in the form of the collection of more than one hundred ballad stanzas in A Sweet Nosegay: "Whitney's groupings in the stanzas concentrate overwhelmingly on power, the regulation of social behaviour, and range from the value and treatment of friends to the danger of ambition and the powerlessness of the poor in a legal system determined by wealth" (102). Virtually nothing is known of Whitney after the publication of her last work, and whether her identity was covered over in marriage or whether she died soon thereafter remains unknown.

At the opposite end of the social scale was Mary Sidney. In addition to fostering the talents of authors and artists at her home at Wilton, Sidney was an accomplished author in her own right, figuring among the most influential literary figures in late-sixteenth-century England. Numerous contemporary writers acknowledged the significance of Sidney's innovative work in the poetic and dramatic genres, but her literary impact has only recently been rediscovered by such scholars as Margaret P. Hannay and Mary Ellen Lamb (indeed, Robin P. Williams has gone so far as to claim that Sidney wrote the plays we attribute to Shakespeare). Perhaps because much of her work was based in translation, recent scholarship is only now beginning to understand the full significance of her work, most notably her prodigious and innovative achievements in adapting French and Italian poetic forms to English. She translated Philippe du Plessis-Mornay's Discourse of Life and Death and Petrarch's Triumph of Death. Her translation of Robert Garnier's Marc Antonie provided an early and influential experiment in both Senecan drama and blank verse.

Sidney presents a strikingly stoic figure in her Cleopatra, one that reads inter-estingly in contrast to Shakespeare's later depiction in *Antony and Cleopatra*. Although Sidney's play was a closet drama (meant for reading and performance among an elite coterie in the privacy of noble households, rather than for professional performance on the public stage), the text of Sidney's play was extremely popular. In addition to circulating in manuscript among her literary coterie, the printed version went through five editions between 1592 and 1607.

Also unrecognized until fairly recently has been the significance of Sidney's editorial work on the posthumous editions of Philip Sidney's *The Arcadia*, which included extensive revision and additions to her brother's prose pastoral romance. In addition to these achievements, Sidney also composed several original works, including "The Doelful Lay of Clorinda" and "To the Angel Spirit," both elegies she wrote on the death of her brother Philip. She also composed "A Dialogue Between Two Shepherds . . . in Praise of Astraea," which was intended to make up part of the entertainments planned for a state visit by Queen Elizabeth I to Wilton (the visit was cancelled, and consequently the dialogue was not presented). In the pastoral dialogue, however, Sidney engages the contemporary debate over whether language has the ability to capture the truth or whether poetry is merely a form of lying (a debate begun at least as far back as Plato).

Born into a family known for its literary talent, Sidney's niece, Lady Mary Wroth, continued the legacy of her famous aunt, as well as her uncle Philip Sidney. Wroth was a lady-in-waiting first to Elizabeth I in the final years of her reign, and then to Queen Anne, in whose court she participated in numerous masques and entertainments. Her major works, *The Countess of Montgomery's Urania* and the lengthy sonnet sequence appended to the first part of the *Urania*, follow in the tradition set by her uncle Philip in his prose romance *The Arcadia* and his sonnet sequence *Astrophil and Stella*, the former of which Mary Sidney worked on revising and editing while Mary Wroth was a child and frequently in residence at Wilton.

In *Pamphilia to Amphilanthus*, a sequence of eighty-three sonnets, including a crown of linked sonnets and nineteen songs, Wroth presents the first Petrarchan sonnet sequence by an Englishwoman. In rewriting the conventions of Petrarchan love, Wroth provides the first extended presentation in English of female subjectivity in this genre. In sonnet sequences by earlier English male writers, such as Philip Sidney, Edmund Spenser, and Shakespeare, the beloved is typically presented as the mute object of the male gaze and desire, and only rarely does she speak in the poems. Whereas male-authored sonnet sequences typically focus on the point of view of the male lover and his alternating states of pain and ecstasy as his beloved rejects or acknowledges him, Wroth's sequence portrays the voice of the female lover as she suffers in her desire. Pamphilia means "all loving," and she is a figure of unwavering constancy in the face of the fickleness and disregard of her beloved Amphilanthus, which means "lover of two." As in Shakespeare's sonnet #116, Pamphilia's constancy is an unwavering and extended demon-stration of the claim "Love is not love / Which alters when it alteration finds, / Or bends with the remover to remove: / O no! it is an ever-fixed mark / That looks on tempests and is never shaken" (116.2–6). Ultimately, Pamphilia's love never wavers, regardless of whether her beloved reciprocates.

While the sonnet sequence stands as a separate work, the characters of Pamphilia and Amphilanthus figure prominently in Wroth's pastoral romance as well. *The Urania* is an ambitious project, with hundreds of characters and multiple plots. It was also a sometimes highly critical fictional account of court life, including not only her parents' happy marriage and her own more complicated relationships with her deceased husband, Robert Wroth (who appears as Rustic), and her cousin and lover, William Herbert (who appears as Amphilanthus), but also a number of current court scandals. In particular, Lord Edward Denny objected to the work, which he claimed was a roman à clef aimed at slandering his family by paralleling in fiction details of recent events in his life. He thus demanded that she retract the book from publication. In the unfinished second part of *The Urania*, Pamphilia and Amphilanthus exchange vows in a private marriage ceremony. As Josephine Roberts observes, Wroth's work calls into question the validity of "exclusively monogamous relationships and how widely such unions need to be acknowledged" (110). Aside from its historical interests, *The Urania* provides two female points of view on the question of love and constancy, thus creating a sense of variedness among women. Urania, the title character, urges a more moderate view of love and the limits of constancy, a position juxtaposed with the extremity of Pamphilia's immoderate constancy, which Urania claims as excessive.

In addition to the prose romance and sonnet sequence, Wroth also composed *Love's Victory*, which follows the trials and tribulations of four pairs of lovers as they are manipulated by Venus and her son Cupid.

Elizabeth Cary was also an extremely learned author in her time. She composed texts in a range of genres, and all of her works engaged, either implicitly or analogously or directly, the religious and political issues of her day. In addition to her closet drama *Mariam, Fair Queen of Jewry* and several works that seem to have been lost, Cary also composed a dramatically presented prose history of Edward II, which was written sometime around 1627. As a recusant (i.e., she professed Catholicism against English rules of conformity to the Anglican Church), her translation of *The Reply of the Most Illustrious Cardinal of Perron, to the Answer of the Most Excellent King of Great Britain*, published in 1630, directly engages the most significant questions of religion in her day. Her most commonly read work now is *Mariam*, which she composed around 1603–1609. Written for private performance or presentation rather than the public stage, *Mariam* tells the story of King Herod's trial of the constancy and obedience of his wife, Mariam, his court officers, and his family members. Rumors arrive that he has been put to death after having been summoned to Rome by Caesar. With the exception of Herod's wicked sister, Salome and his former wife, Doris (who, along with her children by Herod, has been displaced by Mariam as Herod's new wife), nearly everyone in the play has cause for joy at his death: Herod's brother Pheroras can marry his true love, rather than the niece with whom Pheroras has been politically matched by Herod; Mariam's mother gloats, seeing Herod's death as just revenge for his having killed many of her kinfolk and usurping the throne by marrying her daughter, whom she sees as racially superior to Herod; and the sons of Babus, whose escape Constabarus aided in contradiction to Herod's order that he kill them, can return from hiding.

The character of Mariam, however, is conflicted between her personal emotions and her duties of wifely obedience and constancy. She is pleased by Herod's death for a number of personal reasons, including his having murdered several of her family members and his tyranny over her—he had even ordered her execution by her former brother-in-law Josephus, whom Herod had put to death at Salome's instigation so that she could take Constabarus as a new husband. But Mariam's failure to mourn Herod's death calls into question her own virtue. Interpreting her absence of love for Herod as a form of being unchaste, she sees herself as having betrayed him in her mind, even though she has not betrayed him with her body. In fascinating contrast to the character of Mariam is her sister-in-law Salome, who orchestrates the execution of two husbands for a succession of lovers, advocates for the ability of women as well as men to call a divorce, and fiercely counters the racial slurs made against her by both Mariam and her mother. Claiming the title of "custom breaker," Cary's Salome is clearly a villain in the play, and her wickedness is juxtaposed against Mariam's complex, yet ultimate, purity. Nonetheless, Salome could be said to escape punishment, for she survives while Mariam is executed and Herod descends into madness. Cary's play stands in striking complement and contrast to a number of Shakespearean plays, most notably *Othello* and *Antony and Cleopatra*, but the general questions raised by Cary also resonate throughout most of Shakespeare's plays.

One popular genre for women writers was books for their children, providing educational and life advice within a context endorsed by their positions as mothers. A number of these books were printed for the edification of others—though often not until after the death of the author, perhaps indicating the stigma against women making their writings public. Nevertheless, many of the mother's advice books were quite popular, undergoing several editions. Elizabeth Grymeston's *Miscellanea, Meditations, Memoratives* (1604), written for her son Bernye, blends classical learning with Christian piety, attesting to Grymeston's impressive education, her skill as a compiler, and the depth of her maternal love. Dorothy Leigh's *The Mother's Blessing, or the Godly Counsel of a Gentlewoman Not Long Since Deceased, Left Behind for Her Children* (1616), another extremely popular volume, was published nineteen times between 1616 and 1640. Although ostensibly written for Leigh's sons, the first printed edition was dedicated to Princess Elizabeth, the eldest daughter of King James and Queen Anne. In her work, Leigh advocates not only that one's own children be taught to read, so that they may better "serve God, their king, and country," but also that servants be taught to read as well. Significantly, the possibility of death and a mother's duty to her children is partly what opened a space authorizing women to write. Similarly popular was Elizabeth Joceline's *The Mother's Legacy to her Unborn Child by Elizabeth Joceline* (1624). Anxious that she would die in childbirth, Joceline composed the book as a postmortem gift, conveying in writing the spiritual and moral guidance she feared (rightfully so, it happens) she would not be able to provide for her unborn child. Joceline's work is interesting because her ideas distinguishing between her vision for the upbringing of a son and that of a daughter reveal a somewhat conflicted relationship to her own education, which was apparently impressive. Addressing her husband, she outlines her aspirations for her unborn child. If it is a son, she hopes he will become a minister; if it is a daughter, she recommends an education focused on piety and good housewifery. Although she ultimately leaves it to her husband's discretion if he desires a learned daughter, she argues that scholarly learning is unnecessary—and potentially dangerous—for women, comparing a learned woman to a small boat equipped with a main sail, "which runs it under water" (494).

WOMEN WRITERS AND THE *QUERELLE DES FEMMES*

The misogynist suspicions underlying Joceline's concern that her daughter will fall prey to what she believes is women's supposedly innate inclination toward sin trace their roots back to medieval debates about the pros and cons of women. Many of these ideas can be found imbedded in works ostensibly on subjects other than women. Anti-theatrical polemics, for example, sometimes included sections specifically addressed to women, revealing misogynist assumptions about the female sex. Stephen Gosson's *School of Abuse* (1579) encourages women to stay home rather than risk their reputations gadding about in the public playhouses, suggesting that their natural inclinations toward depravity will be overwhelmingly enticed by the pastimes available in the theater districts of the London suburbs. Philip Stubbes's *Anatomie of Abuses* (1583) objected to cross-dressing, especially fearing men are made effeminate by wearing women's clothing. He objected to the fashion of women wearing masculine clothing as well, citing Deuteronomy 22 that those who wear the clothing of the opposite gender "are an abomination unto the Lord."

However, there also existed a specific genre known as the *querelle des femmes* (literally, "argument about women"). This genre of debate grew from ancient and medieval roots, sometimes drawing explicitly on these literary antecedents. For example, the title page of *The Deceit of Women to the Instruction and Example of all Men* (1561), a heavily illustrated sixteenth-century collection of stories about women who caused the downfall of men, reproduces the image of Phyllis (Aristotle's wife) riding him like a beast (the illustrations also include a wife driving a nail into the head of her sleeping husband, Judith with the severed head of Holofernes, and Samson and Delilah, to name a few). While pre-reformation attacks on women tended also to be anti-matrimonial, later attacks continue to warn of the dangers and hindrances of wives, but without the possible escape route of monastic celibacy. Frequently satirical, such attacks presented women as by nature prone to drinking, lascivious behavior, gossiping, idleness, wasting household goods (often on alcohol, lovers, and fancy clothing), gadding about, and failing to fulfill their duty of tending the home. Early modern debates about women took place in a variety of secular and religious genres.

As Linda Woodbridge has pointed out, however, the debate was often approached as a purely rhetorical exercise, one in which the writers' main purpose was to hone their skills in argumentation rather than a heartfelt expression of opinion (6). Consequently, some of the pairings are known or suspected to have been written by the same author, with one text producing the thesis and the other the antithesis. For example, Francis Utley, Linda Woodbridge, and others have argued convincingly that Edward Gosynhill wrote both the 1541 *Mulierum Paean* ("The Praise of Women") and the 1542 countersatire *The Scholehouse of Women*, tapping into the growing market for such pamphlets (Utley 251–256; Woodbridge 25). Diane Purkiss has likewise argued that Constantia Munda and Esther Sowernam were the pseudonyms of male writers seeking to cash in on the Swetnam controversy of 1615–1617.

As in the past, such misogynist attacks also provoked defenses. In response to an assertion made publicly in Oxford that it is lawful for a husband to beat his wife, for example, William Heale published *An Apologie for Women* (1609), in which he countered the argument with civil and canon law (an "apology" is a formal defense, rather than an expression of regret). Implicit in many of the works advocating education for women, including those by Erasmus and Vives, is a defense of womankind. Other pro-woman educational theorists also wrote works that specifically defended women, and a number of these were quite popular. Thomas Elyot's Latin text, for example, was translated as *The Defense of Good Women* (1540) by Richard Hyrde, who was the tutor of Thomas More's daughters and also translated Vives's text on educating women. The flipside of such views of women—purportedly in praise of good women—also continued in stories that traced their origins to medieval literatures and authors such as Chaucer. *The Nutbrown Maid* (1503) and *The Ancient True and Admirable History of Patient Griselda* (1619) attest to the continuing popular taste for tales of female constancy in the face of tribulation and adversity.

It is important to note, however, that defenses of women are not necessarily what we might call feminist. Often, as the title of Elyot's work demonstrates, women are divided into "good" and "wicked," with good women being those who are chaste, silent, and obedient, and the wicked being those who are sexually active outside marriage, sharp-tongued, and of independent will.

Yet this period is also what Katherine Henderson and Barbara McManus have called a "landmark because for the first time in England women began to write in their own defenses and for the first time anywhere significant numbers of women began to publish defenses" (Henderson and McManus 4). In response to a 1567 satiric pamphlet by Edward Hake, a London lawyer who depicted maid-servants as "light," dishonest, and prone to prostitution, a coauthored "Letter sent by Maydens of London" was published defending maidservants from the charges against their chastity and honesty (Fehrenbach 285–304). In 1589 Jane Anger responded to an apparently now-lost pamphlet entitled *Boke his Surfeit in Love* (1588). (While Anger's name may sound like a pseudonym, there are at least six Jane Angers in the archives who could have been educated well enough to have written the pamphlet, and many scholars currently attribute the work to a female author.) Anger's text blends classical and biblical references to support her arguments against the earlier misogynist polemic. She emphasizes the evils of male lust and the sexual double standard, juxtaposing the harms caused by male sin against the invaluable nature of women's domestic activities as nurturers, nurses, and housewives.

While as far as we know, *Boke his Surfeit in Love* (1589) elicited no other responses in addition to Jane Anger's, an pseudonymous pamphlet appeared in 1615 titled *The Arraignment of Lewd, Idle, Froward, and Unconstant Women* that sparked an extensive round of rebuttals and even a play. Purportedly by Thomas Tell-Troth, the text presents an anthology of stories of depraved women and a collection of biblical and classical quotations condemning women's wickedness. The volume concludes with a particular focus on "the vanity of widows," which the author calls a "bear-baiting" (i.e., the supposed "sport" in which a bear is chained to a stake in a pit and dogs trained to fight are set on it; bear-baiting gardens flourished in the same neighborhoods making up the early modern theater district). In 1617 three responses to *The Arraignment* appeared in print— the first and most important being that of Rachel Speght, the daughter of a Calvinist minister who was not yet twenty years old, according to the dedicatory poem prefacing her text.

To begin, Speght unmasked Joseph Swetnam, a London fencing master, as the author of *The Arraignment*. Second, she dismantled Swetnam's metaphor of "bear-baiting," pointing out that if women were the "bear," then that made Swetnam the attacking dog. Thus she titled her work *A Mouzell for Melastomous* (A Muzzle for Black-Mouth), labeling Swetnam in her subtitle as "The Cynicall Bayter of, and foule mouthed Barker against Evah's Sex." Carefully reasoned and thoroughly argued, Speght's point-by-point response demonstrates an extensive knowledge of the Bible and its commentaries, a brilliant wit, and a keen sense for the genre of sermon composition. Chief among her criticisms of Swetnam, whose pamphlet she describes as "irreligious and illiterate," are that his condemnation of God's creation of women is blasphemous, his logic is faulty, he is a poor reader of scripture, his grammar is poor, and he is ungrateful to women as a source of life in this world. Significantly, a copy of Speght's text exists containing extensive marginalia in a contemporary hand. While it is not known who the author of the marginalia is, the hostility of the comments provides vivid insight into the anxiety produced when women did not silently acquiesce to misogynist attacks. For the most part, the annotations do not engage Speght's use of scripture but primarily spew additional misogynist venom. Barbara Lewalski has appended the marginalia to her edition of Speght's *A Mouzell*, and sums the annotations thus:

> Whoever he was, the annotator's strategies for dealing with the first Englishwoman to publish a serious polemic defending women are familiar enough—early versions of what have proved to be quite durable methods for trying to keep subversive women in their place. Several rejoinders condescend to Rachel's youth and female ignorance. Many more are explicit sexual put-downs: puns on female genitalia, rude references to body parts or to sexual intercourse, double entendres, and slurs on Rachel's chastity—attacks which take on special force since they are directed against a known young unmarried woman, highly vulnerable to insinuations of unchastity and indecorum. (Speght 92–93)

In addition to Speght's response, two other pseudonymous texts appeared in 1617. Both texts were published under pseudonymous names punning on the original text, and it remains uncertain as to whether they were written by women or men in the guise. *Ester Hath Hang'd Haman* purports to have been written by Esther Sowernam, whose first name alludes to the biblical figure, thus countering Swetnam's claim that there have been no good women, while her last name provides a punning opposite (sour name) to Swetnam's (sweet name). On her title page, Sowernam makes the riddling assertion (like Mariana in *Measure for Measure*) that she is "neither Maide, Wife, nor Widdowe, yet really all, and therefore experienced to defend all." Sowernam counters with stories of good women drawn from the Bible and from classical antiquity. Sowernam states that she was already working on a reply to Swetnam when she was given Speght's newly published response to read. While Sowernam mostly praises the earlier work, she also faults it for conceding to the distinction between good and bad women, thus compelling her to add her reply to the debate as well.

The next text to be published mentions both the earlier responses by Speght and Sowernam: Constantia Munda's *The Worming of a Mad Dog or a Sop for Cerebus the Jailor of Hell*, which is dedicated to the author's mother, Prudentia Munda. Both names are probably fictional, as the first means "pure constancy" and the latter "pure prudence," and the work is both much more erudite and boisterously insulting in its tone. As late as 1620, the controversy continued to rage with the performance of a play called *Swetnam the Woman-Hater, Arraigned by Women*, in which women hold a trial at which they condemn and muzzle the character of Swetnam.

Importantly, Rachel Speght went on to write another book, *Mortalities Memorandum with a Dreame Prefixed* (1621), consisting of two long poems composed in honor of her recently deceased mother and her godmother, to whom she dedicates the book. Speght also claims she was compelled to write a second book in order to prove that she (and not her father, as some claimed) had written *A Mouzell*. It is also possible that, given her marriage to William Procter in the same year, she may have been seeking patronage, perhaps from her godmother or other readers of the volume. The prefatory poem is especially interesting, presenting an allegorical dream vision in which the poem's speaker (also named Rachel) is led to Erudition's Garden, where women's learning is defended as a godly endeavor and contextualized in terms of the parable of talents and a catalogue of learned female poets, orators, astronomers, rhetoricians, and philosophers. In the poem, the dreamer is called away, however, by a horrible beast that she must muzzle with the help of Esther and the daughter of Prudence (alluding, of course, to Swetnam and the other pamphlets in the controversy). Seeing the dog securely muzzled and wormed, the dreamer continues on her way only to encounter the allegorical figure of Death, who is laying waste to entire countries and devouring vast numbers of people, regardless of degree or sex. Without warning, Death suddenly slays the dreamer's mother, and her tears awaken her to learn her mother's death is true. The main poem, 756 lines of iambic pentameter, provides an extended meditation on death, its origins in Eden, and its benefits for Christians as a release from worldly pain and tribulations. Such meditation, according to Speght, is valuable for making Christians ready for death, which is inescapable, impartial, and unexpected. The work is an important tribute not only to her mother, but to women in general.

Although Aemilia Lanyer's *Salve Deus Rex Judaeorum* ("Hail God, King of the Jews") and "The Description of Cooke-ham," published together in 1611, do not engage a specific misogynist polemicist, her work nonetheless also contributes to the praise and defense of women. Her work also exemplifies how gentlewomen participated in the early modern system of patronage. Like many of her male contemporaries, including Shakespeare, Lanyer's prosperity depended on forging successful connections with the nobility and other members of the inner court circle. *Salve Deus* clearly is a forthright bid for patronage from some of the most powerful women in the Jacobean court. Lanyer's volume of poetry assumes a highly educated female readership, praises women's achievements, and critiques aggressive masculinity. In the prefatory material to the title poem itself, Lanyer attributes great learning and wisdom to the women in general, but particularly to the company of nine specific women she addresses with individual dedications.

Aemilia Lanyer was the daughter of Baptista Bassano, a Jewish Italian musician in the court of Elizabeth I, and an Englishwoman named Margaret Johnson. Lanyer probably gained her education while in the service of Susan Bertie, the Countess Dowager of Kent, and at some point after 1587, she became the mistress of Elizabeth I's Lord Chamberlain, Henry Cary. In 1592 she became pregnant and therefore was married to Alphonso Lanyer, a court musician and captain in the navy of the queen, and then later in the navy of James I. After the death of Elizabeth, Lanyer seems to have spent time in the household of Margaret Clifford, the Countess of Cumberland, to whom she assigns as the primary dedicatee and for whom she wrote "To Cooke-ham," the country house poem appended to the end of the volume. Following the death of her husband in 1613, Lanyer also briefly ran a school in London.

Stylistically and formally, Lanyer's work is especially significant for its use of dramatic presentation and its feminization of various poetic forms—most notably her incorporation of the *querelle des femmes*, her use of elegiac form to depict the general condition of women, and her reworking of the blason in her description of Christ. Both the biblical *Song of Songs* and later French erotic poetry provide important first models for the blason, a poem cataloging the various body parts of the beloved.

By the time of Lanyer's work, however, male poets emphasized more thoroughly the erotic elements of the Canticles, transforming the genre into a voyeuristic cliché of the male gaze and a metaphor for sexual and other earthly desires. Donne's Elegy 19, for example, "To His Mistress Going to Bed," as well as his "Sun Rising," links the riches of the beloved's body to the riches of the newly discovered worlds of the empire and colonies.

By the early modern period, authors were also satirizing the genre, and Shakespeare is no exception. Dromio of Syracuse in *A Comedy of Errors*, for example, compares his beloved to the world, but his analogies transform the holy eroticism of Solomon into an insultingly bawdy and scatological inventory of Nell's body parts (*Comedy of Errors* 3.2.106–144). Similarly, in Sonnet 130, "My mistress's eyes are nothing like the sun," Shakespeare turns the conventions on their head, reducing each hyperbolic feature to a more mundane perspective on his beloved's breath, hair, gait, and so forth. The illustration on the title page of *The Extravagant Shepherd* (1660) renders the metaphors of the blason literal, presenting a grotesque female figure with pearls for teeth, globes for breasts, and golden wires for hair. Lanyer's translation of the feminine features of the beloved figure of Christ as bridegroom reworks the erotic language of the blason, reclaiming the holy purposes of the Canticles and drawing away from the more common misogynist uses of the genre (*Salve Deus* 1305–1320).

Nearly 2,000 lines long, the central poem *Salve Deus* presents the trial and crucifixion of Christ from the point of view of the women present. Distributed throughout the central poem's depiction of the crucifixion are Pilate's wife's plea for Christ and her defense of Eve, the tears of the daughters of Jerusalem, the Virgin Mary's sorrow, and numerous praises of the Countess of Cumberland, who is repeatedly aligned spiritually with the virtuous women present at the crucifixion. The extended section titled "Eve's Apology" most directly partici-pates in the debates about women by providing a formal defense of the female sex (761–840). Calling for the return of women's sovereignty, Pilate's wife argues that men's misuse of power, most notably in their crucifixion of Christ, outweighs any harm caused by Eve and negates men's claims of authority over women. The final section of the poem is "The Description of Cooke-ham," which forms an elegiac farewell to the Countess of Cumberland's country estate. A major theme in Lanyer's poem on Christ's passion is the misuse of power on the part of men. She aligns true speech with Christ and the women who model themselves on his virtues, contrasting this against the twisted words of the men present at the crucifixion. As Janel Mueller argues, Lanyer "uses her portrayals of Christ and actual good women to trace the impact of feminine or feminized virtue on the masculine side of a range of standing dichotomies that mark con-ceptions of social and political relations: public/private, mind/body, culture/nature, reason/passion" (117). These portraits, along with those drawn from the archives of history and the writing of other Renaissance women, provide an important context for understanding Shakespeare's depictions of wives, daughters, and the occasional mother or sister (who are almost always imagined primarily in relation to men).

WORKS CITED

Becon, Thomas. *Catechism. Renaissance Woman: A Sourcebook.* Ed. Aughterson, Kate. New York: Routledge, 1995.

Ben-Amos, Ilana Krausman. *Adolescence and Youth in Early Modern England.* New Haven: Yale UP, 1994.

Bergeron, David M. "Women as Patrons of English Renaissance Drama." *Readings in Renaissance Women's Drama Criticism, History, and Performance, 1594–1998.* Eds. S. P. Cerasano and Marion Wynne-Davies. New York: Routledge, 2002. 69–80.

Brace, Patricia. "Isabella Whitney, A *Sweet Nosegay.*" Ed. Anita Pacheco. *A Companion to Early Modern Women's Writing.* Oxford: Blackwell, 2002. 97–109.

Cary, Elizabeth. *The Tragedy of Mariam, the Fair Queen of Jewry, with the Lady Falkland Her Life, by One of Her Daughters.* Eds. Barry Waller and Margaret W. Ferguson. Berkeley: U of California P, 1994.

Clifford, Anne. *The Diaries of Lady Anne Clifford.* Ed. D. J. H. Clifford. Wolfeboro Falls, NH: Alan Sutton, 1991.

Cressy, David. "Literacy in Seventeenth-Century England: More Evidence." *Journal of Interdisciplinary History.* 8.1 (1977): 141–150.

Dolan, Frances E. "The Household: Authority and Violence." *The Taming of the Shrew: Texts and Contexts.* Ed. Frances E. Dolan. Boston: Bedford, 1996. 200–243.

Duncan-Jones, Katherine. *Ungentle Shakespeare: Scenes from His Life.* London: Arden, 2001.

Erickson, Amy Louise. *Women and Property in Early Modern England.* New York: Routledge, 1995.

Ezell, Margaret. *Writing Women's Literary History.* Baltimore: Johns Hopkins P, 1993.

Fehrenbach, R. J. "A Letter Sent by Maidens of London (1567)." *English Literary Renaissance* 14.3 (1984): 285–304.

Froide, Amy M. *Never Married: Singlewomen in Early Modern England.* Oxford: Oxford UP, 2005.

Hannay, Margaret P. "'Doo What Men May Sing': Mary Sidney and the Tradition of Admonitory Dedication." *Silent but for the Word: Tudor Women as Patrons, Translators, and Writers of Religious Works.* Ed. Margaret P. Hannay. Kent: Ohio State UP, 1985. 149–165.

———. *Philip's Phoenix: Mary Sidney, Countess of Pembroke.* Oxford: Oxford UP, 1990.

Hull, Suzanne W. *Chaste, Silent & Obedient: English Books for Women, 1475–1640.* San Marino, CA: Huntington Library, 1982.

Joceline, Elizabeth. *The Mothers Legacie, To Her Unborne Childe* (1625). Edinburgh: William Blackwood, 1852.

Kemp, Theresa D. "Women's Patronage-Seeking as Familial Enterprise: Aemilia Lanyer, Esther Inglis, and Mary Wroth." *Literature Compass* 4.2 (2007): 384–406.

Lamb, Mary Ellen. *Gender and Authorship in the Sidney Circle.* Madison: U of Wisconsin P, 1991.

Lewalski, Barbara. "Exercising Power: The Countess of Bedford as Courtier, Patron, and Coterie Poet." *Writing Women in Jacobean England.* Cambridge: Harvard UP, 1993. 95–123.

McIntosh, Marjorie. *Working Women in English Society, 1300–1620*. Cambridge: Cambridge UP, 2005.

McNeill, Fiona. *Poor Women in Shakespeare*. Cambridge: Cambridge UP, 2007.

Mendelson, Sara H. "Women and Work." *A Companion to Early Modern Women's Writing*. Ed. Anita Pacheco. Oxford: Blackwell, 2002. 58–76.

Mendelson, Sara H., and Patricia Crawford. *Women in Early Modern England, 1550–1740*. Oxford: Clarendon, 1998.

Mueller, Janelle. "The Feminist Poetics of *Salve Deus Rex Judaeorum*." *Aemilia Lanyer: Gender, Genre, and the Canon*. Ed. Marshall Grossman. Lexington: UP of Kentucky, 1998. 99–127.

Overbury, Thomas. "The Chambermaid." *The Overburian Characters*. Ed. W. J. Paylor. Oxford: Blackwell, 1936.

Prior, Mary. "Wives and Wills, 1558–1700." *English Rural Society, 1500–1800: Essays in Honour of Joan Thirsk*. Eds. J. Chartres and D. Hey. Cambridge: Cambridge UP, 1990. 201–225.

Purkiss, Diane. "Material Girls: The Seventeenth-century Woman Debate." *Women, Texts and Histories, 1575–1760*. Ed. Clare Brant and Diane Purkiss. London: Routledge, 1992. 69–101.

Rienstra, Debra K. "Mary Sidney, Countess of Pembroke, *Psalmes*." *A Companion to Early Modern Women's Writing*. Ed. Anita Pacheco. Oxford: Blackwell, 2002. 110–124.

Roberts, Josephine A. "'The Knott Never to Bee Untide': The Controversy Regarding Marriage in Mary Wroth's Urania." *Reading Mary Wroth: Representing Alternatives in Early Modern England*. Ed. Miller and Waller. Knoxville: University of Tennessee Press, 1991. 109–132.

Rowley, William, Thomas Dekker, and John Ford. *The Witch of Edmonton* (1621). Ed. Peter Corbin and Douglas Sedge. Manchester: Manchester UP, 1999.

Speght, Rachel. *The Polemics and Poems of Rachel Speght*. Ed. Barbara Kiefer Lewalski. Oxford: Oxford UP, 1996.

Stretton, Tim. *Women Waging Law in Elizabethan England*. Cambridge: Cambridge UP, 1998.

Travitsky, Betty. *The Paradise of Women: Writings by Englishwomen of the Renaissance*. Westport, CT: Greenwood, 1981.

Tudor, Elizabeth. *Queen Elizabeth I: Selected Works*. Ed. Steven W. May. New York: Simon and Schuster, 2005.

Utley, Francis. *The Crooked Rib: An Analytical Index to the Argument about Women in English and Scots Literature to the End of the Year 1568*. Columbus: Ohio State UP, 1944.

Vives, Juan Luis. *Instruction of a Christian Woman. Renaissance Woman: A Sourcebook*. Ed. Aughterson, Kate. New York: Routledge, 1995. 168–171.

Walter, John. "Grain Riots and Popular Attitudes to the Law: Maldon and the Crisis of 1629." *An Ungovernable People: The English and Their Law in the Seventeenth and Eighteenth Centuries*. Eds. John Brewer and John Styles. London: Hutchinson, 1980. 47–84.

Wayne, Valerie. "Introduction" to Edmund Tilney, *The Flower of Friendship, A Renaissance Dialogue Contesting Marriage*; 1573. Ithaca: Cornell UP, 1992. 1–94.

Williams, Robin P. *Sweet Swan of Avon: Did a Woman Write Shakespeare?* Berkeley: Peach Pit P, 2006.

Woodbridge, Linda. *Women and the English Renaissance: Literature and the Nature of Womankind, 1540 to 1620*. Champaign-Urbana: U of Illinois P, 1984.

Wrightson, Keith. *English Society: 1580–1680*. New Brunswick: Rutgers UP, 1982.

3

WOMEN IN SHAKESPEARE'S WORKS

A brief exchange between the Duke and Lucio during the final scene of *Measure for Measure* is telling of how women were predominantly imagined in Shakespeare's plays, if not in the larger early modern world. In this scene, the Duke pretends to sort out the charges made against Angelo. Because the Duke has spent most of the play disguised as a friar and is part of the conspiracy which will happily resolve the play, he actually knows the truth that is about to be revealed. Angelo is charged with fornication, or having illicit sex with someone who is not his wife—a crime punishable by death in the play.

Angelo has bargained with Isabella, a devout and virgin nun, to exchange sex for the remittance of the death sentence imposed against her brother, Claudio, who has been condemned to die for impregnating his fiancée Juliet before their wedding day. Although he believes Isabella has upheld her end, Angelo reneges on his part of the vile bargain. Mariana, who previously was engaged to Angelo until he broke it off when her dowry and brother were both lost in a shipwreck, is brought in as a witness to counter Isabella's sexual charges as false—as in fact they are. For the two women have conspired along with the disguised Duke to arrange a "bed trick," in which Angelo is led to believe that his silent assignation in the dark is with Isabella, but unwittingly he has consummated the marriage with his fiancée Mariana.

As she is being questioned, Mariana states that she is neither married, nor a maid, nor a widow—to which the Duke concludes, "Why, you are nothing then: neither maid, widow, nor wife?" (5.1.176). Imagining an identity outside these three categories, however, Lucio interjects, "My lord, she may be a punk [prostitute]; for many of them are neither maid, widow, nor wife" (5.1.177–178). Lucio's accusation is, of course, ironically comedic, since he is described in the cast list as a "fantastic" (a showy, extravagant young man of fashion and pleasure), and he has fathered a child by Kate Keepdown, a prostitute who works in Mistress Overdone's brothel (3.1.427–431). While a handful of characters do fall outside these main categories, most of the women in Shakespeare's plays tend to be shaped for better or for worse as maids (those who are to be married), wives (those who are married), and widows (those who were once married). Those female characters who do act upon the stage for very long often must battle against the imposition of sexual reputations that would render them either "punks" or "nothing, then."

Despite their relatively few lines, the women in Shakespeare's plays loom surprisingly large onstage and in our imaginations: Rosalind and Portia, Ophelia and Desdemona, and Lady Macbeth and Cleopatra—just to name a few. The kinds of female characters we see onstage and the kinds of dramatic scenarios they enact are largely a result of two key factors: Shakespeare wrote for an English stage on which only males acted (potentially limiting the number of female characters he might cast), and he wrote for the tastes of audiences keen for stories ranging across a male-centered vision of human experience, rather than for experiences central to most women's lives. Nearly all the major female characters are presented in terms of their connections to men. Shakespeare's plays contain very few young children (mostly royal princes and other heirs), and none of these are girls. Young female characters central to the plays are almost without exception adolescent or young women moving toward marriage. Many are daughters, and the presence or absence of fathers often plays a crucial role in the narratives they enact. A common source of dramatic tension arises from conflict between daughters and fathers. For some fatherless daughters, especially those of wealth and high rank, the absence (whether permanent or temporary) can open up space for a variety of female freedoms, as in the case of Rosalind in *As You Like It*, Beatrice in *Much Ado About Nothing*, and Olivia in *Twelfth Night*, all of whom take on a kind of independence and agency in choosing their mates. For fatherless characters of lower ranks, however, to be without male protection of uncle or brother as well can render them vulnerable to exploitation, as in the case of *Much Ado About Nothing*, where Margaret is used by Don John and Borachio in their plot against Hero (and indeed, Hero herself is as good as dead during the time that her father turns against her in his belief that she has been sexually active). The ultimate success of Helena in *All's Well that Ends Well* is in large part due to the King taking on the role of surrogate father. Maids are defined by their virginity, a quality they must defend against their own desires, the deceitful desires of men, and the destructive malice of slander. Fathers (and sometimes brothers, standing in for fathers) are often crucial in this defense.

While fathers often play key roles, Shakespearean daughters are more often than not motherless (e.g., Katherine in *Shrew*, Hermia, Lear's daughters, Desdemona, Jessica, Ophelia, Rosalind, and Celia, to name a few). Juliet, Perdita (who only meets her mother and father at the end of the play), and Anne Page are exceptions to the general trend—as is Portia, who is both motherless and fatherless. When female characters are mothers, they are more likely to be mothers to sons. (Gertrude, the Countess Roussilion, Volumnia, and the Duchess of Gloucester come most readily to mind when we think of Shakespearean mothers—though Elizabeth Woodville is given compelling speeches on behalf of both her sons and her daughter in *Richard III*.) Likewise, with the striking exception of Lear's daughters and Katherine and Bianca in *Shrew*, Shakespearean sisters are typically siblings to brothers rather than to other females (e.g., Imogen,

Ophelia, Isabella, and Viola). Very few sisters appear in Shakespeare's plays, although characters with sisterlike bonds are somewhat more numerous. Indeed, for both male and female characters, marriage is commonly depicted as the disruption of homosocial friendships. The comedies especially often romanticize and normalize companionate heterosexual marriages in favor of (and sometimes at the cost of) such pairs of female friends, as Hermia and Helena in *Midsummer Night's Dream* and Rosalind and Celia in *As You Like It*. When presented in companionate pairs, however, female characters are more likely to be lady and servant, as in the case of Portia and Nerissa in *Merchant of Venice* or Desdemona and Emilia in *Othello*. *The Merry Wives of Windsor* is perhaps unique in presenting a postmarital vision of female friendship between relative equals.

COMEDIES

A Midsummer Night's Dream

Battles between the sexes—between husbands and wives as well as between fathers and daughters—run throughout the romantic comedy of A *Midsummer Night's Dream*. As the play opens, Duke Theseus eagerly anticipates his upcoming nuptials with Hippolyta, the captured queen of the recently defeated Amazons. Military conquest is linked to romantic conquest in Theseus's promise to change the tune of their encounter: "Hippolyta, I wooed thee with my sword, / And won thy love doing thee injuries. / But I will wed thee in another key — / With pomp, with triumph, and with reveling" (1.1.16–19). Hippolyta, however, is given no lines to express what she might think of all this, and the possibility for her reply is cut short by the arrival of Egeus, who brings complaint against the disobedience of his daughter Hermia. While Egeus has approved Demetrius (a young man who, it turns out, has already wooed and abandoned Helena, a young Athenian woman), Hermia has chosen a lover contrary to her father's wishes. Because her wish runs contrary to that of her father, her speech is filled with words like "entreat," "pardon," "plead," and "beseech" (1.1.59–64).

According to the rules of patriarchy, fathers have complete control not only over their daughter's choices, but over their daughter's very selves. It does not matter that Lysander is acknowledged by all to be Demetrius's equal (or even superior) in every respect; nor does it matter that Demetrius is known for his infidelity, having wooed and abandoned Helena. The determining factor that makes Demetrius the more suitable lover is that he has the approval of her father. As Duke Theseus warns Hermia, the cultural ideology asserts the supremacy of the father's decision:

> Be advised, fair maid.
> To you your father should be as a god,
> One that composed your beauties, yea, and one
> To whom you are but as a form in wax,
> By him imprinted, and within his power
> To leave the figure or disfigure it. (A *Midsummer Night's Dream* 1.1.46–51)

Contests over love and the arrangement of marriages provide the central theme of action for a number of Shakespeare's unmarried heroines, and dramatic tension often arises from the conflict between choices made by fathers (or parents) and daughters. Parental control over daughters' desires and fortunes runs through several plays. In *The Merry Wives of Windsor*, Master Page vows that his daughter will inherit no money from him unless she marries the man he approves: "the wealth I have waits on my consent, and my consent goes not that way" (*Merry Wives* 3.2.49–65). Lord Capulet similarly vows to disown Juliet if she does not consent to marry Prince Paris, who is her father's choice.

The conflict between daughterly duty and freedom of choice emerges through the dramatic lives of a number of Shakespeare's characters who must grapple with pressure to marry husbands chosen against their will, or just pressure to marry in general. While Shakespeare's fathers may demand a godlike obedience, his theatrical daughters often rebel, eloquently attesting to the sovereignty of female will. Hermia boldly and poignantly chooses death or the cloistered life: "Ere I will yield my virgin patent up/ Unto his lordship whose unwished yoke/ My soul consents not to give sovereignty" (*MND* 1.1.80–82). Fortunately for Hermia, however, *A Midsummer Night's Dream*'s plot turns comic, and the brutal ultimatum to either face death or conform to her father's choice is lost among the magical shenanigans that ensue in the forest. Although the question of choice in marriage is both on the surface of the plot involving the pairs of young lovers and disrupted by its links to madness and magic, the play ends on a note of joyful union. By the end of the play, Hermia is matched happily with Lysander, and Helena with Demetrius, and both couples are married in the temple with the Duke and Hippolyta (who, as the Duke overrides Hermia's father's will in favor of his daughter's in 4.1.183, is once again intriguingly silent concerning her own thoughts about the question of choice in marriage).

Although rarely acted onstage, childhood sometimes is recalled in memory, usually as a phase on the way to marriage, as when the Nurse in *Romeo and Juliet* recalls her weaning of Juliet and the bawdy punning of her husband's response to the toddler's falling on her face rather than backward as she will when she is "com'st to age" (1.3.18–65). In *A Midsummer Night's Dream*, girlhood provides an important subtext to the major plot of true love freely chosen. In this context, girlhood is a stage of life to be left behind, along with the bonds of girlish friendships, in favor of heterosexual marriage. Hermia fondly hearkens back to the days when she and Helena "Upon faint primrose beds were wont to lie, / Emptying our bosoms of their counsel sweet" (*MND* 1.1.215–216). The place in the woods just outside of Athens where the two once shared their girlish secrets is transformed into the point of elopement as Hermia and Lysander prepare to escape the iron hand of Athenian law. Ironically, Helena betrays Hermia's last shared confidence, somehow hoping to gain Demetrius's gratitude in exchange for alerting him to the flight of the woman for whom he rejected Helena. Later, in the midpoint of the play where romantic rivalry entirely displaces the bonds of female friendships, Helena accuses

Hermia of forgetting the ties of their younger days and allying with the men against her:

—O, is all quite forgot?
All schooldays' friendship, childhood innocence?
We, Hermia, like two artificial gods,
Have with our needles created both one flower,
Both on one sampler, sitting on one cushion,
Both warbling of one song, both in one key,
As if our hands, our sides, voices, and minds,
Had been incorporate. So we grow together,
Like to a double cherry: seeming parted,
But yet an union in partition,
Two lovely berries moulded on one stem.
So, with two seeming bodies, but one heart,
Two of the first—like coats in heraldry,
Due but to one and crowned with one crest.
And will you rent our ancient love asunder,
To join with men in scorning your poor friend? (*MND* 3.2.202–217)

Helena's memory centers on needlework and songs "warbled"—domestic activities suitable to young women of their social standing. "Sweet playfellows," however, are quickly left behind for the promise of heterosexual love and the duties and privileges of married life.

That the bonds of marriage and sisterhood are at odds with one another provides a subtext for both Hippolyta and Titania as well. As queen of the Amazons, Hippolyta has been separated from her band of warrior sisters, and the play does not comment on any of the details of her previous warrior life. At the heart of the battle between Titania and Oberon, however, is a conflict over the hierarchy of duties. The king and queen of the fairies are at such war with one another that even the natural world is reeling in response, with earthquakes, floods, pestilences, and famine (2.1.82–117), creating a macrocosmic pandemonium that mirrors the disorder of the fairy realm. According to Oberon, the conflict is simply over "a little changeling boy" which he begs "to be my henchman" (2.1.120–121). Titania, however, claims that her refusal to relinquish her "young squire" is for the sake of his mother, who was a "vot'ress" of her order and faithful companion who died giving birth to the boy (2.1.122–137). It is upon this "injury" that Oberon resolves to "torment" his wife by causing her to fall in love with some vile thing, thus humiliating her until she agrees to his will (2.1.146–185).

Although Titania and Oberon are fairies rather than human characters, the marital strife between them is resolved in a manner that ultimately demonstrates Oberon's superior skills in magic (and psychology as well, perhaps). By the end of the play, Oberon brings Titania back under his control by using a method akin to shrew-taming. Using a love juice, he causes Titania to fall in love with the first thing she wakes to see—which happens to be Bottom the weaver, whom Puck has transformed into an ass. Thus, not only has Titania fallen in love with a low-class character, but one who has been literally rendered bestial. Bottom's bestiality, as Dympna Callaghan observes, not only comments on the nature of men from the class of "rude mechanicals" but also presents the spectacle of an aristocratic woman degraded by an excessive sexuality (*Shakespeare Without Women* 146–151). Oberon, however, must carefully walk the line between humiliating Titania and permanently defiling her. Ultimately, she gives in to his demands, and he releases her from the hateful spell:

> When I had at my pleasure taunted her
> And she in mild terms begged my patience,
> I then did ask of her her changeling child;
> Which straight she gave me, and her fairy sent
> To bear him to my bower in fairy land.
> And now I have the boy, I will undo
> This hateful imperfection of her eyes. (4.1.54–60)

Having resolved all the problems, magically matching lover with lover and reinstating the conventional patriarchal hierarchy in the fairy marriage, the play ends with a blessing on the marriages. The fairy blessing, which according to Titania has been rehearsed "by rote" (5.2.27), echoes the wishes made in marriage homilies of the time for healthy children and marital peace.

As You Like It

Like *A Midsummer Night's Dream*, *As You Like It* resolves the play's various conflicts through marriages in the play's final act. Attended by Hymen, the god of marriage, Rosalind bestows herself on first her father and then on her beloved, Orlando. While paternal authority seems usurped, Hymen steps in and takes control from Rosalind (5.4.114). Hymen bestows a blessing on each of the four couples, and each blessing presents a different facet of early modern views of marriage. He promises that for Rosalind and Orlando, "no cross shall part," adding a Christian overtone that creates a vision of marriage that is eternal under the eyes of God, but also perhaps one in which conflicts must be endured. Celia and Oliver are said to be "heart in heart," meaning that marriage should be a tie of love, or perhaps a reminder that they are equals. Phoebe, however, is given the injunction of obedience and told that "to his love you must accord or have a woman to your lord." Audrey and Touchstone are likewise given a less than ideal prospect, for they "are sure together as the winter to foul weather," providing a more cynical view of marriage as stormy and unpredictable.

This comedy also plays on the idea of love at first sight. By the end of the first act, the play's main characters, Orlando and Rosalind, have met and fallen head over heels in love, but circumstances conspire to keep them apart—just long enough to provide a romantic solution to both the problems of primogeniture and the question of marriage according to romantic inclination rather than according to parental mandate. Orlando is the middle son of the late Rowland de Boys. While the eldest brother, Oliver, has sent the youngest son off to university, he maliciously refuses to provide Orlando with an upbringing appropriate to his social status as a gentleman. When Oliver plots his youngest brother's murder, Orlando must flee to the Forest of Arden.

Meanwhile, the Duke's family has similarly fallen prey to the discontent bred by primogeniture. Duke Frederick has usurped his elder brother, the rightful Duke Senior, who resides with a faithful band of followers in the Forest of Arden as well. Duke Frederick originally retains his niece Rosalind as a companion for his daughter Celia, but as Rosalind's presence increasingly reminds the people of the younger duke's usurpation, he banishes her. Because they have been closer than sisters (1.3.70–73), Celia insists on accompanying Rosalind, and both disguise themselves as they also flee to the Forest of Arden, taking Touchstone the court fool with them. Through a marvelous chain of events, including the fortuitous repentance of both Oliver and Duke Frederick (who not only repents his wicked ways but decides to become a monk), Celia's fortunes are made through her match with the reformed Oliver, and Orlando's likewise through his match with Rosalind, who is once again an heiress.

Of particular interest in this play are the cross-dressing and role-playing that take center stage during the numerous forest scenes. In order to flee the court secretly and to travel in safety on the highway, Celia and Rosalind disguise themselves—Celia as a rural shepherdess named Aliena, and Rosalind as her "brother," Ganymede. Rosalind's costume of doublet and hose affords her character the combined privilege of gender and class. Appearing to be a male accompanying a female, the cousins can travel more safely than they could alone with the sole protection of a court fool. Upon arriving in Arden, moreover, Rosalind is able to purchase without question or opposition a local sheep farm that has recently been put up for sale.

The play's major concern, however, is with the wooing of Rosalind and Orlando—made seemingly "genuine" through Rosalind's cross-dressing. Disguised as Ganymede, Rosalind claims an education at the hands of her uncle, who "read many lectures against" love and the "many giddy offenses" of women (3.2.312–318). Rosalind is able to wittily test Orlando's love for her, probing the depth and truth of his affection as she attempts to cure him of his love. She presents him with a series of misogynist points of view about women, and in response to each one, Orlando claims his Rosalind will not act that way. In her anti-love tutorial with Orlando, Rosalind (playing the part of Ganymede who is in turn playing the part of Rosalind) claims that a husband's "destiny" is to wear horns, echoing Touchstone's similar claim and resonating with the male bonding over horns enacted by her father's banished courtiers in the woods. Orlando's answer is that "Virtue is no horn-maker, and my Rosalind is virtuous" (4.1.55). Perhaps most telling is the question concerning how tightly Orlando expects to constrain his wife. Rosalind's words, when attributed to her instead of Ganymede, provide a poignant promise of the power of female sovereignty and the futility of stifling women's freedom:

> The wiser, the waywarder. Make [close] the doors upon a woman's wit,
> and it will out at the casement. Shut that, and 'twill out at the key-hole. Stop that,
> 'twill fly with the smoke out at the chimney. (4.1.138–141)

Heard in the masculine voice of Ganymede, however, the words align too closely
with the ancient cliché that three things will drive a man from his home: smoke,
a leaky roof, and a shrewish wife. As Ganymede, the picture painted is one of
misogynist stereotypes about women as fickle, petulant, shallow, unfaithful, and
deceitful. As Rosalind finishes her session of playing the part of "Rosalind" in this
fashion for Orlando, Celia declares that she has gone too far. Her depiction of
how women are is completely slanderous, according to Celia:

> You have simply misused our sex in your love-prate. We
> must have your doublet and hose plucked over your head, and
> show the world what the bird hath done to her own nest. (4.1.172–174)

Celia's complaint suggests that Rosalind's masculine privilege has gone to her
head, and she needs to be revealed as a woman. Her swaggering machismo has
become too misogynistic.

Indeed, Rosalind's disguise not only enables her to become the young master
of a sheep farm, it apparently gives her the privilege to speak authoritatively and
as an expert against womanhood. In relation to her interactions with Phoebe,
especially, it gives her the privilege granted to patriarchs in other plays who deny
(or attempt to deny) female characters the right to marry according to their
desire. In many respects, Rosalind and Phoebe echo each other as they cut
through the extremities of the lover's claim, deflating the metaphors and exposing
their ridiculousness. Early on, Rosalind (as Ganymede) claims that Orlando
cannot be in love, for he lacks the lover's lean cheek and disheveled appearance
by which lovers are known (3.2.338–347); later, when Orlando claims he will
die if Rosalind rejects him, she scoffs that love does not have the power to kill:
"Men have died from time to time, and worms have eaten them, but not for love"
(4.1.91–92). Phoebe similarly rejects the lethal power of love, although she
claims she flees Silvius because she "would not injure" him (3.5.9). Exasperated
and unable to escape Silvius's unremitting wooing, Phoebe gives in to frustration
and voices a wish that her eyes might in fact have the power to kill:

> Now I do frown on thee with all my heart,
> And if mine eyes can wound, now let them kill thee.
> Now counterfeit to swoon, why now fall down;
> Or if thou canst not, O, for shame, for shame,
> Lie not, to say mine eyes are murderers. (3.5.15–19)

Overhearing the exchange, Rosalind (as Ganymede) steps forth and delivers a
somewhat shocking attack on Phoebe's character and her right to choose a lover:

> Who might be your mother,
> That you insult, exult, and all at once,
> Over the wretched? What though you have no beauty, . . .
> Must you be therefore proud and pitiless? . . .
> But, mistress, know yourself: down on your knees,

And thank heaven, fasting, for a good man's love:
For I must tell you friendly in your ear,
Sell when you can: you are not for all markets:
Cry the man mercy; love him; take his offer:
Foul is most foul, being foul to be a scoffer. (3.5.36–64)

Of course, the scene provides an opportunity for Phoebe to fall in love with Ganymede, opening up the comedic sexualized possibilities of her apparently misdirected love (as well as the question of how true love at first sight really is, given that these famous lines are Phoebe's). Significantly, even before Rosalind's arrival in the forest, Phoebe was rejecting Silvius's love, thus highlighting privileges of sex and class status as the source of the power underlying Rosalind's command to the privileges of sex and class status. While women in many plays assert—and even die—for the right to choose their own mate rather than have one imposed upon them, these women are typically of higher status. According to Rosalind/Ganymede, however, Phoebe is "not for all markets" and must take what comes her way without attempting to bargain.

Rosalind's disguise also raises a key question explored throughout the play: what is the relation between biological sex and culturally constructed gender? As the two cousins prepare to leave the court, Rosalind exclaims that her costume will make her as much a man as any:

A gallant curtle-axe upon my thigh,
A boar-spear in my hand; and—in my heart
Lie there what hidden woman's fear there will—
We'll have a swashing and a martial outside,
As many other mannish cowards have
That do outface it with their semblances. (1.3.111–126)

The answer in this passage partly depends on who we imagine as "the mannish cowards." If these are men who must act manly, it would seem that gender is a masquerade not inherently attached to sex. However, "mannish" was also used to describe a woman "having characteristics stereotypically associated with men" (OED, "mannish" 2a). On one level, then, the play suggests a natural correlation between sex and gender as Rosalind's ability to maintain the fiction of masculinity breaks down. As she and Celia arrive in the Forest of Arden, both are exhausted but, as Ganymede, Rosalind must bear the hardship in a manly way:

I could find in my heart to disgrace my man's apparel
and to cry like a woman; but I must comfort the weaker vessel,
as doublet and hose ought to show itself courageous to petticoat:
therefore courage, good Aliena! (2.4.3–6)

Later, when Celia reports that Orlando is in the forest—and the secret admirer who has been posting bad love poetry on the trees—Rosalind cannot keep quiet long enough for Celia to tell what she knows. According to Rosalind, just because she's dressed like a man doesn't mean she has a man's disposition, suggesting a biological difference between her outward masculinity and her inward femaleness (3.2.178–180). In response to Celia's frustration at being repeatedly interrupted, Rosalind exclaims, "Do you not know I am a woman? When I think, I must speak. —Sweet, say on" (3.2. 227–228). When Rosalind/Ganymede faints at the sight of Orlando's bloody napkin, it appears that her female interior can no longer sustain the masculine "counterfeit"—she lacks, as Oliver suggests, "a man's heart" (4.3.163–164).

The fact, however, that Shakespeare's Rosalind would have been played by a boy actor—who played a girl playing a boy playing a girl—is playfully acknowledged throughout the text, but especially in the epilogue (a twist impossible to recreate in modern performances with women actors in the part). As Phyllis Rackin has argued, "The 'ambivalent figure' of Rosalind . . . refuses to choose between actor and character or between male and female" ("Androgyny" 36). When Rosalind appears at the end of the play to deliver the epilogue, she claims "It is not the fashion to see the lady the Epilogue" (Epilogue, 1–2). In a production, it is entirely up to the director to determine whether her character is dressed as Rosalind (who presumably has changed out of her Ganymede costume upon her re-entrance with Hymen in 5.4.105), or whether the actor reveals himself at any point during the epilogue. Yet a number of words and images in the final speech call attention to the question of gender that has been posed throughout. "What a case am I in then," she ponders (Epilogue 6). "Case" can mean "predicament" or "situation," suggesting the conflict between her role as a "lady" and her role as the speaker of the epilogue.

But "case" is also a grammar term, indicating perhaps a relationship between gender and sex somewhat akin to the grammatical relationship between words in inflected languages. It can also refer to an outer covering or protective exterior to something—here, suggesting that the exterior body (dressed as Rosalind) encases the interior of the actor's male self. The person onstage is "not furnished like a beggar" (Epilogue, 8), further suggesting the limits or constraints of costume and character. Indeed, as Juliet Dusinberre insightfully reminds us, the play as acted in Shakespeare's time would have contained four female characters played by male actors (Celia, Phoebe, and Audrey, as well as Rosalind), although most modern critical discussion has focused on the character of Rosalind (251–252).

It is also well worth remembering the significance of Rosalind's chosen name here, for Ganymede is a name not only conventional to pastoral romances, but also, as the name of Jove's cupbearer, a conventional signifier of homosexual love. As Rosalind "conjures" the men and the women in the audience, she further toys with the homoerotic possibilities of her character's ambiguous gender at this point, offering ("If I were a woman") to kiss the men in the audience who please her. That she calls her offer "kind" (Epilogue 18) also pulls in two directions, suggesting on the one hand that her offer is merely generous (our modern sense of the word "kind"), as well as the early modern sense of the word as natural. That Rosalind bids farewell with a "curtsy" further complicates the reading, as curtsying is explicitly performative, even ceremonious. So while the marriages with which the play happily ends resolve the gender of Rosalind and the social unrest caused by primogeniture, Rosalind's epilogue unsettles the performance part of identity.

Twelfth Night

Twelfth Night incorporates a number of themes in common with *As You Like It* and *The Merchant of Venice*, including cross-dressed heroines and questions of true love. Like Rosalind, Viola disguises herself as a male throughout much of the play, and initially her reasons are ones of safety. When Viola lands in Illyria, she believes her brother Sebastian is dead, and she needs to not only protect herself as a lone woman but also to seek employment. As an unknown woman, Viola knows that the dangers to her reputation put her in too precarious a situation, and she is more likely to find employment as a male, regardless of whether it is in Olivia's or Orsino's household. Thus she disguises herself as Cesario, an identity she carries through most of the play. Like Rosalind, Viola's speech nods frequently to her performance of a role, and consequently the performance of the actor's role in her. Refusing to tell Olivia where she comes from, Viola claims, "I have studied, and that question's out of my part" (1.5.139–140). A source of the play's comedic humor therefore derives from the mistaken loves that develop as a consequence of the heroine's disguise. Olivia is pursued by Orsino, who is lovesick; later she is pursued by Malvolio, who is the butt of a household prank, and Sir Andrew, who pursues her for profit. Olivia, however, mistakenly falls in love with Cesario, who has been sent by Orsino to woo the grieving lady on his behalf. Olivia's ultimate confession of her love for Cesario, of course, provides the comedic opportunity for Cesario/Viola to swear (as did Rosalind) that no woman shall ever be mistress of his/her heart. Meanwhile, Viola/Cesario falls in love with Orsino. Consequently, s/he is reluctant to woo on behalf of the one she wants to marry (1.4.40).

The play also flirts with sexual possibilities inherent in boy actors playing female parts, female characters posing as males, and the erotic attractions that develop in the context of mistaken identities. As Cesario, Viola draws the attractions of both men and women. Malvolio describes him/her as "between boy and man," "well-favored," and one whose "mother's milk were scarce out of him" (1.5.142–144). More significantly, Orsino seems unwittingly drawn to the youth and even stresses his apparent lack of manliness: "Diana's lip / Is not more smooth and rubious [ruby red]; thy small pipe [voice] / Is as the maiden's organ, shrill and sound, / And all is semblative [like] a woman's part" (1.5.29–33). Orsino's speech is filled with potentially bawdy double entendre, with "sound" meaning whole and unbroken, and "organ" meaning literally "the voice" but also a common slang for sexual organs. Orsino seems unwittingly drawn to Viola/Cesario's intact maidenhead, which makes her the suitable love partner she becomes by the end of the play. Like Rosalind, Viola's male disguise enables her to witness Orsino in an unfeigned state, thus creating the impression that their love is genuine.

Later, in Viola and Orsino's discussion of the best age difference between husband and wife, the sexual punning continues. Orsino recommends younger wives "For women are as roses, whose fair flower / Being once display'd, doth fall that very hour" (2.4.37–38). To which Cesario replies, "And so they are: alas, that they are so; / To die, even when they to perfection grow!" (2.4.39–40). Orsino's analogy alludes to the flower of virginity—which, as Cesario notes, women must lose (with "to die" meaning also orgasm) in order for them to attain the married state prescribed by early modern culture.

While Orsino seems subliminally drawn to Cesario, Olivia seems unafraid of his "masculinity" even as she is infatuated with him (and interestingly, Viola's initial claim that she will pose as a eunuch seems left behind). Despite the potential danger to a lady's reputation in holding company with a strange man without escort, Olivia sends her household away so that she may hold a private interview with Cesario, who then convinces Olivia to unveil herself. While the disguise opens the possibility of frank and honest talk in the play, it also enables dialogue filled with the conventional echoes of concerns and themes found in courtly love poetry. Having convinced Olivia to unveil, Cesario praises her beauty after having been assured that "God did all" and her "red and white" coloring is not the product of cosmetics (1.5.207–210).

Cesario also accuses her of cruelty and vanity for not returning Orsino's love: "Lady, you are the cruell'st she [woman] alive / If you will lead these graces [her beauty] to the grave / And leave the world no copy" (1.5.211–213). Like the young man in the *Sonnets*, Olivia is urged to marry and reproduce. Olivia, however, continues in the vein of courtly literature and replies with a self-blason, promising to provide a detailed inventory in her will before she dies, listing each body part in number (1.5.214–218). That Olivia blasons herself initiates a later tendency to take on a (modestly appropriate) dominant role in the courtship process. It is possible that the hidden gender equality between Cesario and Olivia partly enables Olivia's more aggressive wooing later of Sebastian, whom she believes to be Cesario.

The Taming of the Shrew

Even in its own time, *The Taming of the Shrew* elicited discomforted responses, including most notably John Fletcher's explicit reply in *The Tamer Tamed, or the Woman's Prize*, which carries forward Shakespeare's story in which Katherine has been tamed to death and the widowed Petruchio remarries only to find his match in his second bride Maria. Today, the play continues to resonate, attracting and troubling audiences with its romanticized and slapstick depictions of domestic violence. For some readers, Katherine and Petruchio are perfectly matched. Indeed, Petruchio seems, on a certain level, to admire Katherine's feistiness—at least when it is leveled at others. In response to her breaking a lute over Hortensio's head, he claims he loves "her ten times more than e'er [he] did" (2.1.159). Others, including feminists, see the play as promoting a misogynist agenda still discernible even in our supposedly post-feminist age.

Although it is frequently omitted in modern performance, *The Taming of the Shrew* opens with an induction, or an extraneous scene intended as a commentary (or setup) for the play to follow. On one level, the prank played on Christopher Sly in the induction to *Shrew* is purely for the Lord's amusement—it is another aristocratic pastime like hawking or hunting or music. On another level (and at the same time), the prank also serves as a spectacular demonstration of the Lord's control over those beneath him—not just the drunken tinker, but also the servants and the players the lord commands to stage the illusion. If Sly is properly costumed and fitted with the props of an aristocrat, surrounded by a troupe of supporting actors to play his "madam wife" and a household full of servants, and coached in matters of manners and speech, "Would not the beggar then forget himself?" the Lord asks (Induction 1.37). To which the First Huntsman replies, "Believe me, lord, I think he cannot choose" (Induction 1.38).

As an induction, then, we might consider its relation to the larger play to follow: Is the tale of Petruchio's taming of Katherine a lesson for would-be lords in the proper way to interact with one's wife (to tame them by "policy" rather than by beating them)? Or is the analogy we're to draw between Christopher and Katherine—in other words, does she "forget herself" (and if so, which self does she forget—the shrewish one, or some self beneath the shrew)? While the opening induction calls attention to the performativity of social roles, including gender and class, the absence of a closing frame at the end of the play proper (just after Katherine gives her final speech) potentially naturalizes our sense of Katherine's taming by allowing us to forget that we are, along with Christopher Sly, watching a play.

The play proper begins with a dilemma for the local Paduan admirers of Bianca Minola, an apparent paragon of female desirability: Bianca unfortunately cannot marry until her shrewish older sister has been espoused. Katherine is admittedly an unappealing character in many ways: she beats and binds Bianca in revenge against her preferentially treated sister, and she strikes Petruchio. Bianca, conversely, is initially put forward as the ideal—submissive to her father, perceived as silent and obedient. When Lucentio first meets Bianca, he is drawn to her seeming silence, which he takes as a sign of her "mild behavior and sobriety" (1.1.70–71). The ridiculous echoes of courtly love lyrics in Lucentio's rhapsodies over Bianca, however, call into question the validity of his assessment. Bianca's ordering of her tutors, along with her quick discernment of the secret love messages from the two tutors and her clear preference for Cambio/Lucentio over Litio/Hortensio, suggest that she is not as innocent and conforming to her father's will as she seems (3.1.16–23). While Bianca does not rage like Katherine, the play in some respects foreshadows her later revelation as a shrew when she refuses to come at her husband's call in the final scene of the play.

The common early modern theme of women as a commodity runs throughout the play. Male characters in *Shrew* vie with one another in a bidding war for Bianca, staking farms, houses, argosies, money, and (by proxy, in the case of Tranio, who is disguised as Lucentio) inheritances to be had on a father's death (2.1.335–337). In the final scene of the play, they bet on their wives' performances as if they were placing gentlemen's wagers on horses and hounds.

When we first meet Petruchio, we learn that he has come to "wive it wealth-ily in Padua" (1.1.70), and he agrees to woo Katherine if her dowry is good enough to outweigh her personality. As Grumio remarks concerning Petruchio, "nothing comes amiss so money comes withal" (1.2.78). The negotiations with Katherine's father, Baptista, are handled as if a business deal. Claiming he is too busy for a lengthy courtship, Petruchio provides the credentials of his family (his father and Baptista knew each other) and then immediately cuts to the question of dowry (2.1.112 ff.). Once they are married, Petruchio literally claims Katherine as his property, barring her kin from intervening when he demands she not stay for her own wedding reception:

> I will be master of what is mine own.
> She is my goods, my chattels. She is my house,
> My house-hold stuff, my field, my barn,
> My horse, my ox, my ass, my anything,
> And here she stands, touch her whoever dare.
> I'll bring mine action on the proudest he
> That stops my way in Padua. (3.3.100–106)

While this scene is often presented as slapstick, it also bears remembering that none of the other characters intervenes. It is possible that the seeming absurdity of Petruchio's claims may have rendered the other characters dumbfounded, but his claims nonetheless are legally valid ones for the time—her father no longer controls her.

While the play affords more lines to Petruchio's thoughts on his taming project, we are given some small insight into Katherine's thoughts on the few occasions when she directly expresses her response to the process of being tamed into a proper wife. She poignantly voices her opposition to being silenced and rendered unheard—first to her father, and then later to Petruchio, once they are married; but she is a character full of words that no one hears. In her initial encounter with Petruchio, she is witty and clever as she verbally banters with her unwelcomed suitor, like Beatrice with Benedick in *Much Ado*. It could be said at first that the verbal game seems headed for a draw, with both characters equal contestants in this intricately choreographed ver-bal sparring match. Unable to persuade Katherine or corner her into consent-ing to marry him, however, Petruchio simply stops the encounter, in essence playing his trump of masculine privilege, and asserts that it has already been decided that she will marry him regardless of what she wants ("will you nill you"):

> And therefore setting all this chat aside,
> Thus in plain terms: your father hath consented
> That you shall be my wife, your dowry 'greed on,
> And, will you, nill you, I will marry you.
> . . .
> For I am he am born to tame you Kate,

And bring you from a wild Kate to a Kate
Conformable as other household Kates.
Here comes your father. Never make denial.
I must and will have Katherine to my wife. (2.1.260–272)

That Katherine remains unwilling to marry Petruchio, however, is rendered moot as Petruchio frames her resistance as a game they have agreed to play in public (2.1.296–297). Katherine's response to Baptista is to question his paternal love: "Call you me daughter?" (2.1.277). In spite of Baptista's earlier claim that his consent hinges on Petruchio obtaining Katherine's love, "for that is all in all" (2.1.127), Baptista blithely confirms the deal: " 'Tis a match" (2.1.311). The marriage goes forward in spite of her vehement and repeated protests.

The expectations for female submissiveness are made clear when it appears that Petruchio has left Katherine at the altar. Rather than being outraged at the affront to his daughter's honor, or even acknowledging that one might be upset to have been left at the altar, especially when the engagement was forced, Baptista gives Katherine permission to weep, "for such an injury would vex a very saint, / Much more a shrew of thy impatient humour" (3.2.27–29). Seemingly a woman's proper response is to have none. Once she is finally married, Katherine is further pressured to relinquish her own will and desire. Nonetheless, she continues to assert her sovereignty:

Why, sir, I trust I may have leave to speak,
And speak I will. I am no child, no babe.
Your betters have endured me say my mind,
And if you cannot, best you stop your ears.
My tongue will tell the anger of my heart,
Or else my heart concealing it will break,
And rather than it shall, I will be free
Even to the uttermost, as I please in words. (4.3.73–80)

Ultimately, however, Petruchio wins as he teaches her to speak not what is in her heart but what her husband wills. Katherine is to be domesticated—"made conformable like other household Kates" (2.1.270), and by the end of the play, she can teach other women what she has learned.

The heart of the action, as indicated by the play's title, is the taming of Katherine. Shakespeare's play was one of many plays interested in the question of how to establish sovereignty and obedience in marriage (and, given the analogical way of seeing domestic and political governance, in the general society as well). In the context of such debates about marital relations and the resolution of domestic disputes between husband and wife, *The Taming of the Shrew* presents a fantasy vision in which the husband demonstrates his ability to govern well and train his wife as his co-governor. In the early scenes of the play, Katherine gives as good as she gets in response to the disparagement she receives on all sides (from not only the suitors who disdain her in favor of the more conventionally appealing—that is, seemingly silent—Bianca, but also from her father). By the play's end, Katherine has been "made conformable" to a "household Kate," one who delivers a verbal reprimand on behalf of her husband to her wayward sister and the widow.

Petruchio's means of compelling his wife to submit utterly to his will differs strikingly from those used by the husband in a work like *A Merry Jest of a Wife Lapped in Morel's Skin*, where the wife is thrown down stairs, beaten until she is bloody, and then sewn into the salted hide of a dead horse named Morel. If Petruchio's method is more psychological and less bloody than those seen in *A Merry Jest*, however, it is nonetheless still based in physical coercion, violence, and the threat of violence. In keeping with the advice against beating wives given, for example, in the *Homily of the State of Matrimony* (1563), Petruchio does not beat Katherine. He is not directly violent, yet violence hovers constantly around the perimeters of the play.

Although the play makes an explicit point that Petruchio does not hit Katherine (although she strikes him), he repeatedly beats and abuses his servants. This household violence taking place all around Katherine somehow seems to elicit her pity and kindness. As reported by Grumio, Petruchio's roughness with the servants on the way home from Padua following the wedding ceremony seems to inspire in Katherine a gentleness as she seeks to intervene on their behalf—a role often endorsed for women and even linked to that of the Virgin Mary. Petruchio himself explicitly likens his methods to taming a wild hawk, describing his "reign" as having "politicly begun"—meaning both shrewdly or skillfully but also according to the rule of law—a means endorsed by much of the religious and conduct literature on the topic (4.1.52 ff.).

While Petruchio does not beat Katherine, his physical control over her body nonetheless resonates with (at worst) hints of torture and (at best) mind control or brainwashing. He deprives her of sleep and food (interestingly, these are deprivations also used in witchcraft investigations, as well as in other contexts involving brainwashing, such as war and cult indoctrinations). Petruchio's methods involve both the withholding of things to punish Katherine for her unwanted behavior and the granting of rewards when she offers the behavior he wants from her. At each step, he entices her with clothing and trips to visit her family, threatening her with their withholding. It seems not to occur to anyone in the world of the play other than Katherine that she might have ultimate sovereignty over her self, her freedom of movement, or access to the basic necessities of life such as food, sleep, clothing, and companionship. Her taming brings great prestige and reward to Petruchio—and even in many respects to Katherine, who is able to wield patriarchal power on behalf of her lord against other women.

The final acts of the play illustrate Katherine's process of slowly learning to self-correct so as to get what she wants by pleasing her man, but the price is the complete and absolute subordination of her experiences to his authority. Having determined that they will travel to Padua without the new clothes brought by the tailor and haberdasher, Petruchio cancels their trip when Katherine corrects him concerning the time of day. Petruchio insists:

Look, what I speak, or do, or think to do,
You are still crossing it. Sirs, let't alone.
I will not go today, and ere I do
It shall be what o'clock I say it is. (4.3.186–189)

Once they are finally on the road to Padua, the lessons continue. Petruchio insists that Katherine agree with whatever he says, even if it contradicts verifiable facts: "It shall be moon, or star, or what I list" (4.6.7). In order to move forward (and at Hortensio's urging), Katherine assents: "What you will have it named, even that it is, / And so it shall be still for Katherine" (4.6.22–23).

In a sign that Katherine may still have her wits about her (and raising the possibility of an ironic final speech), she later cleverly plays on Petruchio's earlier demand that she concede the sun as the moon when they encounter (unbeknownst to them) Lucentio's father Vincentio. She demonstrates a marvelous agility as she quickly follows her husband's verbal steps, addressing Vincentio first as if he were a fresh young maid and then, having been corrected by Petruchio, claims, "Pardon, old father, my mistaking eyes / That have been so bedazzled with the sun / That everything I look on seemeth green. / Now I perceive thou art a reverend father. Pardon, I pray thee, for my mad mistaking" (4.6.46–49). Just before entering into the banquet (where the truth of Lucentio's deceit and Bianca's elopement are just coming to dramatic light), Petruchio tests Katherine once more by asking her to kiss him. When she balks at the demand for a public display of affection, he threatens to turn back home, and so once more she relents to his will.

If the previous scenes have depicted Katherine's training—her taming—then the banquet scene is her final exam—which, from Petruchio's perspective, she aces. Lucentio and Hortensio are shocked to learn that their wives are in fact closet shrews. Not only is Katherine alone in coming at her "keeper's call," she also performs additional tricks at Petruchio's command, thus winning his "wager better yet, / And show more sign of her obedience, / Her new-built virtue and obedience" (5.2.120). He "charges" her to "tell these headstrong women / What duty they do owe their lords and husbands" (5.2.134–135), and, like a good lieutenant, she does. Her longest soliloquy, Katherine's final speech ventriloquizes the patriarchal party line on wifely submission, perfectly articulating the gender stereotypes justifying male dominance. Performance, of course, leaves open the possibility for the lines to be delivered with subversive irony rather than as evidence of successful brainwashing. The question of whether the play's continued appeal to modern audiences is puzzling or illustrative is still worth pondering.

The Merry Wives of Windsor

Whereas *The Taming of the Shrew* culminates in Katherine's collusion with patriarchy against her sister and the widow, in *The Merry Wives of Windsor*,

Mistresses Ford and Page put their witty heads together to fight back, shaming a "greasy knight" for his unwanted sexual advances and restoring an overly jealous husband to his right mind. Plots that in other plays follow a tragic trajectory, such as the jealousy of husbands, the unbearable condition of enforced marriage, and the taming of an unruly wife, are translated into festive comedy in *The Merry Wives*.

Indeed, much that is ugly and misogynistic in early modern culture is laid to rest (at least momentarily) through the folksy holiday shenanigans that transpire in Windsor Forest, concluding the play. Through a merry shaming ritual, the wives not only put an end to Sir John Falstaff's sexual harassment but also tame Mistress Ford's overly jealous ("horn-mad") husband, and amid the holiday humor Anne Page's clandestine marriage of choice is given blessing rather than a curse.

Merry Wives presents a remarkable portrait of post-marital female friendship—one especially worth noting within the canon of Shakespearean plays for several reasons. While many of the plays present the disruption of female friendships as (a sometimes seemingly natural) by-product to heterosexual marriage, here it forms the central foundation to the play's major plot: the revenge against Falstaff and the taming of the overly jealous ("horn-mad") Mr. Ford. Unlike in the relationships between mistress and attendant, such as those between Desdemona and Emilia in *Othello* or Portia and Nerissa in *Merchant of Venice*, Mistresses Ford and Page are social equals, making them more like friends in our modern concept. As Mr. Ford remarks to Mistress Page, "I think if your husbands were dead you two would marry," to which she replies, deftly switching the unstated object of the verb from each other to another man, "Be sure of that—two other husbands" (3.2.11–13).

The intimacy of their friendship is demonstrated in their response to Falstaff's letters to them. Rather than bring the matter to their husbands or hide them in fearful shame, they immediately seek each other out to plot their response. The two women are rightfully indignant at Falstaff's affront to their virtue, but their response is neither pious or prudish. The women plot, as Mistress Ford puts it, "to entertain him / with hope, till the wicked fire of lust have melted / him in his own grease" (2.1.58–59). Yet, in spite of their strength as characters, the fact that we never learn their given names is particularly significant: they are, from start to finish, the wives of Page and Ford. Unfortunately, the feminine role of hostess on behalf of her husband—welcoming and making her husbands' associates comfortable in the home—is partly at the heart of the troubles the wives face with Falstaff. In the end, the two wives prove themselves to be strong defenders of their reputations—and, consequently, their husbands' stake in them as property. As wives, their status as property is uniquely complex among household goods. They are responsible for the good management of their households, which includes not only keeping good care of the house but also good management of themselves (and their morality). It is especially interesting that this latter form of good household management includes a kind of safekeeping from pirates like Falstaff.

While this play ends with comedy, spousal anxiety about a wife's role as social intermediary generates much more tragic results in plays like *Othello*, where Desdemona's efforts to heal the rift between her husband and Cassio is read in a warped fashion and construed as blatant infidelity. Similarly, in *The Winter's Tale*, Hermione's skill in convincing her husband's childhood friend Polixenes to put off his duties as king of Bohemia unexpectedly sparks Leontes's murderously jealous rage.

In the first scene of *Merry Wives*, we see Mistress Page and her daughter similarly perform such welcoming duties at the command of Master Page. Anne Page brings in the wine for Slender, Shallow, Evans, and the other, while Mistress Page is asked by her husband to "bid these gentlemen welcome" (1.1.157, 1.1.162). Later, Anne encourages the company to dinner, and must repeatedly press Slender to come to the table. As we soon learn, however, Anne is not at all fond of this suitor, thus making her kindness purely a matter of manners rather than personal affection. But it is precisely the expectations of this kind of ingra-tiating behavior that puts women in the double bind of having to fend off unwanted advances by those, like Falstaff, who intentionally misread the cour-tesy of Mistresses Page and Ford. Concerning his plot to woo Mistress Ford for the sake of monetary profit, Falstaff informs Pistol and Nim,

> I spy entertainment in her; she discourses,
> she carves, she gives the leer of invitation: I
> can construe the action of her familiar style; and
> the hardest voice of her behavior, to be Englished
> rightly, is, "I am Sir John Falstaff's." (1.3.37–41)

Literally mistranslating the two women's courtesy as affection peculiar to him, Falstaff imagines they will be the solution to his current financial woes. That culturally the possibility exists for such misreading can be seen in Master Ford's own claims (in the ugly guise of Master Brook) that it has been rumored "that though she [Mistress Ford] appear honest to me, yet in other places she enlargeth her mirth so that there is shrewd construction made of her" (2.2.197–199).

The conventionally ugly notion of women as a commodity is also given comedic rendering in *Merry Wives of Windsor*. Falstaff pursues the two Windsor women because, as he claims, they are courteous, familiar, and they "bear the purse" (1.3.46 and 1.3.58–59). Indeed, the romantic link between wooing and profiteering is brought together in Falstaff's parody of the conventional idea that a beloved is one's entire world:

> She is a region in Guiana, all gold and bounty. I will
> be cheater to them both, and they shall be
> exchequers to me; they shall be my East and West
> Indies, and I will trade to them both. (1.3.59–62)

Like the narrator in John Donne's poem "Sun Rising," who claims that his beloved is the entire world and its wealth, including "both th' Indias of spice and mine" (line 17), Falstaff also claims that the two wives will be his "East and West Indies" (the east being a source of spices and the west being the source of gold and diamonds). His analogy between Page's wife and Guiana (the land between Venezuela and Brazil) is particularly interesting, as Guiana was fabled as the location of El Dorado (the lost city of gold), which even in Shakespeare's time was seen by many as a myth. In his accounts of his travels to the region, Walter Raleigh had compared Guiana to an unassailable virgin (interestingly ironic in light of both the sacking of the New World and Falstaff's efforts to sack Mistresses Page and Ford). Raleigh's exaggerated claims about the wealth to be had there, however, also were met with skepticism.

In the subplot concerning the espousal of the Pages' daughter Anne, we find the mixing of the conventional themes of women as a commodity and the question of choice in marriage merged to comedic effect. Anne Page's inclusion in the theme of women as a commodity is central to the play's humor—and heightened drama—as Anne's virtues (her "good gifts") are conflated with her dowry of £700 over which her suitors vie, and Anne's parents each favor a different suitor, neither of whom is Anne's choice. Mistress Page favors Dr. Caius, a French physician who is substantially older than Anne, while Master Page promotes Master Slender, the doltish nephew of the local justice, whose only motive in wooing seems to be a desire to please his uncle by matching his annual income of £300 to Anne's dowry. Although Master Page claims he will give no dowry unless Anne marries according to his will, her personal choice is young Master Fenton, who, as Mistress Quickly observes, "smells April and May" (*Merry Wives* 3.2.58). Even Master Fenton confesses, however, that while initially he was drawn by Anne's wealth, he quickly has grown to love her for herself, making him clearly the most suitable of the suitors (*Merry Wives* 3.4.13–18). Happily, the couple manages to override Anne's parents' efforts to force her into a loveless marriage. Amid the merriment in Windsor Forest, Mr. Page is content with Anne's elopement and even patiently takes Fenton's chastisement of them for disregarding their daughter's feelings in the first place (5.5.194–210).

The early modern view that women are of insatiable sexual appetites and that marriage is inextricably linked to cuckolding is rendered insanely hysterical in Master Ford's expression of his ideas about his wife and marriage in general. While Master Page is a more reasonable man, Master Ford immediately takes the bait when Pistol and Nim inform against Falstaff. In the guise of Master Brook, Ford sets Falstaff on even more hotly in chase of his wife, even ironically providing him with the money needed to "lay siege to the honesty" of his Mistress Ford (2.2.208). In a scene that will be echoed in Iago's urging to Roderigo to "put money in your purse" in the later play *Othello*, Master Ford as Brook offers Falstaff money and urges him to "spend it, spend it; spend more; spend all I have" (2.2.206–207). At the heart of Ford's derangement is the misogynist idea that for a woman to say yes once is to leave her ineligible to ever say no to any who seeks to have sex with her—that is, to fall once would make his wife irredeemably a whore:

O, understand my drift. She dwells so securely on the
excellency of her honour, that the folly of my soul dares not
present itself: she is too bright to be looked against. Now,

could I come to her with any detection in my hand, my desires
had instance and argument to commend themselves: I could
drive her then from the ward of her purity, her reputation, her
marriage-vow, and a thousand other her defences, which now
are too too strongly embattled against me. What say you to't,
Sir John? (2.2.214–222)

Quickly Ford is rendered "horn-mad," ranting to himself that to be married is
to be made a cuckold: "There's a hole made in your best coat, Master Ford. This
'tis to be married; this 'tis to have linen and buck baskets! Well, I will proclaim
myself what I am. . . . Though what I am I cannot avoid, yet to be what I would
not shall not make me tame. If I have horns to make me mad, let the proverb go
with me—I'll be horn-mad" (3.5.121–130). Mistress Ford, however, is without
question honest, and consequently Ford's test—and Falstaff's assault—of course
fails. Mistresses Page and Ford ultimately prove that "Wives may be merry, and
yet honest too."
   At the heart of the play is the restoration of harmony overturned by Master
Ford's ugly misogyny and Falstaff's inept sexual harassment of the two wives. The
play's comedic resolution, however, depends upon Falstaff's presence as a kind of
scapegoat, taking on the punishment for both male and female (potential)
transgressions in the play. Falstaff, beaten as Herne the Hunter, pays not only his
own sins but for those of Master Ford as well. Although Master Ford is the would-be
cuckold, and potentially the most misogynist character in the play, it is Falstaff
who wears the horns and is publicly humiliated for his ill treatment of women.
That the wives' plot for Falstaff's final punishment is borne in collusion with
their husbands represents in particular a reincorporation of Master Ford back
into the companionate fold of marriage. But the women's potential unruliness is
also subjected to symbolic punishment—and again this happens through and on
the body of Falstaff when, disguised as the Old Woman of Brainford in the
second scene of the fourth act, he is beaten by Master Page. That the scene is
played for slapstick both displaces the Ford's potential violence against his wife
and presents the potential for domestic violence as humorous.

The Merchant of Venice

   Young women whose fathers are dead or absent face a particular form of either
danger or freedom, depending on the extent to which they are provided with
alternative protection and control. In The Merchant of Venice, Portia's father
asserts his power over her from beyond the grave. Portia's husband is to be chosen
by a sort of lottery in which each suitor gambles all in exchange for a chance to
select the winning casket (which contains Portia's portrait) from among three
treasure chests. As Portia complains to Nerissa, her waiting woman, "I may neither
choose who I would nor refuse who I dislike; so is the will of a living daughter
curved by the will of a dead father" (Merchant 1.2.20–22). Portia's desire or choice
(her "will") is controlled by her father's will, which is both the legal document
and his desire.

Although the lottery imposed by her father's will limits her freedom by barring her from "the right of voluntary choosing," it also affords her a measure of protection against the men who pursue her. An extremely witty character, Portia cleverly navigates her distaste for her various suitors with the cultural demands that she play nice by speaking to her suitors in language filled with double meaning.

From the perspective of some male characters in the plays, romantic interests are linked to financial ones. The courting of a wealthy maiden is presented in metaphors of venture capitalism—a profit earned in exchange for hazarding other wealth or life (or both). In the opening of *The Merchant of Venice*, Bassanio uses both capitalist and classical metaphors of profit to persuade Antonio to lend him the money needed to properly woo Portia:

> Nor is the wide world ignorant of her worth,
> For the four winds blow in from every coast
> Renowned suitors, and her sunny locks
> Hang on her temples like a golden fleece,
> Which makes her seat of Belmont Colchis' strand,
> And many Jasons come in quest of her. (*Merchant* 1.1.167–172)

Portia's hair is the blonde typical of lovely ladies pursued in romantic adventures, a color that also signifies her wealth through Bassanio's comparison of it to the golden fleece sought by Jason and the Argonauts. The various suitors to Portia must not only come appropriately attended and attired, but must ultimately also be willing to risk their fortunes for the chance to marry Portia, for the rules demand that all those who "hazard" and lose must agree "Never to speak to lady afterward/ In way of marriage" (*Merchant* 2.1.40–42). Since the production of lawful heirs is a key obligation for any man with property or title (not to mention entire kingdoms, as the case for Portia's suitors), such a bargain truly means to win or lose all.

Not only does the play address the conversion of women into wealth, but it also links this idea to questions of both interracial marriage and religious conversion—most notably in the figure of Shylock's daughter, Jessica, but in Portia as well. The repeated descriptions of both Portia and Jessica introduce the question of race in the play. Portia's rejection of the Prince of Morocco underscores her character's racism and highlights the play's anxiety about miscegenation. She comments after his departure, "A gentle riddance. Draw the curtains, go. / Let all of his complexion choose me so" (2.7.78–79). Portia's lines pun on "gentle" and "gentile" as well as categorizing the prince by his race, or "complexion." The subplot concerning Jessica similarly links various notions of conversion. Jessica betrays Shylock on several levels, stealing his jewels but also stealing away from the house to marry the Christian Lorenzo and converting to his religion. Disguised as a male page and "gilded" with ducats, she elopes into the night with Lorenzo, linking love and economic advancement with conversion (*Merchant* 2.6.49–50). As Lindsay Kaplan notes, however, while both women are subject to their father's wills, Jessica is allowed to break the parental bonds that tie her to her father—and is even praised for doing so. As Kaplan queries, "why might Jessica's disobedience be approved while Portia's might not be?" (17).

TRAGEDIES

Othello

The idea of woman in the abstract (that is, a notion of what women signify) and the male fear of becoming uxorious (that is, excessively devoted or submissive to women) is perhaps as central to *Othello* as the actual female characters in the play. Like the admonishments made in our own time against adolescent male athletes who run or throw "like a girl," male characters in *Othello* must prove they neither resemble women nor are they ruled by them.

When, for example, Iago complains to Roderigo about Othello's choice of lieutenant, he claims that Cassio is "almost damned in a fair wife" (although Cassio later denies his intentions to marry Bianca, whom he calls a "customer," meaning a common woman or prostitute). Iago also complains that Cassio knows as much about war as a spinster (i.e., a woman who makes a living by spinning) (1.1.22–25). Similarly, drawing on the language of housewifery, Othello assures the Duke that Desdemona's presence will not "corrupt and taint [his] business" for the state (1.3.269–273). In persuading Cassio to ask Desdemona to intercede with her husband on his behalf, Iago claims she will succeed because Othello's "soul is so enfettered to her love" (2.3.317). And when Cassio goes to seek reconciliation with the Othello, he shoos Bianca away lest the general see him "womaned" (3.4.189).

Additionally, *Othello* takes up many of the themes of female sexuality and desire we have seen developed in a number of the comedies, including the initial drama of conflict between fathers and daughters. *Othello*, however, follows these themes to their tragic conclusions rather than happily resolving the conflicts between generations and patriarchy.

As in *A Midsummer Night's Dream*, *Othello* opens with a daughter's rebellion, her "gross revolt," and Desdemona resembles in many respects the clever and outspoken heroines of the comedies. Like Hermia, she bravely chooses her lover rather than submitting to the arrangements of her father. Desdemona's strength and forwardness stands in striking contradiction to the image that Brabanzio has of her. When her father questions her as to whom she most owes obedience, she surprises him (and perhaps the rest of the assembly) in her answer, which illuminates the shifting obligations women owe between fathers and husbands. Claiming "a divided duty" and the precedent set by her mother, she "challenges" her right to "prefer" her husband before her father (1.3.178–188). Before the Duke, her father, and the entire Venetian assembly, she acknowledges her choice of Othello as a "downright violence and storm of fortunes" (1.3.248). She negotiates with the Duke to remain with Othello during his upcoming assignment rather than "be left behind, / A moth to peace" (1.3.254–255). Like Rosalind, Desdemona is a sexual being who insists she not be "bereft" of the "rites" of marriage that a separation from Othello would cause (1.3.254–256). Later, in

Cypress, Desdemona defends Emilia from Iago's claims that she is a shrew, then wittily banters with him when he dilates his accusations to encompass the female sex in general (2.1.106–165).

Like Egeus in A *Midsummer Night's Dream*, Brabanzio imagines his daughter as an inanimate treasure which has been "stol'n" by force or witchcraft. Until he hears it with his own ears, Brabanzio cannot fathom that Desdemona might be "half the wooer" (1.3.175). In his eyes, his daughter is "a maid / So tender, fair, and happy, / So opposite to marriage that she shunned / The wealthy curlèd darlings of our nation" (1.2.67–69). That Desdemona is white and Othello is black, moreover, provides an extended expression of the anxiety over miscegenation that is only briefly engaged in *The Merchant of Venice* when Portia expresses her racist relief at escaping a match with the Prince of Morocco. Yet Desdemona's love is not simply color-blind, as she must negotiate Othello's race in her attraction to him: "I saw Othello's visage in his mind," she explains (1.3.253).

Elsewhere, the whiteness of Desdemona's skin, her fairness, is repeatedly emphasized throughout the play, both as proof of her beauty and her virtue, but it also is presented in "monstrous" contrast with Othello's blackness. Through the warped eyes of Iago, Othello is "an erring barbarian" and Desdemona a "supersubtle Venetian" (1.3.350). Whereas Jessica in *The Merchant of Venice* is "saved" through her marriage to the Christian Lorenzo, Desdemona is "topped" by Othello's blackness. According to Brabanzio, Desdemona is "A maiden never bold, / Of spirit so still and quiet that her motion / Blushed at herself" (1.3.94–96). From his perspective, she has heretofore matched the prescriptions for female passive obedience advocated in early modern conduct manuals.

By the single act of her clandestine marriage to Othello, however, Desdemona steps outside of the prescribed behaviors that define good women. Although the couple enters into what appears to be a companionate marriage, the absence of her father's blessing opens Desdemona to the charges of deceit and infidelity laid generically against her sex. But while Egeus is rendered silent and his claim of the "ancient privilege" mercifully overruled by the end of A *Midsummer Night's Dream*, the ugly misogyny and foul racism spun by Iago in the opening scene of *Othello* are taken up by Brabanzio—and finally, with lethal consequences, by Othello.

An interpretive question for this play is how to resolve the conflict between Desdemona's unconventionality and strength of personality, which leads her to choose her mate without her father's authority, and the misogynist notions of unbridled female sexuality that underlie Othello's doubts of her chastity. This crux is further complicated when, in answer to Emilia's question of "who hath done this deed?" Desdemona replies, "Nobody; I myself" (5.2.128–129). Perhaps she is implying responsibility; perhaps she is alluding to her condition as *femme covert*; the meaning is intriguingly unclear.

In certain respects, Desdemona is a passive object of exchange in the battle among men. She is merely "the fair paper . . . made to write whore." However, the play also engages in a uniquely female tragic drama concerning the difficulties faced by early modern women in negotiating their culture's misogyny on the one hand, and enacting the ideals of companionate marriage and the cultural definitions of a good wife on the other.

As Iago comments to Cassio, Desdemona is noted for her free and generous spirit, and it is precisely this amiableness that opens her to danger. Like Falstaff in *Merry Wives*, who mistakes the friendliness and welcome that Mistresses Page and Ford bestow on him as an associate of their husbands, Iago twists Desdemona's generosity to seem an unwholesome liberality. What does it mean for a woman to be "free" with her favors? Like Leontes in *The Winter's Tale*, Othello ends up reading his wife's efforts to intercede on his behalf as an attraction to his friend Cassio. He believes Iago's claim that "she repeals him for her body's lust" (3.3.330). Moreover, Desdemona's diligence in pursuing the reconciliation between her husband and Cassio seems to recall the language and actions of the shrew. As she vows lightheartedly before Emilia, her words echo contemporary critiques of "curtain lectures":

> My Lord shall never rest.
> I'll watch him tame and talk him out of patience.
> His bed shall seem a school, his board a shrift.
> I'll intermingle everything he does
> With Cassio's suit (3.3.24–26)

Throughout scenes three and four of act three, as Desdemona presses Cassio's case to her unwilling husband, there arises a potential similarity with harping shrews. Contemporary works ranging from Vives's *Instruction of a Christian Woman* to Elizabeth Cary's *Tragedy of Mariam* insist that it is not enough for women to be chaste and obedient in their actions; they must also be so in thought and appearance. In the social economy of the play, a woman's sexual virtue is everything. While the audience knows that Desdemona is innocent, these cultural imperatives make possible Othello's deadly error in reading the evidence against his wife.

Emilia's character, too, is tested on the grounds of what it means to be a good wife, especially in relation to her giving of the dropped handkerchief to her husband. While she knows that her mistress will be exceedingly distraught at its loss, her obligation to her husband's will surpasses those to Desdemona. It is not until the final moments of the play that she realizes the fullness of her error. The handkerchief of white "spotted" with red strawberries becomes a fetish for both Desdemona's purity and the blood of her virgin hymen. Once lost, the handkerchief provides Iago with the material he needs to create the illusion of "ocular proof" that Othello demands. Too late, Emilia speaks the truth, and in doing so she must overcome her husband's command that she be silent—and his accusations that she is a whore when she disobeys. Yet she persists. "'Tis proper I obey him [Iago]," she pleads to the assemble gentlemen, "but not now" (5.2.204). Emilia's truth vindicates Desdemona, but it is too late and even costs her own life.

Ironically, Emilia is particularly astute at laying bare the sexual double standard. In her earlier conversation with Desdemona about whether some women might indeed be unfaithful to their husbands, Emilia's keen-witted practicality stands in stark contrast to Desdemona's romantically unrealistic—and ultimately deadly—ideals for female fidelity. In claiming she would not betray her husband for jewelry, clothing, or other love tokens, Emilia nonetheless raises the question concerning the limits to which a wife might go toward the betterment of her husband: "Uds [God's] pity, who would not make her husband a cuckold to make him a monarch" (4.3.70–76). Continuing, Emilia critiques husbands and the sexual double standard in a speech reminiscent of Shylock's "hath not a Jew eyes" speech. She lists the various economic, emotional, and physical injuries that husbands do to their wives without the expectation that they might seek "revenge." Yet, she exclaims, "Let husbands know / Their wives have sense like them" (4.3.92–93). Her words, however, die with both the speaker and the listener.

With only a handful of lines, Bianca is clearly a minor character. From the perspective of the play's masculine drama, she is there merely as a pawn in the game among men. As a courtesan, she of course represents the opposite of Desdemona's marital fidelity. But while Desdemona is ostensibly the play's "white" character, the courtesan's name means literally "white," ironically calling into question the distinguishing lines between good and bad women (and, as a number of critics have noticed, Desdemona's name encompasses the word "demon").

However, Bianca's interaction with Emilia just after Cassio is wounded highlights in brief sketch the ways in which women are pitted against women, colluding with patriarchy in the pursuit of privilege. Drawn into the street by the ruckus, Bianca is distraught to learn that her lover, Cassio, has been wounded. Iago, however, attempts to draw attention from himself by impugning Bianca: "Gentlemen, all, I do suspect this trash / To be a party in this injury" (5.1.85–86). Emilia, likewise drawn into the street by the disturbance, also turns against Bianca, calling her a "strumpet." Bianca claims she "is no strumpet, but of life as honest / As you that thus abuse me" (5.1.124–125), to which Emilia exclaims, "As I? Faugh! Fie upon thee!" (5.1.126). In a binary system, there can be no "honest" women without "whores" to mark their difference. Early modern England had no respectable category for an unmarried but sexually active woman like Bianca. Yet, of the three female characters in the play, intriguingly it is Bianca who escapes death.

Romeo and Juliet

As in life, noble and aristocratic women figure in Shakespeare's plays as political pawns exchanged between men to create alliances. In *Romeo and Juliet*, Juliet's parents have arranged a politically advantageous marriage with Paris, a wealthy kinsman of the prince. Given the deep rift between the Capulets and the Montagues, however, the more naturally occurring love between Romeo and Juliet stands ironically in contrast to the tradition of using marriages to heal potentially deadly political rifts.

Moreover, *Romeo and Juliet* contrasts in particularly ironic ways with the failed arranged marriage in a play like *Antony and Cleopatra*. In *Antony and Cleopatra*, Agrippa proposes mending the fractured bond between Antony and Caesar by means of Antony's marriage to Caesar's sister Octavia, and in a futile attempt at political reconciliation, Caesar "bequeaths" Octavia (2.2.116–160). Caught between her family and her new husband, Octavia is presented poignantly weeping in a fruitless attempt to prevent Antony from fighting with Caesar (3.4.1–38). Poor Octavia fails even more dismally when she is sent by Antony to make peace with her brother, who insists that her lack of a proper entourage demonstrates Antony's disdain for her, a lack of esteem and love that is clearly shown in his returning to Egypt—and Cleopatra—rather than to Athens (3.6.39–99).

Elsewhere in Shakespeare's plays, however, the fact that women have wills of their own, even as they follow the rules of gendered decorum and cultural obedience to fathers and husbands, is reflected both implicitly and explicitly throughout the tragedies and comedies. Fathers are often the last to realize their daughters have wills of their own. Like Egeus in *A Midsummer Night's Dream* and Brabanzio in *Othello*, Juliet's parents are given the impression that their daughter has not been eagerly seeking her chance to marry. Having not yet met Romeo, Juliet claims that her choice is to forgo marriage. Once she is confronted with love at first sight in Romeo, however, Juliet's rejection of marriage in the abstract shifts to a personal desire for the particular man. Wooed by Romeo below her bedroom balcony, Juliet moves between her own desire for Romeo and cultural expectations that preclude virtuous maidens from having such bold desires:

> Thou knowest the mask of night is on my face,
> Else would a maiden blush bepaint my cheek
> For that which thou hast heard me speak tonight.
> Fain would I dwell on form, fain, fain deny
> What I have spoke; but farewell, compliment.
> Dost thou love me? I know thou wilt say 'Ay',
> And I will take thy word. Yet if thou swear'st
> Thou mayst prove false. . . .
> . . .O gentle Romeo,
> If thou dost love, pronounce it faithfully;
> Or if thou think'st I am too quickly won,
> I'll frown, and be perverse, and say thee nay,
> So thou wilt woo; but else, not for the world. (*R&J* 2.1.127–139)

Even as she asserts the genuineness of her feeling, Juliet's adherence to conventions of female virtue is called into question by several ambiguities and aural puns.

To begin, Juliet does not claim that she is blushing—only that she would be blushing if her face were not hidden by "the mask of night." The potentially shifting meanings of "fain" in her next lines further call into question the authenticity of her virtue according to conventional standards. While editors typically gloss this word as "happily" or "gladly," the word may also mean that she is "required or obliged." This sense of obligation rather than willingness is intensified by the rest of the line, which claims she must/will "dwell on form." Here she claims she will happily/dutifully focus on the formalities of how men and women interact. However, "form" (or formalities) have the potential for implying the absence of intrinsic meaning or authenticity. The ambiguity between real love and formalities is further intensified by the possible aural pun between "fain" and "feign" ("to pretend or to counterfeit"). Because her desire runs contrary to conventions of female virtue, she is willing to pretend to be coy—to "frown, and be perverse, and say thee nay" (2.3.138). Thus while she seeks to affirm the genuineness of Romeo's feelings of love, her own end up being rendered potentially ambiguous as she reveals that she knows how to play the game, and that she will "fain" do so in order to get him to pursue her.

Juliet's sexuality contrasts with both that of her mother and the Nurse, both of whom represent mother figures in the play. On the one hand, Lady Capulet represents the stereotype of the aristocratic woman. Wed at an early age (her character seems to be twenty-eight years old), she advocates her daughter's marriage as a vehicle for maternity and social duty. Her marriage to Lord Capulet is, apparently, not primarily one of companionship. Moreover, Lady Capulet's maternity itself is strongly class-bound in its depiction, as her relationship with her daughter is presented as extremely hierarchical and formal. Lady Capulet not only represents a fading attitude toward relations between husbands and wives, but also a fading notion of motherhood. That she did not nurse her daughter aligns her with an older view concerning maternal breastfeeding, which a number of Shakespeare's contemporaries—including, apparently, his own wife, Anne— had increasingly begun to promote. Indeed, the Nurse seems to hold a more intimate and emotional relationship with Juliet, but also seems to confirm the dangers of handing over one's children to women of the lower classes (one of the arguments made in polemics promoting maternal breastfeeding).

Hamlet

Gertrude in *Hamlet* is another rare example of a Shakespearean mother. But in this play, Shakespeare provides neither of his female characters, Gertrude or Ophelia, with interior monologues or expressions of their own passions and insights, as he does for a number of his heroines in other plays. Yet both, but especially Ophelia, have exercised the minds of countless writers and painters.

Within the confines of the play, both characters primarily react to and obey the men as they struggle for power. Gertrude's initial presence is that of a care-filled mother, concerned about what strikes her as Hamlet's excessive melancholy and grief over his father's death. Hamlet, however, is seemingly overwhelmed by female sexuality—both his mother's and that of Ophelia. His mother's remarriage repulses him, and his negative reaction fails to take into account the early modern woman's need for male protection. It is possibly this need for male support that motivates Hamlet's mother's desire that Hamlet remain with her in Denmark; later, this need may be part of Ophelia's descent into madness and her final suicidal plunge into the river. Rather than considering this social construct, Hamlet focuses on popularly imagined, misogynist reasons for a widow to remarry: seeing his mother as a creature of "appetite," he claims she has hurried "with such dexterity to incestuous sheets!" (1.2.157). Just before Hamlet kills Polonius, who is hiding behind the arras in Gertrude's room, he urges her to leave "the rank sweat of an enseamed bed, / Stewed in corruption, honeying and making love / Over the nasty sty –" (3.4.82–83). She pleads with him to stop, but when (at the prompting of the ghost) he asks her how she is, her reply is to ask Hamlet how he is. Readers are not made privy to what Gertrude thinks of her late husband's death or of her remarriage. As a good mother, her main concern is Hamlet's condition.

Similarly, we are given very little insight into Ophelia's thoughts about what is happening in the Danish court or with her relationship with Hamlet. Ophelia at first seems to be poised precariously to move up in rank through her relation to Prince Hamlet. In the opening scenes of the play, however, both Laertes and Polonius are highly concerned about Ophelia's sexual status, and Ophelia presents herself as ideally feminine in her acquiescence to their cautions. Laertes reminds Ophelia that Hamlet, as the Danish heir, cannot marry based on love "as unvalued [i.e., common] persons do," but must marry according to the needs of the state and the Danish people (1.3.19). Although Ophelia is the daughter of the Lord Chamberlain (who holds a powerful and high-rank position), were Hamlet to marry her, she would not provide Denmark with potentially necessary political alliances with other nations. Polonius likewise warns that Hamlet "is young, / And with a larger tether may he walk / Than may be given" to Ophelia (1.3.125–126). Consequently, both brother and father warn Ophelia that she must guard her sexual reputation, and not trust too heavily on the aims of Hamlet's love.

Ophelia has little to say throughout all of this—as well as later, when Polonius sets her to spy on Hamlet. While she does venture to challenge her brother to heed his own advice to keep reputation safe, her most common reply is that she is listening and that she promises to obey. When Hamlet berates her, infamously directing her to join a nunnery (where she would live a life of sexual abstinence—or, if Hamlet were using the Elizabethan slang for a brothel, where she would join ranks with other prostitutes), she momentarily muses on her own state, but half her speech is given over to lamentation for Hamlet's overthrown reason (3.1.122; 3.1.129–160). Even when Hamlet asks, as he lies with his head in Ophelia's lap while they watch the *Mousetrap* play, whether she has taken his words to mean something crude, she replies that she "think[s] nothing, my lord" (3.2.98–138). And he builds upon Ophelia's "nothing" with additional bawdy puns.

It is, perhaps, this emptiness that makes Ophelia so intriguing a figure and yet one so difficult to locate precisely. As Elaine Showalter has argued, "There is no 'true' Ophelia for whom feminist criticism must unambiguously speak, but perhaps only a Cubist Ophelia of multiple perspectives, more than the sum of all her parts" (92). Indeed, Ophelia seems most full as a character when she is mad.

Macbeth

Macbeth puts in contrast two sorts of wives and women—good wives and witches—and in the process raises questions about the power of women and their suggestions. The witches gathered in the opening scene of the play utter what seems to be nonsense until the apparent truth of their claim that Macbeth shall be named Thane of Cawdor lends an aura of authenticity to the claim that he shall be king. As Banquo warns, however, "oftentimes, to win us to our harm / The instruments of darkness tell us truths" (1.3.121–122). The play leaves open the question of whether the power of suggestions made by the witches—and later by Lady Macbeth—is responsible for Macbeth's downfall.

Regardless of their power to sway Macbeth, both the witches and Lady Macbeth represent the perversion of early modern notions of natural woman-hood and good housewifery. The witches gathered in the opening scene of the play resemble those typically found haunting the early modern English imagination. They are too manly in their acts and looks. As Banquo claims, "You should be women, / And yet your beards forbid me to interpret / That you are so" (1.3.43–44). They have been killing livestock and wreaking havoc on their neighbors. A common context for accusations of witchcraft involved the denial of charity, and here one of Shakespeare's witches plots revenge against a sailor whose wife has refused to share her chestnuts. Not only will she cause his ship to be "tempest-tossed," but like other witches imagined at the time, the first witch also plans to bewitch him sexually: "I'll do, I'll do, and I'll do" (1.3.9) and she will "drain him dry as hay" (1.3.17). The witches also enact a perverted form of domesticity in concocting their stew filled with odiously exotic ingredients. They bake and boil, using their kitchen skills to blend "poisoned entrails" in a broth made of venomous toad stewed "in the charmed pot" (4.1.9). And they call upon their familiars to assist them in their devilish deeds (4.1.44–48).

Through an excessive wifely ambition and an evil perversion of feminine gender roles, Lady Macbeth's character is implicitly linked with the witches in the play (and in some productions, the casting even doubles her character with that of Hecate's), despite her lack of the type of outward features that identify the hags on the heath as witches: nothing in the text suggests that Lady Macbeth is sprouting a beard, nor does she apparently cook anything. Nonetheless, she mirrors the witches in her attempt to take on a psychological masculinity and her perversion of the wifely duties of hospitality. She conjures spirits to "unsex" her, to transform her feminine self into manly savagery. She wants to be filled "from the crown to the toe top-full / Of direst cruelty," her blood to be made "thick," and her spirit to be made remorseless, and the nurturing milk of her breasts exchanged for "gall" (1.5.40–42). She wants "no compunctious visitings of nature / [to] Shake [her] fell [cruel] purpose" (1.5.43–44). Indeed, later she makes her infamous claim to Macbeth that had she vowed to do so (as Macbeth has vowed to murder Duncan), she would willingly dash out the brains of her nursing infant (1.7.54–55). She urges her husband's swift return so that she may, witchlike, "pour [her] spirits in [his] ear" (1.5.23–24). She is the extreme possibility of the shrewish wife, nagging Macbeth to follow through with the murder and repeatedly questioning his manhood (the right form of manhood itself being a strong theme throughout the play).

Having taken on an inward masculinity, Lady Macbeth further perverts her wifely duties, not only assuming the upper hand in the marriage but also providing a deadly form of hospitality to those who enter Glamis Castle. Lady Macbeth tutors her husband in the arts of deceit: "bear welcome in your eye, / Your hand, your tongue; look like the innocent flower, / But be the serpent under't" (1.5.61–64). She insists that Macbeth put the "night's great business into [her] dispatch [management]" (1.5.66).

Lady Macbeth is presented in the role of hostess on several occasions. Unaware of the murder that awaits him, Duncan calls attention to Lady Macbeth's hospitality, calling her "honoured hostess" and "fair and noble hostess" (1.6.10, 24). Aligned with the mythical sorceress Circe, Lady Macbeth premeditates the ruin of Duncan by disarming his bodyguards with "wine and wassail [carousing]" and drowning them in "swinish sleep" (1.6.64–67). Combining the talents of witches and hostesses, Lady Macbeth drugs the guards' posset (a drink of mulled milk and wine), but she cannot bring herself to kill Duncan because he resembles her father (2.2.6–7). Later, following the murders of Duncan and Banquo, Macbeth acknowledges his wife as hostess, and she welcomes the thanes who have gathered after being summoned to acknowledge Macbeth as their new king. Lady Macbeth presents a vision of domestic efficiency, quickly "dispatching" (in both the sense of undertaking them herself and the early modern sense of managing their execution) the various evil tasks needed to promote her husband. Immediately after Duncan's murder, she confidently assures her husband that "A little water clears us of this deed. / How easy it is then!" (2.2.65–66). Yet ultimately, Lady Macbeth succumbs fatally to the madness inspired by her murderous deeds, unable to rid herself of the "damned spot" that stains both her hands and her soul.

Lady Macduff's brief appearance in the play places her in contrast with the witches and Lady Macbeth. While the scene demonstrates Macbeth's increasing degeneration into evil—he has now turned to murdering women and children—the scene also graphically depicts the fragility of motherhood's power in a world, like that depicted in *Richard III*, that is overpowered by a tyrant's evil.

No longer in a position where her skills in housewifery are needed, Lady Macduff's situation is one of desolation and crisis. Although she harshly criticizes her husband to Ross, claiming Macduff is a traitor who lacks affection for his family (he "wants the natural touch"; 4.2.8–9), the scene evokes strong pathos as she puts up a brave front for her son who is so young he does not even merit his own name. In her witty banter with her prattling child, she claims that husbands are infinitely replaceable, and should she find herself a widow, she can buy "twenty at any market price" (4.2.40).

Lady Macduff, however, ultimately proves herself a good and loyal wife, defending Macduff's reputation from the murderers' claims against him. When the murderers seek to know where her husband is, she replies that she hopes he is in "no place so unsanctified" as the one where she is presently and about to be murdered. Moments later, in perhaps one of the most horrific scenes in Shakespeare's works, the murderers savagely kill Lady Macduff's son in front of her (and we learn later that Lady Macduff, who has fled offstage following the brutal murder of her son, has also been killed). Whereas in *Richard III* the actual murders of children occur offstage, leaving the group of childless mothers onstage to compete in their lamentations, here the focus is on the brutality of the deed (and the lamentation takes place later, when Macduff, who is urged by Malcolm to "dispute it like a man," claims he "must also feel it as a man" (4.3.221, 223). Lady Macduff's purpose is primarily to highlight Macbeth's depravity and to illicit Macduff's guilt and righteous vengeance.

SHAKESPEARE AND HISTORICAL WOMEN

Much early criticism examining Shakespeare's uses of history focused on the question of the accuracy of his depictions (for example, pointing out such infamous anachronisms as the references to clocks in *Julius Caesar* and billiards in *Antony and Cleopatra*, or that Margaret of Anjou spent the final six years of her life in Paris, dying in1482 one year before Richard III claimed the throne). Little attention was given to the accuracy of his gendered representations. Shakespeare, however, was a playwright and poet, rather than a historian. Insofar as this section looks at Shakespeare's use of history, I will focus primarily on his thematic and dramatic use of history, rather than on his historical accuracy.

For the English of Shakespeare's time, Roman history was linked legendarily to the birth of Britain, and the English saw themselves as the descendants of the Romans, which had in turn derived its origins from Troy. The major chroniclers from the medieval period through later historians contemporary with Shakespeare included the story of the myth of Britain's founding by Brutus (Aeneas's grandson) after the fall of Troy. For the educated elite of early modern England, classical antiquity provided not only literary types and character archetypes, but also a historical root for the English. The English saw their history as deriving from, and therefore linked to, the classical past. Shakespeare's contributions to this history are to be found primarily in his plays based on Plutarch: *Julius Caesar*, *Antony and Cleopatra*, and *Coriolanus*, but also *Titus Andronicus* and the poem *Rape of Lucrece*.

For the most part, however, female characters play peripheral roles, both in Shakespeare's Roman plays in particular and more generally in the dominant historical traditions concerning classical antiquity. Only a handful of female characters appear in these plays; they appear briefly and are usually given only a few lines, and nearly all of them are the wives, daughters, sisters, and mothers of more prominent aristocratic male characters. As in the histories of ancient Rome, for example, Shakespeare's Octavia, Lavinia, and Portia function in the plays primarily as objects of exchange in marriages meant to weave political alliances and to ensure dynastic continuity. Characters like Tamora and Volumnia, who wield power—or attempt to do so—are presented by Shakespeare as wicked—even depraved or perverse. It is perhaps not surprising that Cleopatra, Shakespeare's most prominent and complex female character drawn from the period of classical antiquity, is neither Roman nor depicted as appearing in Rome. If she can be said to be heroic, however, it is not in the classic tradition of stoicism given male characters.

Cleopatra

While drawing on the traditions handed down by hostile writers, most notably Plutarch, Shakespeare provides a complex figure in his depiction of Cleopatra: On the one hand, her romance with Mark Antony stands among the greatest love affairs in English literature. On the other hand, her failure to rule properly is repeatedly staged and even juxtaposed with Caesar's more valorous, yet shrewd, statesmanship.

Shakespeare's Cleopatra wields her powers in service to love and to the neglect of her country. While she is not given supernatural powers in Shakespeare's version, traces of her witchlike qualities remain in the power she exerts over Antony in general—and in particular, in Antony's attempt to break free of her after the failed naval battle. He calls her a "spell," uses the word "Avaunt!" (meaning "begone") to cast her away from him, and threatens to let his legal wife, the "Patient Octavia plow thy visage up / With her prepared nails!" (4.12.30–39). Scratching to draw blood was held by those who believed in witches to be a way to diminish a suspected witch's power.

Caesar is austere in his pursuits, cunning in his diplomacy, and noble in demeanor, even with messengers of the enemy. In contrast, Cleopatra revels luxuriously in courtly pastimes of music, billiards, and angling (fishing). She moons romantically over her absent lover and maltreats messengers whose messages displease her.

Although Britain is not mentioned in Shakespeare's *Antony and Cleopatra*, the play can be seen as working through the larger questions of national identity that occupied the British during this period. The portraits of Cleopatra and Egypt created by Shakespeare and other early modern writers participate in what postcolonial critic Edward Said has redefined as "orientalism." Orientalism, according to Said, consists of the discourses by which Western writers have imposed on the people of the East an identity of inferiority and exoticism as a means of defining the people of the West as the opposite. Writing at the dawn of the English empire, Shakespeare juxtaposes a rational and right-conquering Rome, embodied in the character of Octavian, against not only the luxurious and eastern colonial territory of Egypt, embodied in the despotic figure of Cleopatra, but also against the figure of Marc Antony, who succumbs to the dangers of "going native" rather than maintaining control of the colonized lands. Egypt and Cleopatra (who is herself metonymically called "Egypt" in the play), represent—as Coppelia Kahn and others have suggested—the danger of being feminized by the colonized other (Kahn 118–119).

The Rape of Lucrece, Titus Andronicus, and Cymbeline

In spite of women's generally peripheral status, a woman figures significantly at the center of several versions of emergent nationhood as depicted by classical authors—and in turn taken up by early modern writers, including Shakespeare in two of his very early works which were set in the ancient world: *The Rape of Lucrece* and *Titus Andronicus*.

In each of these stories, the abduction and rape of a prominent woman sparks revolution and the emergence of a new nation-state. Paris's abduction of Helen from her husband Menalaeus sparked the Trojan War, while the revenge exacted on the Tarquins by Lucrece's family in response to her rape marked the expulsion of the Tarquins and the emergence of the new Roman Republic. Shakespeare's early works raise similar political questions, staking contesting empires' claims to power over the fetishized body of a woman in both *The Rape of Lucrece* and *Titus Andronicus*. In both works, the assault on the noblewoman of the opponent's house is claimed and perceived as an assault upon the opponent, and ultimately the desecration of the woman is simultaneously perceived as an attack on the nation.

While Shakespeare's early poem on Lucrece and his incorporation of the story of Lavinia in *Titus Andronicus* develop the image of the raped woman as the inspiration for nationhood, Shakespeare radically transformed the image near the end of his writing career, in the historical romance of *Cymbeline*. *Cymbeline* was probably written sometime after 1606; although classified generically with the romances, it most directly broaches the link between Roman and English history that lies submerged in the other Roman plays.

On the one hand, the play's dizzying array of plots, reversals, misrecognitions, and recognitions recalls the conventions of transformation drawn from Ovid's *Metamorphoses* and found in a number of his other plays. The play also incorporates numerous features of folk and fairy tales, including the wicked stepmother (named simply "the Queen") who sends poisoned gifts, stolen princes who act according to their innate nobility in spite of having been raised rustically as shepherds, and Imogen's keeping house for rustic men in a cave, which calls to mind Snow White's housekeeping for the dwarves. On the other hand, as a story of the *pax Romana* ("peace with Rome"), the play's resolution focuses on Britain's sovereignty, and the soothsayer's riddling prophecies (5.5.232–237 and 5.6.453–458) call more concretely to mind the myths of national origins at work in *Cymbeline*.

In presenting a more fully developed "English sensibility" in the later play, Shakespeare likewise transforms his incorporation of the story of Philomela in *Titus* and *Cymbeline*, merging it in significantly different ways for both Lavinia and Imogen. In Ovid's *Metamorphoses*, King Tereus lusts after his sister-in-law, Philomela, whom he rapes. When she vows to make known his crime, Tereus cuts out her tongue so that she cannot tell what has happened to her. However, Philomela employs her skill in needlework to create a sampler depicting the crimes against her, and thus she informs her sister Procne of her husband's betrayal. In revenge for the attack against her sister, Procne murders Itys, Tereus's son by her, and cooks him in a stew that she serves to Tereus. When Tereus learns what Procne has done, he flies after the two sisters to kill them, but all three are transformed into birds: Tereus a hoopoe, Procne a swallow, and Philomela a nightingale.

In *Titus*, Lavinia has met "a craftier Tereus" (4.1.40). Deprived of her hands, which the rapists have cut off along with her tongue, Lavinia uses a copy of *The Metamorphoses* to convey what otherwise she might have stitched into a sampler to report the crime against her (*Titus* 2.4.11–57). As Charles and Michelle Martindale point out, the play adapts and transforms not only the story of Philomela, but the Ovidian story of Virginia as well (Martindale 51). Whereas Procne enacts revenge on behalf of her sister, Titus, rather than Lavinia, strikes revenge against Tamora by cooking her sons and feeding them to her (*Titus* 5.2.195 ff.). Moreover, in Titus's murder of Lavinia to dispel her "shame," Shakespeare also incorporates and transforms the story of Virginia, who was murdered by her father as a way to avoid the defilement threatened by Appias (5.3.35–47).

In *Cymbeline* Imogen's body becomes a fetish and signifier of Britain, much like the bodies of Lucrece and Lavinia, which are made metonymies for nation. Thus, the integrity of her chastity and any assaults on it are simultaneously individual and metonymically an attack on Britain, and the play twice threatens Imogen with defilement: Cloten (in Posthumous's clothing) pursues her with the intent to rape her; and Iachomo plots to create the illusion that he has debauched her when his bet with Posthumous fails. However, insofar as Imogen is Britain, it is unimaginable to present a successful assault on her, and both attackers are foiled: Cloten is killed by Imogen's brothers (who are as yet ignorant of each others' identities), and Iachomo repents after confessing his foul deceit.

Moreover, the allusions to the story of Philomel and Procne, as well as to the ancient virtues of stoicism, are likewise adapted to a more contemporary English sensibility. The story of Philomel and Procne, for example, are to be read but not necessarily enacted. While Iachimo lurks hidden in the chest, Imogen goes to bed reading Ovid's *Metamorphoses* (2.2.12–45). Posthumous's failed attempt to have his allegedly defiled wife murdered and Imogen's rejection of suicide in the face of dishonor further demonstrate the distinction between the classical stoicism of Rome and a more native (and perhaps implicitly Christian) sensibility of constancy Shakespeare attributes to a newly emerging Britain (3.4.77–79).

The First Tetralogy

In turning to England's history in the two centuries prior to his own time, Shakespeare presents the national story in eight plays covering the period from 1398 to 1485, beginning with King Richard II and ending with the defeat of Richard III by Henry VII, the first Tudor king and grandfather to Elizabeth I. Scholars often divide these eight plays into two tetralogies, or sets of four plays. The first tetralogy, written earlier, deals with the later period and includes the three parts of *Henry VI* and *Richard III*; the second tetralogy was written slightly later than the first, and these plays move back in time to the deposition of

Richard the II and work forward to the victories of Henry V in France (*Richard II*, the two parts of *Henry IV*, and *Henry V*).

According to Jean E. Howard and Phyllis Rackin, the plays of the first tetralogy "imagine the past as a world where marriages are dynastic and the state is organized around, and is conceived as inseparable from, the body of the monarch" (30). As warriors, seductresses, witches, and monstrous adulteresses, the women in these plays pose threats on various fronts to the monarchical body.

In *I Henry VI*, all three women are French, reduced to their sexuality, and representative of a threat to the English. The beautiful Countess of Auvergne lures Talbot into her castle, but her scheme fails when his army is hidden nearby and waiting to rescue him from her trap. Joan of Arc is the most prominent figure, and the transformation of her reputation throughout the play is particularly intriguing. At first among the French, she is the divinely sent virgin, "[a]ssigned . . . to be the English scourge" (1.3.108). After Joan passes the Dauphin's test and beats him at combat at arms in the first act, the Dauphin calls Joan both an Amazon and a Deborah (a judge in the Old Testament who led a victorious Israelite army). The French call her "la pucelle," meaning the maid or virgin; but for the English, the word puns with "puzzle," a slang term for whore. By the end of the play, Joan's character's actions confirm the English claims that she is a witch and a whore.

In the final act, the French are losing the battle and have turned against Joan. She conjures her demons, but when the fiends appear, they refuse to speak to her or to give her aid. Although she offers her blood, body, and soul, they forsake her (5.3). At her execution (5.6), she first denies her shepherd father, claiming a royal and even celestial parentage (5.6.37–41). When the only mercy from the English is a call for additional wood and pitch "so her torture may be shortened" (5.6.58), Joan claims instead to be pregnant, thus abandoning her identity as the virgin warrior. If Joan were pregnant, she would be reprieved long enough to deliver the baby before being executed (or perhaps to escape). She frantically switches from one alleged father to another, naming first the Dauphin, then Alencon, and finally Rene the King of Naples, further damning her as a whore before the English burn her at the stake as a heretic.

The stage cleared of Joan, Margaret of Anjou arrives to be captured by Suffolk— and to capture the English soldier's body and soul. Margaret's beauty undoes Suffolk, and because he is already married and cannot have her, he decides he will match her with King Henry VI. The play ends by foreshadowing the further chaos and war to come in the next play.

Part two of *Henry VI* opens by recalling the bad political bargain Suffolk has made on behalf of the English king: Henry is to marry Margaret, who brings no dowry— and the lands of Maine and Anjou that had been won by Henry's father, King Henry V, are to be returned to the King of Naples. As York puts it: "I never read but England's kings have had / Large sums of gold and dowries with their wives— / And our King Henry gives away his own, / To match with her that brings no vantages" (1.1.124–127). Consequently, a rift opens as the War of the Roses between the English nobles begins, and civil riot from the commons erupts in Jack Cade's rebellion.

While no female characters are central to the Jack Cade plot, and women have no rights in his vision of a new commonwealth, they figure among the horrors promised by the tyrannical rebellion: the unrelenting rape of the country's women (4.7.111–136). Things among the nobles, however, are hardly better as they vie with each other for control of the country. While the women in the first play opposed England, the main female characters here represent the two sides of the internal factions of English nobles at war with one another. Both Queen Margaret and Eleanor Cobham, the Duchess of Gloucester, possess ambitions far outreaching those of their husbands. So long as Henry and Margaret have no heir, Eleanor and her husband, Gloucester, stand third from the throne. After having a dream that she is seated upon the coronation throne, Eleanor hires a witch and an occultist to foretell the future health of the king (a capital crime, and one for which her husband's enemies have set her up). Eleanor is arrested, forced to do public penance by walking through the streets of London in a sheet and carrying a lighted candle, and then exiled, while her accomplices are burned at the stake for treason. At the instigation of Margaret and Suffolk, Gloucester is also murdered, but Suffolk is banished as a result. After he is beheaded at sea, Suffolk's severed head is returned to England, where Margaret roams the rest of the play carrying it and vowing revenge for the death of her lover, which she will exact in the next play.

The third part of Henry VI features three female characters, but Elizabeth Woodville and Lady Bona now take the place Margaret held as a proposed royal wife at the end of the first part of Henry VI. And, in some respects, Margaret has stepped into the role of Joan of Arc, raising an army because Henry is politically too weak to fight against those who would depose him. In spite of her strong motivations on behalf of her son, whom Henry VI disinherits in his negotiations with the Duke of York, Margaret is presented throughout the play as a vision of cursed and unnatural—even monstrous—masculinity. Following Clifford's murder of young Rutland, the youngest of the sons of York, Clifford and Margaret capture and then torture Rutland's father, the Duke of York. Taunting him with a handkerchief dipped in his son's blood, Margaret stabs York to death. In the ensuing battles, however, Margaret's son Edward Prince of Wales is killed, and the victory swings to the York side. The play ends by foreshadowing another cycle of death and misery in the future reign of Richard III.

The women of Richard III are ultimately and pathetically impotent. The play opens with the Yorks' victory over the Lancastrians and the enthronement of Edward IV. While Richard claims that war has been traded for lovemaking, the peace of victory is short-lived as he begins his bloody path to the throne. In Richard III, the roles of women all center on loss; they are all widows and orphans (although Anne marries Richard, he has killed her husband and father-in-law). In Shakespeare's plays, women without men are powerless and particularly vulnerable, and all have lost at least a father, a husband, or a son. In Richard III, Margaret's character is no longer the wife of a king, mother to an heir, or lover to a nobleman. Nor is she rousing armies and torturing soldiers, as she did in the plays of the earlier tetralogy; she is now witchlike, a ghost haunting the castle as she curses Richard and foretells the doom awaiting those who have taken place of power after her. Lady Anne, bereft of father and husband, is cornered by Richard, who seduces her into believing she has no alternative but to marry him; later, when he determines that marriage to his niece, the princess Elizabeth, will strengthen his hold on the throne, he has it reported that his wife is "sick and like to die" (4.2.58). The Duchess of Gloucester likewise can do little but curse her son's evil. Elizabeth Woodville knows from the moment Edward IV begins to die that her future, and that of her children, is cast in the shadow of her brother-in-law, Richard—who is, as she warns her grown sons, "[a] man that loves not me, nor none of you" (1.3.472). Princess Elizabeth, who marries Henry Tudor, thus uniting the noble houses of England, is the lone survivor of female success. However, even she is merely a ghost character, not even listed among the play's cast of characters (though some productions place her physically onstage).

The Second Tetralogy

In the second tetralogy, the female characters have been fully reduced to hostages, pitiful victims, and their Cassandra-like voices go unheeded as they foretell doom. No longer acting on the events of the play (albeit often unsuccessfully), the women in *Richard II*, the two parts of *Henry IV*, and *Henry V* function as images of sorrow or sources of comedy. Often, they are metonymies of a nation—and therefore property owned by and fought over by men.

In *Richard II*, the Duchess of Gloucester asks her brother-in-law Gaunt to exact revenge on those responsible for the murder of her husband and his brother. Because Gaunt believes the King to be the one who ordered the murder, there can be no revenge: as "God's substitute, / His deputy anointed," the king can be tried and punished only by God. While Gaunt and other male characters in the play feel the conflict between state allegiances and familial ones— between the body politic and the personal bodies of their loved ones—the female characters are the ones who clearly see the right choice to be family, rather than state. The Duchess, however, assigning warlike actions to men alone, feels she has no other recourse than to vainly seek her brother-in-law's assistance. When that fails, she leaves the stage "desolate . . . and [to] die" (1.2.73).

The remaining women are similarly powerless to affect meaningful change in the political situations around them. Although Queen Isabel resists the efforts of Bushy, Green, and Bagot to cheer her, claiming hope is a "cozening . . . flatterer, / A parasite" (2.2.69–70), when she overhears the gardeners discuss the country's sorry state, she curses them for bringing her bad news. Unlike Queen Margaret of the *Henry VI* plays, Queen Isabel does not rally armies, but can only merely "grace the triumph of great Bolingbroke" (3.4.98) and attempt to comfort her husband as he is escorted to the Tower of London. Like the other women in the play, she sees the matter in personal terms, whereas the men see things in terms of politics. When she begs that Bolingbroke's men banish them both and send the king with her into exile, Northumberland replies, "That were some love, but little policy" (5.1.84).

Later, Aumerle's parents are similarly caught between the body politic and the personal body of their son, who appears to have been plotting treason. While York sees his duty as clearly to the king, the Duchess sees hers to her son, even to the point of causing her to disobey her husband's command that she stay out of the matter. The scene before the newly crowned Bolingbroke, however, is nearly slapstick in its humor as the Duchess and Duke hop up and down on bended knee, the one begging mercy and the other begging for his son's execution. That Bolingbroke pardons Aumerle, however, is a matter of policy rather than the kinship and love promoted by the Duchess.

Although they appear onstage, women in the second tetralogy are, according to Howard and Rackin, "strategically peripheralized" (30). In the opening scene of I Henry IV, Westmoreland arrives to report the atrocities performed by Welsh women who had castrated the bodies of thousands of dead English soldiers. We do not see the "beastly shameless transformation" of the English corpses enacted onstage, and the threat to English masculinity posed by women grows increasingly symbolic (1.1.44). Women who actually appear onstage in the two parts of the Henry IV plays inhabit opposite ends of the social spectrum. Lady Percy (or Kate, as her husband, Hotspur, calls her) and Lady Mortimer (who appears in the first part) are members of the elite aristocracy, while Mistress Quickly is hostess of the Boar's Head Tavern, and Doll Tearsheet (who appears in the second part) is a prostitute. Both sets of women seem to pose a threat to English masculinity, drawing men from their warlike pursuits. Hotspur is the most heroic of the characters and therefore most resistant to the charms of domesticity. When his wife, Kate, complains about having been banished from her husband's bed, his response is to call for his horse and leave in the morning for his heroic destiny with death at the hands of Prince Hall on the battlefield.

Although Lady Mortimer cannot speak English, nor can Mortimer speak Welsh, she nonetheless poses an important diversion for her less than heroic husband. Having been captured by Owen Glendower, Mortimer has married the daughter of his Welsh captor, and their inability to converse in a common language highlights the physical aspects of the match over the intellectual aspects. Mortimer is ultimately emasculated by his desire for his wife. As Lady Mortimer sings a Welsh ditty and both Mortimer and Percy loll with their wives, they are distracted from their warlike mission. "Shakespeare's Welsh interlude," according to Howard and Rackin, "replaces the unspeakable horror of castration with the theatrical performance of seduction" (170).

In the second part of Henry IV, the now-widowed Lady Percy chastises her father-in-law, whose failure to send troops to his son Hotspur in the previous play has resulted in Hotspur's death (2.3). But in this play, the monstrously comic whores are given greater stage time, especially in the following scene. In the Boar's Head Tavern, Doll's status as diseased is bantered about, while Mistress Quickly is introduced to Pistol, to whom she will be married in Henry V. Both women are the butt of the play's bawdy humor, and the source of much diversion for the play's character most lacking in heroic masculinity, Falstaff. By the end of II Henry IV, however, Mistress Quickly and Doll Tearsheet have been arrested by

Emma Thompson as Princess Katherine and Kenneth Branagh as Henry V (1989). Photofest.

the Beadle, and Falstaff's claim that he will deliver Doll from prison indicates his inability to stay clear of feminizing charms. Ultimately, however, both aristocratic and common women are powerless against England's rising, masculine power under Henry V.

In *Henry V*, Mistress Quickly appears briefly in the second act of the play, but her death by venereal disease is reported in the final act. The tides have turned drastically, and the women in *Henry V* are primarily objects of exchange in the manly game of war. Our vision of the French Princess Katherine is prefaced by Henry's awful threat to the Governor of Harfleur: if the Governor does not surrender the city to the English, Henry's soldiers will not stop until they have mowed "like grass / Your fresh-fair virgins and your flowering infants" (3.3.13–14). Henry in effect holds hostage the city's women, vowing to let loose "hot and forcing violation" upon Harfleur's "pure maidens" (3.3.11–14). Harfleur's "shrill-shrieking daughters" and howling "mad mothers," claims Henry, will have none to blame but the Governor.

As Jean Howard and Phyllis Rackin have shown, this scene's prefacing of the following scene, in which Princess Katherine learns English with her tutor in preparation for her marriage to King Henry, highlights the ways in which "Katherine, in effect, becomes the potential rape victim we never actually saw at Harfleur. . . . Like the French territory she symbolizes, Katherine is preparing to be occupied, although her occupation will be called marriage" (8). Her language lesson, which provides the theatrical opportunity for Shakespeare's bawdy punning between the French and English words, focuses on her body parts, each of which will come under English control through Henry. As the French King sums it in response to Henry's claim to have been blinded to war by love, "you see them [i.e., the French cities] perspectively, the cities / turned into a maid; for they are all girdled with / maiden walls that war hath never entered" (5.2.321–323).

Although the play's ending on a matrimonial note links it to the romantic comedies, the juxtaposition of martial violence with Henry's martial courtship of Princess Katherine raises potentially unsettling issues in relation to the particular comedies it echoes. Like both Petruchio in *Taming* and, oddly enough, Falstaff in *Merry Wives*, Henry claims he can only woo but as a soldier. Moreover, both Petruchio and Henry demand a public kiss from their Kates, in spite of each woman's reluctance to do so. While Princess Katherine's acquiescence in the final scene (to both the kiss and her betrothal) seems to epitomize early modern notions of female obedience, her insistence that the marriage pleases her "as it shall please de roi mon pere" (5.2.230) also raises doubts about the fidelity of enforced marriage and calls into question the happiness of the ending.

POEMS AND SONNETS

Shakespeare seems to have put his major energy into writing (and perhaps publishing) his nondramatic verse during times of plague, when London officials closed the theaters and other public gathering places in an effort to stave off the spreading epidemics. Both *Venus and Adonis* and *Rape of Lucrece* were written during the 1593 and 1594 closings of the theaters, providing Shakespeare with the opportunity to demonstrate his non-dramatic poetic skills and to seek patronage by writing poetry in the style of the Roman poet Ovid.

As we have seen, *Rape of Lucrece* reworks the origins of the Roman Republic. In *Venus and Adonis*, Shakespeare turns his attention to Ovid's story (X: 510–559 and 705–739). Shakespeare's version participates in a contemporary vogue for playing with the comedic potential in the courtly conventions of hunting and love as depicted in the classical stories of Apollo and Daphne; the comedic potential within the tragic pathos of the reluctant male youth who dies before he is yet ripe for love; and the reversal of gender roles typically found in stories involving the abduction and/or rape of a beautiful young woman by a male god.

Shakespeare's poem similarly highlights the comic effect of the role reversals, in spite of the ultimately tragic ending. Venus stalks the reluctant youth as her prey. Unlike her conventionally frail sisters, Venus is Amazonian in her strength, abducting the unwilling Adonis by tucking him neatly under her arm. Indeed, the poem can be read as a spoof of conventional poetic love and its reversals as well. These reversed roles are presented in their extreme, even to the point of their ultimate limitations. For example, in spite of the fact that Venus is an extremely experienced lover and no wilting virgin, she cannot rape Adonis. Reaching the point at which she cannot continue in her masculine mode of aggression, she is compelled to plead. Yet ironically, this too is a conventional role for Petrarchan male lovers, but where typically the lover blasons the merits of his female love, Venus, unfortunately, must blason herself (lines 140–48).

In 1609 plague once again closed the London theaters, and *Shake-speares Sonnets* was published. The volume includes 154 fourteen-line poems, along with the appended longer poem, *A Lover's Complaint*. If read as a narrative sequence, the sonnets involve the tumultuous affairs of a triangle of lovers. The sequence's characters include the older poet-narrator—a beautiful, unmarried, young man whom the narrator at one point calls "my lovely boy" (126.1) and a married woman who is lover to both men. The first 126 sonnets are typically seen as concerning the young man, with many of them urging him to marry and reproduce, while the remaining twenty-eight are taken to concern the woman, who is mistress to them both.

Interpreting the sequence as primarily autobiographical in nature, some readers have attempted to discern details about Shakespeare's life and feelings from the sonnets. This desire to sort out the true characters and events behind the sonnets may partly arise from the seemingly intimate nature of love poetry in general. However, as Arthur Marotti has shown, the early modern sonnet sequence was not merely a vehicle for expressing the "private tragic-comedy of love"; rather it provided male writers of the period with a means for pursuing "social, political, and economic suits in the language of love" (400, 397). Even if the sonnets can be unlocked for their biographical details, it is also probable that the poems were meant to further Shakespeare's ambitions as a courtier. Moreover, as Katherine Duncan-Jones and others have pointed out, biographical readings of the sequence as the story of Shakespeare's "tragic love" often ignore the obsessive wordplay in the poems and consequently overlook the extraordinary misogyny of many of the sonnets in the latter half of the sequence. Indeed, most of the more "positive" visions of love are in those sonnets that seem to be addressed to the young man. Such readers, according to Katherine Duncan-Jones, "are oblivious to the sheer nastiness of many of the 'dark lady' sonnets, which can . . . be seen to encompass not so much passionate devotion to a distantly cruel mistress as an elaborate mockery of a woman who is no more than a sexual convenience" (51). It is perhaps especially useful to remember that in his plays, Shakespeare created a vast range of character types—murderers and rapists, kings and drunkards, and mothers and whores, to name just a few—who are not likely to reflect his biography in a simple way. It is quite possible that the sonnets are likewise poetic fictions.

Nevertheless, readers throughout the centuries have spent a great deal of time pondering the true identity of the woman figured in the sequence, if such a thing exists. Many women have been suggested as the possible mistress of the sequence: Mary Fitton was a maid of honor to Queen Elizabeth I and gave birth to a child fathered by William Herbert (a patron of Shakespeare's theatrical company and among those proposed as the identity behind the sonnet sequence's "young man"). Her portrait shows her as a fair-skinned, but dark-haired beauty. Another possibility has been named in Luce Morgan (also known as Lucy

Negro), a woman of African ancestry who was for a time favored by Queen Elizabeth, receiving costly fabric for gowns on at least three occasions between 1579 and 1581. She seems to have turned to the business of prostitution, for she was committed briefly in 1599 to Bridewell Prison during one of the periodic crackdowns on London brothel keepers. The courtier poet Aemilia Lanyer has also been suggested. Lanyer was a member of the Italian-Jewish Bassano family, who were musicians in both the Elizabethan and Jacobean courts, and she was the mistress of Henry Cary, Lord Hunsdon, who was one of the patrons of Shakespeare's theatrical company. In addition to these women, others have argued in favor of Queen Elizabeth I, Penelope Rich (the "Stella" of Philip Sidney's sonnet sequence, *Astrophil and Stella*), as well as Shakespeare's landlady, and the wife of one of his Stratford friends. Because of the puns on the name of "Anne" and "Hathaway" in the final couplet of Sonnet 145, Shakespeare's wife, Anne, has also been proposed as the possible mistress of the poems. The narrator languishes in near despair as the mistress begins to breathe "forth the sound that said 'I hate,'" but then she pities him and alters her words: "'I hate' from hate away she threw, / And saved my life, saying 'not you'" (145.13–14). Interestingly, many critics (especially those inclined to see the Shakespeares' marriage—and marriage in general—as unhappy) have disparaged this sonnet as being of poor quality—perhaps a piece of his juvenile work, or perhaps not even his at all.

Although she is never specifically called "dark" nor "lady" in the sequence, the woman of Shakespeare's sonnet sequence has come to be known as the "Dark Lady." As Margreta de Grazia, Linda Boose, Imtiaz Habib, and others have pointed out, however, calling her "dark" obscures and closes off the range of potential meanings for this figure. "Why," asks Linda Boose, "is the sonnet woman's 'black' always referred to its other connotative possibilities and never to its racial one?" (49). The details actually provided in the sonnets concerning her physical appearance suggest she is not the typical blue-eyed, pale-skinned blonde of Petrarchan sonnet convention. His "mistress' eyes are raven black" (127.9), "her breasts are dun [brown]" (130.3), and "black wires grow on her head" (130.4). While critics have traditionally imagined that she is a dark-complexioned white woman—either English or perhaps of Mediterranean descent—it is quite possible that she was of African or Arab descent. Regardless of whether she refers to a real person, Shakespeare certainly imagined women of color and issues of race and miscegenation (cohabitation, marriage, or sexual relations between members of differing races) in a number of his plays. Indeed, as de Grazia has argued, the possible racial issues (as well as the critical resistance to it), rather than the homoerotic attachment to the young man of the first 126 sonnets, are the sequence's true scandal.

Given the physical description Shakespeare attributes to the woman of his sonnets, his choice to flip the poetic conventions of the traditional sonnet beauty seems a natural one (bearing in mind, of course, that the anti-Petrarchan beauty had already become itself a poetic convention even from the time of Petrarch). Playing with the conventional features of the beloved, the narrator claims that times have changed and beauty has been redefined (e.g., Sonnets 127 and 130):

> In the old age black was not counted fair
> Or if it were, it bore not beauty's name;
> But now is black beauty's successive heir,
> And beauty slandered with a bastard shame. (127.1–4)

In the process of extolling the beauty of his beloved, both in spite of and because of her blackness, he also condemns women's use of cosmetics, which makes "foul" faces appear "fair" with "art's false borrowed face" (127.6). Shakespeare also takes the opportunity to challenge the exaggeration and outright falsehood told by other love poets. In Sonnet 130, for example, his "mistress' eyes" may be "nothing like the sun," but her physical appearance is honest and true "As any she belied with false compare" (130.14). In Sonnet 131, he claims "Thy black is fairest in my judgment's place" but then concludes it is her "deeds" that are "black" (131.12–13).

Indeed, many of the sonnets transform the mistress's physically black complexion into a negative metaphor of blackness, presenting it as a visual signifier of her inner moral depravity and demonizing her in the process. In Sonnet 144, he compares his two loves to the good and bad angels of medieval morality plays: "The better angel is a man right fair; / The worser spirit a woman colored ill" (144.3–4). The sonnet goes on to accuse the woman of corrupting the young man's purity, and even implies through the sexual puns on "hell" (vagina as a place of damnation) and "fire . . . out" (to inflame with infection) that she has perhaps given him a venereal disease (144.12–14). In Sonnet 147, the imagery of disease continues in his claim that his "love is as a fever" and his conclusion that he is "Past cure . . . / For I have sworn thee fair, and thought thee bright, / Who art as black as hell, as dark as night" (147.9–14).

Although the narrator admits he is not monogamous, the sonnets depict the woman as both sexually diseased and promiscuous as well. She apparently is already married, having broken her "bed-vow" (152.3), and several sonnets implies that she may also be a prostitute. However, we might bear in mind that even in our own time to call a woman "whore" still works to denigrate someone regardless of her actual sexual activity (cf. Stanton, 80–82). Claims of the woman's promiscuity underlie Sonnet 127, a poem that seems at first glance a charmingly playful conceit in which the narrator envies the keys on the virginal (a harpsichord-like instrument, but one also carrying sexual connotations at the time), which are touched and "tickled" by his beloved. Here the keys are twice called "jacks," a word for not only the virginal's keys but a generic term for men (as in "Jack and Jill," but also in our modern slang term "John" to denote a prostitute's customer), linking the envy back to the mistress's other lovers and even providing a hint at prostitution. Sonnet 129, according to Dympna Callaghan, "takes the tone of bitter and arguably misogynist disgust at having consummated their relationship. . . , [and the] first line of this sonnet . . . is probably the most compact expression of repugnance at ejaculation in the English language" (144–145).

Sonnets 135 and 136 both beg the woman to include the narrator among her many lovers, making more than a dozen sexual puns on the word "will" (a man's name and perhaps specifically Shakespeare's; a wish or desire; and also a male sexual organ—like "willy" or "Johnson"). In Sonnet 137, she is "the bay where all men ride" (137.6), "the wide world's common place" (137.10), and a "false plague" (137.14). Ultimately, as Phyllis Rackin observes about the misogynist disgust to be found in the sonnets, "What matters . . . is not Shakespeare's personal feelings, which remain unknowable, but their contribution to a misogynist legacy that persists even in the twenty-first century, in the epidemic of anorexia as teenage girls starve their developing bodies, and in the agonies of self-loathing that drive mature women to endure the painful mutilations of liposuction and plastic surgery" (*Shakespeare and Women*, 106). Indeed, the legacy of Shakespeare's works to the ongoing cultural representation of women's identity, both positive and negative, is a question that has occupied Shakespearean scholarship from the beginning.

WORKS CITED

Boose, Linda. "'The Getting of a Lawful Race': Racial Discourse in Early Modern England and the Unrepresentable Black Woman." *Women, "Race," and Writing in the Early Modern Period*. Eds. Margo Hendricks and Patricia Parker. New York: Routledge, 1994. 35–54.

Callaghan, Dympha. *Shakespeare without Women*. New York: Routledge, 2000.

———. *Shakespeare's Sonnets*. Oxford: Blackwell, 2007.

Duncan-Jones, Katherine, ed. "Introduction." *Shakespeare's Sonnets*. London: Arden, 2007. 1–106.

Dusinberre, Juliet. "Women and Boys Playing Shakespeare." *A Feminist Companion to Shakespeare*. Ed. Dympna Callaghan. Oxford: Blackwell, 2000. 251–262.

de Grazia, Margreta. "The Scandal of Shakespeare's Sonnets." *Shakespeare Survey* 46 (1994): 35–49.

Habib, Imtiaz. *Shakespeare and Race: Postcolonial Praxis in the Early Modern Period*. Lanham, MD: UP of America, 2000.

Howard, Jean E. and Phyllis Rackin. *Engendering a Nation: A Feminist Account of Shakespeare's English Histories*. New York: Routledge, 1997.

Kahn, Coppelia. *Roman Shakespeare: Warriors, Wounds, and Women*. New York: Routledge, 1997.

Kaplan, M. Lindsay. "Introduction." *The Merchant of Venice: Texts and Contexts*. New York: Macmillan, 2002. 1–22.

Marotti, Arthur. "'Love is Not Love': Elizabethan Sonnet Sequences and the Social Order." 49 ELH (1982): 396–428.

Martindale, Michelle and Charles. *Shakespeare and the Uses of Antiquity: An Introductory Essay*. New York: Routledge, 1994.

Rackin, Phyllis. "Androgyny, Mimesis, and the Marriage of the Boy Heroine on the English Renaissance Stage." *PMLA* 102 (1987): 29–41.

———. *Shakespeare and Women*. Oxford: Oxford UP, 2005.

Said, Edward. *Orientalism*. New York: Vintage, 1979.

Showalter, Elaine. "Representing Ophelia: Women, Madness, and the Responsibilities of Feminist Criticism." Eds. Patricia Parker and Geoffrey Hartman. *Shakespeare and the Question of Theory*. London: Methuen, 1985. 77–94.

Stanton, Kay. "'Made to write "whore" upon?': Male and Female Uses of the Word 'Whore' in Shakespeare's Canon." *A Feminist Companion to Shakespeare*. Ed. Dympna Callaghan. Oxford: Blackwell, 2000. 80–102.

4

SHAKESPEAREAN WOMEN
IN PERFORMANCE

BEFORE 1660

The oft-repeated adage that women did not act on the English stage during Shakespeare's time must be called into question; the facts of the matter are actually more complicated than this simple assertion. As Phyllis Rackin notes, "the all-male companies can be better described as a novelty . . . [for] European professional companies included women, and . . . women regularly performed in a variety of English theatrical venues, ranging from aristocratic masques to local festivals" (Rackin 315). The subject of theatrical performance during this period is therefore perhaps best approached with questions, along with a continual awareness that we are working mostly from a set of educated hypotheses.

To begin, it is important to note that nearly all the parts on stage—not just those of women—were played by "someone else." That is, like the women's parts, the parts of kings, lords, fairies, ghosts, Italians, Romans, Moors, and famous people would also have been played by actors who were not these characters offstage. In an age of sumptuary laws regulating the use of particular styles and fabrics of clothing according to not only sex but also (and more importantly) social standing, a good many early modern people would have been extremely anxious at the idea of actors pretending to be anyone other than who they were "by nature." Conversely, many of Shakespeare's contemporaries were infinitely intrigued by the artistic and social possibilities of cross-dressing across not only gender lines, but class lines as well. There are some general—but not absolute— rules for describing the relation between women and theatrical performance in general and Shakespearean texts in particular during sixteenth and seventeenth centuries.

While Englishwomen did not generally perform on the professional stages of London, they are believed to have performed in local festivals, pageants, and other civic and folk drama during this period. In his study of theatrical practices in Lincolnshire, for example, James Stokes shows that "current research for the REED (Records of Early English Drama) Lincolnshire volume confirms that women were major, indeed co-equal, contributors in a variety of ways to the entertainments associated with traditional culture in Lincolnshire" (25). Women also are known to have participated in the production and performance of guild plays in York and Gloucestershire, as Gweno Williams, Alison Findlay, and Stephanie Hodgson-Wright have shown (45–67). Bella Mirabella similarly argues that women's theatrical activities are revealed in the records involving female mountebanks (from the Italian, "one who climbs on a bench"), or itinerant sellers of medicines and other folk remedies (89–105). These women, and their husbands whom they accompanied, used sleights of hand, storytelling, and other types of performance on makeshift public stages to sell their wares.

Noble and aristocratic women also appeared on private stages, where they danced, sang, and performed in a wide range of courtly entertainments and other theatrics. Queen Anne was an especially avid fan of masques and performed in many of them with her ladies-in-waiting. For Queen Anne, the masques provided a not merely a form of entertainment and occupation, but a crucial means of staging political positions. As Clare McManus has shown, for example, Queen Anne, by making use of the deceased Queen Elizabeth I's clothing as costume in masques, presented herself as the former Queen's successor in courtly authority (109). Perhaps most spectacular was the series written by Ben Jonson, with costumes and stage settings designed by the famous architect Inigo Jones. These included *The Masque of Queens* (1605), *The Masque of Blacknesse* (1605), and *The Masque of Beauty* (1609). In *The Masque of Blackness*, the ladies blackened their faces and wore headpieces of tightly coiled black "hair" to perform as Moors, thus creating an early example of blackface theatrical. Robert White's masque, *Cupid's Banishment*, was commissioned by Lucy Countess of Bedford and "Presented to Her Majesty By the younge Gentlewomen of the Ladies Hall in Deptford at Greenwich The 4th of May 1617" (Cerasano and Wynne-Davies 76). In 1656, perhaps as a reflection of newly developing tastes among aristocrats in European exile, William Davenant's opera starring Mrs. Edward Coleman as Ianthe was performed at Rutland House.

The claim that there were no women on the English professional stage before the Restoration also needs a small bit of qualification. Richard Madox reports going on February 22, 1582, "to the Theatre to see a scurvy play set out all by one virgin, which there proved a freemartin ['fyemarten'—i.e. a hermaphrodite or imperfect female] without voice, so we stayed not the matter" (cited in Wickham et al. 343). Also, Spanish, Italian, and French theater companies regularly included female players among their troupes. While English actresses may not have performed on the public stages of England before the Restoration, continental women did. Henry Herbert, the Master of Revels, records in his account book on November 22, 1629, that he received £2 to allow a French theatrical company with female players to perform at three playhouses over the course of three days (Wickham et al. 584). One of these may have been the performance scathingly described by the anti-theatrical Puritan polemicist William Prynne four years later: "some French women, or monsters rather, on Michaelmas term 1629 attempted to act a French play at the playhouse in Blackfriars—an impudent, shameful, unwomanish, graceless, if not more than whorish attempt"

(Wickham et al. 526–527). However, in 1635 a French company, including actresses, gave repeat performances during Lent (something the local theatrical companies would have been prohibited from doing) at the Phoenix Theater, as well as at the royal venues of Somerset House and Whitehall Palace.

In our own time, films such as *Shakespeare in Love* (1998) and *Stage Beauty* (2004) have depicted women as forbidden by law to perform onstage. Despite popular representations to the contrary, however, women's exclusion from English professional troupes seems to have been a matter of cultural convention rather than of law (though the definitive breaking of the custom happened when Charles II issued a royal proclamation explicitly permitting women to act in the theaters—a move somewhat akin, perhaps, to affirmative action laws and constitutional amendments that make illegal discriminatory practices that have previously been permitted by custom).

Here again, the possible reasons for such custom before the Restoration are many—and often contradictory. None are conclusive. Some factors may have been economic and professional. English professional theater companies consisted of members who came from the artisan and trades class, and memberships in these guilds brought some measure of privilege. There was, however, no actors' guild at the time, and it is possible that company members continued to renew their memberships in the trade guilds as a way of taking on apprentices. Instead of learning to be bricklayers, grocers, drapers, and so forth, Stephen Orgel suggests, they learned to be actors (64–74.). Women's exclusion may be related to the male dominance of the guilds, on which the acting companies modeled themselves. However, women did in fact belong to trade guilds—sometimes in substantial numbers, depending on the particular time and region—complicating our ability to view the role of guilds as a primary factor.

While London theatrical troupes resisted the apprenticeship of women into their companies, other economic factors may have further contributed to women's reluctance to participate. It is important, for example, to remember that acting was not seen as a particularly estimable profession. Anti-theatrical polemicists, such as William Prynne, explicitly linked theaters, bear-baiting arenas, and brothels; in fact, these venues were located in close proximity in the South Bank suburbs of London. Nor was acting a particularly lucrative profession; the real money was to be had by the investors or shareholders of the company. Andrew Gurr's survey of estimates for actors' wages during this time suggests they may have ranged from £10 (equivalent to that of an unskilled day laborer) to £20 per year (*Shakespeare Company*, 100–102). Out of the more than one thousand players acting between 1590 and 1642 for whom we have names, only around twenty ever attained a secure financial status. Moreover, those rare men such as Shakespeare, Edward Alleyn, and Will Kempe who did significantly advance were seeking gentleman status, which would enable them to retire from the disreputable profession of the theater.

Combined with cultural prohibitions against public visibility for "good" women, the stigma against acting was intensified for women and contributed further to the profession's improbability as a female career choice. It is possible that female actors were perceived as less able than male actors to shake off the personal taint of a wicked or immoral character as merely a role, thus giving men greater license to enact a wider range of roles. Moreover, since the more common situation for actors in general was one of subsistence, it is also probable that lower-class women would have been more easily able to find employment in the unsavory professions of prostitution and thievery than they would have as actors.

In addition to economics, another factor involved in the opposition to female actors might derive from a male audience's erotic preference for boys. As Stephen Orgel notes, "the homosexual, and particularly the pederastic, component of Elizabethan erotic imagination is both explicit and for the most part surprisingly unproblematic" in a majority of early modern English plays (70). Orgel, for example, points to Thomas Middleton and Thomas Dekker's *The Roaring Girl* (1608), where no comment is made by other characters in response to Sebastian's remark that he prefers kissing his fiancée, Mary, when she is disguised as a boy, rather than when she is dressed as herself (70–71). This is not to say, however, that opponents to the theater did not object to boys playing female parts. Indeed, many of the objections made by anti-theatrical polemicists centered on the homoerotic potential of this theatrical practice, suggesting that the tastes of audience members may have been a factor.

Other reasons for women's exclusion include conflicts between the public nature of acting and the cultural prescriptions that women not expose themselves to public view and interactions. The question of whether audience members perceived the performance as that of a boy playing a girl also remains open. While certain roles, such as Rosalind in *As You Like It* and Portia in *The Merchant of Venice*, clearly call to mind and play with the illusion being created on stage, other roles might have been presented and perceived in a more naturalistic way. Such players may have passed realistically as females, depending on the talent of the actor combined with such factors as makeup, available lighting, and the distance of the audience members from the stage. Some scholars have argued that the practice of males performing women's parts opened up a wider range of disrespectable female roles precisely because actual women weren't enacting such shocking behaviors.

While we know that males performed all the parts, the question of whether boys or men acted the major female roles remains hotly contested. Some of the debate arises from the question of what age is meant by the term "boy." Working from the assumption that a boy actor was eight to twelve years of age, some scholars have insisted that adult male shareholders must have taken the major female parts (e.g., Force 71–99; Rutter 124–25, 224–25; and Rosenberg). Presuming boys that young would not yet be skilled enough to portray such mature characters as Cleopatra or Lady Macbeth, some scholars have argued that adult male actors in the company would have insisted on keeping the large female parts, rather than assigning them to apprentices. Moreover, modern theatrical cross-dressing also suggests the possibility that older males might have convincingly played the parts of women.

Conversely, some scholars have argued that boys, rather than adults, played the women's parts. These arguments point out that early modern males reached puberty at a much later age than males do now, and that a boy could be anywhere from eight to eighteen years old, with some males retaining into their twenties the ability to speak and sing in a feminine voice. Prepubescent males, especially if they were "painted" with cosmetics and well-trained as actors, could easily pass as women. Working from playlists for non-Shakespearean performances, David Kathman has shown that "of the forty-plus named actors known to have played female roles for adult companies, those whose age we can determine were all between twelve and twenty-two years old, with the normal range being roughly thirteen to twenty-one" (Kathman 244). Stanley Wells concurs, concluding that, given the presence of boy actors in the companies, Shakespeare "would not waste the resources of his company by calling upon adult males to play parts that make use of the talents of his boys" (Wells 15).

Additionally, some scholars, such as Joy Leslie Gibson, have argued that the parts were written precisely with boy actors in mind. While we don't know for certain the assignment of most of the parts in Shakespeare's company, Thomas Whitfield Baldwin has cross-referenced surviving information to hypothesize the lists (Baldwin 229). As Stephen Booth has pointed out, we know "from such things as the tracks of a tall blond boy actor and a short dark one in the early comedies that Shakespeare wrote with his casts in mind" (Booth "Speculations" 105). The most familiar instance here is, of course, Hermia, who is described as small and dark, and Helena, who is described as tall and blond, in A *Midsummer Night's Dream*.

Some interesting speculation has also been made concerning possible doubling of roles. Stephen Booth makes note of the idea, initiated in 1904 with Wilfred Perrett, that the roles of both Lear's daughter and the fool were played by the same (boy) actor, giving an added dimension to the beginning of Lear's last speech: "My poor fool is hang'd" (Booth "Speculations" 104; 126–27). Turning his attention to A *Winter's Tale*, Booth proposes an intriguing alternative to the typical doubling between Mamillius, the son who dies of grief over his father's treatment of his mother, and Florizel, the Prince of Bohemia. Booth suggests that instead one actor might have taken the roles of both Mamillius and Perdita, the daughter who is fantastically restored after having been abandoned as an infant on the coast of Bohemia (Booth "Speculations" 117–120). The theme of loss and recovery evoked in the play's final scene would be deepened by such a doubling between the lost son and the lost-but-found daughter. Booth also briefly outlines a rationale for doubling the roles of Maria and Sebastian in *Twelfth Night*, suggesting that as the reason behind Maria's absence on stage at the end of the play—because the actor playing her was already on stage as Sebastian (Booth "Speculations" 120).

While actual Englishwomen may have appeared infrequently on public stages, they did appear as members of the audience, and part of the experience of going to the theater involved being seen as much as seeing a play. As previously noted, aristocratic women performed in private productions, and A *Midsummer Night's Dream* and *Hamlet* mirror the reality of elite women's attendance at private performances by professional troupes. However, women attended the public playhouses as well. Moll Frith (who came to be known as Moll Cutpurse) is a notorious example of a woman who not only frequented plays (dressed as a man) but also sat upon the stage at the Fortune and at the Swan (as was customary for some men who wished not only to see the play but be seen at the play). While at the Fortune, dressed as a man, Frith played upon a lute and sang while on the stage. Thomas Middleton and Thomas Dekker immortalized Moll Frith in their play *The Roaring Girl* (ca. 1607–1610). Middleton and Dekker depict Moll as in fact quite virtuous in spite of the title's deeming her a "roaring girl," the feminized version of a "roaring boy" which was the term given to young men who frequented the theater district, carousing and brawling and committing petty crimes.

Women also attended the theater without masculine disguise. As part of the framing of his satire of bourgeois London theatrical tastes, Francis Beaumont's hilarious *The Knight of the Burning Pestle* likewise depicts a local citizen and his wife, Nell, choosing seats upon the stage, where they watch—and rewrite—the professional troupe's theatrical production. Drawing evidence from plays by Shakespeare as well as his contemporary playwrights, Richard Levin has also argued for awareness in the plays of the presence of women in the audiences of public theaters (164–171). Jean Howard also documents the presence of bourgeois women as paying customers at public theaters, and in particular raises the question of their impact on both theatrical practices on stage and the performance of gender and class in society (73–92). Andrew Gurr likewise combines documentary evidence from not only the plays, but also extra-theatrical documents, such as letters, legal records, and polemics against the theater, to provide a picture of what playgoing was like in Shakespeare's London (see especially 64–74). Gurr attributes "[t]he high proportion of women at the playhouses . . . to the popularity of playgoing for the illiterate," noting that women were across all classes the least likely to be able to read (Playgoing 65).

While sixteenth- and seventeenth-century English professional troupes may have barred women from their companies as players, women were involved in other aspects of the business of theater. Women were employed as ticket takers—known as "gatherers"—while aristocratic and royal women on occasion issued patents to playing companies (Cerasano and Wynn-Davies 158–159). Records also indicate that women participated as shareholders, in addition to being gatherers and other laborers in the theater, and as members of the audience. S. P. Cerasano attributes the presence of women as shareholders to the development of theater specifically as a business, like any other business. As the earlier generations of shareholders retired and died out, according to Cerasano, "Increasingly their shares, treated like property, were bequeathed to others," including women (88). Margaret Brayne inherited her husband's share in the Theater—a share large enough to warrant prolonged litigation as the Burbages (the other major shareholders) fought to retain control of it. Similarly, Susan Baskerville inherited her husband's share in Queen Anne's Company in 1612, and in 1634 her son bequeathed his share in the Red Bull Company to her. Baskerville's shares were valued at £80, an amount apparently substantial enough to give her significant control over the theater company—and, some scholars have contended, sufficient to ultimately cause bankruptcy when she attempted to make claim on her share (Cerasano and Wynn-Davies 159).

Not all shares acquired by women were inherited, though. When Edward Alleyn opened the purchase of shares to nonplayers after the first Fortune Theatre burned down in 1621, Francis Juby purchased a share in the second Fortune in 1622. A year later, Marie Bryan and Margaret Gray—like Juby, both widows to theater men—purchased a share and a half-share, respectively. According the indenture between Alleyn and Bryan, Bryan's share was a substantial one, constituting "one twelfth of the second Fortune Playhouse" (Cerasano and Wynn-Davies 174–175).

THE RESTORATION THROUGH THE END
OF THE EIGHTEENTH CENTURY

In 1642, when the English Revolution culminated with the beheading of Charles I and the installation of a Puritan-controlled government that would later be termed the Interregnum (meaning "between the reigns"), actors of both sexes were forbidden to play when the public theaters were closed. But when Charles II and his court returned from exile in France in 1660, they brought with them theatrical tastes heavily influenced by their experiences on the continent— including an appetite for female actors, many of whom were mistresses to the king and his courtiers. In the early years of the Restoration (so termed because the monarchy had been restored), however, male actors continued to take up the female parts as they had in the past, and they were well-received by audiences. For example, Samuel Pepys records in his diary for 1661 that he saw Edward Kynaston play the title role of Epicoene in Ben Jonson's *The Silent Woman*, describing the young actor as "the prettiest woman in the whole house." In 1662, however, Charles officially lifted the traditional ban on female players by issuing a royal proclamation, and eventually female actors became more typically cast than males in female roles. As Michael Dobson observes, with the advent of female actresses on the English stage, "male cross-dressing would hereafter be reserved for broadly comic travesty parts . . . (James Nokes, for example, in the mid-1660s a player of heroines, would be better known thereafter for his performances of Juliet's Nurse)" (Dobson, "Improving" 48).

Between the Restoration and the early eighteenth century, when his popularity made him a national figure of England's greatness, Shakespeare's plays were by and large considered old-fashioned and were rarely performed. With few exceptions, early productions of his plays were not very popular, despite being heavily revised to suit "modern" tastes. The stars of the London stages during the Restoration were more likely to be drawn to the heroines composed by contemporary playwrights than to Shakespearean roles. Although Nel Gwyn's personal account books indicate that she attended several Shakespearean plays, including *The Tempest*, *Macbeth*, *Lear*, and *Hamlet*, Arthur Dasent's chronological list of plays acted at the Drury Lane Theatre in which Gwyn appeared reveals that the King's mistress and the premier actress of the newly reopened theaters never took up a Shakespearean role (301). That may be related to the plays' lack of popularity. John Harold Wilson's list of early English stage actresses, which includes brief biographies as well as the roles they were known to play (including the relatively few Shakespearean roles), similarly indicates that Shakespearean roles were not particularly popular during the early days of the theater's reopening.

When female actors first began playing on English stages, their spectacular presence was shocking and garnered much attention. Consequently, playwrights began to seek ways to further exploit the novelty of women's bodies on stage. "Breeches parts," by playing on the disclosure of the actress's female body beneath the male costume, further intensified the excitement surrounding women's presence on stage. Some have argued that Rosalind (*As You Like It*), Viola (*Twelfth Night*), Imogen (*Cymbeline*), and Portia (*Merchant of Venice*) are not technically breeches parts, because the characters are women disguised as men for safety rather than provocation. Presumably, their cross-dressing is considered less sexy than that of a character like Moll Frith (*The Roaring Girl*).

More popular during this time was the practice of female actors turning conventionally male parts into breeches roles, a practice that has continued on occasion up into the present time (e.g., Sarah Bernhardt's Hamlet and Vanessa Redgrave's Prospero). Such parts were especially popular between the Restoration and the end of the seventeenth century, with nearly one-fourth of all plays during those years containing one or more breeches parts. Breeches parts continued to ebb and flow in popularity throughout the following centuries, though such parts seem to have become less fashionable with the lessening of gendered distinctions in clothing.

The extent to which breeches parts subvert gender roles has been much debated, and a number of critics and scholars have argued that breeches parts disrupt gender hierarchies by allowing women to act in masculine ways, thus calling into question the naturalness of gendered behaviors (e.g., Pearson 104, Woodbridge 154, Dusinberre 233). However, Elizabeth Howe points out that during the Restoration in particular, breeches parts typically were "little more than yet another means of displaying the actress as a sexual object" (Howe 59). Breeches roles were potentially titillating for male viewers, because the costumes revealed much more of the female figure than conventional women's clothing. Any feminist potential in breeches parts was ultimately contained by the revelation of the character's sex (often by revealing her breasts) and the character's resumption of her "properly" feminine gender.

In her 1928 lecture, Virginia Woolf imagined the story of Shakespeare's fictional but "wonderfully gifted sister, called Judith" (49). Woolf's Judith desires the theater as much as her brother, but having fled Stratford to haunt the London stage doors, she is laughed at by the theater men who believe no women could be actresses (49–50). Woolf paints the scene:

> [The theater manager] hinted—you can imagine what. She could get no training in her craft. Could she even seek her dinner in a tavern or roam the streets at midnight? . . . At last—for she was very young, oddly like Shakespeare the poet in

her face, with the same grey eyes and rounded brows—at last Nick Greene the actor-manager took pity on her; she found herself with child by that gentleman and so—who shall measure the heat and violence of the poet's heart when caught and tangled in a woman's body?—killed herself one winter's night and lies buried at some cross-roads where the omnibuses now stop outside the Elephant and Castle. (Woolf 50)

That sexual threats, as well as threats to women's sexual reputation, were part and parcel of women's efforts to take the stage is confirmed in Thomas Jordan's inclusion of a prologue and an epilogue to be spoken by one of the first female actors to play Desdemona in 1660, defending herself from being perceived as a whore. The actor urges the male audience members not to harass her as if she were a whore: "pray, do not run / To give her visits when the play is done" (Jordan 24). "'Tis possible," she reminds them, "a vertuous woman may / Abhor all sorts of looseness, and yet play, / Play on the stage, where all eyes are upon her" (Jordan 24).

Not surprisingly, the sexual reputation of actresses, as they continued to appear more frequently onstage, was still a contested matter—one complicated by the common overlap between actresses and mistresses to the king and his courtiers. Consequently, one response was for the business of theater to keep a strong patriarchal control (or at least the illusion of it) over the women. While some actresses were single, the majority of them were married either to theater managers or other actors. Furthermore, from this time until the mid-nineteenth century, actresses were typically referred to by their married names without including their given names (e.g., Mrs. Pritchard, Mrs. Siddons, and so on).

Interestingly, we do not know the name of the English actress thought to be the first to perform professionally in a Shakespeare play. On December 8, 1660 (two years before Charles's official proclamation allowing women to play), an unnamed woman performed the role of Desdemona in *Othello* at the Cockpit Theater. The most remarkable feature of the play seems to have been the novelty of a female actor in the role of Desdemona, rather than the fact that Shakespeare's work was being performed once again. Although the actor's name has been lost to the certainties of history, the most likely possibilities for the first female player of Desdemona are Margaret Hughes and Anne Marshall, both players in Thomas Killigrew's King's Company (Thomson 206–207). Samuel Pepys records in his diary that he saw Margaret Hughes perform the role nine years later on February 6, 1669.

The most popular plays—and roles—were to be found in more recently written plays. The Shakespearean plays taken up in Restoration repertories that did gain popularity usually were heavily revised to suit contemporary tastes, which often did not find tragic deaths appealing. John Dryden, for example, entirely revamped *Romeo and Juliet* so that it ends happily. Similarly, in Nahum Tate's revision of *King Lear*, not only do Lear and Cordelia survive, but Cordelia is married, happily-ever-after style, to Edgar. Tate's version remained the preferred version for nearly 150 years. When Charles Macready's 1835 production restored

Shakespeare's original text, along with the death of Cordelia (played by Helen Faucit), some viewers found the tragic ending to be utterly shocking.

Two early Restoration adaptations of Shakespeare by John Dryden and William Davenant, however, did prove popular with seventeenth-century audiences. Catering to Restoration tastes, the plays featured not only spectacular costuming and special effects, but expanded roles for women as well, in order to showcase the talents of the troupe's actresses. In addition to fleshing out the role of Miranda, Dryden and Davenant's substantially transformed *The Tempest; or, The Enchanted Island* (1667) featured several additional female roles, including sisters for both Miranda (Dorinda, who like her sister, "never saw man") and Caliban (named Sycorax). Davenant's adaptation of *Macbeth* (1664) likewise developed the female roles—most notably that of Lady Macduff, who becomes a major character within the play. The plays had a fairly successful series of runs, and in 1673 Mary Saunderson (later Betterton) played Lady Macbeth, while Jane Long played the role of the virtuous Lady Macduff. Other popular English actresses from these early days include Elizabeth Barry and Anne Bracegirdle.

The eighteenth century witnessed a renewed and growing interest in Shakespeare as an icon of native literary genius, creating more opportunities for actresses to take on the roles formerly played by boys or men. An important impetus for this eighteenth-century Shakespearean revival came from the Shakespeare Ladies Club, an informal association of "ladies of quality," which formed some time near the end of 1736. The leader of this group of posthumous Shakespeare patrons was Susanna Ashley-Cooper, Countess of Shaftesbury. During the theatrical seasons from 1735 through 1738, the group not only succeeded in persuading theater companies to include an increasingly greater percentage of Shakespearean plays among their repertoires, but they were also an instrumental force behind the swell of public sentiment that resulted in the installation of a life-size monument to the playwright in Poet's Corner in Westminster Abbey (Avery 153–158, Dobson 146–164).

The increased production of printed materials, as well as letters and diaries, throughout the eighteenth century provides us with much more information about theatrical activities and persons during this period than during previous times. In addition to references to plays and players found in private correspondences and diaries, we also have numerous references in newspapers and broadsides, as well as in extended theatrical reviews. The increase in mass-produced engravings depicting various performers in their most famous roles and scenes provide us with visual as well as verbal information.

David Garrick's love for Shakespeare and his lengthy management of the Drury Lane Theatre between 1747 and 1776 further paved the way for a number of actresses to take on the roles of Shakespearean heroines. Hannah (Vaughan) Pritchard performed with Garrick for nearly twenty years, being especially renowned for her portrayal of Lady Macbeth, a role she performed up until the end of her life in 1768. Though most famous for her portrayal of Lady Macbeth, Pritchard excelled at comedic roles as well. She paired popularly with several other actresses of the period, most notably Kitty Clive. Pritchard played Rosalind in *As You Like It*, with Kitty Clive in the role of Celia, and she played Viola in *Twelfth Night*, with Clive in the role of Olivia. Clive and Pritchard also paired in *The Merchant of Venice*, with Clive playing Portia and Pritchard Nerissa. Peg (Margaret) Woffington, another popular actress in Garrick's entourage, began her theatrical career in the role of Ophelia and went on to portray a number of Shakespeare's heroines, including Cordelia and Rosalind.

Just before Garrick's retirement, his company offered an early chance at stardom to Sarah (Kemble) Siddons when she played Portia in *The Merchant of Venice* during the Drury Lane's 1775–1776 season. Siddons came from a theatrical family running several generations back (and forward—her niece, Fanny Kemble, would later become a famous actor too), and she had performed the role of Ariel at the age of eleven in the revised version of *The Tempest* produced on tour by her parents. Unfortunately, her debut as a young adult on the London stage was deemed a failure by both critics and audiences. However, Siddons spent the next four years honing her craft while touring again in the provinces. Her return to the London stage in 1782 was an indisputable success, and she came to be known as the greatest tragedian of her time. As Judith Pascoe suggests, "the cult of Sarah Siddons was in large part the result of a publicity campaign" (Pascoe 28).

Siddons became especially known for her stylistic innovations, most notably in her performance of Lady Macbeth. Hannah Pritchard's rendition of the role, which she had performed to great acclaim for twenty years with David Garrick, had been canonized as the standard by which all subsequent performances were judged. A consummate thespian, Siddons became determined to make the role her own. In her "Remarks on the Character of Lady Macbeth," Siddons wrote of the queen that "in this astonishing creature one sees a woman in whose bosom the passion of ambition has almost obliterated all the characteristics of human nature" (Siddons 123). Her greatest transformation of the role was her decision to put down the candle during Lady Macbeth's sleepwalking scene in order to simulate the hand-washing to which the horrified doctor calls attention: "Look how she rubs her hands" (5.1.23). Although audiences found the change initially to be shockingly dramatic, she played the role—and her particular staging of the scene—to packed audiences for nearly three decades.

Not surprisingly, Siddons came to be seen by contemporary reviewers and audiences as the embodiment of tragic drama. Altogether, she played eighteen Shakespearean roles, most of them tragic (though she did play Rosalind, Olivia, Isabella, Imogen, and Hermione). With the exception of her performances as Lady Macbeth, however, she was most famous for her roles in newly written plays—again, mostly tragedies. William Hazlitt called her "Tragedy personified," and this opinion was given visual confirmation by several leading artists of the time. In 1784 Joshua Reynolds painted her as the "Tragic Muse," and in 1793 William Beechey similarly depicted "Mrs. Siddons with the Emblems of Tragedy."

In addition to her skill as a tragedienne, Siddons was also stunningly successful as a businesswoman, building an impressive fortune from her theatrical activities. Her business acumen, however, was seen by some as unsuitable to women, and she was sometimes severely criticized. In 1784 James Gillray satirized her in a cartoon illustration that, presaging Beechey's more flattering portrait of her, depicted her as Melpomene (Muse of Tragedy) greedily reaching for bags of gold suspended above her outstretched arm.

Siddons's career continued until her official retirement from the stage in 1812; however, she continued to give private readings until her death in 1831.

THE NINETEENTH CENTURY

It was difficult for actresses following Siddons to avoid comparison. While Helen Faucit (later Martin) had some success during the early and mid-nineteenth century—especially in her performances with William Charles Macready—her performances were often compared with lukewarm enthusiasm to those of her predecessor. When Faucit married Theodore Martin in 1851, she retired from the stage. However, she continued to perform in private and charitable productions. Significantly, she also continued to discuss her experiences in acting. A series of her letters and essays written after her retirement from the stage appeared in Blackwood's periodical from 1881 to 1891.

Faucit's remembrances of her Shakespearean roles provide interesting information in the development of how actors approached their parts. The trend toward more naturalistic presentation that gained appeal in the eighteenth century continued to develop even more fully alongside nineteenth-century innovations in thinking and technology. For Faucit, acting was a matter of "personating" or "impersonating" the characters as if they were living (or once-living) human beings. Whereas Sarah Siddons adapted her gestures, voice, and other features of her acting based on what she deemed believable coming from the character, Helen Faucit imagined entire biographies for her characters—childhoods lived before the play begins and (for those who do not die) their days and final moments after the play's ending. Ophelia was, Helen Faucit claims, "one of the pet dreams of my girlhood—partly, perhaps, from the mystery of her madness" (5), and she was eventually able to play Ophelia opposite Macready, in whose company Faucit's career began. Reminiscing of preparations, she writes that "I pictured Ophelia to myself as the motherless child of an elderly Polonius" (9). Defending Ophelia's character from views that read her as weak, Faucit's vision of the flower scene concludes that Ophelia, brought beyond the brink of sanity by the play's many traumas, resorts back to her innocent, pastoral childhood memories (9). She also imagines a childhood for Portia (31–32) and, because "I could never leave my characters when the curtain fell and the audience departed" (48), she also imagines a "fanciful" life beyond the play in which Portia comforts the dying Shylock (48–52). Likewise for Desdemona, Faucit imagines the childhood of her character, attributing personality and motivations for this similarly motherless heroine. She envisions Desdemona as a "thoughtful woman; one whose heart and mind went with her love" (67). Faucit also writes of Juliet, the first Shakespearean heroine she performed: "Of all characters, hers is the one which I have found the greatest difficulty, but also the greatest delight, in acting" (105–106). Perhaps this is because of Juliet's youth and brevity of life, which makes it difficult to imagine beyond the boundaries of the play.

Ellen Terry's stunningly long stage career ran from 1856, when she played Mamillius at the age of nine in Charles Keans's production of *A Winter's Tale* (this was quickly followed by a long stint in the role of Puck in *A Midsummer Night's Dream*), to her last major role as the Nurse in *Romeo and Juliet* in 1919. Terry's circle of friends included imminent artists and thinkers of the day— among them Lewis Carroll; the artist George Frederick Watts (whom she married briefly at the age of sixteen, when he was nearly three decades her senior); the architect-designer Edward William Godwin (by whom she had a son, Edward Gordon Craig, and a daughter, Edith Craig); and Bram Stoker; as well as George Bernard Shaw, whose drama she admired (and he her talent and intellect), and with whom she engaged in a long-standing correspondence. In the early twentieth century, in addition to acting onstage and in film, Terry toured Great Britain, the United States, and Australia as a Shakespearean lecturer-recitalist. When she died in 1928, some 5,000 people lined the sixty miles between Smallhythe, Kent, and London as her ashes were brought to St. Paul's Church in Covent Garden.

From 1874 onward, Terry was the leading Shakespearean actress in London, playing eighteen characters, most of them opposite Henry Irving. The pair also wowed audiences in the United States and on the continent. Opposite Irving, Terry played most of the great Shakespearean parts for women—Ophelia (1878), Portia (1879), Desdemona (1881), Juliet and Beatrice (1882), Lady Macbeth (1888), Cordelia (1892), Queen Katharine (1892), Imogen (1896), and Volumnia (1901). However, she never played Rosalind—because there was no suitable part for Irving in the play. By the time Irving had retired from the stage, it was too late for Terry to play the role.

Terry was in many respects the quintessential Victorian lady: self-sacrificing, sometimes to the point of masochism. Consistently, she yielded to the pre-eminence of her costar Irving. In 1878 Terry wanted her Ophelia to wear a black dress during the madness scene, but she capitulated to Irving's resolute opposition to the idea: "My God! Madam, there must be only one black figure in this play, and that's Hamlet!" Terry comments, "I did feel a fool. What a blundering donkey I had been not to see it before!" (Terry, *Story* 100). In her memoirs, she records sacrificing her vision of Portia in *The Merchant of Venice* in favor of Henry Irving's. "I found that Henry Irving's Shylock necessitated an entire revision of my conception of Portia, especially in the trial scene. . . . I had considered, and still am of the same mind, that Portia in the trial scene ought to be very *quiet*. I saw an extraordinary effect in this quietness. But as Henry's Shylock was quiet, I had to give it up. His heroic saint was splendid, but it wasn't good for Portia" (Terry, *Memoirs* 128). Terry's Portia was a figure of stern justice rather than comic joy.

Such feminine self-sacrifice for the sake of a male-centered sense of art was not unique to Terry during this period. Elizabeth Siddal (Dante Gabriel Rossetti's wife) seriously endangered her health, coming near to contracting pneumonia, as a result of sitting for the now-famous portrait of Ophelia drowning, which

John Everett Millais produced during the years 1851–1852. When the heating lamps for the tub of water went out, Siddal endured hours of posing in the chilled waters rather than interrupt Millais's artistic genius by asking him to have the candles replaced.

While pathetic heroines like Ophelia were Terry's forte, she also gave a turn at some characters that more typically resonate with spunk and vitality with modern audiences. For these characters, however, Terry followed Irving's visions and toned them down to suit Victorian tastes. Until Terry played her, for example, Beatrice in *Much Ado About Nothing* had not been a very popular character with audiences, who saw her as too shrewish. Taking great pains in the crafting of her—taming of her—Terry made Beatrice into an immensely likable character. As Nina Auerbach comments, "Independent and assaultive, Beatrice disturbed Victorian middle-class audiences; they liked heroines who suffered, not termagants who attacked men. . . . Irving dragged Ellen Terry's Beatrice down to the place where audiences could love her without fear" (Auerbach 226).

Perhaps Terry's greatest triumph, because it was her greatest stretch and dramatic manipulation, was Lady Macbeth. For decades, performances of the Scottish queen had followed the vision of Sarah Siddons, playing Lady Macbeth as the "fiend-like queen" and a powerfully sinful virago driven by ambition. During the nineteenth century, a "virago" was more commonly defined as a bold, impudent (or wicked) woman, and rarely taken to mean a manlike, vigorous, and heroic woman. As Nina Auerbach observes in relation to the text of Shakespeare's play, "in the 1880s, a woman who was 'man-like' or 'unsexed' was not heroic but horrible" (252). On both counts, such a figure would run counter to Ellen Terry's sensibilities. Playing to contemporary sensibilities—and to her own—Ellen Terry realized her vision of Lady Macbeth as a creature strained with feminine fragility.

According to Auerbach, Terry's performance of the character provides a radical comment on contemporary sexual roles taken to their extreme. Terry's Lady Macbeth is "not the unnatural woman, but the pliable one who makes herself into all the sweet things she is told to be" (Auerbach 254). She is the quintessential Victorian lady taken to her horrifying extreme. Auerbach compares Terry's portrayal of the Scottish queen with Bram Stoker's depiction of women in *Dracula*: "Lucy, a sleepwalker like Lady Macbeth and a dear giggling English rose, might be Bram Stoker's tribute to his adored Ellen Terry's most audacious performance" (254). Whereas Sarah Siddons imagined Lady Macbeth as a monstrous figure whose humanity has been blasted by "the passion of ambition," Ellen Terry imagined the Lady Macbeth as weak with womanliness, a figure who reluctantly takes on an unaccustomed cruelty in the service of her husband's flawed ambition. As Terry saw her, Lady Macbeth's tragic flaw is her determined acquiescence in the face of what she ultimately knows is Macbeth's inability to succeed. Above all, she is a wife who loves her husband too much.

Given the spectacular nature of Terry's achievement, it is not surprising that her portrayal of Lady Macbeth generated great debate about Shakespeare's character. It also inspired one of the great artists of her time, John Singer Sargent, to persuade her to sit for the striking portrait of her in that role. Concerning her costume and the Sargent portrait, Terry wrote to her daughter:

> I wish you could see my dresses. They are superb, especially the first one: green beetles on it, and such a cloak! The photographs give no idea of it at all, for it is in the colour that it is so splendid. The dark red hair is fine. The whole thing is Rossetti— rich stained-glass effects. I play some of it well, but, of course I don't do what I want to do yet. Meanwhile I shall not budge an inch in the reading of it, for that I know is right. Oh, it's fun, but it's precious hard work, for I by no means make her a "gentle, lovable woman" as some of 'em say. That's all pickles. She was nothing of the sort, although she was *not* a fiend, and *did* love her husband. I have to what is vulgarly called "sweat it," each night. (Terry *Story of My Life* 197)

Although Ellen Terry never managed to get her fill of breeches parts because Henry Irving saw them as detracting from his importance on stage—and Terry most notably regretted that she never had a chance to perform the role of Rosalind in *As You Like It*—other nineteenth-century actresses in Great Britain and in the United States made their careers by specializing in cross-dressed roles. Such now nearly forgotten actresses include Lucy Vestris, Ada Isaacs Mencken, Elizabeth Dickinson, Ada Rehan, and Miss Marriott. Because the character of Romeo tended to be seen as young—and potentially too feminine—to be of substance for major male actors, a number of actresses had presented the Italian lover. In 1829, for example, Ellen Tree played Romeo opposite the Juliet of Fanny Kemble, who claimed that of all the actors she had worked with, Tree was most suited to the role.

American actor Charlotte Cushman gained widespread recognition for her performances of both powerful female characters and more than thirty male parts between the 1830s and 1870s. One motive for her taking the stage was to help care financially for her fatherless family (and acting was a more lucrative, if potentially less respectable, profession for women than journalism). When Cushman died of breast cancer two years following her 1874 farewell performance as Lady Macbeth in New York, the theater community mourned. Sidney Lanyer wrote an elegy to her, and the New York *Daily Graphic* published a pictorial cover tribute to her. In addition to her achievements in acting, Cushman was also an activist for women's rights, managing a theater company (typically a male preserve), demanding comparable pay for her work, and supporting the work of a number of female artists.

Today, Cushman would most probably identify as a lesbian or queer, but these terms were not yet used to describe female homoerotic relationships, although scholars have shown that nineteenth-century British and American culture permitted middle-class women to engage in intensely romantic same-sex relationships, partly because they were seen to be incapable of erotic desire (e.g., Smith-Rosenberg, Faderman). Throughout her life, Cushman entered into several romantic relationships with women, on occasion setting up domestic households ("marriages") with a few of them, a practice that was acceptable in nineteenth-century American and British culture.

Cushman's first long-term relationship was with the journalist and actress Matilda Hays, with whom Cushman spent a decade. (Elizabeth Barrett Browning described their relationship as a "female marriage.") In 1852 Cushman and Hays moved with several other women to Rome, where they established a woman-centered American expatriate community.

In 1857, shortly after a tumultuous break-up with Hays, Cushman began living with sculptor Emma Stebbins, with whom she lived until her death in 1876. Perhaps like many men of her time, Cushman also roamed outsider her "marriage," for during this time Cushman also entered into a romance with a young actress named Emma Crow (who later married Cushman's adopted nephew Edwin).

Considering that she was hailed as the greatest actress of her time, Cushman's physical appearance is especially interesting, as it ran quite contrary to Victorian standards of beauty: she was tall, buxom, and square-jawed—not at all the typical stage beauty. Even when Cushman played female roles, her strength lay in personifying viragos rather than weak victims or conventionally feminine heroines. Her first major success on the stage came in 1836, when she played Lady Macbeth as ruthless and without pity in New Orleans. Cushman was especially known for her powerful renditions of the mysterious gypsy queen Meg Merrilie in Walter Scott's *Guy Mannering*.

Her performances of male characters are particularly intriguing. Contrary to the experiences of most actresses in breeches parts, Cushman's affinity for the roles she played derived more from her natural aptitude for personifying realistically the male characters, rather than from a desire to titillate heterosexual male viewers with a lovely pair of legs. By highlighting both Charlotte Cushman's own attraction to women and her large number of female fans, Faye Dudden's discussion of Cushman's performance of male parts complicates our understanding of both breeches parts and Cushman as an actor. Dudden argues that Cushman's wildly successful portrayal of Romeo was paradoxically made possible by a culture that was accepting of female romantic friendships (primarily because it associated middle-class women with sexual purity)—enabling Cushman's Romeo, for example, to be "more realistically erotic than a man in the same part" (Dudden 99).

Hamlet, Cardinal Wolsey in *Henry VIII*, and Romeo in *Romeo and Juliet* stand among Cushman's highest theatrical achievements. Wildly popular with audiences—especially female audiences—were her performances as Romeo, many of them played opposite her sister Susan Cushman. Romeo was seen as a character whose lovelorn youthfulness was deemed feminine enough to be played by a woman (or, conversely, too feminine to appeal to male actors). Cushman's masculine impersonation here is particularly complex and intriguing. On the one hand, she frequently claimed a kind of paternal motive in taking on the part. In acting the role with her sister Susan, whose husband had abandoned her and her son, Charlotte claimed to be giving Susan "the support I know she required, and would never get from any gentleman that could be got to act with her" (Merrill 112). As Merrill notes, her assertion here resembles her "earlier narrative that she went on the stage merely to support her family . . . [allowing] Charlotte to represent herself as the protector of her sister's respectability, rather than as a possible transgressor of gender norms in her own right" (Merrill 112). In addition, many reviewers praised the sisters' performance as being "without vice" precisely because of

Charlotte Cushman as Romeo and Susan Cushman as Juliet. Lithograph, 1846. Houghton Library, Harvard Theatre Collection.

nineteenth-century notions of female sexuality (or lack of it). The precariousness of female respectability—especially when lacking male familial endorsement—is demonstrated by the fact that later, in order to retain the patronage of their newly acquired circle of friends in Edinburgh, the Cushmans were compelled to present marriage certificates and other documentary evidence proving that Susan Cushman had been married when her son was born (Merrill 113–114).

In spite of these domestic and cultural assurances, however, Cushman also performed the role of Romeo with a number of other leading ladies. Cushman seems to have enjoyed playing this part, and she used the role on occasion to instigate offstage flirtations and petty jealousies with her mistress, Emma Crow. Writing to Crow about her performance with a particular Juliet, Cushman wrote: "I wonder if you would be very jealous if you were to see the performance; . . . she acts Juliet charmingly and would delight you in the abstract idea of Juliet, but as your darling's Juliet, I don't know" (Merrill 129–130).

Cushman's fans included vast numbers of women, many of whom were infatuated by her impersonation of an ideal masculinity that they yearned for in real life, while others were drawn to the woman beneath the role. The subjectivity of desire is especially intriguing in relation to the 1846 lithograph that captures Cushman's Romeo climbing through the open window to Juliet's bedroom. Romeo straddles the window, embracing Juliet, whose hand winds tenderly around her lover's head. But what are readers to make of the parted thighs straddling the open window, especially given their knowledge of the actor's sex (provided by the caption)? The stance may be read as manly. However, it might also hearken to more traditional uses of the breeches part, providing an enticing gesture toward the feminine mysteries hidden by the breeches beneath the skirt.

TWENTIETH-CENTURY STAGE AND FILM

Penny Gay notes that the twentieth century marks "the disappearance of assumptions about the necessity of typecasting"—as witnessed, for example, in the range of Shakespearean roles taken up by Peggy Ashcroft, who is often considered to be the first modern Shakespearean actress (Gay, "Shakespearean Performance," 167). Unlike Dorothy Jordan in the eighteenth century and Ada Rehan in the nineteenth (who were primarily confined to comedic parts) or their contemporaries, Sarah Siddons and Ellen Terry (who conversely were known predominantly for their tragic roles), modern actresses seem granted greater dramatic options. This range of actresses inhabiting the various Shakespearean heroines—and heroes—has resulted in an amazingly diverse range of ways of imagining such characters as Desdemona, Ophelia, Rosalind, and Titania. It has also resulted in opening up a range of roles—both comedic and tragic—to individual actresses.

With a stage and film career spanning more than fifty years, Peggy Ashcroft is often considered to be the first major modern Shakespearean actress and among the twentieth century's finest Shakespearean actresses (indeed, among actresses in general, as she has also won numerous awards for her non-Shakespearean roles on stage and in film). She performed the role of Desdemona in *Othello* opposite

Paul Robeson, controversial for the interracial casting of the play instead of casting Othello in blackface. In 1937, she was chosen to participate in the first known instance of a Shakespeare play to be performed on television, appearing with Greer Garson in a thirty-minute excerpt of *Twelfth Night* broadcast by BBC Television. Ashcroft was known early in her career for her performance in an innovative production of *Romeo and Juliet*, playing Juliet opposite Lawrence Olivier and John Gielgud, who alternated between the roles of Romeo and Mercutio. She performed regularly with the Royal Shakespeare Company (RSC), taking throughout the years nearly all the greatest female roles.

Following Ashcroft, the generation of actresses born in the 1930s enjoyed what could perhaps be considered the heyday for female Shakespeareans during the twentieth century, including Judi Dench, Claire Bloom, Glenda Jackson, Maggie Smith, Diana Rigg, Helen Mirren, Janet Suzman, and Vanessa Redgrave, to name just a few. This period is particularly interesting, because the acting style—not just in Shakespearean plays but on the stage in general—began to shift from a stylized presentation to a more naturalistic representation.

Because a number of these actresses performed in stage productions that were filmed or adapted to film or television by their more famous male counterparts, many of their contributions have taken on an enduring quality. Claire Bloom, for example, performed the role of Lady Anne in Olivier's 1955 version of *Richard III*. In 1999 she also starred in *Shakespeare's Women*, an hour-long documentary in which she does several monologues. Similarly, Maggie Smith (now perhaps most widely known among younger people for her role as Professor McGonnagal in the *Harry Potter* movies) played Desdemona to Olivier's Othello in his 1965 filmed version of that play.

If genre was not the determining factor in the twentieth century, age certainly played a key part in determining the assignation of female Shakespearean roles, and many Shakespearean actresses moved away from the more youthful parts (such as Portia, Rosalind, Ophelia, and Juliet) as they aged into more mature characters (such as the Countess in *All's Well*, Cleopatra, and Mistress Quickly). Nevertheless, some of the century's finest actresses are among this group.

A number of actresses from this generation are known both for innovations in their performance and in their directorial work with Shakespeare's plays. South African actor and director Janet Suzman joined the Royal Shakespeare Company in the early 1960s, following the rave reviews she received for her performance as Joan of Arc in a two-year run of *The War of the Roses* (based on the trilogy of Henry VI plays). During the 1970s, Suzman performed to acclaim in numerous productions directed by Trevor Nunn (who was her husband at the time). Her roles included Portia; Ophelia; Kate; Beatrice; Celia and Rosalind in separate productions; Lavinia; and Cleopatra. In the late 1980s, Suzman also began to direct, and she is most noted for her multiethnic castings in both England and South Africa. Particularly striking was her 1987 *Othello*, which ran at the height of South African apartheid at the Market Theatre in Johannesburg (this production is available on recording).

As with Suzman, Vanessa Redgrave's first Shakespearean role was in the 1960s; as she took on the character of Imogen in the 1962 RSC production of

Cymbeline. Since then she has performed as Rosalind, Viola, Cleopatra (opposite a black Antony in the 1995 production), and Lady Macbeth in various productions over the past decades. In 2000, Redgrave performed as Prospero in Mark Rylance's production of *The Tempest* at the Globe in London. Redgrave's Prospero, according to Penny Gay, "was neither 'masculine' nor 'feminine', artist or magus, but rather a watchful parent to both Miranda and Ariel . . ." (Gay, "Women and Shakespearean Performance," 172).

Without question, Judi Dench stands among the most important Shakespearean stage actresses of the twentieth century (and, indeed, among the most significant actors of the period in general). She began in 1957 at the Royal Court Theatre in Liverpool, where she played Juliet in Franco Zeffirelli's stage version of *Romeo and Juliet*, Ophelia, and Princess Katherine in *Henry V*. Four years later, she joined the RSC, where she played nearly every major female role in the Shakespearean canon, including Rosalind in *As You Like It*, Isabella in *Measure for Measure*, Lady Macbeth, and Beatrice in *Much Ado About Nothing*. In 1976 she performed a chilling Lady Macbeth opposite Ian McKellen's Scottish king in Trevor Nunn's minimalist production, which was filmed in 1977 (it is still available on video and DVD). Her 1987 Cleopatra garnered numerous awards. Among her many awards in stage, as well as film, is her 1998 Academy Award for Best Supporting Actress for her performance of Queen Elizabeth I in *Shakespeare in Love*. She continues to perform with the RSC, and in 2006 she played Mistress Quickly in *The Merry Wives of Windsor*. Judi Dench is, in the words of Russ McDonald, "our most distinguished interpreter of Shakespeare's heroines . . ." ("Look to the Lady" 104).

While the women's movement had an impact on individual performers, it has had surprisingly little effect on the structures of Shakespearean theater companies as institutions or, with some striking exceptions to the majority, on the ways in which Shakespearean texts are performed onstage and in film. "In the 1980s and 1990s," according to Penny Gay,

> there was plenty of evidence, in interviews with and articles by Shakespearean actresses, that the perspectives of second-wave feminism had influenced their thinking about the characters and stories of Shakespeare's plays. The question arises, however, as to what difference, if any, this new awareness has made to what the twenty-first-century audience sees. Little in the record of Britain's Royal Shakespeare Company in recent years indicates any change in the relation between women performers and the Shakespeare industry. The few plays directed by women have been disliked or ignored by critics and other opinion-makers. . . . Actresses who break the mould of audience's expectations—and make a success of it—remain, at the beginning of the twenty-first century, disappointingly rare. (Gay, "Changing Shakespeare," 314–315)

Among the rarities are the performances of Kathryn Hunter and Fiona Shaw. Known for the nearly limitless range of her ability to transform into different ages and even sexes, Hunter's roles have ranged from Juliet and Cleopatra to Richard III and King Lear.

Fiona Shaw (another Shakespearean actor perhaps more widely recognized for her role in the *Harry Potter* film series—she plays Aunt Petunia) also is known as an actor with great range. Working with Juliet Stevenson in 1985, Shaw was cofounder of the short-lived Royal Shakespeare Company Women's Group, which attempted to address the sexist politics of the RSC and theater in general both on stage and off (Werner 50–68). Ultimately, the group chose a non-Shakespearean project for its first and only production.

Nonetheless, Shaw's feminist sensibilities have informed her work on the Shakespearean stage. In 1987 her feminist reading of *Taming of the Shrew* conflicted with director Jonathan Miller's vision for the production. In Tim Albery's 1989 production of *As You Like It*, however, she performed the role of Rosalind as a critique of gender stereotyping, providing a subversive presentation of androgyny in Rosalind's disguise as Ganymede. As Lizbeth Goodman describes Shaw's performance, her "characterization of Rosalind illustrates one way in which performers today may reclaim the power to wear the costume, rather than be subsumed into it. Her costume is not a sign representing her but rather a disguise she uses to subvert expectation" (Goodman 212). Like a number of her contemporary players who have taken on male roles, Shaw played the lead in Deborah Warner's 1995 production of *Richard II*, which was adapted for television in 1997.

In the late twentieth and early twenty-first centuries, there has also been a revival in the number of all-male productions of Shakespeare. Sometimes, as in the case of the Globe Theatre in London, which often presents one such production per season, the all-male productions ostensibly are aimed at using authentic methods of Elizabethan dramaturgy. As part of the Globe's all-male Men's Company, Mark Rylance has played both leading male and female roles, including Cleopatra in 1999 and Olivia in *Twelfth Night* in 2002 (as well as male roles such as the title character in an all-male production of *Richard II*). Other well-received all-male productions have included a number of productions by Declan Donnellan's Cheek by Jowl Company, including *As You Like It*, which starred Adrian Lester as Rosalind in 1991, and *Twelfth Night* which toured Russia in 2006.

DESDEMONA

A number of parts, including both male and female roles, have accumulated important histories of their own with regard to female actors on stage and in film. The representation of Desdemona, for example, gained significance as the possibility of biracial casting was brought to the fore in the mid-nineteenth century. It is not until then that the role of Desdemona seems to take on particular interest. As Lois Potter notes, "By the end of the eighteenth century it was already agreed that Emilia was the better of the two women parts" (Potter 50). Once the question of race in relation to Desdemona emerged explicitly in the mid-nineteenth century with the first biracial casting in major productions, however, the role became immensely intriguing to audiences and theater critics. In April 1833, the year marking the abolition of slavery in the British colonies, Aldridge played Othello opposite the popular actress Ellen Tree (Kean) at Covent Garden. Significantly, newspaper critics made openly racist comments about Aldridge. Critics responded with openly racist reviews regardless of whether they were praising his work or condemning it. One critic protested "in the name of propriety and decency" about the decision to pair Aldridge with Tree, adding that he disliked Tree being "pawed about on the stage by a black man" (Marshall and Stock 232–233).

Interestingly, however, the question of Desdemona's death is at the heart of her role for many actresses—and its violence linked to racist stereotypes not only of blackness but also nineteenth-century notions of Mediterranean masculinity. As Fanny Kemble observed wryly "the Desdemonas I have seen, on the English stage, have always appeared to me to acquiesce with wonderful equanimity in their assassination. On the Italian stage, they run for their lives" (Kemble 378). The productions starring Italian actors Ernesto Rossi and Tommaso Salvini, for example, were noted for the extreme violence and physicality of their murder

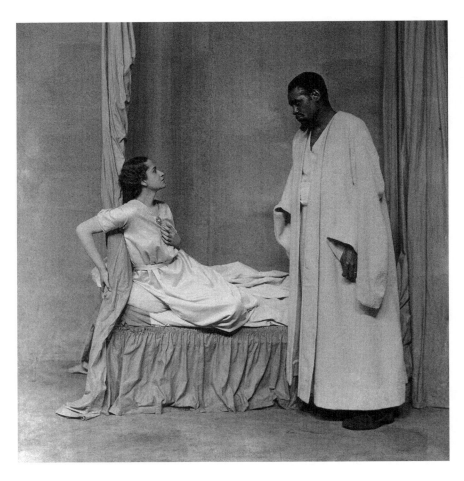

Peggy Ashcroft as Desdemona and Paul Robeson as Othello (1930). Bettmann/Corbis (U237503AP-A).

scenes. Kemble, however, expressly preferred the English version in which "The terrified woman cowers down upon her pillow like a poor frightened child. Indeed the whole scene loses its most pitiful elements by allowing Desdemona to confront Othello standing, instead of uttering the piteous pleadings for mercy in the helpless prostration of her half recumbent position" (Kemble 378).

Audiences in Eastern Europe similarly responded with mixed emotions to Ira Aldridge's performances—both titillated and horrified by his graphic method of

Peggy Ashcroft as Desdemona, Paul Robeson as Othello, and Maurice Brown as Iago (1930). Bettmann/Corbis (U237503P-A).

Emil Jannings as Othello and Ica von Lenkeffy as Desdemona in Dimitri Buchowetzki's silent film version (Germany 1922). Photofest.

portraying the murder of Desdemona. In 1852 Aldridge embarked on a tour of major European cities followed by an extended tour of Russia, where he played Othello opposite a number of white Ophelias. As he had in the British productions, Aldridge's Othello dragged his Desdemonas around the stage by their hair before smothering them. In 1858 a cartoon alluding to the violence of Aldridge's Othello shows Ira Aldridge as Othello and Desdemona in front of a judge with the following caption:

> Des: Save me! This savage one day will really suffocate me! Judge: You must be more careful, Mr. Othello. If you do actually suffocate her, what will happen then? Othello: Nichevo. Just you give me another Desdemona better than this one. (Marshall and Stock 233)

While actors of African descent played the role of Othello in minor venues, it was nearly a hundred years before another interracial casting of the play was produced on a main London or New York stage.

Peggy Ashcroft's debut as Desdemona at the Savoy in September 1930, playing opposite Paul Robeson's Othello, is particularly important to the history of theater, for this was the twentieth century's first interracial casting of the play in a major London venue. The performance was fraught with the history of prior performances, especially that of Aldridge, and the production met mixed reviews. As Robeson recalled, the recurrent question of "how the public will take to seeing a Negro make love to a white woman" affected his performance in the early days of the production: "For the first two weeks in every scene I played with Desdemona that girl couldn't get near to me, I was backin' away from her all the time. I was like a plantation hand in the parlor, that clumsy" (cited in Duberman 135). Although there was talk of bringing the production to the United States, it was not until 1942 that Robeson played the role opposite Uta Hagen in New York and in Boston. Central to the performance of Desdemona's character, as it is central to the doubt in Othello's mind, is the paradox of her chastity on the one hand and her self-initiated passion on the other. According to Peggy Ashcroft, her main concern in presenting the character was to find a balance between two extreme views of Desdemona's character: the "alabaster angel or wilting lily" versus the overly flirtatious and ungovernable woman (Billington 39).

Oliver Parker's 1995 film subtly plays on the doubts about the compatibility of Desdemona's fidelity and passion in the opening frames of the film, which do not begin with Roderigo's complaint to Iago, but rather by visually linking Desdemona to not only secret, but illicit love. As the film opens, it is night, and the camera follows several gondolas traveling on the canal, the unlit waterways providing cover for the clandestine assignations of several pairs of lovers. Perhaps the women in the boats are courtesans—in one gondola, a white woman dozes as a black man dons a white mask, obscuring his visage at the moment when the camera's view approaches; in another boat, we see a graceful feminine hand draw close a curtain, obscuring our view of the deeds inside. We first see Desdemona as she debarks from one of the gondolas and then runs through the dark, somewhat menacing Venetian streets to her elopement. The manner in which Parker prefaces our first view of Desdemona links her to these more illicit, seemingly temporary and purely sexual, couplings at the moment she vows fidelity to Othello.

At the center of any production's position on the question of race and sexuality in *Othello*, and central to the question of Desdemona's character, is the presentation of her murder. For many (especially earlier) critics and performers, Desdemona's appeal to audiences hinges on her passivity and apparent lack of self-preservation in the face of her husband's rage. Yet audiences have not been entirely willing to watch even the passive death up close. As James R. Siemon's review of the staging of this scene demonstrates, "complex interactions between the desire to see and the need to be protected from unmediated vision reveal themselves through" the positioning of the bed on stage (Siemon 40). The audience's level of comfort with viewing Desdemona's death determines the location of the bed on stage and its distance from audience, with many productions locating the bed far upstage away from the audience and obscured by low lighting. Moreover, as Siemon notes, "in most eighteenth- and nineteenth-century productions, the Othello, who according to the Shakespearean text rolls his eyes and gnaws his lip in paroxysms of agitation, becomes too refined to strangle Desdemona with his bare hands" (Siemon 46).

Claire Danes as Maria and Billy Crudup as Edward "Ned" Kynaston in *Stage Beauty* (2004). Photofest.

The medium of film, however, seems to demand that the death scene be visually presented up close. Consequently, the question of whether Desdemona dies in a stylized manner or more naturally becomes even more crucial to the representation of the scene and of our understanding of her character. Richard Eyre's 2004 film, *Stage Beauty*, grapples precisely with the issue of Desdemona's death. Set in the 1660s, at the dawn of the restoration of King Charles II and the moment when women replace men in female parts on English stages, *Stage Beauty* follows the falling career of the historical person Edward (Ned) Kynaston, one of the last stars specializing in female roles (most popularly Desdemona), and the rising fame of his dresser, the fictionalized Maria, who takes the stage as Desdemona under the guise of Mrs. Margaret Hughes, the first female actress on the English public stage. Kynaston's career as a player of female parts is seemingly at an end, along with his style of acting. As Kynaston and Maria vie for the right to play Desdemona, the film also presents a fictional history for the shift from the stylized presentation of artifice popular in the early modern period to a more naturalistic representation of psychological realism and emotional authenticity (akin to Constantin Stanislavsky's "system," or its later offshoot of Method acting). The film's problematic suggestion that Kynaston's sexuality is "straightened out" through his love affair with Maria also merits further discussion, possibly within the context of the differences between early modern and modern (or postmodern) concepts of sexuality and the question of male playing women's roles onstage.

Early in the film, Kynaston's manner of acting relies on an abstract sense of beauty, one that removes feeling and naturalism from it. In response to Maria's question as to why he won't play men, Kynaston's reply echoes numerous earlier opinions linking women's death and beauty:

> Men aren't beautiful. What they do isn't beautiful, either. Women do everything beautifully, especially when they die. Men feel far too much. Feeling ruins the effect. Feeling makes it ugly. Perhaps that's why I could never pull off the death scene. I . . . could never feel it in a way that . . . wouldn't mar the . . . I couldn't let the beauty die. Without beauty, there's nothing. Who could love that?

Kynaston's mode of performing Desdemona is highly artificial and extremely styl-ized, with certain scenes, including the death scene, staged in tableau vivant (frozen momentarily like photographs). Eventually, however, the preferred method of acting shifts from a presentational one based on formalized imitation (e.g., "the five positions of female subjugation") to a claim that authentic emotions are at the heart great acting; beauty is replaced by artistic truth.

Kynaston, aiming to further perfect his Desdemona, asks Maria how she dies as Desdemona. Unfortunately, his professional question comes in the middle of the couple's lovemaking, and she is offended. Nevertheless, she answers:

> Your old tutor did you a great disservice, Mr. Kynaston. He taught you how to speak and swoon and toss your head but he never taught you to suffer like a woman or love like a woman. He trapped a man in woman's form and left you there to die! I always hated you as Desdemona. You never fought! You just die beautifully. No woman would die like that no matter how much she loved him! A woman would fight!

Yet as the film progresses Nell Gwyn (the king's mistress) and Samuel Pepys con-vince Kynaston that he must teach Maria to leave behind her imitation of his arti-ficial manner of acting and take on a truer rendition, one that is more realistic. In tutoring Maria, Kynaston also "naturally" learns to act the male part of Othello. On stage, before an audience that includes King Charles II and Nell, Kynaston and Maria's portrayal of the murder scene is anything but emblematic or stylized. Rather, Maria's Desdemona frantically scrabbles across the stage in an attempt to evade Kynaston's Othello. Maria's Desdemona does not "die beautifully": she fights, and the performance is horrifying and disturbing to watch for both the film's fictional audience and the film's viewers. As Kynaston's Othello smothers Desde-mona, it is not clear that Kynaston is not actually killing Maria—while personally he is not sexually jealous of Maria, Kynaston is professionally jealous of her for having displaced him from the role of Desdemona. The audience in the film is wide-eyed and gaping as they eventually learn that they have just watched a monumental performance, one signaling the shift to a more realistic, representa-tional rather than presentational performance style. As Maria as Desdemona mutters her final gasping farewell, the King stands in ovation, crying "Brava! Brava!"

With few exceptions, however, nearly all film productions of this scene ulti-mately find difficulty in avoiding stage business that renders Desdemona's murder aesthetically beautiful rather than artistically true. Orson Welles's *Othello* (1952) stars Suzanne Cloutier as a very blonde and pale Desdemona. In this film production, Desdemona dies "beautifully" and with little fight or even movement. Othello enters the bedchamber, with Desdemona lying on the bed as if it were a bier. Although she is awake when he enters, she feigns sleep—further enhancing the sense of self-control over her fear. Because the film is black and white, the fairness of Desdemona's skin is highlighted by the use of light and shadow. Desdemona is lighted as if glowing amid the darkness of the bedchamber and in contrast to Othello's darkness. Desdemona does not rise even when she says the line, "Talk you of killing"; she remains prone upon the bed until Othello accuses her of giving Cassio the handkerchief, but then she quickly lies back down on the bed. While the music is an intensely dramatic chorus of voices, Desdemona offers little resistance as Othello covers her face with a semiopaque white cloth and literally stops her breath with his kiss.

Sergei Yutkevich's 1955 Russian version, with Sergei Bondarchuk as Othello and Irina Skobtseva as Desdemona, likewise presents a very blonde and pale Desdemona, laid out on her bed as if already dead upon a bier or monument. We see very little physical resistance on Desdemona's part to her impending murder, and the actual murder takes place behind the curtains of the bed, beyond the viewer's sight. The film, in black and white, also highlights the juxtaposition between the dark Othello and the very white Desdemona.

Jonathan Miller's 1981 version, starring an embarrassingly darkened Anthony Hopkins as Othello and Penelope Wilton as Desdemona, casts Desdemona as dark-haired but pale. Desdemona is lying in bed asleep when Othello approaches her ("It is the cause . . .") and sits upon her bedside. She doesn't wake until he kisses her ("She wakes," to which Desdemona says "Who's there . . ."). Here, the staging is quite unrealistic as she doesn't budge, even in sleep, to brush away her husband's beard as he paws at her. As in other somewhat stylized versions, Desdemona remains prone in bed. She sits up at "I hope you will not kill me," but her rising seems motivated more because Othello has walked away from the bed rather than because she is moved by emotion. Her most strident moment is when she pounds her fists on the bed to punctuate her denial that she ever gave her handkerchief to Cassio. The camera focuses on Othello's face, seemingly in an epileptic fit as he suffocates Desdemona, and we see only her hand weakly grasping as Othello comes out of his trancelike state. Nor does the camera show Desdemona as Othello, weeping, finishes killing her at "I would not have thee linger in thy pain."

While the 1996 Metropolitan Opera version of Giuseppe Verdi's *Otello* and Oliver Parker's 1995 film version have attempted to gesture toward the violence of Desdemona's murder, both ultimately insist on retaining a stylized beauty to her death. Parker's version, starring Laurence Fishburne and Irene Jacobs, presents Desdemona's death with great and disturbing violence, but in the end, she dies with great beauty. Jacobs's Desdemona hits Othello before he overpowers her and smothers her with a pillow. During her death struggles, Desdemona beats with her hands and even brings her foot up in a failed attempt to fend off the attack. In the end, however, her hand elegantly caresses Othello's cheek as it falls beautifully upon the pillow. In the 1996 *Otello*, starring Placido Domingo and

Renee Fleming, a blonde Desdemona puts up a mild fight as Othello strangles her (rather than suffocating her with a pillow). Like that of Irene Jacobs and hundreds before her, Fleming's Desdemona dies beautifully in the end as well: her hand floats elegantly down to rest on the bed, signifying her death. Even the 2001 youth adaptation O, set on a southern prep-school campus and starring Julia Stiles as Desi and Mekhi Phifer as Odin, likewise renders the death of the film's heroine in surprisingly passive terms.

THE PRINCE OF DENMARK AND THE WOMEN OF HAMLET

Throughout the centuries, women have taken on a number of male Shakespearean roles, including Romeo (perhaps most famously by Charlotte Cushman), Prospero from *The Tempest*, King Lear, and even Shylock from *Merchant of Venice*. A number of actresses throughout the centuries have been particularly drawn to Hamlet.

As recently as 1999, for example, Angela Winkler won Germany's Best Actress Award for her performance in the title role of *Hamlet 2000* (1999), a version highly redolent with post–Berlin Wall local and global politics. In 1993 Michael Sheridan's post-punk/post-feminist production of *Hamlet's Nightmare*, starring Irish actor Olwen Foure in the title role, used the story of a dysfunctional family to explore the enduring abusive familial subtexts of English and Catholic imperialism in Ireland. The play had originally cast the part of both Ophelia and Death for Sinéad O'Connor, the Irish activist, artist, and singer who has been highly critical of both the Catholic Church and the British government, but she withdrew from the production during rehearsals.

During the eighteenth century, however, the role of Hamlet had already been performed by women, in part because of its appeal to contemporary tastes for novelty and breeches parts. Fanny Furnival, who played the role in Dublin on April 28, 1741, is the first recorded female player to assume the role of the Danish prince. Sarah Siddons took on the role several times, beginning in 1776 and then again in 1802 while on tour in Ireland, though she never played the part in London. The risqué associations with breeches parts brought with them a potential tinge of disrepute, and it is in connection with this role alone that Siddons faced public criticism of her sexual reputation. Although her duel scenes with Laertes received critical accolades, the wife of the actor performing the role of Laertes accused her of having an affair with her husband, claiming that the extensive time the pair spent choreographing the fencing scene was merely a ruse to cover their illicit activities. The Dublin press and other publications had a field day with the scandal.

The vogue for female Hamlets—as well as the attendant controversy surrounding the role—continued to increase during the nineteenth century, when nearly fifty female players are known to have taken on the role of Hamlet between 1802 and 1899. In the mid- to late nineteenth century, the role became linked to the emergent feminist agenda and especially the New Woman movement. Among the most noted actresses drawn to the character of Hamlet during the nineteenth century are Charlotte Cushman and Sarah Bernhardt.

Lafayette – Photo – London.

SARAH-BERNHARDT (HAMLET.)

Sarah Bernhardt as Hamlet (ca. 1885–1900). Library of Congress (LOT 3120 (F) [P&P].

Cushman's rendition of Hamlet was audacious and bold—she even went so far as to borrow the costume of her chief rival in the role, the famed actor Edwin Booth, when she performed in Boston in 1861. Rather than seek the femininity within the role, as many actresses before and since have done, Cushman played Hamlet by fully embodying the masculinity in the character. Her performances were for the most part met with rave reviews, many of them remarking upon the absolute excellence of her acting and refraining from implying that her performance was only relatively good—for a woman, that is.

In 1885 Sarah Bernhardt had played the role of Ophelia in a disastrous production of *Hamlet,* with Phillipe Garnier in the title role. Bernhardt claimed the role "brought nothing new to me in the study of character," preferring the greater intellectual depth to be found in male parts, and especially in Hamlet (Bernhardt, *Art* 139). "But," she continues, "a woman can only interpret a male part when it represents a mind in a feeble body. A woman would not be able to play Napoleon, Don Juan, or Romeo" (141). In 1899, at the age of fifty-four, she took on the role of the Danish prince herself, which played in France as well as in both England and the United States to mixed reviews. While a number of critics praised the audacity of the choice and the fineness of her acting, one reviewer sarcastically suggested that Henry Irving, a leading male actor of the time, be cast as Ophelia.

Bernhardt herself explained that Hamlet appealed to her more than Ophelia because of his complexity: "Generally speaking male parts are more intellectual than female parts. . . . No female character has opened up a field so large for the exploration of sensations and human sorrows as that of Hamlet" (Bernhardt, *Art* 139). Bernhardt played several renditions of the character and in 1900 performed "The Duel Scene from *Hamlet*" in one of the earliest examples of Shakespeare on film, which was played at the 1900 Paris Exposition. As film began to flourish as an artistic medium, the number of film versions of *Hamlet* increased, including the 1920 film version starring Danish actor Asta Nielsen.

Many women who have played Hamlet have been drawn to the character's supposedly feminine side (deriving from such stereotypical feminine traits as his inwardness, melancholia, madness, and his reluctance to act). Yet some feminists have questioned the linking of these traits to femininity as potentially misogynistic. Despite playing Richard II in 1995, for example, Fiona Shaw refused several offers to play Hamlet, characterizing the part as a "role of male consciousness" and not a fruitful one in which female actors might "tap the natural androgyne in themselves" (Shaw xxiii–xxiv). As Sue-Ellen Case and others have observed, the tradition of gendering the universal human subject as male imprisons women in the position of object and excludes them from full subjectivity.

> Scanning the 'masterpieces' of theatre, with their focus on the male subject, one can see that women are called upon to identify with Hamlet, Oedipus, Faust and other male characters imbued with specifically male psychosexual anxieties. The idea that these are 'universal' characters represses the gender inscription in the notion of the self. Yet the dominance of the self as male has taken its historical toll on women . . . . (Case 135)

Erika Munk has similarly commented on the implied misogyny behind the tradition of women playing Hamlet:

> Hamlet, stereotyped as a waffling neurotic prone to violent fits, is considered proper for women to enact, unlike Lear, Henry V, Caesar, Coriolanus, or Falstaff. (Peter Pan is a woman's role for similar reasons.) . . . as long as men are not clamoring to play Mother Courage or Juliet or Amanda Wingfield, Hamlet as woman reemphasizes the universalist pretensions of maleness, the specific limitations of femaleness in our culture. (Munk 80)

Presently, in mainstream popular culture, *Hamlet* remains the prerogative of male actors. In spite of Hamlet's associations with the "feminine," male actors have often seen the character as a watershed role (Irish actor Fiona Shaw has called *Hamlet* a "sacred cow" in England, though not Ireland), including popular stage and film stars such as Mel Gibson, Kevin Kline, Kenneth Branagh, and Ethan Hawke. Women, for the most part, are excluded from participating—and apparently have been perceived as a threat to the role's import. Tony Howard enumerates several of the scores of rumors concerning prospective pop culture female Hamlets that emerged in the 1990s: "None of those performances materialized but the multimedia threat was there—and the threat, the guerrilla assault on hierarchy via pop culture, bawdry, Girl Power and Hamlet, was the point" (Howard 252).

The case of acclaimed television, stage, and film actor Diane Venora's performance in three productions of *Hamlet* provides a telling history in relation to the question of women in the role of Hamlet and women more generally in Shakespearean productions. Venora has played Hamlet, Ophelia, and Gertrude. In 1982 she played the lead in Joseph Papp's production of *Hamlet* at the prestigious New York Shakespeare Festival, the first woman to play the role in that particular venue. As the partial transcript of Carl Charlson's documentary of the rehearsals reveals, throughout the rehearsal and production, there was much tension between Venora's and Papp's visions of how Hamlet should interact with Ophelia, especially in the nunnery scene (Howard 276–280). Indeed, the question of how Hamlet interacts with the female characters in the play is made interestingly complex when Hamlet is played by a woman. In depicting the relationship between Hamlet and Gertrude and Ophelia (regardless of the sexes of the actors involved), many productions collapse Hamlet's negative responses into a general hatred of women ("woman, thy name is frailty").

However, a number of female actors, including Charlotte Cushman in the nineteenth century, have stressed the tension as personal and individual rather than generically based in misogyny. Such was Venora's vision of Hamlet and Ophelia, for example, in the twentieth-century production of *Hamlet*. While Papp wanted a noble, classical Hamlet, Venora was drawn to his passion, his rage, his disillusionment, and his fear. Ultimately, "critics found Venora's scenes with the other women 'unusually violent.' Hamlet ripped letters and tossed keepsakes in Ophelia's face; he threw her to the back of the stage, menaced her like a stalker, choked her and limped off sobbing. In the 'particularly ugly' Closet scene Hamlet punched Gertrude in the ribs and dragged her down" (Howard 278).

Julia Stiles as Ophelia (2000). Photofest.

Venora would go on to play traditional roles in more conventional productions of *Hamlet*. In 1990 Venora played (as the back cover of the 2001 Image Entertainment DVD puts it) a "heartbreaking" Ophelia opposite Kevin Kline's "elegant" Hamlet. Only nine years later, she was apparently no longer young enough to continue the role of Ophelia, and in 1999 she played Gertrude opposite Ethan Hawke as Hamlet in Michael Almereyda's film version of the play. The film's translation of the play into a global corporate setting, combined with its explicit postmodern aesthetic, promises to speak to late-twentieth-century concerns, but ultimately (and disappointingly) the film is retrograde in its gender politics. Although the minor character of the soldier Marcello is made a woman, Marcella is also reduced to the role of playing Horatio's girlfriend. Almereyda's direction of Julia Stiles's Ophelia is perhaps most disappointingly conventional in terms of both vision and voice. In spite of Stiles's fine acting, her Ophelia's lines have been diminished to the point that she is played as a weak, nearly voiceless and childlike character, floating ephemerally through the film before her final scene where she floats face up, drowned in the reflecting pool in front of a New York sky scraper.

Almereyda's lingering shot of Ophelia floating stands in a long line of similar images drawn from the plays, and the dead Ophelia has been an especially favorite source of inspiration for artists. Such examples include the pre-Raphaelite John Everett Malais's portrait of Ophelia in the stream, W. G. Simmonds' similar portrait, John William Waterhouse's several painted versions, and Henrietta Rae's 1890 portrait showing Ophelia handing out the flowers. Dead women's bodies are figured in many stage productions and works of art as icons of the beautiful. Many productions, for example, follow the convention of lingering over Cordelia's dead body, presented in tableau fashion draped in the arms of King Lear, and painters such as Friedrich Pecht (1876) and James Barry (1786) put the image to canvas (Cordelia's meeting with and comforting her father also proved a popular image). Although Juliet is frequently represented on the balcony, the vision of her dead body (in the tomb and in final funeral procession) seems to have had equal appeal with painters and illustrators. Desdemona's death is also rendered to conform to romanticized notions of female death and the beautiful, presenting her either asleep before the murder, or still and unrealistically "unmarred" after death. Alexandre Marie Colin's (1829) portrait of Othello and Desdemona, but also film stills such as those taken from Ashcroft and Robeson, show Othello standing while Desdemona shrinks (very white) in her bed; Rossetti drew her singing Willow as Emilia brushes her hair (1875–1880).

VANISHING WOMEN IN RICHARD III

While *Richard III* has proved a cinematically popular play, with three successful film versions in the late twentieth century, it is also interesting to note the handling of the female characters. The filmed versions by Laurence Olivier, Al Pacino, and Richard Loncraine each radically diminish—or eliminate—the roles and voices of female characters.

The role of Lady Anne, typically presented in romantic fashion, seems to be of the most interest among the directors. The Laurence Olivier 1955 version of *Richard III* eliminates nearly all of the women's speaking parts except for the role of Anne, which is played by Claire Bloom. The king's mistress, Jane Shore, is added as a non-speaking character who appears briefly to dampen the new queen consort's celebration, a detail that makes sense only to audience members who have read the play or know the story from English history. Queen Margaret's part is entirely eliminated, and Elizabeth Woodville's character is reduced to a dumbshow presenting of the coronation of King Edward IV. Gone are both the prophecies and lamentations of women in a kingdom where the fate of children is so bloody. In the remaining role for Lady Anne, the focus is on the romanticizing of heterosexual domestic violence in the wooing scene with Richard. The swelling music and framing of the scene replicate the film strategies of contemporary dramatic romantic films of the 1950s.

While Pacino's 1996 documentary, *Looking for Richard*, retains the women's roles for Queen Margaret, Elizabeth Woodville, and Lady Anne, his production nevertheless seems less interested in the power of the female characters than the homosocial engagements of collusion, betrayal, and war. During a scene in which the characters do a reading of the scene preceding the death of Edward IV, the actors discuss the character of Queen Elizabeth Woodville. The men suggest that she is hysterical, but Penelope Allen, the actor playing Queen Elizabeth, counters that she "is not weak or hysterical because that diminishes her—and him [Richard]." Instead, Allen argues, Elizabeth "knows damn well" what everyone else is denying: that Richard loves none of them. Allen then slides into character, and literally stuns her fellow actors with the power of her performance.

Yet Pacino's vision of the play is for the most part uninterested in the strength of women's roles. This is especially clear when Pacino prefaces the introduction of his choice for Lady Anne with his vision of the character as one who is very young and easily manipulated by Richard. Pacino's choice, Winona Ryder, is thirty years his junior, and the music, lighting, and framing of his wooing scenes with her are presented in a cynically romanticized fashion (with, not surprisingly, multiple takes of the kiss).

Richard Loncraine's 1995 version, starring Ian McKellen, similarly reduces the female parts, eliminating Queen Margaret's Cassandra-like ranting and prophecies. Some of Margaret's lines are reassigned to the Duchess of Gloucester (played by Maggie Smith) and to Queen Elizabeth Woodville (played by Annette Bening). The main focus of the film is the maneuvering among the men. Like Pacino and Olivier, Loncraine seems most able to imagine the part of Lady Anne, played by Kristin Scott Thomas. However, Loncraine's handling of the wooing scene between Richard and Anne is perhaps the most adept at offering a reasonable motive for Anne's shifting demeanor toward Richard and her acceptance of his proposal. While Loncraine retains the giving of the ring and the kiss, Thomas's final action in the scene is to salute her new lord. The effect is not one of seething romantic attraction but rather a matter of political survival and national duty on the part of a fatherless and widowed royal woman.

KATHERINE MINOLA AND JULIET

While Lady Anne is fatherless and widowed, Katherine Minola in *The Taming of the Shrew* and Juliet in *Romeo and Juliet* both rebel against their fathers as they enter into newly made marriages, one forced and the other clandestine. Given mainstream directors' currently apparent disinterest in comedies such as *As You Like It*, *Twelfth Night*, and *Merry Wives*, all of which offer great potential in female roles, Juliet and Katherine remain perhaps the most intriguing and potentially rich female roles for actors to play on film.

Romeo and Juliet's popularity might be related, according to Deborah Cartmell, to its seeming to be "the straightest: no gender bending, no woman falling in love with other women, no mixing of races" (42). This is certainly the case in scenes where Shakespeare (played by Joseph Fiennes) and Viola (played by Gwyneth Paltrow) rehearse the parts of the star-crossed lovers in John Madden's 1999 *Shakespeare in Love*. Like the contemporary historical romance of *Stage Beauty*, *Shakespeare in Love* straightens out the homoerotics of boy players of female parts in the Renaissance. While *Shakespeare in Love* and *Stage Beauty* both address the theme of women's desire to act during a time when it was prohibited, both films end up straightening the historical figures of William Shakespeare and Ned Kynaston.

The exception in terms of race (though not sexuality) for *Romeo and Juliet*, of course, would be the 1961 musical adaptation, *West Side Story*, directed by Robert Wise and Jerome Robbins. While the film likewise presents the story of heterosexual romance developed and then destroyed, *West Side Story* infuses the question of race by making the rival families Anglo and Puerto Rican gangs. Set in twentieth-century New York, Romeo becomes Tony, a member of the Anglo Jets, while Juliet becomes Maria, played by Natalie Wood, who is a member of the recently immigrated Puerto Rican gang known as the Sharks. The film translates

Shakespeare's story of family rivalries to address questions of immigration and race relations (in the context of which, the casting of white actors to play Puerto Rican roles is worth noting).

Franco Zeffirelli's 1968 version, on the other hand, stresses the generational conflict over the cross-familial, a theme perhaps likely to appeal to viewers of the "flower power" generation. Filmed in Italy and noted for being visually gorgeous, the film is also famous for its age-appropriate casting of the actors. Zeffirelli cast fifteen-year-old Olivia Hussey as Juliet, which she played with an aura of innocent sexual awakening, blossoming in rebellion against parental authority. Baz Luhrmann's 1996 *Shakespeare's Romeo + Juliet* continued the trend in casting young actors— including Claire Danes, who was seventeen at the time she played Juliet.

Inspired by MTV and action-flick genre films, Luhrmann's modernization of the play situates the romance amid the conflict between rival business families in a fictionalized Verona Beach. Like Hussey's Juliet, Danes's version of the character depicts the emergence of sexuality from a purity of innocence. While much of the conflict takes place in scenes of postmodern excess juxtaposed with scenes of urban wasteland, Danes's Juliet is repeatedly costumed or framed in the whiteness of pearl-colored gowns, angel's wings, and the white coral in the fish tank through which she peers. While the world inhabited by Luhrmann's Romeo and Juliet is racialized, the film does not seem to consciously engage the politics attendant on its use of race, and in many ways the lovers are artificially insulated from that aspect of culture.

In spite of *The Taming of the Shrew*'s ability to discomfit viewers and readers, the play is oddly among the most produced and filmed of all Shakespearean plays.

Olivia Hussey as Juliet and Leonard Whiting as Romeo (1968). Photofest.

Claire Danes as Juliet (1996). Photofest.

As Diana E. Henderson observes, the frequency with which it appears on stage and film puts "*Shrew* in a select league with the 'big four' tragedies, . . . outpacing those comedies scholars usually dub more 'mature'" (149).

In the late twentieth and early twenty-first centuries, there have been two basic solutions to the discomfort inspired by the domestic violence of *The Taming of the Shrew*. One solution, especially in stage productions, has been to transform the slapstick comedy into a tragedy by exposing the brutality of Petruchio's methods. Such productions explicitly link Petruchio's actions to torture and to brainwashing, and they emphasize the psychological destruction of Katherine's character. The Royal Shakespeare Company has staged a number of such interpretations of the play, including Charles Marowitz's 1973 production in which, after being raped by her husband, Katherine delivers her final speech in chains; Michael Bogdanov's 1976 version; and Di Trevis's version highlighting the economics of Petruchio's patriarchal oppression of Katherine. In 1985 the Medieval Players (a professional touring group that disbanded in the mid-1990s) staged an all-male production of the play to show that tamed shrews are a male fantasy. In the shocking finale of a 1989 Turkish production, Katherine concluded her submission speech by slitting her wrists (Elson 74–75).

The other general solution to the discomfort produced by the play is to tone down the violence (to varying degrees of success) and to make it a play about mutual taming, with Petruchio learning to love alongside Katherine. From the beginning of film, this has been a popular route to take. Sam Taylor's version of *The Taming of the Shrew* was among the earliest pictures with sound and the first "Shakespeare talkie."

Released in 1929 and starring the married stars known as "America's Sweethearts," Douglas Fairbanks and Mary Pickford, the film is interesting in terms of the

Elizabeth Taylor as Katherine Minola and Richard Burton as Petruchio (1967). Photofest.

Elizabeth Taylor as Katherine Minola and Richard Burton as Petruchio (1967). Photofest.

history of not only Hollywood films, but also in terms of gender issues surrounding such questions as suffrage in the United States, Britain, British commonwealths, and other countries around the world in the 1920s. In our first glimpse of Katherine, she is standing at the top of a staircase brandishing a whip. Her character is in many ways the more physically aggressive of the two throughout much of the film, and it is only after much brawling that the couple comes to a potentially more egalitarian relationship. After breaking Petruchio's head with a stool, Katherine nurses the injured Petruchio and then throws her whip into the fireplace in a gesture symbolic of reconciliation. That she has not been tamed, however, is clearly indicated in the film's final scene. Pickford delivers the last lines of the submission speech in an exaggerated and overly dramatic—even by early talkie standards—fashion, one that potentially implies an irony that is made explicit in the delivery of her last lines. As she claims that women are "bound to serve, love, and obey," Pickford puts her hands in a prayer position and raises her eyes, perhaps heavenward but perhaps in an eye-roll at the ludicrousness of wifely submission. On the word "obey" she turns directly to Bianca and winks. Bianca, now an insider to her sister's meaning, registers the point and nods in smiling comprehension.

Like the Sam Taylor version, Franco Zeffirelli's 1967 version of *The Taming of the Shrew* drew upon the star power of that generation's hot Hollywood couple, Richard Burton and Elizabeth Taylor. For viewers, the film developed and made even more entertaining the tales of the Burton-Taylor romantic battles that filled the tabloids. Katherine begins the film wild and shrieking, her untamed hair flying as she rages through the house. Through a number of key scenes, the film makes clear the mercenary nature of Petruchio's interest in marriage with Katherine. The film displaces some of the domestic violence onto objects and even animals (Petruchio beats Katherine's donkey at one point), but not all the violence is eliminated as, for example, when Petruchio twists Katherine's arm behind her back to ensure her acquiescence.

While Zeffirelli's version is most remarkable for the lushness of its scenery and his use of visual imagery, it is also significant in its use of camera work to provide Katherine with a response not given literally in the lines of Shakespeare's text. Indeed, as Diana Henderson notes, for someone called a shrew, Katherine "seldom gets a word in edgewise" (159). Nevertheless, through its focus on Taylor's face, and especially her famously beautiful eyes, Zeffirelli's camera work also attends to Katherine's emotional response to key moments in the narrative, providing her with an interiority usually made possible through monologue but for the most part not available to her character in the play's text. Visually, Zeffirelli provides us with insight into Katherine's response, for example, to Petruchio's eagerness for the wealth of her dowry, the loss of family and home as she embarks upon her journey toward Petruchio's home during a thunderstorm, and her realization that housekeeping is one possible domain in which she might rule. While the newly domesticated Katherine offers her hand in the submission speech in the film's final scene, Burton's Petruchio takes it, lifting her up to his side in the process. Zeffirelli's film, however, is hardly a feminist text.

Particularly interesting is the way in which filmed versions of the past few decades present a view in which being a man-hating feminist is what makes Katherine a shrew—and taming her is a matter of teaching her to be a man-loving feminist (though these versions also frequently present Petruchio worthily rare among men of such love).

Will MacKenzie's 1986 Emmy-winning episode of Moonlighting, "Atomic Shakespeare," provides a slapstick updated, seemingly feminist, version of the play. Drawing on the battle-of-the-sexes relationship between the show's main characters, Cybil Shepherd's Maddie Hayes takes on the role of Katherine while Bruce Willis's David Addison plays Petruchio. In further keeping with the series in general, the episode also draws on Cybil Shepherd's public reputation as a strong woman and a feminist—a characteristic often perceived as "bitchy," that modern equivalent of "shrewish." In setting the play in sixteenth-century Italy but including a subtitle that simultaneously calls attention to the setting as "a facsimile," the episode sits somewhat uneasily with the question of whether women's struggle for equality is a thing of the past. Updated for modern sensibilities, the show downplays the details of the dowry. At one point the dowry is literally displaced as Petruchio mixes up the marital document for his contract requesting a higher salary and more power in the series. Additionally, the conditions of the bet are changed to entail giving up the dowry, suggesting that the idea of women as property is perhaps an element of the original play that is difficult to negotiate in modern terms, but one not yet entirely erasable.

Heath Ledger as Patrick "Pat" Verona and Julia Stiles as Katarina "Kat" Stratford (1999). Photofest.

On the one hand, like Elizabeth Taylor's Katherine, the Katherine played by Maddie Hayes played by Cybil Shepherd is explicitly shown as domesticated. With her hair in a head rag, Katherine cooks and cleans, taking on the role of domestic worker in Petruchio's filthy home (he claims it is the cleaning lady's century off). On the other hand, Katherine is given an eloquent speech arguing that marriage is a matter of "fifty-fifty" and that women want "respect and to be held in higher esteem as wife and partner" ("Atomic Shakespeare"). Moreover, Katherine's submission speech is replaced with Petruchio's "witness to a revelation." Confessing the error of his ways, Petruchio claims he has learned from Katherine that women's "gifts be so much more / When allowed to be freely given"; and he concludes, "Kate never needed to be tamed, / She merely needed to be loved" ("Atomic Shakespeare"). Thus, the demand for respect and equality is translated into love.

Like the "Atomic Shakespeare" episode of *Moonlighting*, Gil Junger's 1999 teen flick, *10 Things I Hate About You*, also translates Renaissance "shrew" into modern-day raging feminist. The need for the female lead's obedience likewise becomes her need to learn how to love. Starring Julia Stiles as Kat Stratford and Heath Ledger as Patrick Verona, the film resituates the story in terms of the coming-of-age angst of high school. Kat is extremely intelligent, outspoken, khaki-wearing, and a fan of angry female rock of the indie persuasion.

Although Kat's character claims fandom to such Riot Grrrl bands as Bikini Kill and The Raincoats (interestingly given the film's Seattle setting, Sleater-Kinney is missing from the list), the film's actual soundtrack consists of the "lite" version bands, including Letters to Cleo, who perform at the film's Skunk Club and on the school's rooftop (the latter filmed in a spectacular helicopter shot as the final credits roll). Indeed, the film's taming enacts a mainstream mass-media co-option of third-wave feminist Riot Grrrl into what Elizabeth A. Deitchman terms a "de-fanged Girl Power femininity" (480).

Kat's difference from her sister, Bianca, is apparent from the moment we see them juxtaposed in separate cars in the film's opening scene: Kat arrives second at a stoplight, where her revved engine stereo blasts out Joan Jett's lyrics "I don't give a damn about my reputation," drowning out the pop sounds coming from the car belonging to Bianca and her friends. Bianca is the antithesis of Kat: not threat-eningly smart, she is popular, boy-crazy, sun-dressed, and seemingly a daddy's girl. The father in the film is Dr. Stratford (a gynecologist and single parent who knows firsthand the ugly reality of teen maternity), who delightedly strikes a deal in which his more affable daughter, Bianca, cannot date until her femi-nazi sister Kat does. Importantly, the film also makes Patrick among the most appealing of the characters. He is at first uninterested in the date-for-pay proposition and does not take on the deal until he discovers that he is interested in Kat; indeed, Patrick seems least interested in transforming her, but rather wins her by pleasing her.

Altering the tradition in which both Katherine and Petruchio are tamed together, it turns out that neither Kat nor Patrick are wild and in need of taming; they are simply misunderstood and in need of love. The rumors about Patrick's mysterious life before enrolling at Padua High School (that he lit a state trooper on fire, spent a year in San Quentin, and sold his liver on the black market to buy a pair of speakers) all turn out to be false: he spent the past year in Milwaukee watching Wheel-of-Fortune and making Spaghettios for his dying grandfather. Kat's seemingly mindless man-hating is in fact a matter of specific responses to specific injuries against her (e.g., Bobby Ridgeway's attempt to grope her in the lunch line and Joey Donner's refusal to accept her decision to not have sex with him a second time). While Patrick learns to be honest with Kat, Kat learns to let her guard down. With the main characters having learned to love (not obey), the film replaces the traditional capitulation speech of the play with a sonnet—a homework assignment and the play's title: "10 Things I Hate About You." When the English teacher calls for someone "brave enough" to read their homework, Kat volunteers, enumerating all the things she hates. "But," her final couplet concludes, "mostly I hate the way I don't hate you. / Not even close, not even a little bit, not even at all" ("10 Things").

In Sally Wainright's BBC 2005 modernization of the play, Katherine and Bianca Minola are clearly adults and living on their own, while Baptista's char-acter has been replaced by a widowed mother, played by former supermodel Twiggy. Wainwright casts Shirley Henderson (experienced in British "period piece" drama, but also known for her role as Moaning Myrtle in the *Harry Potter* films) as Katherine Minola, a successful British politician known for being a "ball-breaker." Here the feminist needs to learn not obedience but to "be nice."

In contrast to the politically powerful Katherine, her sister Bianca (played by Jaime Murray) is a supermodel with a worldwide following and a penchant for younger men. Bianca initiates the bet in an attempt to bring a halt to the unrelenting marriage proposal from her business manager, Harry. Trying to get rid of Harry so she can begin her assignation with her Italian boy toy, Lucentio (a college student who speaks no English), Bianca glibly exclaims she will marry when her sister does. Ironically, because the British people supposedly tend to prefer their political leaders married, Katherine is about to begin looking for a mate.

Thus Katherine's motives for marrying are as mercenary as those of the Petruchio character, the penniless sixteenth Earl of Charlbury, played by Rufus Sewell (he is never actually called Petruchio). While he needs to marry well so he can afford to keep his decrepit family estate, she sees his title as politically useful. When the Earl arrives late to his marriage, he is dressed in drag (he is, it turns out, a cross-dresser). Unlike in the play and in earlier film versions (such as those starring Elizabeth Taylor or Cybil Shepherd), where the bride is physically forced (even tied up, in the case of "Atomic Shakespeare"), Henderson's Katherine chooses to continue with the wedding for her own political reasons, complicating the situation of forced matrimony. Rather than having her mouth stopped (by a gag or a kiss), Henderson's Katherine vows, "to smash his skull through his gullet into his chest cavity on the first available opportunity; oh yes, I will" ("Shakespeare Retold").

Like earlier versions, the film displaces domestic violence into other scenarios. Although Sewell's character hits other people (a trait which Katherine, herself a violent character, finds attractive), he does not hit her. Katherine strikes him during their first meeting in the elevator, in response to which he promises that he will hit her if she hits him again. But later, when she strikes him while on their honeymoon in Italy, he grabs her hand and then gives her a painful flick in the face.

Interestingly, Sewell's character deprives Katherine of her clothing (he "misplaces" her luggage), but most significantly, he deprives her of sex. He chases her into the bedroom, where it looks as if he will force himself on her. Pinned on the bed, she screams at him, "just do it," at which point he stops, stands up, and says he will not have sex with her until she "starts being nice." He leaves her clearly confused, disappointed, and frustrated. Later, Katherine has a heart-to-heart with Harry (whom the Earl has called in from England to help him figure out his new marriage). Harry explains his friend's character and behavior as honest, but with very poor timing. And while Harry argues that being married to an eccentric aristocrat is not going to hurt Katherine's political career, he also asks her whether she married him because it would look good or because she loves him. In answer to Harry's question of whether her career or her love is more important, she momentarily quibbles, but then answers "love." The couple finally reconciles, and the film plays on Shakespeare's original scenes involving the sun and the moon and the mistaking of a man for a "young maid."

Upon returning to England, Katherine discovers that both her sister and mother are planning to marry: Bianca is to marry Lucentio, and Mrs. Minola (who turns out to be the film's counterpart to the play's rich widow) is engaged to Harry. The question of prenuptials gets conflated with the question of obedience in the film's penultimate scene, when Katherine gives the capitulation speech to her mother and sister. The speech, taken in large chunks verbatim from the original, is an ambiguous blend of irony (the Earl hardly fits any of the details of manly virtue in the lines she quotes from the play) and an odd assertion of conservative gender roles and equality (she is willing to place her hand beneath his foot because she knows he would never ask it, and because he would be willing to do the same).

In the final scene, which takes place in the same elevator where the couple first met, he asks whether she regrets not signing the "post-natal thingy," to which she answers no—because they are not worth the paper they are written on (but even if they were, she wouldn't). She then informs him that she is pregnant—with triplets—and that she is not giving up her career. The film ends with a series of photos detailing their lives beyond the film: several of a very pregnant Katherine and her husband in front of the now-renovated Charlbury estate; a sequence in which the Earl is feeding their toddler triplets (all boys, of course) as Katherine leaves for work; a series of the exhausted parents, asleep on a sofa in front of the television while the toddlers are mischievously still wide awake; a series of what look like campaigning activities; and a final shot of the family in front of number 10 Downing Street (the British prime minister's home—comparable to the White House). Thus, the film concludes, women can be strong and find love, too—though it seems also necessary to be nice and to find a man willing to stay at home.

So long as the stage and film industries remain male-dominated and generally conservative when it comes to sexual politics, it is not likely we will see women taking on prominent Shakespearean roles that break gender conventions in large-scale, mainstream venues. Although she is addressing the conditions for female stage directors of Shakespeare, Elizabeth Schafer's comments apply more broadly to female film directors as well. The fact that female directors, whether on stage or in film, tend more often to work outside the mainstream and main stage venues, "has long-term implications: not only are production resources more limited, and access to a pool of performers experienced in playing Shakespeare less attainable, but also, and crucially from the point of view of theatre historians, the archiving treatment is different. [Women's works] are far more susceptible to being forgotten" because of the resources that go into preserving and archiving materials related to theatrical production (Schafer 3–4). However, the impacts of feminism and the increasing numbers of female producers and directors, as well as new technologies, may make possible a more women-centered Shakespeare.

The hopes Diana E. Henderson holds out for the possibilities of film in relation to *Taming of the Shrew* in particular could be broadened more generally to apply to Shakespearean texts and the relatively low number of lines and speaking parts for women in his plays. Henderson argues that the "use of camera and voice . . . could be employed . . . in ways that might lead away from a co-opted and conservative gender politics" (151). As Henderson proposes, it is quite possible that we will encounter in the new millennium "a more experimental filmic rendering" of Shakespearean texts (Henderson 165).

WORKS CITED

Auerbach, Nina. *Ellen Terry: Player in Her Time*. NY: Norton, 1987.

Avery, Emmett L. "The Shakespeare Ladies Club." *Shakespeare Quarterly* 7.2 (1956): 153–158.

Baldwin, Thomas Whitfield. *The Organization and Personnel of the Shakespearean Company*. New York: Russell and Russell, 1961.

Bernhardt, Sarah. *The Art of the Theatre*. Trans. H.J. Stenning. New York: Dial P, 1925.

Billington, Michael. *Peggy Ashcroft*. London: John Murray, 1988.

Booth, Stephen. "Speculations on Doubling in Shakespeare's Plays." *Shakespeare: The Theatrical Dimension*. Eds. Philip C. McGuire and David A. Samuelson. New York: AMS P, 1979. 104–131.

Cartmell, Deborah. *Interpreting Shakespeare on Screen*. New York: Macmillan, 2000.

Case, Sue-Ellen. "Towards a New Poetics." *The Routledge Reader in Gender and Performance*. Eds. Lizbeth Goodman and Jane de Gay. New York: Routledge, 1998. 143–148.

Cerasano, S. P. "Women as Theatrical Investors: Three Shareholders and the Second Fortune Playhouse." *Readings in Renaissance Women's Drama: Criticism, History, and Performance, 1594–1998*. Ed. S. P. Cerasano and Marion Wynne-Davies. London: Routledge, 1998. 87–94.

Cerasano, S. P., and Marion Wynne-Davies. *Renaissance Drama by Women: Texts and Documents*. London: Routledge.

Dasent, Arthur Irwin. *Nell Gwynne, 1650–1687*. NY: Benjamin Blom, 1924.

Dobson, Michael. "Improving on the Original: Actresses and Adaptations., *The Oxford Illustrated History of Shakespeare on Stage*. Eds. Jonathan Bate and Russell Jackson. Oxford: Oxford UP, 1996. 45–68.

———. *The Making of the National Poet: Shakespeare, Adaptation, and Authorship, 1660–1769*. Oxford: Clarendon, 1992. 146–164.

Duberman, Martin Bauml. *Paul Robeson*. New York: Alfred A. Knopf, 1988.

Dudden, Faye E. *Women in the American Theatre: Actresses and Audiences, 1790–1870*. New Haven: Yale UP, 1994.

Dusinberre, Juliet. *Shakespeare and the Nature of Women*. London: MacMillan, 1975.

Elson, John. *Is Shakespeare Still Our Contemporary?* New York: Routledge, 1989.

Faderman, Lillian. *Surpassing the Love of Men: Romantic Friendship and Love Between Women from the Renaissance to the Present*. New York: Harper, 1998.

Faucit Martin, Helena. *On Some of Shakespeare's Female Characters*. Edinburgh: W. Blackwell and Sons, 1885.

Force, James H. *Art Imitates Business: Commercial and Political Influences in Elizabethan Theatre*. Madison: U of Wisconsin P, 1993.

Gay, Penny. "Changing Shakespeare: New Possibilities for the Modern Actress." *The Cambridge Companion to Actresses*. Eds. Maggie B. Gale, John Stokes. Cambridge: Cambridge UP, 2007. 314–326.

———. "Women and Shakespearean Performance." *The Cambridge Companion to Shakespeare on Stage*. Eds. Stanley Wells and Sarah Stanton. Cambridge: Cambridge UP, 2002. 155–173.

Gibson, Joy Leslie. *Squeaking Cleopatras: The Elizabethan Boy Player*. Sutton: Sutton P, 2000.

Goodman, Lizbeth. "Women's Alternative Shakespeares and Women's Alternatives to Shakespeare in Contemporary Theater." *Cross-Cultural Performances: Differences in Women's Re-visions of Shakespeare*. Ed. Marianne Novy. Urbana: U of Illinois P, 1993. 206–226.

Gurr, Andrew. *Playgoing in Shakespeare's London*. 3rd ed. Cambridge: Cambridge UP, 2004.

———. *The Shakespeare Company, 1594–1642*. Cambridge: Cambridge UP, 2004.

Henderson, Diana E. "A Shrew for the Times." *Shakespeare: The Movie*. Eds. Lynda E. Boose and Richard Burt. London: Routledge, 1997. 148–168.

Howard, Jean E. "The Materiality of Ideology: Women as Spectators, Spectacles, and Paying Customers." *The Stage and Social Struggle in Early Modern England*. London: Routledge, 1994. 73–92.

Howard, Tony. *Women as Hamlet: Performance and Interpretation in Theatre, Film and Fiction*. New York: Cambridge UP, 2007.

Jordan, Thomas. "A Prologue, to introduce the first Woman that came to act on the Stage in the Tragedy call'd The Moor of Venice." *A Royal Arbor of Loyal Poesie* (1664). *Illustrations of Old English Literature*. Vol. 3. Ed. J. Payne Collier. New York, Benjamin Blom, 1866. 24–25.

Kathman, David. "How Old Were Shakespeare's Boy Actors?" *Shakespeare Survey* 58 (2005): 220–246.

Kemble, Fanny. "Salvini's *Othello*." *Temple Bar* 71 (1884): 368–378.

Levin, Richard. "Women in the Renaissance Theatre Audience." *Shakespeare Quarterly* 40 (1989): 165–174.

Marshall, Herbert, and Mildred Stock. *Ira Aldridge: The Negro Tragedian*. Carbondale: Southern Illinois UP, 1968.

McDonald, Russ. *Look to the Lady: Sarah Siddons, Ellen Terry, and Judi Dench on the Shakespearean Stage*. Athens: U of Georgia P, 2005.

McManus, Clare. *Women on the Renaissance Stage: Anna of Denmark and Female Masquing in the Stuart Court 1590–1619*. Manchester: Manchester UP, 2002.

Merrill, Lisa. *When Romeo Was a Woman: Charlotte Cushman and her Circle of Female Spectators*. Ann Arbor: U of Michigan P, 1999.

Mirabella, Bella. "'Quacking Delilahs': Female Mountebanks in Early Modern England and Italy." *Women Players in England, 1500–1660: Beyond the All-Male Stage*. Eds. Pamela Allen Brown and Peter Parolin. Burlington, VT: Ashgate, 2005. 89–105.

Munk, Erika. "Drag: 2 Women." *Village Voice*, March 12, 1985. 79–80.

Orgel, Stephen. *Impersonations: The Performance of Gender in Shakespeare's England.* Cambridge: Cambridge UP, 1996.

Pascoe, Judith. *Romantic Theatricality: Gender, Poetry, and Spectatorship.* Ithaca: Cornell UP, 1997.

Pearson, Jacqueline. *The Prostituted Muse: Images of Women and Women Dramatists 1642–1737.* New York: St. Martin's P, 1988.

Potter, Lois. *Shakespeare in Performance: Othello.* Manchester: Manchester UP, 2002.

Rackin, Phyllis. "Afterword." *Women Players in England, 1500–1660: Beyond the All-Male Stage.* Eds. Pamela Allen Brown and Peter Parolin. Burlington, VT: Ashgate, 2005. 315–319.

Rosenberg, Marvin. "The Myth of Shakespeare's Squeaking Boy Actor—Or Who Played Cleopatra?" *Shakespeare Bulletin* 19.2 (2001): 5–6.

Rutter, Carol Chillington. *Documents of the Rose Playhouse.* Manchester: Manchester UP, 1999.

Schafer, Elizabeth. *Ms-Directing Shakespeare: Women Direct Shakespeare.* NY: Palgrave, 2000.

Shaw, Fiona. "Foreword." *The Routledge Reader in Gender and Performance.* Eds. Lizbeth Goodman and Jane De Gay. New York: Routledge, 1998. xxiii–xxv.

Siddons, Sarah. "Remarks on the Character of Lady Macbeth." *Life of Mrs. Siddons.* Thomas Campbell. New York: Harper and Brothers, 1834. 123–135.

Siemon, James R. "'Nay, that's not next': *Othello,* V.ii in Performance, 1760–1900." *Shakespeare Quarterly* 37.1 (1986): 38–51.

Smith-Rosenberg, Carroll. "The Female World of Love and Ritual: Relations Between Women in Nineteenth-Century America." *Signs* 1 (1975): 1–29.

Stokes, James. "Women and Performance: Evidences of Universal Cultural Suffrage in Medieval and Early Modern Lincolnshire." *Women Players in England, 1500–1660: Beyond the All-Male Stage.* Eds. Pamela Allen Brown and Peter Parolin. Burlington, VT: Ashgate, 2005. 25–44.

Stanley Wells. "Boys Should Be Girls." *Foreign Literature Studies* 28.1 (2006): 10–15.

Terry, Ellen. *Four Lectures.* London: Martin Hopkinson, 1932.

———. *Ellen Terry's Memoirs.* Ed. Edith Craig and Christopher St. John. New York: Putnam's, 1932.

———. *The Story of My Life.* New York: Schocken Books, 1982.

Thomson, Peter. "English Renaissance and Restoration Theatre," in *The Oxford Illustrated Guide to Theatre.* Ed. John Rusell Brown. Oxford UP, 1995. 173–219.

Werner, Sarah. "Punching Daddy, or the Politics of Company Politics." *Shakespeare and Feminist Performance: Ideology on Stage.* New York: Routledge, 2001. 50–68.

Wickham, Glynne, Herbert Berry, and William Ingram, eds. *English Professional Theatre, 1530–1660*. Cambridge: Cambridge UP, 2000.

Williams, Gweno, Alison Findlay, and Stephanie Hodgson-Wright. "Payments, Permits and Punishments: Women Performers and the Politics of Place." *Women Players in England, 1500–1660: Beyond the All-Male Stage*. Eds. Pamela Allen Brown and Peter Parolin. Burlington, VT: Ashgate, 2005. 45–67.

Wilson, John Harold. All the King's Ladies: Actresses of the Restoration. Chicago: U of Chicago P, 1958.

Woodbridge, Linda. Women and the English Renaissance: Literature and the Nature of Womankind, 1540–1620. Champaign, IL: U of Illinois P, 1984.

Woolf, Virginia. *A Room of One's Own*. New York: Harvest, 1929.

5

SCHOLARSHIP AND CRITICISM

To survey the topic of women in Shakespeare from a feminist perspective is to consider not only women as images in the plays and poems, but also to consider women as readers of and writers about Shakespearean works. Prior to the feminist movements beginning in the mid-1970s, a great deal of criticism had examined the role of women in Shakespeare, and some of this criticism had even rewritten ("corrected") a number of the representations of women in his works.

However, most of these changes and responses were not feminist, for feminism is not merely a matter of giving attention to women. Indeed, among the points Virginia Woolf makes in describing her experiences searching for information about women in *A Room of One's Own*, for example, is how deeply misogynistic much writing on women can be. Criticism that explicitly labeled itself "feminist" appeared more and more frequently as the impact of the women's movement of the 1960s and 1970s began to resonate in the universities. Quickly, scholars and critics began working to articulate what a feminist methodology might mean or look like.

In 1981 Elaine Showalter suggested two broad sweeping phases of feminist criticism, one androcentric and the other gynocentric. "The first mode," which she labeled feminist critique, "is ideological; it is concerned with the feminist as *reader*, and it offers feminist readings of texts which consider the images and stereotypes of women in literature, the omissions and misconceptions about women in criticism, and woman-as-sign in semiotic systems" (Showalter 182). This mode of criticism looks to (mostly male) canonical literature and studies the images of women, celebrating positive ones and castigating negative ones. Shakespeare was, of course, a prime author to examine in terms of images of women. Not surprisingly, we find writers looking at images of women in his works almost immediately.

The second mode of criticism, which Showalter terms gynocriticism, however, takes as its focus the study of women *as writers*, and its subjects are "the history, styles, themes, genres, and structures of writing by women; the psychodynamics of female creativity; the trajectory of the individual or collective female career; and the evolution and laws of a female literary tradition" (Showalter 184–185).

With respect to Shakespeare, both the question of women as characters and women as writers are central. While truly feminist scholarship does not appear in great quantities until the latter part of the twentieth century, glimpses of it emerge now and then from the beginning. However, interestingly, in relation to Showalter's phases of criticism is the fact that the earliest points of connection to be made between women and Shakespeare do not center on images of women, but rather concern women as writers who saw themselves as following in Shakespeare's footsteps. In recent years, female poets, fiction writers, and playwrights have continued to be inspired by Shakespeare, writing works that creatively revise and write back to these earlier works. Because creative texts (e.g., poems, plays, stories) imply a critical response to the power of Shakespeare's representation of women's lives, they have been included in this survey of scholarship and criticism related to women in Shakespeare.

THE SEVENTEENTH AND EIGHTEENTH CENTURIES

Among the earliest critical responses to Shakespeare in the generation following his death are a handful of women writers who turned to the playwright himself—rather than his female characters—as a source of validation for their own writing. As Marianne Novy points out, "[i]n the seventeenth and much of the eighteenth century, before Shakespeare was enshrined in the literary canon, he had a cultural image as an outsider to many established institutions. He lacked university education; he wrote in the popular form of the drama, rather than the most prestigious form of the epic; and he broke many of the rules of dramatic construction favored by literary critics. . . . [T]here are good historical reasons why women writers, and even women readers, might feel analogously outside literary institutions and might take this Shakespeare as a model who showed that they could succeed anyway" (Novy *Women's Re-Visions* 2–3).

Shakespeare's reputation for lacking advanced formal education thus provided a precedent for women writers like Aphra Behn and Margaret Cavendish. Cavendish referenced Shakespeare's lack of advanced formal education in "A General Prologue to all my Playes" (1662) as a way to legitimize her own dramatic efforts:

Yet Gentle Shakespear had a fluent Wit,
Although less Learning, yet full well he writ;
For all his Playes were writ by Natures light,
Which gives his Readers, and Spectators sight.
But Noble Readers, do not think my Playes,
Are such as have been writ in former daies;
As Johnson, Shakespear, Beamont, Fletcher writ;
Mine want their Learning, Reading, Language, Wit:
The Latin phrases I could never tell,
But Johnson could, which made him write so well.
Greek, Latin Poets, I could never read,
Nor their Historians, but our English Speed;

I could not steal their Wit, nor Plots out take;
All my Playes Plots, my own poor brain did make. (iv)

Cavendish's claim that her works are not like those of the learned earlier writers credits her with an originality and "natural light" akin to Shakespeare's.

Aphra Behn similarly uses Shakespeare's low-level educational background as justification for her own attempt to write for the theaters. In the preface to her *The Dutch Lover*, she addresses her "Good, Sweet, Honey, Sugar-candied READER, (which I think is more than any one has call'd you yet.)" (A2). Behn (perhaps facetiously) argues that plays are merely entertainment and do not contain "learning" or moral improvements, nor need they be constrained by "musty rules of Unity" (not paginated). Writing plays, according to Behn, is a suitable endeavor for the unlearned and for women. "Plays have no great room for that which is mens great advantage over women, that is Learning: We all well know that the immortal Shakespears Playes (who was not guilty of much more of this than often falls to womens share) have better pleas'd the World than Johnsons works, though by the way 'tis said that Benjamin was no such Rabbi neither; for I am inform'd his Learning was but Grammar high" (not paginated).

Thus, Shakespeare's rise in status during the eighteenth century, along with the increased availability of his works, was particularly important to women's participation in not only scholarly and critical discussions concerning Shakespeare, but in the art and craft of creative writing as well. The elevation of Shakespeare's status as the national figure of England's greatness involved numerous activities, including the production of dozens of scholarly editions and hundreds of critical commentaries aimed at establishing Shakespeare as the English Homer. Shakespeare was available nearly everywhere, even as his reputation shifted further from popular culture and more toward high culture.

The erection of Shakespeare's monument in Poets' Corner of Westminster Abbey in 1741 and David Garrick's 1769 Stratford Jubilee heightened the nation's bardolatry. This process of canonizing an English author—one who wrote in English rather than in Greek or Latin—had a particularly significant hand in providing female writers with an entrance into important critical and literary discussions. As long as ancient languages and literatures were the primary focus of criticism and scholarship, only an elite—and mostly male—minority who possessed a classical education would be able to participate. Men and women who were literate in English but lacked training in Greek and Latin could nevertheless read and write about Shakespeare, the English Homer.

From the beginning, women not only used Shakespeare as a model to justify their own work as playwrights, but also contributed more generally to the critical debates concerning Shakespeare. In her epistolary and prefatory materials to her 1664 *CCXI Sociable Letters*, Margaret Cavendish defends the range and realism of Shakespeare's dramatic characters. Her "Letter CXXIII" in *CCXI Sociable Letters* is the first extended piece of criticism ever published on Shakespeare. "Letter CXXIII" defends Shakespeare's plays from the charge that they are base, containing only "Clowns, Fools, Watchmen, and the like" (244). Cavendish counters that the detractor

> Understands not Playes, or Wit; for the Express Properly, Rightly, Usually, and Naturally, a Clown's, or Fool's Humour, Expressions, Phrases, Garbs, Manners, Actions, Words, and Course of Life, is as Witty, Wise, Judicious, Ingenious, and Observing, as to Write and Express the Expressions, Phrases, Garbs, Manners, Actions, Words, and Course of Life, of Kings and Princes; and to Express Naturally, to the Life, a Mean Country Wench, as a Great Lady, a Courtesan, as a Chaste Woman, a Mad man, as a Man in his right Reason and Senses, a Drunkard, as a Sober man, a Knave, as an Honest man, and so a Clown, as a Well-bred man, and a Fool, as a Wise man; nay, it Expresses and Declares a Greater Wit, to express, and Deliver to Posterity, the Extravagancies of Madness, the Subtlety of Knaves, the Ignorance of Clowns, and the Simplicity of Naturals, or the Craft of Feigned Fools, than to Express Regularities, Plain Honesty, Courtly Garbs, or Sensible Discourses, for 'tis harder to Express Nonsense than Sense, and Ordinary Conversations, than that which is Unusual; and 'tis Harder, and Requires more Wit to Express a Jester than a Grave Statesman; yet Shakespeare did not want wit, to Express to the Life all Sorts of Persons, of what Quality, Profession, Degree, Breeding, or Birth soever; nor did he want Wit to Express the Divers, and Different Humours, or Natures, or Several Passions in Mankind; and so Well he hath Express'd in his Playes all Sorts of Persons, as one would think he had been Transformed into every one of those Persons he hath Described; and as sometimes one would think he was Really himself the Clown or Jester he Feigns . . . (245–246)

After listing a vast range of all the various sorts of characters, including women, Cavendish concludes, "nay, one would think that he had been Metamorphosed from a Man to a Woman, for who could Describe Cleopatra Better than he hath done, and many other Females of his own Creating, as Nan Page, Mrs. Page, Mrs. Ford, the Doctors Maid, Bettrice, Mrs. Quickly, Doll Tearsheet, and others, too many to Relate?" ("Letter CXXIII" 246).

As early critics continued to debate Shakespeare's place, not all of their writings were entirely favorable. Many of these early critics scrutinized his depiction of female characters and his revision of earlier literary portraits of women. For example, Charlotte (Ramsay) Lennox's three-volume *Shakespear Illustrated* (1753) studies Shakespeare's plays in relation to his source materials, devoting considerable attention to the female characters. Admired in her own time as a novelist, Lennox provides English translations of the presumed sources alongside plot summaries for each of the plays studied, followed by critical analyses in which she provides a comparative evaluation.

Surprisingly, Shakespeare does not always win out in the comparison, with Lennox frequently preferring the source materials' handling of characters or themes over Shakespeare's. Concerning *Cymbeline*, for example, Lennox finds great fault (and in the process reveals a strong class bias) in Shakespeare's rewriting of Boccaccio's story in which a drunken merchant bets on his wife's fidelity. She attributes "all the Absurdities of this part of Shakespeare's Plot" to his giving "the Manners of a Tradesman's Wife, and two Merchants intoxicated with Liquor, to a great Princess [Imogen], and *English* Hero [Posthumous], and a noble Roman" (I: 156).

Although she declares that overall *Measure for Measure*'s source has been "altered for the worse," she does find Shakespeare's Isabella appealing—interestingly, for many of the same reasons that modern critics often find her troubling. Whereas modern critics and productions grapple uncomfortably with Isabella's refusal to give up her honor to save her brother's life, Lennox sees this steadfastness as her chief virtue. However, the difficulty for Lennox lies in the vehemence with which Isabella, whom she calls "a mere vixen in her Virtue," berates her brother for his sin. According to Lennox, such a strong response is implausible for a "modest tender Maid." Lennox's work soon fell into obscurity, despite favorable reviews by Samuel Johnson. One possible reason may have to do with Lennox's view, which is not always laudatory and sometimes quite harsh in its criticism. Such a critical stand may not have suited what eventually became the dominant eighteenth-century move to enshrine Shakespeare as *the* national poet.

Much more popular—and positive in its assessment of Shakespeare's achievement—was Elizabeth (Robinson) Montagu's *An Essay on the Writings and Genius of Shakespear, Compared with the Greek and French Dramatic Poets: With Some Remarks upon the Misrepresentations of Mons. de Voltaire* (London: J. Dodsley, 1769). Montagu was an important literary patron and hosted the great thinkers and writers of the age in literary salons held in her home. She was also the leader of the Bluestockings, a women's literary and educational society. The Bluestockings encouraged women to write, and several women associated with this group, including Montagu, Joanna Baillie, and Henrietta Bowdler, wrote on Shakespeare.

Participating in the neo-Aristotelian debates concerning dramatic conventions, Montagu's *Essay* presents a nationalistic defense of Shakespeare's plays from critical attacks by Voltaire, "a great wit, a great critic, and a great poet of a neighboring nation, [who has] treated [Shakespeare] as a writer of monstrous Farces, called by him Tragedies; and barbarism and ignorance attributed to the nation, by which he is admired" (2). Montagu argues that Shakespeare's plays cannot be judged by classical or French standards, for the genius of his works lies in their originality. Comparing him to that other "prodigious" native monument, Stonehenge, she stresses the naturalness of his work (11). Like a number of readers before her, Montagu particularly admires Shakespeare's ability to capture the emotions of his characters: "Shakespear, seems to have had the art of the Dervise, in the Arabian tales, who could throw his soul into the body of another man, and be at once possessed of his sentiments, adopt his passions, and rise to all the functions and feelings of his situation" (35).

Any "barbarism" or "irregularity" in Shakespeare's plays, Montagu therefore insists, is a feature of his naturalness. Whereas she sees Shakespeare's drama as virile and original, she describes French drama as "effete" and characterized by "extravagant sentiments" and a slavish adherence to Aristotle's unities of time and place and to "the decorums of . . . Rank" rather than "the nature of . . . Man" (5, 36). In response to what she saw as distasteful features of Shakespeare's work,

Montagu historicizes such features, encouraging her readers to see Shakespeare in the evolution of English greatness. She characterizes the Elizabethan era as "a time when learning was tinctured with pedantry; writing was unpolished, and mirth ill-bred" (9–10).

Although her work was initially published anonymously, Montagu's identity was soon revealed, and during the following thirty years, *An Essay* was reprinted six times in English and translated into German, French, and Italian. Her work was praised by the actor David Garrick, who recommended her work as convincing evidence of Shakespeare's place as the greatest dramatic poet in the world.

Early responses by both male and female critics soon turned to questions of character. Women writing on Shakespeare especially sought out and romanticized what they saw as admirable female characters and criticized those they saw as falling short of "ideal" in terms of feminine qualities. Though not as popular as Montagu's work, Elizabeth Griffith's *The Morality of Shakespeare's Drama Illustrated* (1775) was well-received enough to merit a second edition.

The daughter of a comic actor and theater manager, Griffith experienced her greatest success as a playwright whose work was produced at Covent Garden Drury Lane from 1764 to 1779. Following Montagu's position, Griffith argues that Shakespeare is best understood as "a *model*, not a *copy*; he looked into nature, not into books, for both men and works" (vi). Intrinsic to Griffith's defense of Shakespeare's greatness is her claim that his works provide important moral lessons. Thus her focus is on illuminating the moral point underlying each play—though she confesses, however, that with regards to *Measure for Measure* she "cannot see what moral can be extracted" (35). Nevertheless, she presumes Shakespeare must have had a moral in mind and thus she proceeds "to collect together the dispersed maxims, sentiments or morals, which may be gathered from the field at large" (35).

Griffith is especially interested in character (and female characters in particular) as moral exempla for women. Some characters are models to be emulated, while others are to be taken as negative exempla, or lessons in what not to be. In her "general postscript" summing up Shakespeare's greatness as a moral philosopher and the superiority of example over precept, she makes an intriguing comment about the significance of the fact that English theater is typically viewed in the evening: "the impressions [of the performances] accompany us to our couch, supply matter for our latest reflections, and may sometimes furnish the subject of our very dreams" (527). Although she is of course following the ancient view that great literature both delights and teaches, Griffith's work points forward to modern discussions of how literature works on the human psyche.

Modern histories of Shakespearean criticism have tended to neglect the early work of women, even though these female writers' interpretations do not typically vary radically from those of their male peers, and even though some of their works were extremely influential during their time. Sometimes this neglect appears to be the result of women's work having been dismissed by contemporary male rivals who were then taken at their word by a long line of later (often, though not always, male) scholars and critics. Although generally admired by a number of respected authorities on Shakespeare, Elizabeth Montagu's work, for example, had a notable and powerful detractor in Samuel Johnson.

As Fiona Ritchie suggests, Johnson's response seems to derive from envy and "his dissatisfaction at having to share his position as Shakespeare's most eminent critic" (Ritchie 76). In other cases, the lack of interest in women's critical work seems derived from critical biases dismissive of the topics and ideas that are central to women's interests. Sometimes it is simply a matter of gender bias, as seems to be the case with Elizabeth Griffith, who has only been recently recognized as being the first to suggest that *The Tempest* was not an early play (as most of her contemporaries believed) but rather, as is now the general consensus, one of Shakespeare's last plays (Griffith 2). In other instances, female scholars worked anonymously, or their work was misattributed— sometimes intentionally so, as in the case of Henrietta Maria Bowdler. Bowdler was the first editor of *The Family Shakespeare*, and her work was first published anonymously in 1807; Bowdler's brother, Thomas, subsequently published the second edition under his name "so as to preserve the reputation of his unmarried sister" (Dobson 137).

The lack of attention to women's critical work may also be related to what Karen Grevitz has suggested is a paradoxical relation between gender and genre faced by female writers during the early periods. As Grevitz notes, the works of Charlotte Lennox, Elizabeth Montagu, and Elizabeth Griffith did not differ radically from those written by male contemporaries. However, the neglect and dismissal of these women's works reveal that literary criticism—and its requisite strong, authoritative authorial voice—was still a contested genre in which for women to work (Grevitz 64). For example, "although Charlotte Lennox's skeptical approach in *Shakespear Illustrated* was more acerbic than the time usually produced, it was also generally consistent with an atmosphere that still allowed negative assessments of Shakespeare's drama" (Grevitz 62). Grevitz attributes Montagu's greater success to the difference in attacks, with Montagu directing most of her critical energies against the French Voltaire, "offering her work as a nationalistic defense of a great cultural icon rather than a work of independent, intellectual acumen establishing a place by criticizing male, English scholars" (67). The retrieval and reassessment of work by early women Shakespearean scholars and critics continues.

THE NINETEENTH CENTURY

Despite being met with disregard and sometimes outright hostility, women continued to participate as editors and critics in the bourgeoning industry in Shakespeare scholarship. As in earlier generations of Shakespeare scholarship produced by women, many nineteenth-century writings of female Shakespeareans resonate (sometimes ironically) with questions being currently posed in the field. For example, in her 1857 *The Philosophy of the Plays of Shakespeare Unfolded*, Delia Bacon claimed that Shakespeare's plays were written by a consortium of authors, a theory that was unfortunately conflated with its author's madness and eventually taken as the ultimate example of a crackpot theory. As Juliet Fleming observes, however, "Bacon's proposition that 'Shakespeare' was the name not of an author but of a book produced by multiple hands and collaborative intellectual practices is no longer scandalous within a discipline that is currently itself working to think outside the author function" (19).

Perhaps not surprisingly, we find that among the earliest critical responses to Shakespeare's female characters were those by actresses who had performed these roles onstage. In order to perform a role, an actor must first interpret his or her character; consequently, these discussions of Shakespeare's women tended to be character-based. At the beginning of the nineteenth century, Elizabeth (Simpson) Inchbald, an actress, playwright, and novelist, was asked by Thomas Norton Longman to provide the prefaces for his twenty-five-volume series *The British Theatre: A Collection of Plays* (London: Longman, 1806–1809), including those for the twenty-four plays by Shakespeare. In her prefaces, Inchbald frequently brings to bear her experiences as both an actor and a playwright, discussing matters of dramatic performance and literary style, and approaching Shakespeare's work as both a reader and a writer. Helena Faucit similarly based her discussions on her experiences as a Shakespearean actor. Faucit saw Shakespeare's female characters as natural and lifelike, disagreeing with "those who maintain that Shakespeare was governed, in drawing his heroines, by the fact that they were acted by boys. . . . As if Imogen, Viola, and Rosalind were not 'pure women' to the very core" (329).

For non-actors writing about Shakespeare's female characters, the question of the realism and the morality of Shakespeare's characters also continued to be central during the nineteenth century. A great deal of early work on Shakespeare focused on addressing perceived inadequacies or flaws in his depictions, often correcting them by rewriting the tales and the characters. Among the most popular works related to Shakespeare during the nineteenth century were those that presented revised and adapted versions of Shakespearean tales and heroines, rendered suitable for youthful—and especially female—readers. Henrietta Bowdler (of the family whose name became synonymous with texts expurgated of offensive, obscene, or indelicate parts from the original—in other words, "bowdlerized") produced the first edition of *The Family Shakespeare* in 1807. Her brother and later at least five other family members across three generations continued to produce expurgated editions of Shakespeare's works. As Bowdler explains in her preface, her intent is to "make the young reader acquainted with the various beauties of this writer, unmixed with any thing that can raise a blush on the cheek of modesty" (I: 7). Sexual references, both direct and punning, were eliminated along with three whole plays (*Measure for Measure*, *Troilus and Cressida*, and *Antony and Cleopatra*). The Bowdlers's editions, however, were merely one set among hundreds of expurgated and expunged editions published for the more delicate tastes of the nineteenth century.

Mary Lamb co-authored with her brother Charles *Tales from Shakespeare: Designed for the Use of Young Persons*, which appeared in 1807 and was aimed at young, mostly female audiences for whom the original texts would be too unseemly. Mary Lamb wrote fourteen of the twenty tales, along with most of the prefatory materials. She proposes that girls read the *Tales* (boys are not addressed because they typically have free rein among the books in their fathers' libraries) first, and then their brothers should read carefully chosen, chaste excerpts from Shakespeare's original text. The volumes were so popular that by the end of the eighteenth century, they had been published more than seventy times, as well as translated into numerous languages, including Bengali. *Tales from Shakespeare* is still readily available for purchase even in the twenty-first century.

Indeed, paraphrases aimed at young readers formed a large subgenre in the larger nineteenth-century Shakespeare industry. Caroline Maxwell's *The Juvenile Edition of Shakespeare* appeared in 1828, promising a text devoid of "any incident, passage, or even word which might be thought exceptionable by the strictest delicacy, . . . and on no occasion has the fair purity of the youthful mind been for one moment forgot" (Maxwell iv). In 1833 Elizabeth Wright Macauley, an actress-turned-preacher, published her *Tales of the Drama*, which drew upon many early modern playwrights, including Shakespeare. According to Macauley, she translated the plays into "the more popular form of narrative," taking great care to "render the whole strictly obedient to the most refined ideas of delicacy" (5, 6). Similarly, Amelia E. Barr published her *The Young People of Shakespeare's Dramas* in 1882.

A number of works were written specifically for girls and women. Victorian culture linked Shakespeare and an agenda of moral instruction for women. The various characters in the plays were provided as examples of behavior to either imitate or avoid. Although girls and young women were presented with Shakespeare's plays in order to improve themselves, the Shakespeare they read was highly selective and heavily "improved" by editing and paraphrasing. It was rarely Shakespeare in the unadulterated original.

Viewing the experiences and conditions of Shakespeare's characters as reflective of those faced by real women, Anna Brownell (Murphy) Jameson titled her book *Characteristics of Women, Moral, Poetical, and Historical*, rather than giving it a more narrow focus on Shakespeare's fictional characters. Within her discussion, Jameson moves seamlessly from her claims about the defining "characteristics of women" to the individual Shakespearean female characters she saw as exemplifying women's generally repressed status. Dedicated to the famed actress Fanny Kemble, the two-volume study was extremely popular. *Characteristics of Women* appeared in over forty printings in four editions in both England and the US between 1832 and 1911 (the title in later editions was changed to *Shakespeare's Heroines* and *Shakespeare's Female Characters*). Jameson's original title, however, most clearly indicates her view that womanhood is exemplified in Shakespeare's female characters. The work is prefaced by a fictional dialogue between Alda (a figure for the author) and Medon, a gentleman (Jameson *Shakespeare's Heroines*, 47–74). According to Alda, "Shakespeare's characters combine history and real life; they are complete individuals, whose hearts and souls are laid open before us: all may behold, and all judge for themselves" (*Shakespeare's Heroines*, 55). Her description of the usefulness of Shakespeare's characters as models of womanhood makes them comparable, as Medon exclaims, "to those exquisite anatomical preparations of wax, which those who could not without disgust and horror dissect a real specimen, may study, and learn the mysteries of our frame, and all the internal workings of the wondrous machine of life" (Jameson, *Shakespeare's Heroines* 56).

Jameson engages critics of her day in the question of whether "Shakespeare's women are inferior to his men" by concluding that artistically, they are drawn equally well, but "[i]f these people mean that Shakespeare's women are inferior in power to his men, I grant it at once; for in Shakespeare the male and female characters bear precisely the same relation to each other that they do in nature and in society—they are not equal in prominence or in power—they are subordinate throughout" (Jameson, *Shakespeare's Heroines* 57). She also takes a positive stand on the question of whether Shakespeare sufficiently represents the range of women's experience. Both Medon and Alda list a number of female friendships among Shakespeare's heroines, as well as instances of affection between older and younger women (Jameson, *Shakespeare's Heroines* 71). Alda's character continues by raising a question that, interestingly, some current feminists such as Coppelia Kahn have posed concerning whether heroism is defined in different terms for men and women (Jameson, *Shakespeare's Heroines* 71; Kahn *Roman Shakespeare*).

> Portia, Isabella, Beatrice, and Rosalind, may be classed together, as characters of intellect, because, when compared with others, they are at once distinguished by their mental superiority. In Portia it is intellect, kindled into romance by a poetical imagination; in Isabel, it is intellect elevated by religious principle; in Beatrice, intellect animated by spirit; in Rosalind, intellect softened by sensibility. (Jameson, *Shakespeare's Heroines* 77)

Jameson claims it is difficult to name one as superior to the rest, but ultimately decides Portia unites "in a more eminent degree than the others, all the noblest and most loveable qualities that ever met together in woman" (Jameson, *Shakespeare's Heroines* 77). Though Jameson sees Portia as exemplifying womanhood at its most perfect in her combination of intellect, morality, and sentiment, she also declares that such a woman "probably never existed—certainly could not now exist" (Jameson, *Shakespeare's Heroines* 92).

Isabella comes a close second to Portia in perfection. Jameson provides an interesting commentary on Isabella's desire for a stricter restraint in the convent, which provides her with the occasion to make a positive comparison with St. Theresa and to negatively compare the types of women exemplified by Desdemona and Ophelia to Isabella. "In the convent, (which may stand here poetically for any narrow and obscure situation in which such a woman might be placed,) Isabella would not have been unhappy. . . . Such women as Desdemona or Ophelia would have passed their lives in the seclusion of a nunnery, without wishing, like Isabella, for stricter bonds, or planning, like St. Theresa, the reformation of their order, simply, because any restraint would have been efficient, as far as *they* were concerned" (Jameson, *Shakespeare's Heroines* 110; emphasis in original). Though less perfect than Portia and Isabella, Beatrice and Rosalind also figure as fine examples of womanhood, according to Jameson.

In volume two, the "characters of affection," Hermione, Desdemona, Imogen, and Cordelia, must all face false accusation of infidelity (Cordelia's being filial rather than marital). While Hermione is praised, Jameson does suggest that she (and Paulina as her helper) go too far, and perhaps are even cruel, in keeping Hermione in hiding so long past the point of Leontes's sorrowful regret and repentance. In her discussion of Lady Macbeth, who figures among the "characters of history," Jameson takes on several critics who have claimed that the queen is naturally cruel and wicked from the beginning. Jameson, however, claims such a figure is not fit for poetry (and so Shakespeare would never have created her), and, echoing Sarah Siddons's view, argues that Shakespeare's Lady Macbeth is flawed by an excessive love for her husband (Jameson, *Shakespeare's Heroines* 358–360).

Nineteenth-century women continued to demonstrate interest in scholarly and critical approaches to Shakespeare's works. The work of Mary Cowden (Novello) Clarke shows that, in spite of their more scholarly efforts, however, women are most likely to be remembered for their creative approaches to Shakespeare. Clarke is perhaps the first female professional Shakespearean scholar, earning her living by producing all areas of Shakespeareana: concordances, editions, critical studies, as well as the extremely popular *Girlhood of Shakespeare's Heroines* (1850–1852), which first appeared serially and then in a five-volume set. Clarke was the first woman to produce a scholarly edition of the plays. She also produced the first concordance to his works, and in 1879 went on to coauthor the highly respected *The Shakespeare Key*. However, Mary Cowden Clarke is perhaps most famous (or notorious) for *The Girlhood of Shakespeare's Heroines* (1850–1852), which presents fictionalized childhoods for Shakespeare's female characters. M. Leigh Noel's 1885 *Shakespeare's Garden of Girls* also provided girlhood prequel stories for Shakespearean heroines.

THE TWENTIETH AND TWENTY-FIRST CENTURIES

In the early twentieth century, some scholars continued to argue in favor of Shakespeare's realism and to pursue the question of how well Shakespearean heroines might serve as model for feminine behavior. However, a number of writers (especially early feminists) also began to conclude that representations of women by Shakespeare are limited in depth and range, and of limited use as models for modern female writers. During the centuries following the eighteenth, when the number of female writers began to increase exponentially, the increasing variety of representations of women by female writers partly illuminated both the brilliance and the limits of Shakespeare's portraits of women.

While Woolf clearly admired Shakespeare's work, for example, she ultimately argued that women's experiences and reality are only minimally reflected in his female characters. "It is true," according to Woolf, "that women afford ground for much speculation and are frequently represented; but it is becoming daily more evident that Lady Macbeth, Cordelia, Ophelia . . . and the rest are by no means what they pretend to be. Some are plainly men in disguise; others represent what men would like to be, or are conscious of not being; or again they embody that dissatisfaction and despair which afflict most people when they reflect upon the sorry condition of the human race" ("Men and Women," 65). Especially missing is a sense of the full range of women's lives, including the significance of female friendships, which is crowded out by an overemphasis on their relations to men in much of Shakespeare's writing—and in much of the writing by men in general that had hitherto dominated the field of literature: ". . . and thus the splendid portrait of the fictitious woman is much too simple and much too monotonous. Suppose, for instance, that men were only represented in literature as the lovers of women, and were never the friends of men, soldiers, thinkers, dreamers; how few parts in the plays of Shakespeare could be allotted to them; how literature would suffer! . . . —literature would be incredibly impoverished, as indeed literature is impoverished beyond our counting by the doors that have been shut upon women" ("A Room of One's Own," 87).

At the same time, many women continued to write scholarship and criticism on Shakespearean texts and theatrical history. Not all work by women, however, was gender specific, and some work by men in the nineteenth and early twentieth centuries sought to bring women into a more central focus. In 1874, for example, F.J. Furnivall, a pioneer in modern philology and cocreator of the *Oxford English Dictionary*, founded the New Shakespeare Society (among numerous other learned literary societies), which included women as equal members alongside men. As Juliet Fleming points out, many of these women gave papers on such topics as the function of similes in particular plays, questions of authorship, Shakespeare's use of medieval sources, and versification—topics that are not intrinsically woman-centered (Fleming 8–9). Nevertheless, a good many of the papers by both men and women read in the New Shakespeare Society also explored the topic of woman's nature in the plays. And women were among the many editors working under Furnivall in his nearly-countless projects.

Moreover, early in the twentieth century, two American women, Charlotte Endymion Porter and Helen Armstrong Clarke, edited three editions of Shakespeare: *The Pembroke Edition* 12 vols. (New York: 1903); *The First Folio Edition of the Works of William Shakespeare* 40 vols. (New York: 1903–1913); and *The Complete Works of William Shakespeare Reprinted from the First Folio* (London: 1906). Scholars also explored Shakespeare's historical context, including inquiry into the women in his life. Mary Rose, the Custodian of the Shakespeare Birthplace Trust from 1909–1921, for example, wrote a brief history of the women in Shakespeare's family. In 1912, Frank Harris published *The Women of Shakespeare*, in which he identified various characters from the plays with key women from his life, including his mother, Mary Arden; his wife, Anne; his daughter, Judith; and Queen Elizabeth I's lady-in-waiting Mary Fitton, whom Harris believed to be Shakespeare's mistress.

For the most part during the first half of the twentieth century, however, few studies focusing specifically on women in Shakespeare appeared. Although a handful of articles and a few books can be found sprinkled across the early decades, it wasn't until the latter half of the twentieth century that the subject of women took on significance in terms of scholarly inquiry and debate among professional Shakespeareans. The late 1970s proved to be a watershed era in the history of Shakespearean criticism as increasing numbers of women—and men—in the academy began to bring feminist questions to the study of Shakespeare's plays and poems. In 1975 Juliet Dusinberre published *Shakespeare and the Nature of Women*, the first full-length explicitly feminist study of Shakespeare. Meanwhile, Carolyn Ruth Swift organized the first special session on "Feminist Criticism of Shakespeare" at the 1976 annual meeting of the Modern Language Association (MLA). In the following years, special sessions on the topic continued to be organized for MLA and other regional conferences. Swift also joined with Gayle Greene and Carol Thomas Neely to coedit *The Woman's Part: Feminist Criticism of Shakespeare*, and in 1981 the journal *Women's Studies* devoted an entire issue to the subject (volume 9.1–2). Feminist criticism and theory has had an undeniably invigorating influence on the study of Shakespeare in the past century, and it has played a crucial role in the continuing interest in Shakespeare's works.

As Neely (and other feminist critics) pointed out early on, though, feminist criticism is not a single methodology, but rather employs many methods. Indeed, it is this characteristic that has made it difficult to precisely define the approach but also one that opens it up to vitality, adaptation, and growth. Neely's early attempt to define what feminist criticism of Shakespeare might mean drew upon the terminology used by historians Gerda Lerner and Joan Kelly to offer three "modes" of Shakespearean criticism: compensatory, justificatory, and transformational criticism (terms appear on p. 5). "Compensatory criticism" works from the assumption that women (and women characters) are worthy of critical attention. Thus critics working in this mode seek images of strong female characters in the play, emphasizing their virtues and on occasion rescuing them from previous interpretations that may have trivialized or demonized them. In addition to Dusinberre's book, early examples of this compensatory criticism include early essays by Coppelia Kahn on *The Taming of the Shrew*, L.T. Fitz [Linda Woodbridge] on *Antony and Cleopatra*, Shirley Nelson Garner on *Othello*, and Joan Klein on *Hamlet*.

Neely cautions, however, that criticism in the compensatory mode poses a number of dangers and limitations: "Influenced by their own battles for equality, feminist critics may overcompensate and attribute inappropriately or too enthusiastically to women characters qualities traditionally admired in men—for example, power, aggressiveness, wit, and sexual boldness. Reversing but not discarding the conventions and their feminism, they may compromise both their interpretations and their feminism. The mode also may find it difficult to deal with women who are not heroines and with the men who are important to all of Shakespeare's women, whether powerful or powerless" (Neely "Feminist Modes" 7).

Thus "justificatory criticism" seeks to account for the actions of female characters (as well as male characters) in the context of early modern patriarchal structures. Important examples of the justificatory mode of criticism include essays by Rebecca Smith on *Hamlet's* Gertrude, Joan Klein on Lady Macbeth, Gayle Greene on Cressida, Clara Claiborne Park on comedic heroines, and David Leverenz on Ophelia. Here as well, Neely notes the potential difficulties of this type of criticism:

> Justificatory critics differ over whether Shakespeare defends patriarchal structures, attacks them, or merely represents them. Such criticism may be led to make the structures more monolithic or oppressive than they are, to minimize both the freedom of action of individual women within them and the part such women play in determining their shape; the result may be depressing—and also imbalanced. (Neely 9)

Building on the first two modes, "transformational criticism" seeks to interrogate the interactions between female characters and the patriarchal structures that constrain, and sometimes enable, them. The goal is to transform criticism and how we see the relation between literature and culture.

A pressing question for early feminists focusing on images of female characters concerned whether we might view Shakespeare as a feminist (or protofeminist). Linda Bamber, for example, argues in *Comic Women, Tragic Men: A Study of Gender and Genre in Shakespeare* that, while Shakespeare writes from a masculine perspective, his plays nonetheless value the feminine, especially in their depiction of comedic heroines. While Gayle Greene similarly argues that Shakespeare, especially in his comedies, is more liberal than other early modern writers, she concludes that typically even Shakespeare's heroines are ultimately assimilated into the patriarchy.

In its optimism regarding Shakespeare's gendered representations, Juliet Dusinberre's *Shakespeare and the Nature of Women* exemplifies the compensatory mode of Shakespearean criticism. Historicizing Shakespeare's work in terms of contemporary ideas such as Puritan notions of spiritual equality between men and women, the presence of Queen Elizabeth I on the throne, and humanist theories about education, Dusinberre argues that the culture that produced early modern drama—not just that of Shakespeare—"is feminist in sympathy" and Shakespeare's "attitudes toward women are part of a common stock to be found in the plays of almost all of his contemporaries" (Dusinberre 5). Thus, Shakespeare's strong female characters are the result of the playwright's genius sparking off the ideological catalyst of his time. Focusing on Shakespeare's cross-dressed comedic heroines and the figures of forgiveness in the romances, Dusinberre presents Shakespeare as a proto-feminist, exploring the possibility of women's emancipation through "his skepticism about the nature of women" (Dusinberre 305).

Dusinberre's view of Shakespeare as a protofeminist was followed by other feminist critics who sought out strong female characters in the plays and argued that Shakespeare presents female characters that challenge early modern (and even modern) conventions for female behavior. Irene Dash, for example, employs close-reading techniques in *Wooing Wedding, and Power: Women in Shakespeare's Plays* to examine strong women characters in ten plays. Dash's book is divided into sections on courtship, illustrated by *Loves Labors Lost* and *The Taming of the Shrew*; sexuality, illustrated by *Romeo and Juliet*, *Othello*, and *A Winter's Tale*; and women of power, illustrated by the *Henry VI-Richard III* tetralogy and *Antony and Cleopatra*. Dash seeks to redeem the "strong, attractive, intelligent women [who] come to life in Shakespeare's plays" from past producers and literary "critics, [who have been] limited by their own perceptions of a woman's role" (1–2). According to Dash, Shakespeare created lifelike individuals in both his male and female characters. "But," she continues, "that kind of individuality in the women has seldom intrigued critics" (Dash 255).

By redeeming Shakespeare's characters, Dash also redeems their relevance for modern, feminist audiences. Moving between ideologies in early modern texts and performances by female actors, Dash argues that the plays continue to "offer insight into women's perceptions of themselves in a patriarchal world" (6). Especially interesting is Dash's analysis of prompt books that reveal some of the interpretive choices made by past productions—including some which, troubled by strong complex women such as Kate in *Shrew*, Cleopatra, and Queen Margaret in *Richard III*, have evaded the difficulties posed by such women by constraining them on stage or by cutting them altogether.

Marilyn French's *Shakespeare's Division of Experience*, on the other hand, is more ambivalent than Dusinberre and Dash about Shakespeare's position on gender, seeing him as for the most part constrained by culturally assigned gender roles. French examines Shakespeare in relation to a theory of binary gender principles, according to which certain basic human qualities such as mercy, compassion, and intuitiveness are perceived as feminine, while others such as prowess, bravery, and individualism are perceived as masculine. Though these gender principles are not inescapably linked to biological sex, French argues, society assigns certain roles according to gender and demands their enactment. Thus, female characters who act in accordance with their assigned principles bring life and mercy to counter-balance the potential lethalness of the masculine principle; female characters who transgress their assigned principle, however, are monstrous.

Seeing a progressive questioning and development, French maps the "received" ideas as they appear across the early to late plays. "More than any other poet," French argues, "Shakespeare breathed life into his female characters and gave body to the principle they are supposed to represent. Yet his dis-ease with the sexuality supposedly incarnate in women grew, as he aged, into a terrified loathing. More than any other poet of his time, according to French, Shakespeare was tormented by the consequences of power. Yet he could not imagine the world being run in any way so that power could be checked and restrained, except by the internalization, in a governing class, of the qualities of the feminine principle" (French 31). Unwilling to define Shakespeare as a feminist, French concludes that the playwright's ideas about women were as progressive as they could be, given the times.

Other feminist Shakespeareans writing in the early 1980s took the position that the plays reflected a specifically masculine perspective, countering the view of Shakespeare as androgynous poet. Rather than seeing Shakespeare as a writer able to embody all human points of view and create plays that reflect the realities of male and female experiences, such critics argued that Shakespeare wrote from a particular—and gendered—point of view.

In *Still Harping on Daughters: Women and Drama in the Age of Shakespeare*, for example, Lisa Jardine argues that the plays present a moderately enlightened view of women, but one also strongly marked by anxieties generated in response to changing attitudes and conditions for women as a result of Protestantism and humanism. In *Love's Argument: Gender Relations in Shakespeare*, Marianne Novy likewise argues for an ambivalent, and changing, relationship between the images of women in the plays and patriarchal culture of Shakespeare's time.

In *Broken Nuptials in Shakespeare's Plays*, Carol Thomas Neely demonstrates that marriages have a strong influence on the themes and structures of the plays. While the movement toward marriage is central in the comedies, according to Neely, the disruption of marital relations often stands at the center of the tragedies. In the romances, the restoration of broken marriages is emblematic of harmony in the plays. According to Neely, these contradictory depictions of marriage reflect the culture's contradictory attitudes toward women and the complexity of their status, which is one of both power and subordination.

Early feminist Shakespearean criticism that focused on anxieties in the plays often took a psychoanalytic approach, responding not only to Shakespeare's works but also to the work of earlier mainstream psychoanalytic readers of literature by calling into question the "universality" of earlier psychoanalytic analyses that presented a particularly masculine development as generally human. Key figures in feminist psychoanalytic criticism of Shakespeare include Coppelia Kahn, Janet Adelman, Murray Schwartz, Gayle Greene, Peter Erickson, Meredith Skura, Carol Neely, and Valerie Traub.

In *Man's Estate: Masculine Identity in Shakespeare*, Coppelia Kahn examines in psychological terms the patriarchal structures of the early modern family. According to Kahn, the central actions of the plays focus on the social and psychological development of men within a patriarchal world. Drawing on social historian Lawrence Stone's depiction of sixteenth-century England as structured through patrilineage, primogeniture, and patriarchy, Kahn traces the "dilemmas of masculine selfhood" as they are staged across the plays. She begins her analysis with adolescent masculinity in "Self and Eros in *Venus and Adonis*," then moves on to "Masculine Identity in the History Plays," where she argues that masculine identities develop in relation to other men. Given the dynastic concerns generated by men's place in the patriarchal world described by Stone, Kahn provides an important context for the recurring anxiety about female fidelity—and cuckoldry— that runs throughout the plays. Additionally, Kahn reads *Romeo and Juliet* and *The Taming of the Shrew* as respectively tragic and comic versions of marriage as a male rite of passage, with the latter being interpreted as Shakespeare's satire on the male urge to control women. Her final chapters focus on Shakespeare's early modern handling of the male stage of fatherhood, contrasting the tragic visions presented in *Coriolanus* and *Macbeth* with those in the late romances of *The Winter's Tale* and *The Tempest*.

Among the most influential of psychoanalytic approaches has also been that
of Janet Adelman. In her now-classic study of male anxiety and fantasies of
maternal sexuality, "'Anger's My Meat': Feeding, Dependency, and Aggression in
Coriolanus," Adelman argues that the fierce warrior personality of Coriolanus
derives from his mother, from whom he desperately craves approval. In her book-
length study, *Suffocating Mothers: Theories of Maternal Origin in Shakespeare's
Plays, Hamlet to The Tempest*, Adelman draws on the objects-relations theories
of psychologists D. W. Winnicott and Melanie Klein in order to study the
construction of male identity and the representation of women through the
attendant fantasies of female sexuality in Shakespearean tragedy after *Hamlet*.
Before *Hamlet*, as Adelman notes, mothers are for the most part absent, and
where women do appear, female power is sublimated through heterosexual
romance and holiday inversions. However, according to Adelman, "the mother
occluded in these [early] plays returns with a vengeance in *Hamlet*" as the women
in the later tragedies become the locus of male terrors and desires concerning the
potential malevolence and contamination of maternal power (10). Starting with
Hamlet, the sin of Cain and Abel (fratricide) is rewritten as the sin of Adam and
Eve (female betrayal).

> Despite Shakespeare's sometimes astonishing moments of sympathetic engagement
> with his female characters, his ability to see the world from their point of view, his
> women will tend to be . . . more significant as screens for male fantasy than as inde-
> pendent characters making their own claim to dramatic reality; as they become
> fused with the mother of infantile need, even their fantasized gestures of inde-
> pendence will be read as the signs of adulterous betrayal. (Adelman, *Suffocating*,
> 35–36)

Adelman reads both *Troilus and Cressida* and *Othello* as "versions of the
morning-after fantasy in which the madonna is transformed into the whore"
(*Suffocating*, 64). While Adelman focuses on tragedy, a genre that she argues is
structured by male fantasies of maternal origin, she includes a chapter on two
"problem plays," *All's Well That Ends Well* and *Measure for Measure*, positioning
them in the midway to Shakespeare's attempt to resolve the gender issues worked
out in his plays. Central to this endeavor, according to Adelman, are the bed
tricks in the two plays, in which Bertram and Angelo unwittingly sleep with
their own wives. "Through a version of homeopathic cure, the two bodies of the
bed trick allow both Bertram and Angelo to enact fantasies in which a virgin is
soiled—one nearly a nun, the other a Diana—only to find out that their sexual
acts have in fact been legitimate, that the soiling has taken place only in fantasy"
(Adelman, *Suffocating*, 77). Not surprisingly, the marriages ending these two
"problem plays" fail to satisfy audiences and readers.

Paradoxically, it is *King Lear*, a play with no mothers, in which, according to
Adelman, Shakespeare confronts most directly and powerfully the fear and desire
of the maternal that is at the heart of masculine identity. Although mothers
appear to be occluded in this play, "in recognizing his daughters as part of himself

he will be led to recognize not only his terrifying dependence on female forces outside himself but also an equally terrifying femaleness within himself—a femaleness that he will come to call 'mother' (2.4.56)" (Adelman, *Suffocating*, 104).

With *Macbeth* and *Coriolanus*, however, Shakespeare returns to the attempt to create a masculine world that successfully eliminates or evades the maternal. In these plays, however, Adelman sees Shakespeare hitting an "impasse," which leads him to seek a solution in the romances (164). Adelman sees Shakespeare at his most successful near the end of his career, in working through his deep ambivalence toward the figure of the mother; in *Pericles, Cymbeline, A Winter's Tale*, and *The Tempest*, Adelman presents Shakespeare as seeking more positive solutions to the dilemmas of *Hamlet*. Yet even here, Shakespeare is ultimately unable to escape his inherited psychic paradigms. While she sees *A Winter's Tale* in particular as "an astonishing psychic achievement," Adelman concludes that Shakespeare is in the end able to only momentarily "undo the legacy of *Hamlet*" (235, 237).

During the 1980s, as feminist Shakespearean criticism developed in tandem with women's historiography and women's literary history, as well as the burgeoning of critical approaches in literary studies in general, there was a marked shift toward scholarship seeking to historicize the plays and to examine female characters in the context of early modern social structures.

In 1987, for example, Lynda E. Boose called to task new historicism's monolithic and male-dominated view of state power, a view that seemed incapable of accommodating a consideration of women. Boose also emphasized that recent feminist Shakespearean scholarship "seemed to promise not only the belated exhumation of Renaissance Woman into a contemporary dialogue that would at last include her, but a newly enfranchised space for latter day Renaissance Man—a space in which he might get beyond being merely soldier, scholar, and poet and dare to explore his entitlements as son, brother, father, and husband" (717).

While questions of the extent to which Shakespeare's characters conform to the gender norms coded in his culture, and to what extent they disrupt or transform those codes, continue to engage Shakespeareans, the question of how his plays interact with other contemporary texts and ideologies—not just in relation to the state, but to the home and other realms inhabited by women as well—has become increasingly important to Shakespearean scholarship. Karen Newman's 1991 *Fashioning Femininity and English Renaissance Drama* revises new historicism by examining "the relationship of gender to power and the state" and the ways in which "gender is used, or alternatively, effaced, in the service of so-called larger political interests" (xvii). The 1991 collection of essays edited by Valerie Wayne and with an afterword by Catherine Belsey, *The Matter of Difference: Materialist Feminist Criticism of Shakespeare*, likewise was a response to the omissions of women and gender in both Marxist and new historicist studies of Shakespeare.

A number of materialist studies have focused on the question of women in relation to early modern theatrical practices. In her groundbreaking study *The*

Stage and Social Struggle, Jean Howard sought to work through the commonality among various critical approaches:

> Despite the differences dividing Marxist, new-historicist, and various feminist practices, a crucial premise uniting the work of all these groups is that no textual production simply gives an objective, impartial, or true account of the world. To represent the world is precisely to present it from a vantage point in contest with other vantage points. While it may be extremely difficult to specify the interests served by a particular representation, it is impossible for political criticism to imagine a representation not implicated in the power relations of a particular society. Consequently, in my analysis of discourses of the theater, I begin by asking the crucial question: *cui bono* [who does it benefit]? Whose interests are served by particular discourses about or representations of theater and theatrical practice? (8)

Howard's work brought to light not only the specter of women and the feminine in the anti-theatrical polemics of the time, but also the significance of women as (to quote the title of one of her chapters) "spectators, spectacles, and paying customers in the English public theater."

Materialist considerations of women and early modern theatrical practices have been more recently pursued in the collection of essays edited by Pamela Allen Brown and Peter Parolin, *Women Players in England, 1500–1660: Beyond the All-Male Stage*. These essays recover the history of women's performances outside of the public stages from which they were customarily barred. Conversely, David Mann's *Shakespeare's Women* focuses on the male actors who were "the original performers of Shakespeare's female roles and how they, and the possibilities and limitations of the representational tradition in which they worked, may have influenced his conception" (1).

Lena Cowen Orlin's work on understanding early modern households has been especially significant in terms of creating a cultural history that includes the spaces inhabited by women. Noting that in its concentration on matters of the state, conventional history has largely ignored the household, Orlin's *Private Matters and Public Culture in Post-Reformation England*, for example, instead turns to early modern domestic tragedies to "materialize the house in all its associations" (9). Caroline Bicks similarly turns her attention to the details of early modern childbirth in *Midwiving Subjects in Shakespeare's England*, highlighting the power of midwives in early modern culture. In a study of *Othello*, Dympna Callaghan likewise explores the role of needlework and laundry as part of housewifery in the play and the times ("Looking Well to Linens"). Catherine Belsey's *Shakespeare and the Loss of Eden* examines representations of the early modern family in Shakespeare's plays, Reformation versions of the Adam and Eve story, and their representations in such artifacts as furniture, tombs, and tapestry work, which she reads closely as texts on an equal footing with the dramatic texts (which she likewise treats as cultural artifacts) (Belsey 17–18).

Indeed, as Dympna Callaghan notes, "Feminist Shakespeareans no longer consider themselves as purely literary scholars but as cultural historians who are especially interested in women's own representations of themselves, which range from poetry to embroidery" (Callaghan, "Introduction," xiv). In many respects this has shifted Shakespeare from the center to the margins.

Naomi Miller, for example, reads the sonnets of Mary Wroth against not only Shakespeare but other early modern sonneteers from England, as well as from the continent—literally changing the subject, as her title indicates. Recent discussions of Shakespearean character and representations of women are likely to be situated in the context of other instances of similar early modern genres (e.g., comedies, tragedies, Petrarchanism, etc.), including examples of those written by Shakespeare's female contemporaries. Misogynist portraits of women in the plays are juxtaposed against the defenses of women in Rachel Speght's polemics and Aemilia Lanyer's vision of Eve in *Salve Deus*; Shakespearean tragedies written for public theater, such as *Othello*, *Antony and Cleopatra*, and *Richard II*, are read in light of Elizabeth Cary's *Tragedy of Mariam*, Mary Sidney's *Antonie*, and other private dramas composed by early modern women; Shakespearean sonnets are read in light of those by Mary Sidney, Anne Locke, and Mary Wroth; while questions of early modern patronage and popular literature includes considerations of Isabella Whitney and Aemilia Lanyer, as well as Shakespeare.

As a consequence of scholarship historicizing Shakespeare's female characters, combined with ongoing developments in feminist theories, recent studies of women in Shakespeare attempt to treat women in more articulated ways, acknowledging the significance of not only gender, but class, race, religion, and other factors as well in imagining who we mean when we say "women." A number of works consider questions of early modern sexuality; lesbianism and female/feminine queerness in the period; and the history of representations of female homoeroticism. Such works focusing on female friendships, as well as never-married or older virgin characters, include Valerie Traub's *Desire and Anxiety* and her *The Renaissance of Lesbianism in Early Modern England*; Marie H. Loughlin's *Hymeneutics: Virginity on the Early Modern Stage*; Mary Bly's *Queer Virgins and Virgin Queans on the Early Modern Stage*; Kathleen C. Kelly and Marina Leslie's collection *Menacing Virgins*; and Theodora Jankowski's *Pure Resistance: Queer Virginity in Early Modern English Drama*. Recent works focusing on historicizing our understanding of Shakespeare in relation to other minority identity categories also include Michelle Ephraim's *Reading the Jewish Woman on the Elizabethan Stage*, Bernadette Andrea's *Women and Islam in Early Modern England*, and Fiona McNeill's *Poor Women in Shakespeare*.

Significantly, many of these studies often focus on women in the margins of Shakespearean texts. Characters like Sycorax in *The Tempest* or the unnamed Moorish woman who is reputedly pregnant with Lancelot Gobbo's child, for example, never appear onstage. Consequently, exploring their meaning likewise entails moving Shakespeare from the center to the margins of critical inquiry. In her groundbreaking work *Things of Darkness: Economies of Race and Gender in Early Modern England*, Kim F. Hall examines the complex issue of gender, race, and colonialism in not only Shakespeare's works, but in the plays, sonnets, and travelogues of other early modern writers, as well as in paintings and jewelry and other cultural artifacts of the period.

Typical of other English sonneteers from the period, Shakespeare uses the poetic "beauty discourse" of "fairness" in the service of a developing white nationalism (Hall 62–122). In *Shakespeare Jungle Fever: National-Imperial Re-Visions of Race, Rape, and Sacrifice*, Arthur L. Little Jr. also examines the rhetoric of masculinity and whiteness in *Titus Andronicus, Othello,* and *Antony and Cleopatra* in terms of early modern England's national-imperial vision of itself. In its allusion to Spike Lee's film, *Jungle Fever,* however, and in its postscript, Little's work argues for the significance of such studies in term of understanding the racial and sexual politics not only in the early modern period, but in our own as well. Similarly, in *Racism, Misogyny, and the Othello Myth*, Celia Daileader argues the political necessity for understanding the continuing cultural obsession with stories patterned on Shakespeare's *Othello* in light of the greater factual occurrence of white male sexual predation upon black females—a phenomenon Daileader terms "Othellophilia":

> My approach to Shakespeare is first and foremost political, and my approach to the literary canon first and foremost revisionist. I argue in this book that Othellophile narratives are less concerned with the praise or blame of their black male protagonists than with the sexual surveillance and punishment of the white women who love them. In other words, Othellophilia as a cultural construct is first and foremost about women—white women explicitly, as the "subjects" of representation; black women implicitly, as the abjected and/or marginalized subjects of the suppressed counter-narrative. (Daileader 10)

Revisionist impulses lie at the heart of most current readings of Shakespeare that are consciously politicized—including feminist readings—both in terms of the meanings we derive from our readings of the texts and in terms of our understanding of Shakespeare's place and worth in our culture.

Editorial practices, however, have not always kept pace with critical practices. While female editors existed in the early centuries of Shakespearean scholarship—including nineteenth-century editors Teena Rochfort-Smith, Jane Lee, Mary Cowden Clarke, Charlotte Endymion Porter, and Helen Armstrong Clarke—feminist editing provides an important scholarly venue in which the meanings we derive from Shakespearean texts and our understanding of their place and worth are negotiated. As Laurie Maquire argues, feminists can make important contributions to what are typically considered to be "the three main components of editorial activity[:] . . . construction of the text, annotation/commentary, and introduction" (61).

Often, unacknowledged assumptions about traditional sexual politics have caused editors in the past to reassign or amend lines because they do not seem appropriately gendered for a particular character or scenario (cf. Maquire 61–63). Especially important are the interpretive imperatives generated by annotations and introductory materials framing the plays. In providing glosses and explanatory notes, for example, "[e]ditors regularly distance themselves from dietary superstitions, medical folklore, and racial stereotypes," according to

Maquire, but they often seem to concur with misogynist statements and viewpoints by describing them as "proverbial" rather than giving them a historical and cultural specificity (66). Lea Marcus, in *Unediting the Renaissance: Shakespeare, Marlowe, Milton,* and Juliet Fleming, in "The Ladies' Shakespeare," and Margreta de Grazia and Peter Stallybrass, in "The Materiality of the Shakespearean Text," similarly provide feminist histories and discussions of the political implications of editorial decisions made during the process of textual editing. Yet even feminist editions maintain the centrality of Shakespeare's texts and the limitations of the images of women in them.

"Feminist criticism," as Elaine Showalter noted several decades ago, "has gradually shifted its center from revisionary readings to a sustained investigation of literature by women. The second mode of feminist criticism engendered by this process is the study of women *as writers,* and its subjects are the history, styles, themes, genres, and structures of writing by women" (184).

It thus might seem that there is little to connect Shakespeare with Showalter's call to gynocriticism, but in fact many feminist artists have produced creative revisions that do just that. An understanding of Shakespeare continues to enhance our understanding of the works of both male and female writers who have composed out of and against the grand monuments of Shakespearean texts. Modernist writers such as Virginia Woolf and Hilda Doolittle, who wrote under the name H. D., imagined themselves in relation to the literary legacy left by Shakespeare. Virginia Woolf's Judith Shakespeare in "A Room of One's Own," for example, is both a fictional portrait by an important modernist woman writer but also a starting point for Woolf's endeavor to understand women of the late sixteenth and early seventeenth centuries.

By the River Avon, by the American poet H. D., which stands as a tribute to Shakespeare, consists of a three-part narrative poem entitled "Good Frend" and a critical essay on Renaissance lyric poetry entitled "The Guest." H. D.'s project, she claims, is a matter of "remembering Shakespeare always, but remembering him differently" (H. D. 31). Prominent among the voices in "Good Frend" is that of Claribel from *The Tempest.* H. D. provides a voice for the previously unheard, "the invisible, voiceless Claribel," the King Naples's daughter whose marriage to the African King of Tunis (on the Mediterranean coast of North Africa) is the occasion for the journey during which the royal party is shipwrecked.

For contemporary poets, such as Rita Dove and Adrienne Rich—to name just two—Shakespeare figures prominently in the critical artistic and political processes of what Rich has described as "writing as re-vision" in the sense of seeing anew (33–49). Novelists have also continued to provide greater depth and insight into minor Shakespearean characters, such as Erica Jong's *Shylock's Daughter: A Novel of Love in Venice* (originally titled *Serenissima: A Novel of Venice*), which puts Jessica at the center of *The Merchant of Venice.*

Another common strategy in rewriting, responding, and writing back to Shakespeare is to not only give voice to characters who are marginalized, as H. D. does for Claribel in *The Tempest,* but also to characters who have been demonized or otherwise represented negatively, such as Lear's daughters Regan and Gonereil, Gertrude in *Hamlet*, or Sycorax in *The Tempest*. Jane Smiley's Pulitzer-Prize-winning novel, *A Thousand Acres*, for example, resituates the story of King Lear on a 1970s Iowan farm in order to explore cultural "amnesia," the patriarchal institution of the family, and the ecological consequences of farming on women's fertility and infant mortality in the American heartland. Told from the point of view of Jenny (Gonereil), Smiley's novel revises our insight into the motivations of Jenny and Rose (Regan), both of whom have been sexually abused by their father, Larry Cook (Lear). The novel unfolds as they struggle with Daddy and Caroline (Cordelia) for control of not only the farm but also the terms of their personal histories. In "Gertrude Talks Back," Margaret Atwood gives voice to Hamlet's mother, who had been mostly mute in Shakespeare's version. In Atwood's version, we learn that Gertrude, rather than Claudius, has killed the king (19).

A number of playwrights have also revised Shakespearean stories for the stage. Interestingly, while *Othello* is a key text in the adaptations by Paula Vogel and Ann-Marie MacDonald, both playwrights have subsumed the play's original racial themes in favor of themes of sisterhood. Paula Vogel's *Desdemona: A Play About a Handkerchief* focuses on the female characters in the play, providing an extremely cynical vision of the private lives of Shakespeare's heroines, who are explicitly classed in terms of British identities. In Vogel's play, Desdemona is even worse than Iago makes her out to be to Othello. A bored rich housewife, Vogel's Desdemona entertains herself by stringing Emilia along with promises of promotion and by secretly "slumming it" in Bianca's brothel as way to spice up her sex life. The action of Vogel's play takes place in a back room of the palace, while the events of Shakespeare's original story continue to play out offstage. *Desdemona* aggressively confronts a number of important—albeit uncomfortable—feminist themes concerning not only sexuality, but also the implications of class inequities on women's relationships. Although centering on the relationships among the play's three female characters, the play refuses to provide a sentimental vision of female solidarity. Instead, *Desdemona* exposes the ways in which women's refusal to reject class and patriarchal privileges renders true sisterhood impossible, even as it renders that failure as lethal to both Emelia and Desdemona, whose murders await them in the Shakespearean plot unfolding simultaneously offstage. Indeed, while Vogel's play stops short of Desdemona's murder, the ending also opens onto the tricky question of whether a character who is in fact as duplicitous and unfaithful as Iago has claimed "deserves" her fate. Is Desdemona's death tragic only if she is innocent?

Ann-Marie MacDonald's much more popular play, *Goodnight Desdemona (Good Morning Juliet)*, provides a more affectionately sweet rendition of Shakespeare's works. MacDonald's play features the journey of self-discovery of Constance Ledbelly, a drab, academic ghostwriter and fledgling professor who has been slogging along for years on a thesis in which she argues that *Othello* and *Romeo and Juliet* were originally comedies. When her mentor betrays her by marrying her rival, Constance is thrown into a deep despair and magically/psychologically transported into the worlds of Shakespeare's plays. Constance's

theories about the plays' original genres are realized as she takes on the role of
the wise fool in the plays, thus helping both Desdemona and Juliet escape their
fatal conclusions. MacDonald's play is filled with duels, cross-dressing, and
thwarted plots of revenge, as the role Constance plays in these revised versions
also leads to her own comedic self-awakening.

Writers coming from colonized and formerly colonized cultures have been
keenly interested in *The Tempest*, despite the fact that Miranda is the only female
figure to physically appear on the island. As previously noted, H. D. gives voice
to Claribel, whose marriage to the Tunisian king is mentioned, although neither
character ever appears on stage. While the figure of Caliban has most thoroughly
occupied the imagination of a number of (mostly male) postcolonial Caribbean
writers, Sycorax and Miranda have also been of particular interest to postcolonial revisionists of Shakespeare's play, especially those seeking to explore the
roles of women in the histories of colonization. Elaine Savory's poem, "Miranda:
The First Voicing," for example, interweaves the voice of Miranda with pieces of
text not only from the play, but from postcolonial poets Kamau Brathwaite and
Derek Walcott, as well as novelists Paule Marshall and Marina Warner. Both an
insider and an outsider to the island's sexual and racial politics, Savory's Miranda
is "Old now & burdened with memories," as she muses upon "four hundred years
& my young arrogance" (Savory 3–5). Gloria Naylor's novel *Mama Day* revises
and transforms the identities born in *The Tempest*, while Paule Marshall's short
story "Brazil" similarly explores the long-term implications of colonization when
a retiring nightclub performer discovers he can no longer find his original
identity beneath the stage persona of the savage Caliban he has enacted for
decades in the clubs of Rio de Janeiro.

In his poems written in the "Sycorax video style" (a computer-generated
typeface that radically shifts in size and font through the work, sometimes putting a single word on a page), Kamau Brathwaite gives voice to Sycorax, who
speaks not only on behalf of her son Caliban, but in promotion of Afro-
Caribbean writers in general. The "Dream Sycorax" poems are intensely difficult to read, fusing classical literary content with linguistic creoles, African
and Caribbean traditions, allusions to jazz greats and Egyptian mythology, and
Creole language. They are presented in a typography that seeks to re-create
the immediacy of spoken language in print. Reclaiming Caliban's inheritance
stolen by Prospero from Sycorax, Brathwaite's poems attempt a return to the
"mother" tongue lost when Prospero and Miranda taught Caliban their language, an event that symbolizes the larger history of colonization. Addressed
to Caliban's twentieth-century editors and literary agents, Sycorax's letters
promote her son's writings, urging the publishers to value Caliban's work for
its literary merits rather than its market value. In the very act of speaking,
however, Sycorax also has to counter a Western worldview, begun with Prospero's enchantment of the island, that has claimed her dead: she must counter
those who "so completently pretending to ffforgettin . . ./ have come to
beLIEve . . . that I don't in fax / Xist" (Brathwaite, "The Dream Sycorax Letter,"
123–125).

British writer Marina Warner's novel *Indigo: Mapping the Waters* focuses on the ramifications of colonization for the colonizers generations after the event, moving back and forth between the events that served as a prequel to Shakespeare's *The Tempest* and the story's sequel in the present day. In her depiction of the events before the seventeenth-century colonial invasion of the island, Warner details the lives of Sycorax, a wise woman and healer, who cultivates the materials used in dying fabrics a deep indigo blue, and her adopted children, Dule (Caliban) and Ariel. Both children have been discarded by white colonizers. Sycorax miraculously rescues Dule from the womb of his dead mother, whose body washed ashore after being thrown overboard by the crew of a slave ship; and she takes in Ariel, an Arawak Indian girl, after white travelers leave her behind on the island. The family's isolated but relatively peaceful lives are disrupted in 1600 when British buccaneer Christopher ("Kit") Everard invades the tropical island. Ariel is seduced by Kit, who betrays her even as she seemingly betrays the islanders. Dule is captured and enslaved, and Sycorax is killed and buried beneath a tree that later becomes a shrine. Everard's descendants govern the colony, and through the centuries they amass a fortune in slave-worked indigo and sugarcane. The twentieth-century parts of the novel follow the lives of Everard's descendants, who have returned to London in the previous generation—including Miranda Everard, whose ancestry is Creole (mixed) and on whom much of the modern-day story centers. The island, however, is not left behind, and the present reverberates inescapably with the past. The voice of Sycorax links the history of the island and the family to the present through the storytelling of Serafine Killebree, the Caribbean maid brought to London with the family at the turn of the century. Serafine has cared for three generations of Everard children, both on the island and in England, including the youngest Everard girls, Xanthe and Miranda. Now in her nineties, Serafine is an ancient figure whose stories "could conjure Enfant-Béate when she wanted, even for those who had never been there, like Miranda" (Warner 51). As Miranda discovers her history and reconnects to the island, the novel explores the consequences of colonial memory and amnesia in the colonizers' descendants.

If, however, the memories to be recovered are those of the indigenous peoples and the transplanted slaves whose traditions have been silenced through the process of colonization, then Shakespeare's plays would seem to have very little to impart indeed. Yet, as Kamau Brathwaite, Michelle Cliff, and other postcolonial writers trained in Western traditions have noted, these traditions are theirs, too. As Jamaican-born writer Michelle Cliff points out in her essay, "Caliban's Daughters," she was trained in the British university system, and the precursor to her first piece of politicized writing was a dissertation thesis "on intellectual game-playing in the Italian Renaissance (which [she] negotiated through six Western languages—five living, one dead—validating [her] intellect all the while)" ("Caliban's Daughters" 38).

Moreover, in forging a new literary future, postcolonial writers often must grapple not only with recovering the past, but with uncovering the lies of the dominant narratives. Both Cliff's novels, *Abeng!* and *No Telephone to Heaven,* follow the life of Clare Savage, a privileged, light-skinned Jamaican girl from her island childhood to her emigration to the United States with her parents, to her university education in England. As Cliff comments, Clare's first name signifies her light-skinnedness and her privilege, while her surname

> is meant to evoke the wilderness that has been bleached from her skin, understanding that my use of the word wilderness is ironic, mocking the master's meaning, . . . [and her] knowledge of history, the past, [that] has been bleached from her mind, just as the rapes of her grandmothers are bleached from her skin. And this bleached skin is the source of her privilege and her power, too, she thinks, for she is a colonized child. ("Caliban's Daughters" 44–45)

In *No Telephone to Heaven*, Clare returns to Jamaica when she is summoned by her friend Harry/Harriet, a transgendered, bisexual black character (who is both Ariel and Miranda). There, she joins a revolutionary group, donating the land she inherited from her grandmother, and is ultimately killed, her body burned into the grounds on the ruins of her grandmother's plantation, eventually becoming one with the Jamaican soil.

But while Shakespeare's *The Tempest* can be said to haunt both of Cliff's novels, there is not a specific presence or point-by-point retelling of the tale. Sexual, racial, and class issues are explored through multiple characters resurrected from *The Tempest* (as well as other stories). The histories of Sycorax, Caliban, and Miranda are not literal, but allegorical. Throughout both novels, Cliff juxtaposes the dominant culture's official version of history—as well as the histories of Bertha Mason in Charlotte Bronte's *Jane Eyre* and Jean Rhys's *Wide Sargasso Sea*, Nanny of the Maroons (whom Cliff calls the "Jamaican Sycorax"), and Pocahontas—against not only Clare's personal story, but also the untold versions of Jamaican history.

As Marianne Novy observes in the introduction to her collection of critical essays about women's re-visions of Shakespeare, "Using fiction as a form of criticism, [female writers] let characters escape plots that doom them to an oppressive marriage or to death; as writers, performers, and directors, they demythologize myths about male heroism and also about female martyrdom, and they imagine stories for figures who are silent or demonized in Shakespeare's version" ("Introduction" 2).

To rewrite Shakespeare's plays is to interpret them. Conversely, to interpret them through criticism and scholarship is also to rewrite them, drawing our attention as readers to new and unexamined elements of the plays. As Margo Hendricks asks, "Who are the immigrant women who resided outside the city [of London], in Spitalfields, Moorfields, in Southwark? Who are the ethnic women who worked the 'stews' and brothels of Renaissance London? What place do these immigrant women have in our 'readings' of Shakespeare's women?" (364–365). That poets, novelists, playwrights, as well as scholars, editors, and critics still find themselves drawn to speak to, for, and sometimes even against Shakespeare's plays attests to their continued relevance and power in our lives.

WORKS CITED

Adelman, Janet. "'Anger's My Meat': Feeding, Dependency, and Aggression in *Coriolanus*." *Representing Shakespeare: New Psychoanalytic Essays*. Ed. Murray M. Schwartz and Coppelia Kahn. Baltimore: Johns Hopkins UP, 1980. 19–49.

———. *Suffocating Mothers: Theories of Maternal Origin in Shakespeare's Plays, Hamlet to The Tempest*. New York: Routledge, 1992.

Andrea, Bernadette. *Women and Islam in Early Modern England*. Cambridge: Cambridge UP, 2008.

Atwood, Margaret. "Gertrude Talks Back." *Good Bones and Simple Murders*. New York: Random House, 1994. 16–19.

Bamber, Linda. *Comic Women, Tragic Men: A Study of Gender and Genre in Shakespeare*. Stanford: Stanford UP, 1982.

Behn, Aphra. *The Dutch Lover*. London: Thomas Dring, 1673.

Belsey, Catherine. *Shakespeare and the Loss of Eden*. New Brunswick: Rutgers UP, 1999.

Bicks, Caroline. *Midwiving Subjects in Shakespeare's England*. Burlington, VT: Ashgate, 2003.

Boose, Lynda E. "The Family in Shakespeare Studies; or—Studies in the Family of Shakespeareans; or—The Politics of Politics." *Renaissance Quarterly* 40.4 (1987): 707–742.

Brathwaite, Kamau. "Asturias." *Black Renaissance/Renaissance Noir* 5.1 (2003): 125–136.

———. "The Dream Sycorax Letter." *Black Renaissance/Renaissance Noir* 1.1 (1996): 120–136.

Brown, Pamela Allen, and Peter Parolin, eds. *Women Players in England, 1500–1660: Beyond the All-Male Stage*. Burlington, VT: Ashgate, 2005.

Callaghan, Dympna. "Introduction." *A Feminist Companion to Shakespeare*. Oxford: Blackwell, 2000. xi–xxiv.

———. "Looking Well to Linens: Woman and Cultural Production in *Othello* and Shakespeare's England." *Marxist Shakespeares*. Ed. Jean E. Howard and Scott Shershow. London: Routledge, 2000. 53–81.

Cavendish, Margaret. *Playes Written by the Thrice Noble, Illustrious And Excellent Princess, The Lady Marchioness of Newcastle*. London: A. Warren, 1662.

Cliff, Michelle. *Abeng!* New York: Penguin/Plume, 1984.

———. "Caliban's Daughters: The Tempest and the Teapot." *Frontiers* 12.2 (1991): 36–51.

———. *No Telephone to Heaven*. New York: Penguin/Plume, 1987.

Dash, Irene. *Wooing Wedding, and Power: Women in Shakespeare's Plays*. NY: Columbia UP, 1981.

Daileader, Celia R. *Racism, Misogyny, and the Othello Myth: Inter-racial Couples from Shakespeare to Spike Lee*. Cambridge: Cambridge UP, 2005.

Dobson, Michael. "Bowdler and Britannia: Shakespeare and the National Libido." *Shakespeare Survey* 46 (2003): 137–145.

Dusinberre, Juliet. *Shakespeare and the Nature of Women* (1975) 3rd ed. New York: Palgrave, 2003.

Ephraim, Michelle. *Reading the Jewish Woman on the Elizabethan Stage*. Surrey: Ashgate, 2008.

Faucit, Helena. *On Some of Shakespeare's Female Characters*, Edinburgh: Blackwood and Sons, 1885.

Fitz, L.T. [Linda Woodbridge]. "Egyptian Queens and Male Reviewers: Sexist Attitudes in *Antony and Cleopatra* Criticism. *Shakespeare Quarterly* 28: (1977): 297–316.

Fleming, Juliet. "The Ladies' Shakespeare." *A Feminist Companion to Shakespeare*. Ed. Dymphna Callaghan. Oxford: Blackwell, 2000. 3–20.

French, Marilyn. *Shakespeare's Division of Experience* New York: Summit Books, 1981.

Garner, Shirley Nelson. "Shakespeare's Desdemona." *Shakespeare Studies* 9: (1976): 233–252.

De Grazia, Margreta, and Peter Stallybrass, "The Materiality of the Shakespearean Text." *Shakespeare Quarterly* 44 (1993): 255–283.

Green, Gayle. "Shakespeare's Cressida: 'A kind of self.'" In Lenz, et al. *The Woman's Part: Feminist Criticism of Shakespeare*. 133–140.

Grevitz, Karen Bloom. "Ladies Reading and Writing: Eighteenth-Century Women Writers and the Gendering of Critical Discourse." *Modern Language Studies* 33.1–2 (2003): 60–72.

Griffith, Elizabeth. *The Morality of Shakespeare's Drama*. London: T. Cadell, 1775.

H.D. [Hilda Doolittle]. *By Avon River*. New York: MacMillan, 1949.

Hendricks, Margo. "Feminist Historiography." *A Companion to Early Modern Women's Writing*. Ed. Anita Pacheco. Oxford: Blackwell, 2002. 361–376.

Howard, Jean E. *The Stage and Social Struggle in Early Modern England*. New York: Routledge, 1993.

Jameson, Anna. *Shakespeare's Heroines: Characteristics of Women, Moral, Poetical, and Historical* (1836). Ed. Cheri L. Larsen Hoeckley. Calgary: Broadview P, 2005.

Jardine, Lisa. *Still Harping on Daughters: Women and Drama in the Age of Shakespeare*. Totowa, NJ: Harvester, 1983; reprinted NY: Columbia UP, 1989.

Jong, Erica. *Shylock's Daughter: A Novel of Love in Venice* [originally titled *Serenissima: A Novel of Venice*]. New York: Norton, 2003.

Kahn, Coppelia. *Man's Estate: Masculine Identity in Shakespeare*. Berkeley: U of California P, 1981.

———. *Roman Shakespeare: Warriors, Wounds, and Women*. New York: Routledge, 1997.

———. "*The Taming of the Shrew*: Shakespeare's Mirror of Marriage." *The Authority of Experience*. Eds. Arlyn Diamond and Lee Edwards. Amherst: U of Massachusetts P, 1988. 84–100.

Klein, Joan. "'Angels and Ministers of Grace': *Hamlet* IV.v-vii." *Allegorica* 1.2 (1976): 156–176.

———. "Lady Macbeth: 'Infirm of purpose.'" In Lenz, et al. *The Woman's Part: Feminist Criticism of Shakespeare*. 240–255.

Lennox, Charlotte. *Shakespear Illustrated: or the Novels and Histories on which the Plays of Shakespear are Founded, Collected and Translated from the Original Authors: With Critical Remarks.* 3 vols. 1753; New York: AMS, reprinted 1973.

Lenz, Carolyn R. S., Gayle Greene, and Carol Thomas Neely, eds. *The Woman's Part: Feminist Criticism of Shakespeare.* Urbana: U of Illinois P, 1980.

Leverenz, David. "The Woman in *Hamlet*: An Interpersonal View." *Signs* 4 (1978): 291–308.

Little Jr., Arthur L. *Shakespeare Jungle Fever: National-Imperial Re-Visions of Race, Rape, and Sacrifice.* Stanford: Stanford UP, 2000.

Macauley, Elizabeth Wright. *Tales of the Drama.* Exeter, NH: Robinson and Towle, 1833.

MacDonald, Ann-Marie. *Goodnight Desdemona (Good Morning Juliet).* New York: Grove, 1998.

Mann, David. *Shakespeare's Women: Performance and Conception.* Cambridge: Cambridge UP, 2008.

Maquire, Laurie. "Feminist Editing and the Body of the Text." Dympna Callaghan. *A Feminist Companion to Shakespeare.* Oxford: Blackwell, 2000. 59–79.

Marcus, Lea Sinanoglou. "The Blue-Eyed Witch" and "The Editor as Tamer: A *Shrew* and *The Shrew*." *Unediting the Renaissance: Shakespeare, Marlowe, Milton.* New York: Routledge, 1996. 1–37; 101–131.

Marshall, Paule. "Brazil." *Soul Clap Hands and Sing.* New York: Athenaeum, 1961. 132–177.

Maxwell, Caroline. *The Juvenile Edition of Shakespeare.* London: Chapple, 1828.

McNeill, Fiona. *Poor Women in Shakespeare.* Cambridge: Cambridge UP, 2007.

Naylor, Gloria. *Mama Day.* New York: Ticknor, 1988.

Neely, Carol Thomas. *Broken Nuptials in Shakespeare's Plays.* New Haven: Yale UP, 1985.

———. "Feminist Modes of Shakespearean Criticism: Compensatory, Justificatory, and Transformational." *Women's Studies* 9.1–2 (1981): 3–15.

Newman, Karen. *Fashioning Femininity and English Renaissance Drama.* Chicago: U of Chicago P, 1991.

Novy, Marianne. *Love's Argument: Gender Relations in Shakespeare.* Chapel Hill: U of North Carolina P, 1984.

———. "Introduction." *Transforming Shakespeare: Contemporary Women's Re-Visions in Literature and Performance.* 1–12.

———. "Women's Re-Visions of Shakespeare, 1664–1988." *Women's Re-Visions of Shakespeare.* Ed. Marianne Novy. Urbana: U of Illinois P, 1990. 1–15.

Orlin, Lena Cowen. *Private Matters and Public Culture in Post-Reformation England.* Ithaca, NY: Cornell UP, 1994.

Park, Clara Claiborne. "As We Like It: How a Girl Can Be Smart and Still Popular." In Lenz, et al. *The Woman's Part: Feminist Criticism of Shakespeare.* 110–116.

Rich, Adrienne. "When We Dead Awaken: Writing as Re-Vision." *On Lies, Secrets, and Silence.* New York: Norton, 1979. 33–49.

Ritchie, Fiona. "Elizabeth Montagu: 'Shakespear's Poor Little Critick'?" *Shakespeare Survey* 58 (2005): 72–82.

Rose, Mary. *The Women of Shakespeare's Family.* London: Ballantyne P, 1905.

Savory, Elaine. "Miranda: The First Voicing." *The Caribbean Writer* 12 (1998): 63–72. http://www.thecaribbeanwriter.org.

Showalter, Elaine. "Feminist Criticism in the Wilderness." *Critical Inquiry* 8.2 (1981): 179–205.

Smith, Rebecca. "'A Heart Cleft in Twain': The Dilemma of Shakespeare's Gertrude." In Lenz, et al. *The Woman's Part: Feminist Criticism of Shakespeare.* 194–210.

Vogel, Paula. *Desdemona: A Play about a Handkerchief* (1994), *Adaptations of Shakespeare: A Critical Anthology of Plays from the Seventeenth Century to the Present.* Eds. Daniel Fischlin and Mark Fortier. New York: Routledge, 2000. 233–254.

Warner, Marina. *Indigo, or Mapping the Water.* London: Chatto & Windus, 1992.

Wayne, Valerie, ed. *The Matter of Difference: Materialist Feminist Criticism of Shakespeare.* Ithaca: Cornell UP, 1991.

Woolf, Virginia. "Men and Women." *Women and Writing by Virginia Woolf.* Ed. Michèle Barrett. New York: Harcourt, 1980. 64–67.

———. *A Room of One's Own.* New York: Harcourt, 1929; 1957.

6

PRIMARY DOCUMENTS

In many areas of early modern English life, the Tudor-Stuart period in England was a time of great change—and consequent backlash against that change. The impact of this instability was keenly felt by women, whose social degrees followed along with those of the families to which they belonged. Their positions also rose or fell in privilege as religions changed with the shifting governmental decrees of succeeding monarchies.

The early modern period was also a time of intense debate about the status of women in particular. Questions about the capacity for human education and salvation posed by both Catholic humanists and Protestant reformers, for example, opened the way to thinking about the nature of women and their role in the human world. The misogyny of the classical and medieval traditions continued to maintain an incredibly strong hold on the religious, philosophical, medical, and political ideologies that shaped women's lives. However, the invention of printing, which resulted in the wider dissemination of printed works and the ideas contained in them, along with rising rates of literacy, meant that women—especially of middling and upper ranks—added their voices to the debates in increasing numbers.

The documents included here provide a small sample of ideas about women and responses to those ideas that circulated during Shakespeare's time. Some of the documents are meant to provide a view of women's lives not depicted in Shakespeare's plays, while others are meant to enhance the depictions he presents on stage. While many of the texts here prescribe behavior for women, a number of them speak back not only to the ideas circulating about women but also engage Shakespeare's depiction of women in particular. In presenting these documents, I have silently modernized spellings, and I have incorporated translation or paraphrase of the original text where it seemed necessary for the understanding of nonspecialist readers.

JUAN LUIS VIVES (1492–1540)

Vives was commissioned by Henry VIII's first queen, Catherine of Aragon, to write a book on education for the royal princess Mary Tudor (later Queen Mary I). The work was translated into multiple languages, including numerous English editions, and it remained an influential text in the discussion of women's education throughout the Renaissance. (*Vives and the Renascence Education of Women*. Ed. Foster Watson. New York: Longmans, Greene, and Co., 1912. 48–55.)

DOCUMENT: "OF THE LEARNING OF MAIDS," FROM *THE INSTRUCTION OF A CHRISTIAN WOMAN*

Of maids, some be but little suited to learning: likewise as some men be unsuited, again some be even born unto it, or at least not unfit for it. Therefore they that be dull are not to be discouraged, and those that be apt, should be heart[en]ed and encouraged. I perceive that learned women be suspected of many: as who saith, the subtlety of learning should be a nourishment for the maliciousness of their nature. Verily, I do not allow in a subtle and crafty woman, such learning as should teach her deceit, and teach her no good manners and virtues: not with standing the precepts of living, and the examples of those that lived well, and had knowledge together of holiness, be the keepers of chastity and pureness, and the copies of virtues, and pricks to prick and to move folks to continue in them. . . . And she that hath learned from inborn disposition or from books to consider . . . [the worth of her chastity as the goodliest treasure], and hath furnished and fenced her mind with holy counsels, shall never find to do any villainy. For if she can find in her heart to do naughtily, having so many precepts of virtue to keep her, what should we suppose she should do, having no knowledge of goodness at all? . . . A woman, saith Plutarch, given unto learning, will never delight in dancing. But here, peradventure, a man would ask, what learning a woman should be set unto, and what shall she study? I have told you, the study of wisdom, which doth instruct their manners, and inform their living, and teacheth them the way of good and holy life. As for eloquence, I have no great care, nor a woman needeth it not, but she needeth goodness and wisdom. Nor is it no shame for a woman to hold her peace, but it is a shame for her and abominable to lack discretion, and to live ill. . . . When she shall be taught to read, let those books be taken in hand, that may teach good manners. And when she shall learn to write, let not her example be worthless verses, nor wanton or trifling songs, but some prudent and chaste sentences, taken out of holy Scripture, or the sayings of philosophers, which by often writing she may fasten the better in her memory. And in learning, as I appoint none end to the man, no more I do to the woman: saving it is meet that the man have knowledge of many and diverse things, that may both profit himself and the commonwealth, both with the use and increase of learning. But I would the woman should be altogether in that part of philosophy, that taketh upon [it] to inform, and teach, and amend the conditions. Finally, let her learn for herself alone and her young children, or her sisters in our Lord [if she is a nun]. For it neither becometh a woman to rule a school, nor to live amongst men, or speak abroad, and shake off her demureness and honesty, either all together, or else a great part; which if she be good, it were better to be at home within and unknown to other folks, and in company to hold her tongue demurely, and let few see her, and none at all hear her.

SIR THOMAS WYATT (1503–1542)

Wyatt was a prominent courtier during the reign of Henry VIII, and he is credited with popularizing the sonnet form in English court. In general terms, this poem is an allegory for unrequited love. "Whoso List" is also believed to be about Wyatt's love for Anne Boleyn. When it became clear that the king had claimed her for his own, Wyatt was forced to withdraw his courtship of her. This poem also illuminates the conflicted position held by wives whose graciousness as hostesses might make them "seem tame" or agreeable when they are in fact the property of their lord. Such is the case, for example, with Desdemona's courtesy to Cassio in *Othello*, Hermione's to Polixenes in *A Winter's Tale*, and Mistresses Ford and Page to Falstaff in *Merry Wives*. (*The Surrey and Wyatt Anthology 1509–1547 A.D.* Ed. Edward Arber. London: Oxford UP, 1900. 3.)

DOCUMENT: "WHOSO LIST TO HUNT"

Whoso list to hunt, I know where is a Hind!
But as for me, alas! I may no more!
  The vain travail hath wearied me so sore,
I am of them that furthest come behind!
Yet may I, by no means, my wearied mind
  Draw from the Deer! but as she fleeth afore,
  Fainting I follow. I leave off therefore,
  Since in a net I seek to hold the wind!
Who list her hunt, I put him out of doubt,
  As well as I, may spend his time in vain!
  And graven with diamonds, in letters plain,
  There is written, her fair neck round about,
Touch me not! for Cesar's I am;
And wild for to hold, though I seem tame!

BALDASSARE CASTIGLIONE (1478–1529)

Castiglione was a prominent Italian courtier in Urbino, Italy. Composed in dialogue form in four books, *The Courtier* defines by discussion the quintessentially perfect courtier. Book three treats the requisite qualities for a "waiting gentlewoman" (note that there is not a complimentary or even neutral equivalent term for female courtiers, "courtesans" being used to indicate prostitutes). Thomas Hoby, a diplomat in service to Elizabeth I, translated the work into English in 1561, and the work appeared in numerous subsequent editions throughout the Renaissance. Elsewhere in *The Courtier*, Castiglione uses the term "sprezzatura" to describe the seemingly effortless performance of a very difficult task or skill, one that in fact has taken a great deal of training, practice, or learning. Interestingly, sprezzatura for women, according to Castiglione, is not a matter of singing or playing instruments with apparent ease. Rather it means seeming to be naturally very beautiful without showing any signs of having been "made up." (*The Book of the Courtier: From the Italian of Count Baldassare Castiglione Done into English by Sir Thomas Hoby, 1561*. Ed. and introduction, Walter Alexander Raleigh. London: David Nutt, 1900. 220–222).

DOCUMENT: FROM THE THIRD BOOK OF *THE COURTIER*, "OF THE CONDITIONS AND QUALITIES OF A WAITING GENTLEWOMAN"

The L[ord] Julian answered: Since I may fashion this woman after my mind, I will not only have her not to practice these manly exercises so sturdy and boisterous [e.g., riding horses, playing tennis, and wrestling], but also even those that are appropriate for a woman, I will have her to do them with heedfulness and with the soft mildeness that we have said is attractive for her. And therefore in dancing I would not see her use too swift and violent tricks, nor yet in singing or playing upon instruments those hard and often divisions that declare more cunning than sweetness. Likewise the instruments of music which she useth (in mine opinion) ought to be fit for this purpose. Imagine with your self what an unsightly matter it were to see a woman play upon a drum, or blow in a flute or trumpet, or any like instrument: and this because the boisterousness of them both covers and takes away that sweet mildness which setteth so forth every deed that a woman doeth. Therefore when she commeth to dance, or to show any kind of music, she ought to be brought to it by allowing her self somewhat to be coaxed, and with a certain bashfulness, that may declare the noble shamefastness that is contrary to being boldly confident. She ought also to frame her garments to this intent, and so to apparel herself so that she appear not foolish and light. But forsomuch as it is lawful and necessary for women to set more by their beauty then men, and sundry kinds of beauty there are, these woman ought to have a judgment to know what manner garments set her best out, and be most fit for the exercises that she intends to undertake at that instant, and with them to array herself. And where she perceives in her a sightly and cheerful beauty, she ought to farther it with gestures, words and apparel, that all may betoken mirth. In like case an other that feeleth herself of a mild and serious disposition, she ought also to accompany it with fashions of the like sort, to increase that which is the gift of nature. In like manner where she is somewhat fatter or leaner then reasonable size, or paler or browner in complexion, to help it with garments, but artfully as much as she can possible, and keeping herself cleanly and handsome, show always that she bestoweth no pain nor diligence at all about it. And because the L. Gaspar doeth also ask what these many things be she ought to have a sight in, and how to entertain, and whether the virtues ought to be applied to this entertainment, I say that I will have her to understand that these Lords have willed the Courtier to know: and in those exercises that we have said are not suitable for her, the lady should know enough about "manly exercises," without actually doing them herself, to be able to recognize and praise their being well done by Gentlemen and other male courtiers. And to make a brief rehearsal in few words of that is already said, I will that this woman have a sight in letters, in music, in drawing or painting, and skilful in dancing, and in devising sports and pastimes, accompanying with that discreet sober mode and with the giving a good opinion of herself, the other principles also that have been taught the Courtier. And thus in conversation, in laughing, in sporting, in jesting, finally in every thing she shall be had in very great price, and shall entertain accordingly both with Jests and feat conceits meet for her, every person that commeth in her company. And albeit staidness, nobleness of courage, temperance, strength of the mind, wisdom and the other virtues a man would think belonged not to entertain, yet will I have her endowed with them all, not so much to entertain (although notwithstanding they may serve thereto also) as to be virtuous: and these virtues to make her such a one, that she may deserve to be esteemed, and all her doings framed by them.

I wonder then, quoth the L[ord] Gaspar smiling, since you give women both letters, and staidness, and nobleness of courage and temperance, ye will not have them also to bear rule in Cities and to make laws, and to lead armies, and men to stand spinning in the kitchen.

The L[ord] Julian answered in like manner smiling: Perhaps too, this were not amiss, then he proceeded. Do you not know that Plato (which in deed was not very friendly to women) giveth them the overseeing of Cities, and all other martial offices he appointeth to men? Think you not there were many to be found that could [have] as well skill in ruling Cities and armies, as men can? But I have not appointed them these offices, because I fashion a waiting gentlewoman of the Court, not a queen.

ISABELLA WHITNEY (FL. 1567–1573)

Whitney is the earliest known nonaristocratic woman to seek a career in writing, a career which she claims in the prefatory materials to her second book that she pursued as a result of losing her position as a servant. (*An English Garner: Ingatherings from our History and Literature*. Vol. 8. Ed. Edward Arber. Westminster: Archibald Constable, 1896. 234–238.)

DOCUMENT: "THE ADMONITION BY THE AUTHOR TO ALL YOUNG GENTLEWOMEN, AND TO ALL OTHER MAIDS, BEING IN LOVE," FROM *THE COPY OF A LETTER LATELY WRITTEN IN METRE BY A YOUNG GENTLEWOMAN TO HER INCONSTANT LOVER* (1567)

Ye Virgins, that from Cupid's tents
   do bear away the foil!
Whose hearts as yet with raging love
   most painfully do boil:

To you, I speak! For you be they
   that good advice do lack;
O if I could good counsel give,
   my tongue should not be slack!

But such as I can give, I will
   here in a few words express:
Which if you do observe, it will
   some of your care redress.

Beware of fair and painted talk!
   Beware of flattering tongues!
The Mermaids do pretend no good,
   for all their pleasant Songs!

Some use the tears of crocodiles,
   contrary to their heart:
And if they cannot always weep,
   they wet their cheeks by Art.

Ovid, within his Art of Love,
   doth teach them this same knack:
To wet their hand, and touch their eyes;
   as oft as tears they lack.

Why have ye such deceit in store?
   have you such crafty wile?
Less craft than this, God knows, would soon
   us simple souls beguile!

But will ye not leave off; but still
   delude us in this wise?
Sith it is so, we trust we shall
   take heed to feigned lies.

Trust not a man at the first sight!
   but try him well before:
I wish all Maids, within their breasts,
   to keep this thing in store.

For trial shall declare this truth,
   and show what he doth think:
Whether he be a Lover true,
   or do intend to shrink.

. . .

The little fish that careless is
   within the water clear,
How glad is he, when he doth see
   a bait for to appear!

He thinks his hap right good to be,
   that he the same could spy;

And so the simple fool doth trust
   too much before he try.

O little fish, what hap hadst thou,
   to have such spiteful fate!
To come into one's cruel hands,
   out of so happy state.

Thou didst suspect no harm, when thou
   upon the bait didst look:
O that thou hadst had Lynceus's eyes,
   for to have seen the hook!

Then hadst thou, with thy pretty mates,
   been playing in the streams ;
Where as Sir Phoebus daily doth
   shew forth his golden beams

But sith thy fortune is so ill
   to end thy life on shore;
Of this, thy most unhappy end,
   I mind to speak no more.

But of thy fellow's chance that late
   such pretty shift did make
That he, from fisher's hook did sprint
   before he could him take.

And now he pries on every bait,
   suspecting still that prick
For to lie hid in everything,
   wherewith the fishers strike.

And since the fish, that reason lacks,
   once warned, doth beware:
Why should not we take heed to that-
   that turneth us to care.

And I, who was deceived late
   by one's unfaithful tears,
Trust now for to beware, if that
   I live this hundred years.

A HOMILY OF THE STATE OF MATRIMONY (1563)

In 1547 the Anglican church produced an official compilation of sermons, *Certain Sermons, or Homilies, Appointed by the Kings Majesty, to be Declared and Read, by All Parsons, Vicars, or Curates Every Sunday in Their Churches. The Second*

Tome of Homilies, in which the marriage homily appeared, followed in 1563. The sermons were a powerful means of spreading orthodox views throughout the country. The homily on matrimony presents a paradoxical view of marriage. On the one hand, marriage is intended to provide the couple with friendship, children, and a means for avoiding sexual sins. However, the relationship is presumed to be fraught with conflict and power struggles. The sermon also holds the view of women as by nature inferior ("the weaker vessel") than men and more inclined to disrupt the household harmony. Nonetheless, the sermon also discourages husbands from beating their wives, a practice that not only disrupts prayer but is also linked to the lower-class mentalities of "the common sort of men." (*Certain Sermons or Homilies Appointed to be Read in Churches in the Time of Queen Elizabeth.* Ed. John Griffiths. London: Society for Promoting Christian Knowledge, 1864.)

DOCUMENT: FROM A HOMILY OF THE STATE OF MATRIMONY (1563)

The word of Almighty God doth testify and declare whence the original beginning of matrimony cometh, and why it is ordained. It is instituted of God, to the intent that man and woman should live lawfully in a perpetual friendly fellowship, to bring forth fruit, and to avoid fornication: by which means a good conscience might be preserved on both parties in bridling the corrupt inclinations of the flesh within the limits of honesty. . . .

. . . You husbands, deal with your wives according to knowledge, giving honor to the wife, as unto the weaker vessel, and as unto them that are heirs also of the grace of life, that your prayers be not hindered. This precept doth peculiarly pertain to the husband: for he ought to be the leader and author of love in cherishing and increasing concord; which then shall take place, if he will use measurableness and not tyranny, and if he yield some things to the woman. For the woman is a weak creature, not endued with like strength and constancy of mind: therefore they be the sooner disquieted, and they be the more prone to all weak affections and dispositions of mind, more than men be; and lighter they be and more vain in their fantasies and opinions. These things must be considered of the man . . . so that he ought to wink at some things, and must gently expound all things, and to forbear.

Howbeit, the common sort of men do judge that such moderation should not become a man: for they say that it is a token of a womanish cowardness ; and therefore they think that it is a man's part to fume in anger, to fight with fist and staff, howbeit, howsoever they imagine, undoubtedly St. Peter doth better judge what should be seeming to a man, and what he should most reasonably perform. For he saith reasoning should be used, and not fighting. Yea, he saith more, that the woman ought to have a certain honor attributed to her; that is to say, she must be spared and borne with, the rather for that she is the weaker vessel, of a frail heart, inconstant, and with a word soon stirred to wrath. And therefore, considering these her frailties, she is to be the rather spared. By this means thou shalt not only nourish concord, but shalt have her heart in thy power and will; for honest natures will sooner be retained to do their duty rather by gentle words than by stripes. . . .

Now as concerning the wife's duty: What shall become her? Shall she abuse the gentleness and humanity of her husband, and at her pleasure turn all things upside down? No surely; for that is far repugnant against God's commandment. For thus doth St. Peter preach to them: Ye wives, be ye in subjection to obey your own husbands. To obey is another thing than to control or command; which yet they may do to their children and to their family; but as for their husbands, them must they obey, and cease from commanding, and perform subjection. . . .

Howbeit, it can scantly be but that some offences shall sometime chance betwixt them: for no man doth live without fault; specially for that the woman is the more frail part. Therefore let them beware that they stand not in their faults and willfulness; but rather let them acknowledge their follies, and say: My husband, so it is, that by my anger I was compelled to do this or that: forgive it me, and hereafter I will take better heed. Thus ought women the more readily to do, the more they be ready to offend. And they shall not do this only to avoid strife and debate, but rather in the respect of the commandment of God, as St. Paul expresseth it in this form of words : Let women be subject to their husbands, as to the Lord: for the husband is the head of the woman, as Christ is the Head of the Church. . . .

Truth it is, that [women] must specially feel the griefs and pains of their matrimony, in that they relinquish the liberty of their own rule, in the pain of their travailing, in the bringing up of their children; in which offices they be in great perils, and be grieved with great afflictions, which they might be without, if they lived out of matrimony. But St. Peter saith that this is the chief ornament of holy matrons, in that they set their hope and trust in God; that is to say, in that they refused not from marriage for the business thereof, for the griefs and perils thereof. . . . O woman, do thou the like, and so shalt thou be most excellently beautified before God and all his angels and saints. . . . For, obey thy husband, take regard of his requests, and give heed unto him to perceive what he requireth of thee; and so shalt thou honor God. . . .

Even so think thou, if thou canst suffer an extreme husband, thou shalt have a great reward therefore; but, if thou lovest him only because he is gentle and courteous, what reward will God give thee therefore? Yet I speak not these things, that I would wish the husbands to be sharp towards their wives; but I exhort the women, that they would patiently bear the sharpness of their husbands. For, when either parts do their best to perform their duties the one to the other, then followeth thereon great profit to their neighbors for their example's sake. For when the woman is ready to suffer a sharp husband, and the man will not extremely entreat his stubborn and troublesome wife, then be all things in quiet, as in a most sure haven. Even thus was it done in old time, that everyone did their own duty and office, and was not busy to require the duty of their neighbors.

But yet to you that be men thus I speak: let there be none so grievous fault to compel you to beat your wives. But what say I your wives? No, it is not to be borne with that an honest man should lay hands on his maidservant to beat her. Wherefore, if it be a great shame for a man to beat his bondservant, much more rebuke it is to lay violent hands upon his freewoman. . . .

But peradventure thou wilt object that the woman provoketh thee to this point. But consider thou again that the woman is a frail vessel, and thou art therefore made the ruler and head over her, to bear the weakness of her in this her subjection. . . .

Understand that God hath given thee children with her, and art made a father, and by such reason appease thyself. Dost not thou see the husbandmen, what diligence they use to till that ground which once they have taken to farm . . .? As for an example, though [the land] be dry, though it bringeth forth weeds, though the soil cannot bear too much wet, yet he tilleth it, and so winneth fruit thereof. Even in like manner, . . . if thou wouldest diligently apply thyself to weed out by little and little the noisome weeds of uncomely manners out of [your wife's] mind with wholesome precepts, it could not be but in time thou shouldest feel the pleasant fruit thereof to both your comforts. Therefore, that this thing chance not so, perform this thing that I do here counsel thee . . . for she is thy body, and made one with thee.

But thou peradventure wilt say, that she is a wrathful woman, a drunkard, a beastly, without wit and reason. . . . Chafe not in anger, but pray to Almighty God. Let her be admonished and holpen with good counsel, and do thou thy best endeavour that she may be delivered of all these affections. But, if thou shouldest beat her, thou shalt increase her evil affections; for frowardness and sharpness is not amended with frowardness, but with softness and gentleness. Furthermore, consider what reward thou shalt have at God's hand: for, where thou mightest beat her, and yet for the respect of the fear of God thou wilt abstain and bear patiently her great offences, the rather in respect of that law which forbiddeth that a man should cast out his wife, what fault soever she be encumbered with, thou shalt have a very great reward. . . .

And although (which can no otherwise be) some adversities shall follow, . . . call upon the help and assistance of God, the Author of your marriage; and surely the promise of relief is at hand. . . . For there is no stronger defense and stay in all our life than is prayer: in the which we may call for the help of God, and obtain it; whereby we may win his blessing, his grace, his defense, and protection, so to continue therein to a better life to come. Which grant us he that died for us all: to whom be all honor and praise for ever and ever. Amen.

ISABELLA WHITNEY (FL. 1567–1573)

In addition to her *Letter . . . to her Inconstant Lover* (1567), Whitney also published a collection of poetic aphorisms (short moral and philosophical statements) titled *A Sweet Nosgay, Or Pleasant Posye: contayning a hundred and ten Phylosophicall Flowers* (1573). Appended to *A Sweet Nosgay* are also a collection of epistles or letters to members of her family along with a fictional last will and testament to the City of London, which reveals Whitney's skills in satire as well as her intimate knowledge of the city, including its less prestigious lanes and alleys. (From *A Sweet Nos[e]gay, or Pleasant Posye, contayning a hundred and ten phylosophicall flowers &c.* London: R. Jones, 1573. C6r–D2r.)

DOCUMENT: "TO HER BROTHER. GEORGE WHITNEY," FROM *A SWEET NOSGAY, OR PLEASANT POSYE, CONTAYNING A HUNDRED AND TEN PHYLOSOPHICALL FLOWERS* &C. (1573)

Good Brother when a vacant time
doth cause you hence to ride:
And that the fertile fields do make,
you from the City bide.
Then cannot I once from you hear
nor know I how to send:
Or where to hearken of your health
and all this would be known.
And most of me, for why I least,
of fortunes favor find:
No yielding year she me allows,
nor goods hath me assigned.

But still to friends I must appeal
(and next our Parents dear,)
You are, and must be chiefest staff
that I shall stay on hear.
Wherefore mine own good brother grant
me when that you are here:
To see you oft and also hence,
I may have knowledge where
A messenger to harke unto,
that I to you may write:
And also of him your answers have
which would my hart delight.
Receive of me, and eke accept,
a simple token bear:
A smell of such a Nosegay as
I do for present bear,
Unto a virtuous Lady, which
till death I honor will:
The loss I had of service hers,
I languish for it still.

Your loving (though luckless) Sister, Isabella Whitney

DOCUMENT: "TO HER BROTHER. BROOKE WHITNEY," FROM *A SWEET NOSGAY, OR PLEASANT POSYE, CONTAYNING A HUNDRED AND TEN PHYLOSOPHICALL FLOWERS* &C. (1573)

Good Brother Brooke, I often look,
to hear, of your return:
But none can tell, if you be well,
nor where you doo sojourn:

Which makes me fear, that I shall hear
your health impaired is:
And oft I dread, that you are dead,
or somthing goeth amiss.
Yet when I think, you can not shrink,
but must with Master be:
I have good hope when you have chance,
you will visit to me.
And so the fear, and deep dispair,
that I of you then had
I drive away: and wish that day
wherein we may be glad.
Glad for to see, but also for me:
will be no joy at all:
For on my side, no luck will bide,
nor happy chance befall.
As you shall know, for I will show,
you more when we do speak,
Then will I write, or yet recite,
within this Paper weak.
And so I end, and you commend,
to him that guides the skies:
Who grant you health, & send you wealth,
no less then shall suffice.

Your loving Sister. Is. W.

DOCUMENT: "AN ORDER PRESCRIBED, BY IS. W. TO TWO OF HER YOUNGER SISTERS SERVING IN LONDON," FROM *A SWEET NOSGAY, OR PLEASANT POSYE, CONTAYNING A HUNDRED AND TEN PHYLOSOPHICALL FLOWERS &C.* (1573)

Good Sisters mine, when I
shall further from you dwell:
Peruse these lines, observe the rules
which in the same I tell.
So shall you wealth posses,
and quietness of mind:
And all your friends to see the same,
a treble joy shall finde.

1. In mornings when you rise,
forget not to commend:
Your selves to God, beseeching him
from dangers to defend.
Your souls and bodies both,
your Parents and your friends:
Your teachers and your governors

so pray you that your ends,
May be in such a sort,
as God may pleased bee:
To live to dye, to dye to live,
with him eternally.

2. Then justly do such deeds,
as are to you assigned:
All wanton toys, good sisters now
exile out of your mind,
I hope you give no cause,
whereby I should suspect:
But this I know too many live,
that would you soon infect.
If God do not prevent,
or with his grace expel:
I cannot speak, or write too much,
because I love you well.

3. Your business soon dispatch,
and listen to no lies:
Nor credit every feigned tale,
that many will devise.
For words they are but wind.
yet words may hurt you so:
As you shall never brook the same,
if that you have a foe.
God shield you from all such,
as would by word or Bill.
Procure your shame, or never cease
till they have wrought you ill.

4. See that you secrets seal,
tread trifles under ground:
If to rehearsal oft you come,
it will your quiet wound.
Of laughter be not much,
nor over solemn seem:
For then be sure they'll count you light
or proud will you esteem.
Be modest in a mean,
be gentle unto all:
Though cause they give of contrary
yet be to wrath no thrall.
Refer you all to god,
that sits above the skies:
Vengeance is his, he will revenge,
you need it not devise.

5. And since that virtue guides,
where both of you do dwell:
Give thanks to God, & try hard
to please your rulers well.
For fleeting is a foe,
experience hath me taught:
The rolling stone doth get no moss
your selves have heard full oft.
Your business being done,
and this my scroll perused,
The day will end, and that the night
by you be not abused.
I some thing needs must write,
take pains to read the same:
Henceforth my life as well as Pen
shall your examples frame.

6. Your Masters gone to Bed,
your Mistresses at rest.
Their Daughters all with haste about
to get themselves undressed.
See that their Plate be safe,
and that no Spoone do lack,
See Doors & Windows bolted fast
for fear of any wrack.
Then help if need there be,
to do some household thing:
If not to bed, referring you,
unto the heavenly King.
Forgetting not to pray
as I before you taught,
And giving thanks for all that he,
hath ever for you wrought.
Good Sisters when you pray,
let me remembered be:
So will I you, and thus I cease,
till I your selves do see.

(quoth) Is. W.

DOCUMENT: "TO HER SISTER MISTERIS ANNE BARRON," FROM A SWEET NOSGAY, OR PLEASANT POSYE, CONTAYNING A HUNDRED AND TEN PHYLOSOPHICALL FLOWERS &C. (1573)

Because I to my Brethren wrote,
and to my Sisters two:
Good Sister Anne, you this might note,
if so I should not do

To you, or ere I parted hence,
You vainly had bestowed expense.

Yet is it not for that I write,
for nature did you bind:
To do me good: and to requite,
hath nature me inclined:
Wherefore good Sister take freely,
These simple lines that come from me.

Wherein I wish you Nestor's days,
in happy health to rest:
With such success in all assays,
as those which God hath blest:
Your Husband with your pretty Boys,
God keep them free from all annoys.

And grant if that my luck it be,
to linger here so long:
Till they be men: that I may see,
for learning them so strong:
That they may march amongst the best,
Of them which learning have possessed.

By that time will my aged years
perhaps a staff require:
And quakingly as still in fears,
my limbs draw to the fire:
Yet joy I shall them so to see,
If any joy in age there be.

Good Sister so I you commend,
to him that made us all:
I know you housewifery intend,
though I to writing fall:
Wherefore no longer shall you stay,
From business, that profit may.

Had I a Husband, or a house,
and all that belongs thereto
My self could frame about to rouse,
as other women do:
But til some household cares me tie,
My books and Pen I will apply.

Your loving Sister. Is. W.

MARGARET TYLER (FL. 1578)

Tyler translated and published the first part of the Spanish romance by Ortunez de Calahorra Diego, *The Mirror of Princely Deeds and Knighthood* (1578). Not much is known for certain about Tyler other than what can be gleaned from the prefatory remarks to her translation. She dedicates her work to Lord Thomas Howard, who was probably the son of Thomas Howard, fourth Duke of Norfolk. Tyler previously had served in the household of the Howards, a prominent Catholic family that became attainted (having lost its privilege to pass on property and hereditary titles) because of the fourth duke's execution in 1572 for treason (in 1584, some of his hereditary rights lost through his father would be restored to the younger Thomas Howard). Tyler's translation of Diego's romance from its Spanish original is doubly significant. First, its publication puts Tyler among the earliest English women to make a serious (if not perfectly timed) bid for literary patronage. Equally significant is Tyler's contribution to the growing English interest in prose romances, a genre which only recently had begun to cross over from the continent but would flourish in the coming decades. In her preface to the romance, Tyler defends the audacity of her writing, her choice of genre, and her decision to publish her work. She claims that if male authors can dedicate such works to women, and women can read them, then they ought to be able to "farther wade" in by producing their own translation. Tyler also follows the notion seen in Castiglione's *The Courtier* that ladies-in-waiting should know about manly deeds (though not partake in them) so they can be knowledgeable in their appreciation. In her hope that her translation "delight" her audience "with some profitable reading," Tyler provides an early English example of the classical tradition that the purpose of literature is to "delight and teach" (a point made a few years later, for example, by Philip Sidney in his *Defense of Poetry*). (*The Mirrour of Princely deedes and Knighthood: Wherein is shewed the worthinesse of the Knight of the Sunne, and his brother Rosicleer, sonnes to the great Emperour Trebetio: with the strange love of the beautifull and excellent Princesse Briana, and the valiant actes of other noble Princes and Knightes. Now newly translated out of Spanish into our vulgar English tongue*, by M.T. London: Thomas East, 1578. A3r–A4v).

DOCUMENT: "M.T. TO THE READER," FROM *THE MIRROUR OF PRINCELY DEEDS*

Thou hast here, gentle Reader, the history of Trebatio an Emperor in Greece: whether a true story of him in deed, or a feigned fable, I know not, neither did I greatly seek after it in the translation, but by me it is done into English for thy profit & delight. The chief matter therein contained is of exploits of wars, & the parties therein named, are especially renowned for their magnanimity & courage. The authors purpose appeareth to be this, to animate thereby, and to set on fire the hearts of young gentlemen, to the advancement of their lineage, by ensuing such like steps. The first tongue wherein it was penned was the Spanish, in which nation by common report, the inheritance of all warlike commendation hath to this day rested. . . . For I take the grace thereof to be rather in the reporters device than in the truth of this report, as I would that I could so well impart with thee the delight which my self findeth in reading the Spanish: but seldom is the tale carried clean from an others mouth. Such delivery as I have made I hope thou wilt friendly accept, that rather for that it is a womans work, though in a secular story, and a subject matter more manlike than seems appropriate to my sex.

But as for the manliness of the matter: thou knowest that it is not necessary for every trumpeter or drummer in the war to be a good fighter. They take wage only to incite others, though they themselves have secret injuries, and are thereby unable. So Gentle Reader if my labor in Englishing this Author, may bring thee to a liking of the virtues herein commended, and by example thereof in thy princes & countries quarrel to hazard thy person & purchase good name, . . . I neither bend my self thereto nor yet fear the speech of people if I be found backward. I trust every man holds not the plow, who wishes the ground were tilled: & it is no sin to talk of Robin Hood though you never shot in his bow: Or be it that the attempt were bold to take part in things pertaining to war, so as the ancient Amazons did, and in this story Claridiana doth, & in other stories not a few, yet to report of arms is not so odious but that it may be borne withal, not only in you men which your selves are fighters, but in us women, to whom the benefit in equal part appertains of your victories. . . .

The invention, disposition, trimming, & what else in this story, is wholly an other mans, my part none therein but the translation, as it were only in giving entertainment to a stranger, before this time unacquainted with our country guise. Indeed, the worst perhaps is this, that among so many foreign texts as daily come over, some more ancient, and some but new set forth, . . . I have notwithstanding made countenance only to this gentleman's text, whom neither his personage might sufficiently commend it self unto my sex, nor his behavior (being light & soldier-like) might in good order acquaint it self with my years.

So that the question now ariseth of my choice, not of my labor, wherefore I preferred this story before matter of more importance. For answer whereto gentle Reader, the truth is, that as the first motion to this kind of labor came not from my self, so was this piece of work put upon me by others, & they which first counseled me to fall to work, took upon them also to be my taskmasters and overseers lest I should be idle, and yet because the refusal was in my power, I must stand to answer for my easy yielding. . . . For they would say that as well the one as the other were all naught, & though peradventure I might pass unknown amongst a multitude, & not be the only one to draw attention or be the odd party in my ill-doing, yet because there is less merit of pardon if the fault be excused as common, I will not make that my defense which cannot help me, & doth hinder other men. But my defense is by example of the best, amongst which many have dedicated their labors, some stories, some of war, some Physic, some Law, some as concerning government, some divine matters, unto divers Ladies & Gentlewomen.

And if men may & do bestow such of their travails upon Gentlewomen, then may we women read such of their works as they dedicate unto us, and if we may read them, why not farther wade in then to the search of a truth. And then much more why not deal by translation in such arguments, especially this kind of exercise being a matter of more heed than of deep invention or exquisite learning, & they must needs leave this as confessed, that in their dedications they mind not only to borrow names of worthy personages, but the testimonies also for their further credit, which neither the one may demand without ambition, nor the other grant without overlightness: if women be excluded from the view of such works as appear in their name, or if glory only be sought in our common inscriptions, it mattereth not whether the parties be men or women, whether alive or dead. But to return whatsoever the truth is, whether that women may not at all discourse in learning, for men lay in their claim to be sole possessors of knowledge, or whether they may in some manner that is by limitation or appointment in some kind of learning, my persuasion hath been thus, that it is all one for a woman to pen a story, as for a man to address his story to a woman.

But amongst all my ill willers, some I hope are not so strict that they would enforce me necessarily either not to write or to write of divinity. Whereas neither durst I trust mine own judgment sufficiently, if matter of controversy were handled, nor yet could I find any book in the tongue which would not breed offence to some, but I perceive some may be rather angry to see their Spanish delight turned to an English pastime, they could well allow the story in Spanish, but they may not afford it so cheap, or they would have it proper to themselves. Of what Natures such men be, I do not wish greatly to dispute, but my meaning hath been to make other partners of my liking, as I doubt not gentle reader, but if it shall please thee after serious matters to sport thy self with this Spaniard's text, that thou shalt find in him . . . delights with some profitable reading. . . .

And thus much as concerning this present story, that it is neither unseemly for a woman to deal in, neither greatly requiring a less staid age then mine is. But of these two points gentle Reader I thought to give thee warning, lest perhaps understanding of my name & years, thou mightest be carried into a wrong suspect of my boldness and rashness, from which I would gladly free my self by this plain excuse, & if I may deserve thy good favor by similar labor, when the choice is mine own I will have a special regard of thy being pleased by my work.

So I wish thee well. Thine to use, M.T.

THOMAS NORTH (1535–1604)

North translated from French into English the Latin works of the Roman historian and biographer Plutarch. Shakespeare relied heavily on North's translation in writing his Roman plays. The selection included here depicts Cleopatra on her barge, a scene also appearing in Shakespeare's *Antony and Cleopatra* (2.2.196–245). (Thomas North. *Plutarch's Lives Englished by Sir Thomas North in Ten Volumes.* Vol. 9. Ed. W.H.D. Rouse. London: J.M. Dent, 1899. 33–34.)

DOCUMENT: FROM *PLUTARCH'S LIVES* ENGLISHED BY SIR THOMAS NORTH (1579)

Therefore, when she was sent unto by several letters, both from Antonius himself and also from his friends, she made so light of it, and mocked Antonius so much, that she disdained to set forward otherwise, but to take her barge in the river of Cydnus; the poop deck whereof was of gold, the sails of purple, and the oars of silver, which kept stroke in rowing after the sound of the music of flutes, oboes, guitars, viols, and such other instruments as they played upon in the barge. And now for the person of her self, she was laid under a pavilion of cloth of gold of tissue, appareled and attired like the goddess Venus, commonly drawn in picture: and hard by her, on either hand of her, pretty fair boys appareled as painters do set forth god Cupid, with little fans in their hands, with the which they fanned wind upon her. Her ladies and gentlewomen also, the fairest of them, were appareled like the nymphs Nereids (which are the mermaids of the waters) and like the Graces; some steering the helm, others tending the tackle and ropes of the barge, out of the which there came a wonderful passing sweet savor of perfumes, that perfumed the wharf's side, pestered with innumerable multitudes of people. Some of them followed the barge all along the riverside: others also ran out of the city to see her coming in. So that in the end, there ran such multitudes of people one after another to see her, that Antonius was left alone in the market-place, in his imperial seat, to give audience: and there went a rumor in the people's mouths, that the goddess Venus was come to play with the god Bacchus, for the general good of all Asia. When Cleopatra landed, Antonius sent to invite her to supper to him. But she sent him word again, he should do better rather to come and sup with her. Antonius therefore, to show himself courteous unto her at her arrival, was contented to obey her, and went to supper to her: where he found such passing sumptuous fare, that no tongue can express it.

RICHARD MULCASTER (1531–1611)

Mulcaster was the Headmaster of Merchant Taylors' School (1561—1586) and dedicated his treatise on educational reform to Elizabeth I. While the bulk of the treatise focuses on the education of boys, Mulcaster does devote some attention to arguing in favor of the education of girls. (Richard Mulcaster, *Positions Wherein Those Primitive Circumstances Be Examined, Which Are Necessary for The Training Up Of Children, Either For Skill in Their Book, Or Health in Their Bodies* (1581). Ed. Robert Hebert Quick. London: Longmans, 1888. 166–182.)

DOCUMENT: "THAT YOUNG MAIDENS ARE TO BE SET TO LEARNING," FROM *POSITIONS* (1581)

And to prove that [maidens] are to be trained, I find four special reasons, whereof any one, much more all, may persuade any their most adversaries, much more me, which am for them tooth and nail. The first is the manner and custom of my country, which allowing them to learn, will be loath to be contradicted by any of her countrymen. The second is the duty, which we owe unto them, whereby we are charged in conscience, not to leave them lame, in that which is for them. The third is their own inclination toward learning, which God by nature would never have given them to remain idle, or to small purpose. The fourth is the excellent effects in that sex, when they have had the help of good bringing up: which commends the cause of such excellence, and wish us to cherish that tree, whose fruit is both so pleasant in taste, and so profitable in trial. What can be said more? Our country doth allow it, our duty doth enforce it, their aptness calls for it, their excellence commands it. . . .

That young maidens can learn, nature doth give them, and that they have learned, our experience doth teach us, with what care to themselves, them selves can best witness, with what comfort to us, what foreign example can more assure the world, then our diamond at home? our most dear sovereign lady and princess, by nature a woman, by virtue a worthy, not one of the nine, but the tenth above the nine. . . .

For the matter what they shall learn, thus I think, following the custom of my country, which in that that is usual doth lead me on boldly, and in that also which is most rare, doth show me my path, to be already trodden. . . .

Reading if for nothing else it were, as for many things else it is, is very needful for religion, to read that which they must know, and ought to perform, if they have not whom to hear, in that matter which they read: or if their memory be not steadfast, by reading to revive it. If they hear first and after read of the self same argument, reading confirms their memory. . . .

As for writing, though it be discouraged, . . . many good occasions are oftentimes offered, where it were better for them to have the use of their pen, for the good that comes by it, then to wish they had it, when the default is felt: and for fear of evil, which cannot be avoided in some, to avert that good, which may be commodious to many.

Music is much used . . . to the parents delight, while the daughters be young . . . [but quickly lost] when the young wenches become young wives. For then lightly forgetting Music when they learn to be mothers, they give it in manifest evidence, that in their learning of it, they did more seek to please their parents, than to pleasure themselves. But howsoever . . . seeing it is but little which they learn, and the time as little wherein they learn, because they haste still on toward husbands, it were expedient, that they learned perfectly, and that with the loss of their penny, they lost not their pennyworth also, besides the loss of their time, which is the greatest loss of all. I meddle not with needlework, nor yet with housewifery, though I think it, and know it, to be a principal commendation in a woman: to be able to govern and direct her household, to look to her house and family. . . .

The greater borne Ladies and gentlewomen, as they are to enjoy the benefit of this education most, so they have best means to undertake it best, being neither restrained in wealth, but to have the best teachers, and greatest helps: neither abridged in time, but to ply all at full. And thus I take my leave of young maidens and gentlewomen, to whom I wish as well, as I have said well of them.

EDWARD ALLEYN (1566–1626) AND JOAN
WOODWARD ALLEYN (1572?–1623)

Edward Alleyn was an actor who, along with Philip Henslowe, held substantial shares in the Fortune and Rose playhouses, rivaling those venues in which Shakespeare had staked his fortunes. In 1592, Alleyn married Henslowe's step-daughter, Joan Woodward. Philip Henslowe's collection of papers has survived, including not only Henslowe's diaries but a number of letters written when Edward was away from home, on the road and touring during times when the London theaters were closed because of plague. These letters, along with entries about business transactions recorded in Philip Henslowe's diary, are particularly suggestive in terms of what they tell us about the important role Joan (and, to a degree, her mother, Agnes Henslowe) played in the family business, early modern marriage in practice (as opposed to the theory of conduct books and marriage manuals), and the process by which a player could become a member of the rising middling sort. During Edward's absences, Joan acted on her husband's behalf, receiving rents and serving as witness to loans and pawns made to her stepfather. As a kind of familial collaboration, Joan's tending of business affairs made possible Alleyn's traveling when the London theaters were closed, which in turn enabled him to further his career. Also recorded in both the diary and the letters are the material means by which the Alleyns would demonstrate their rise in status to the better "sort." Alleyn sends her his waistcoat and his lute and lute books to keep for him because they've become too burdensome to carry with him. We hear of payments for a bedstead and some cushions, and negotiations with the joiner for the building of items such as a court cupboard (designed not only to contain household goods but to display the most prized possessions), a bedstead, and a porthole for the bedchamber. Not only leisure items such as lutes but the more seemingly common household objects—bedsteads, court cupboards, and the like—carried great significance in terms of establishing one's identity as a person of quality. (*Henslowe Papers: Being Documents Supplementary to Henslowe's Diary*. Ed. Walter W. Greg. London: A. H. Bullen, 1907. 34–36; 59–61.)

DOCUMENT: EDWARD ALLEYN TO HIS WIFE, JOAN, WRITTEN AT CHELMSFORD, MAY 2, 1593

My good sweet heart & loving mouse I send thee a thousand commendations wishing thee as well as well may be & hoping thou art in good health with my father mother & sister I have no news to send thee but yet I thank god we are all well & in health which I pray god to continue with us in the country and with you in London, but mouse I little thought to hear that which I now hear by you for it is well known they say that you were by my lord mayor's officer made to ride in a cart you & all your fellows which I am sorry to hear but you may thank your two supporters—your strong legs I mean—that would not carry you away but let you fall in to the hands of such Tarmagants. But mouse when I come home, I'll be revenged on them. Till when, mouse I bid thee farewell. I pray thee send me word how thou dost & do send my hearty commendations to my father mother & sister & to thy own self and so sweet heart, the lord bless thee. From Chelmsford, the 2 of May 1593. Thine ever & no body's else, by god of heaven, Edward Alleyn.

DOCUMENT: EDWARD ALLEYN TO HIS WIFE, JOAN, WRITTEN AT BRISTOL, AUGUST 1, 1593(?)

Emanuel,

My good sweet mouse. I commend me heartily to you and to my father, my mother & my sister Bess, hoping in god that though the sickness be around about you, yet by his mercy it may escape your house, which by the grace of god it shall. Therefore, use this course: Keep your house fair and clean, which I know you will, and every evening throw water before your door, and in your back side, and have in your windows good store of rue and herb of grace, and with all the grace of God, which must be obtained by prayers. And in so doing, no doubt, the Lord will mercifully defend you. Now, good mouse I have no news to send you, but this: that we have all our health for which the lord be praised. I received your letter at Bristol by Richard Collier, for the which I thank you. I have sent you by this bearer, Thomas Pope's kinsman, my white waistcoat because it is a trouble to me to carry it. Receive it with this letter, and lay it up for me till I come home. If you send any more letters, send to me by the carriers of Shrewsbury or to Westchester or to York to be kept till my Lord Strange's players come. And thus sweet heart, with my hearty commendation to all our friends, I cease. From Bristol, this Wednesday after St. James' Day, being ready to begin the play of Harry Cornwall. Mouse, do heartily commend me to Mr. Grigg's wife and all his household and to my sister Phillips. Your Loving husband, E Alleyn

[p.s.:] Mouse, you send me no news of any thing. You should send of your domestical matters, such things as happen at home, as how your distilled water proves or this or that or any thing what you will. And Jug I pray you let my orange tawny stockings of woolen be dyed a very good black for when I come home to wear in the winter. You sent me not word of my garden, but next time you will but remember this in any case: that all that bed which was parsley in the month of September, you sow it with spinach, for then is the time. I would do it myself, but we shall not come home till allholland time, and so, sweet mouse, farewell, and brook our long journey with patience.

This be delivered to Mr. Henslowe, one of the grooms of her Majesty's Chamber, dwelling on the Bankside right over against the Clink.

DOCUMENT: JOAN ALLEYN TO HER HUSBAND, EDWARD ALLEYN, OCTOBER 21, 1603

Jhesus,

My Entire & well-beloved sweet heart. Still it Joys me & long I pray god may I Joy to hear of your health & welfare as you joy to hear of ours. Almighty god be thanked, my own self, your self, & my mother & whole house are in good health

& about us the sickness doth Cease, & likely more & more by gods help to Cease. All the Companies be Come home & are well for all that we know, but that Brown of the Boar's head is dead & dyed very poor. He went not into the Country at all. & all of your own Company are well at their own houses, my father is at the Court, but where the Court is I know not. I am of your own mind, that it is needless to meet my father at Basing-stoke, the uncertainty being as it is, & I commend your discretion. It were a sorry Journey to lose your labor, besides the expenses & Change of Air might hurt you. Therefore you are Resolved upon the best Course. For your Coming home, I am not to advise you, neither will I, use your own discretion. Yet I long & am very desirous to see you, & my poor & simple opinion is, if it shall please you, you may safely Come home. Here is no one now sick near us, yet let it not be as I will but at your own best liking. I am glad to hear you take delight in hawking & though you have worn your apparel to Rags the best is you know where to have better, & as welcome to me shall you be with your rags as if you were in Cloth of gold or velvet: try & see. I have paid fifty shillings for your Rent for the wharf. Mr. Woodward, my Lords bailiff, was not in town but appointed his deputy who Received all the Rents. I had witnesses with me at the payment of the money & have his quittance but the quittance cost me a groat. They said it was the bailiff's fee; you know best whether you were wont to pay it. If not, they made a simple woman of me. You shall Receive a letter from the Joyner himself & a printed bill. & so with my humble & hearty Commendations to your own self, Mr. Chaloners & his wife with thanks for your kind usage, with my good mother's kindest Commendations with the rest of your household, I end praying almighty god still to bless us for his mercies sake & so sweet heart once more farewell till we meet, which I hope shall not be long. This 21st of October 1603.

Your faithful & loving wife, Joane Alleyne

QUEEN ELIZABETH I (1533–1603)

The materials and styles of clothing worn by both men and women were prescribed according to rank and wealth. What a woman could wear was determined by her rank (often dependent upon that of her father or husband) and the disposable income of her father or husband. Cloth of gold or silver tissue, or purple silk, for example, could not be worn by women whose rank was below a countess, except for viscountesses, who could wear cloth of gold or silver in their kirtles (but not purple silk). Women whose husband were under the rank of a gentleman bearing arms could not wear satin in her kirtle; or damask, taffeta (tufted or plain), or grosgrain in her gown, except if she were an attendant upon the wife of a knight or higher rank, and if her husband had sufficient disposable income to warrant the apparel. While the proclamation included here was issued in 1597, sumptuary laws were repeatedly issued and reissued throughout the reigns of Henry VIII, Elizabeth I, and James I, perhaps an indication of their frequent violation and the difficulty of enforcing them. Following the Queen's proclamation was a lengthy table outlining what men and women beneath various ranks could not wear. (*The Gentleman's Magazine and Historical Review*. Ed. Sylvanus Urban. London: John Henries and James Parker, 1860. 259–261.)

DOCUMENT: *PROCLAMATION AGAINST THE INORDINATE EXCESS IN APPAREL* (1597)

By the Queen: Whereas the Queen's Majesty for avoiding of the great inconvenience that hath grown and daily doeth increase within this her Realm, by the inordinate excesses in Apparel, hath in her Princely wisdom and care for reformation thereof, by sundry former Proclamations, straightly charged and commanded those in Authority under her to see her Laws provided in that behalf duly executed: Whereof notwithstanding, partly through their negligence, and partly by the manifest contempt and disobedience of the parties offending, no reformation at all hath followed; Her Majesty finding by experience that by clemency, whereunto she is most inclinable, so long as there is any hope of redress, this increasing evil hath not been cured, hath thought fit to seek to remedy the same, by correction and severity to be used against both these kinds of offenders, in regard of the present difficulties of this time, wherein the decay and lack of Hospitality appears in the better sort in all countries, principally occasioned by the immeasurable charges and expense which they are put to in superfluous appareling their wives, children, and families, the confusion also of degrees in all places being great, where the meanest are as richly appareled as their betters, and the pride that such inferior persons take in their garments, driving many for their maintenance to robbing and stealing by the highway. . . . And albeit her Highness knows how she might justly make great profit from fines and taxes, as well by the executions of her Laws standing in force for the penalties already due, as also against both the said kinds of offenders for their manifest contempt against her Majesties said Proclamations; Yet her Majesty not respecting her advantages in these cases, but seriously intending the reformation of the abuses, and the common good and benefit of all her loving Subjects by these most Royall and Gracious proceedings, hath not only added by these presents such favorable tolerations and qualifications to such points of the former Laws, now standing in force, as by alteration of time may seem in some part hard to be exactly observed, but also hath commanded the due execution of those parts of those Laws that be most agreeable to this time, and easy and necessary to be observed, without charging either kind of the said offenders, for any offence already past, unless it be against such as shall hereafter offend, or not observe the special parts and branches of the Laws now standing in force, and Articles hereafter following, according to such toleration and moderation thereof, as is hereafter expressed and set down.

ANNE CLIFFORD (1590–1676)

Clifford was an extremely well-educated heiress and patron of not only the arts but a number of civic projects as well. Her extensive diaries, memoirs, and other documents make her an important figure in the study of early modern women's writing. Clifford's mother, Margaret Russell, is the primary dedicatee of Aemilia Lanyer's *Salve Deus*. As the only surviving heir to the Earl of Cumberland, Anne Clifford should have inherited the enormous northern estates of Westmoreland when her father died, because this particular entailment determined the succession regardless of sex. However, Anne's father bypassed the entailment, naming his younger brother and his male heirs as the successors. Anne's mother, who was estranged from her husband, fought to restore the inheritance. Following Margaret Russell's death, Anne continued to fight for the return of the rights to Westmoreland, a fight that put her in strong opposition to not only her first and second husbands (she was widowed), but even King James. It wasn't until all the male line on her uncle's side died out that Clifford was able to inherit the lands, which she did following the civil war. The selection here recounts her youth, in the days surrounding the death of Queen Elizabeth on March 20, 1603, her funeral on April 28, and the months preceding the coronation of James I. Throughout the events, the competition for place and status plays a primary role in the narrative she records (*The Diary of the Lady Anne Clifford*. Ed. Victoria Sackville-West. London: W. Heinemann, 1923. 3–6).

DOCUMENT: THE DEATH OF QUEEN ELIZABETH AND THE SUCCESSION OF JAMES I (1603), FROM *THE DIARY OF LADY ANNE CLIFFORD*

In Christmas I used to go much to the Court and sometimes did I lie at my Aunt Warwick's chamber on a pallet, to whom I was much bound for her continual love and care of me, in so much as if Queen Elizabeth had lived she intended to prefer me to be of the Privy Chamber [and recommend me as a maid of honor to the queen], for at that time there was as much hope and expectation of me as of any other young lady whatsoever. A little after the queen removed to Richmond she began to grow sickly, my Lady used to go thither and carry me with her in the coach and using to wait in the Coffee Chamber and many times came home very late. About the 21st or 22nd of March my Aunt of Warwick sent my Mother word about 9 o'clock at night . . . that she should remove to [her house at] Austin Friars, for fear of some commotions, the GOD in his Mercy did deliver us from it. The [24th] Mr. Flocknall, my Aunt Warwick's man, brought us word . . . that the Queen died about 2/3 o'clock in the morning. This message was delivered to my Mother and me in the same chamber where afterwards I was married. [I was at queen Elizabeth's death thirteen years and two months old; Mr. Sackville [my future husband] was fourteen, he being then at Dorset House with his grandfather and that great family. . . .] At about 10 o'clock King James was proclaimed in Cheapside by all the Council with great joy and triumph. I went to see and hear. This peaceable coming-in of the King was unexpected of all sorts of people.

Within two or three days we returned to Clerkenwell again. A little after this Queen Elizabeth's corpse came by night in a barge . . . to Whitehall [Palace], my Mother and a great company of ladies attending it, where it continued a great while standing in the Drawing Chamber, where it was watched all night by several lords and ladies, my Mother sitting up with it two or three nights, but my

Lady [mother] would not give me leave to watch by reason I was held too young. At this time we used to go very much to Whitehall, and walked much in the garden which was frequented by lords and ladies, my Mother being all full of hopes, every man expecting mountains and finding molehills. . . . When the corpse of Queen Elizabeth had continued at Whitehall as the Council had thought fit, it was carried with great solemnity to Westminster, the lords and ladies going on foot to attend it, my Mother and my Aunt of Warwick being mourners, but I was not allowed to be one, because I was not high enough in rank, which did much trouble me then, but yet I stood in the church at Westminster to see the solemnities performed.

A little after this my Lady and a great deal of company . . . went to Theobald's Palace to see the King who used my Mother and aunt very graciously, but we all saw a great change between the fashion of the Court as it is now and of that in the queen's time, for we were all infested with lice by sitting in the chamber of Sir Thomas Erskine. As the King came out of Scotland, when he lay at York, there was a strife between my Father and Lord Burleigh [over] who should carry the sword. It was adjudged on my Father's side because it was an office by inheritance and so it lineally descended to me.

From Theobalds the King went to the Charterhouse, where . . . he created many barons, . . . and for nights they were innumerable. All this spring I had my health very well. My father used to come to us sometimes at Clerkenwell but not often, for he had at this time as it were wholly left my Mother, yet the house was still at his charge.

JOHN FLETCHER (1575–1625)

Fletcher was a highly successful and influential playwright who collaborated with a number of London's most important literary talents, including Shakespeare. Fletcher succeeded as resident playwright to the King's Men following Shakespeare's death. *The Woman's Prize: Or, the Tamer Tamed* is a sequel to Shakespeare's *The Taming of the Shrew*. Petruchio, who is now a widower, has just married his second wife, Maria, and as the play opens the wedding guests take bets on how long it will take for Petruchio to tame his new bride and whether he will tame her to death as he did his first wife, Katherine. Before the marriage can be consummated, however, Bianca arrives to warn Maria of the taming that lies ahead. Maria enlists her more conventional sister Livia (a parallel to Bianca's character in the first play), and the trio mounts a women's rebellion which is later supported by troops of country and city women. Maria vows that Petruchio will not be allowed into her bed until he gives up his desire to master her. In this scene, Maria provides an alternative way of thinking about the analogy Shakespeare's Petruchio makes between taming wives and taming hawks. According to Maria, a woman who "lives a prisoner to her husband's pleasure, / Has lost her making, and becomes a beast"—that is, she forgets God's purpose in creating her. Rather than submit easily, the mature woman (one that "hath wing, and knows it") will not sell herself cheaply. While Shakespeare's Petruchio claims that by depriving his wife, she will come to know her keeper's call, Fletcher's Maria advises women hold out until their demands are met. For them their husbands will "Be glad to fling out trains, and golden ones, / To take her down again." Her speech creates a pun on "trains," which means simultaneously the lines of meat a trainer puts out to lure his hawk, but also the long trailing skirt of a lady's fancy gown and the group of servants or ladies-in-waiting attending her. Maria ultimately succeeds in running Petruchio through his paces and "taming" him. The play ends with the couple happily reconciled and a call for equality, with neither partner exerting tyranny over the other. (*The Woman's Prize: Or, the Tamer Tamed* [ca. 1604–22; publ. 1647]. *The Works of Beaumont and Fletcher 1579–1625.* Ed. George Darley. London: Routledge, 1883. 203–231.)

DOCUMENT: FROM *THE WOMAN'S PRIZE: OR, THE TAMER TAMED* (ACT 1, SCENE 2)

Bianca: Nay, never look for merry hour, Maria,
If now you make it not: Let not your blushes,
Your modesty, and tenderness of spirit,
Make you continual anvil to his anger!
Believe me, since his first wife set him going,
Nothing can bind his rage: Take your own council;
Yon shall not say that I persuaded you.
But if you suffer him—
Maria: Stay! shall I do it?
Bianca: Have you a stomach to't?
Maria: I never showed it.
Bianca: 'Twill show the rarer and the stronger in you.
But do not say I urged you.
Maria: I am perfect.
Like Curtius, to redeem my country, have I leaped
Into this gulf of marriage; and I'll do it.
Farewell, all poorer thoughts, but spite and anger,
Till I have wrought a miracle!—Now, cousin,
I am no more the gentle, tame Maria:
Mistake me not; I have a new soul in me,
Wide of a north-wind, nothing but tempest;
And, like a tempest, shall it make all ruins,
Till I have run my will out!
Bianca: This is brave now,
If you continue it: But, your own will lead you!
Maria: Adieu, all tenderness! I dare continue.
Maids that are made of fears, and modest blushes,
View me, and love example!
Bianca: Here's your sister.
Maria: Here's the brave old man's love—
Bianca: That loves the young man.
Maria: Ay, and hold thee there, wench.
What a grief of heart is't,

When Paphos' revels should up-rouse old Night,
To sweat against a cork, to lie and tell
The clock o' th' lungs, to rise sport-starved!
Livia: Dear sister,
Where have you been, you talk thus?
Maria: Why at church, wench;
"Where I am tied to talk thus: I'm a wife now.
Livia: It seems so, and a modest!
Maria: You're an ass:
When thou art married once, thy modesty
will never buy thee pins.
Livia: 'Bless me!
Maria: From what?
Bianca: From such a tame fool as our cousin Livia!
You are not mad?
Maria: Yes, wench, and so must you be,
Or none of our acquaintance, (mark me, Livia,)
Or indeed fit for our sex. 'Tis bed-time:
Pardon me, yellow Hymen [Roman god of marriage], that I mean
Thine offerings to protract, or to keep fasting
My valiant bridegroom!
Livia: Whither will this woman?
Bianca: You may perceive her end.
Livia: Or rather fear it.
Maria: Dare you be partner in it?
Livia: Leave it, Maria
(I fear I have seen too much) for goodness leave it!
Undress yourself with obedient hands; and get to bed!
Maria: To bed? No, Livia; there are comets
Prodigious over that yet; there's a fellow hang
Must yet, before I know that heat—(don't be startled, wench,)
Be made a man, for yet he is a monster;
Here must his head be, Livia.
Livia: Never hope it:
'Tis as easy with a sieve to scoop the ocean, as
To tame Petruchio.
Maria: Stay!— Lucina [Roman goddess of childbirth], hear me!
Never unlock the treasure of my womb,
For human fruit to make it capable;
Nor never with thy secret hand make brief
A mother's labour to me; if I do
Give way unto my married husband's will,
Or be a wife in anything but hopes,
Till I have made him easy as a child,
And tame as fear! He shall not win a smile,
Or a pleased look, from this austerity,
Though it would pull another jointure from him,
And make him every day another man.
And when I kiss him, till I have my will,

May I be barren of delights, and know
Only what pleasures are in dreams and guesses!
Livia: A strange preface to a learned speech!
Bianca: All the several wrongs
Done by imperious husbands to their wives
These thousand years and upwards, strengthen thee!
Thou hast a brave cause.
Maria: And I'll do it bravely,
Or may I knit my life out ever after!
Livia: In what part of the world got she this spirit?
Yet pray, Maria, look before you, truly!
Besides the disobedience of a wife,
(Which you will find a heavy imputation,
Which yet I cannot think your own) it shows
So distant from your sweetness—
Maria: 'Tis, I swear.
Livia: Weigh but the person, and the hopes you have
To work this desperate cure!
Maria: A weaker subject
Would shame the end I aim at. Disobedience?
You talk too tamely: by the faith I have
In mine own noble will, that childish woman
That lives a prisoner to her husband's pleasure,
Has lost [God's purpose in] her making, and becomes a beast,
Created for his use, not fellowship!
Livia: His first wife [Katerhine Minola] said as much.
Maria: She was a fool,
And took a scurvy course: Let her be named
Amongst those that wish for things, but dare not do 'em;
I have a new dance for him.
Liva: Are you of this faith?
Bianca: Yes, truly; and will die in it.
Livia: Why then, let's all wear breeches!
Maria: Now thou comest near the nature of a woman:
Hang these tame-hearted young hawks, that no sooner
See the bait set out, and hear their husband's holla,
But cry like scavenger birds upon 'em: The free hawk in spirit and plume
(Which is that woman that hath wing, and knows it),
Will make an hundred refusals to take the lure,
To show her freedom, sail in every air,
And look out every pleasure, not regarding
Lure nor quarry till her pitch command
What she desires; making her foundered keeper
Be glad to fling out trains, and golden ones,
To take her down again.
Livia: You're learned, sister;
Yet I say still, take heed!
Maria: A witty saying!
I'll tell thee, Livia; had this fellow tired

As many wives as horses under him,
With spurring of their patience; had he got
A patent, with an office to reclaim us,
Confirmed by parliament; had he all the malice
And subtlety of devils, or of us,
Or anything that's worse than both—
Livia: Hey, hey, boys! this is excellent!
Maria: Or could he
Cast his wives new again, like bells, to make 'em
Sound to his will; or had the fearful name
Of the first breaker of wild women; yet,
Yet would I undertake this man, thus single;
And, spite of all the freedom he has reached to,
Turn him and bend him as I list, and mould him
Into a babe again, that aged women,
Lacking both teeth and spleen, may master him.
Bianca: Thou wilt be chronicled in the history books.
Maria: That's all I aim at.
Livia: I must confess I do with all my heart
Hate an imperious husband, and in time
Might be so wrought upon—
Bianca: To make him cuckold?
Maria: If he deserve it.
Livia: Then I'll leave ye, ladies.
Bianca: Thou hast not so much noble anger in thee.
Maria: Go sleep, go sleep! What we intend to do
Lies not for such starved souls as thou hast, Livia.
I.ivia: Good night! The bridegroom will be with you presently.
Maria: That's more than you know.
Livia: If you work upon him
As you have promised, you may give example,
Which no doubt will be followed.
Maria: So!
Bianca: Good night! We'll trouble you no farther.
Maria: If you intend no good, pray do no harm!
Livia: None, but pray for you! [Exit]
Bianca: Cheer, wench!
Maria: Now, Bianca,
Those wits we have, let's wind them to the height!
My rest is up, wench, and I pull for that [which]
Will make me ever famous. They that lay
Foundations are half-builders, all men say.

FRANCIS BEAUMONT (1584–1616)

Beaumont typically collaborated in playwriting with John Fletcher, but *The Knight of the Burning Pestle* (perf. 1607; publ. 1613) is one of his solo endeavors. In this comedy, the entire play consists of a play-within-a-play. Actually, there are two plays within the larger play: The overall plot of the play concerns a London grocer and his wife, George and Nell, who have come to the theater to see a play. As a grocer, George is a member of one of London's Twelve Great Livery Companies (freemen in the theatrical companies had to be members of one of these companies, the theatrical companies not having the same civic privileges or power). However, upon hearing that the play about to be presented is *The London Merchant*, George becomes certain that the play will be a city comedy meant to satirize people like him—people of the middling sort (e.g., middle class grocers and merchants). He and Nell insist the players change the play immediately, and his wife decides that what they really would prefer to see is a tale of a knight who slays a dragon. In spite of the theatrical company's efforts to carry on as rehearsed with *The London Merchant*, George and Nell foist their servant Rafe onto the stage and into their own play of the *Knight of the Burning Pestle*. By convincing George and Nell that the heraldic device on Rafe's shield should be a burning pestle, the professional players manage to poke some fun at their insistent audience. Grocers typically used pestles (a club-shaped instrument) to grind ingredients for medicines, and pestles commonly figured on signs above shop doors. As a phallic symbol, the pestle on Rafe's shield also denotes his manly prowess as a knight errant. But while the pestle certainly is an appropriate symbol for a grocer errant, a burning one would also have suggested a phallus afflicted with syphilis (and the play continues the joke throughout the performance). The two plays, the professional troupe's *The London Merchant* and the citizens' impromptu performance of *The Knight of the Burning Pestle*, compete against one another, as each story tries to complete its individual plot.

The scene included here is the "Induction," a prelude to the play(s) proper. In the "Induction," we see Nell accompanying her husband to the theater, where both climb onto the stage. Audience members could pay extra to be seated on stage, where they could not only see intimately but also be seen by the rest of the audience. Seated upon the stage, the couple's redirecting of the play comments on Beaumont's perception of the power of audience members as paying customers, including women, on theatrical productions. *The Knight of the Burning Pestle* (perf. 1607; publ. 1613). (*The Knight of the Burning Pestle and A King and No King by Francis Beaumont*. Ed. Raymond M. Alden. Boston: D. C. Heath, 1910. 1–135.)

DOCUMENT: "INDUCTION" TO *THE KNIGHT OF THE BURNING PESTLE* (PERF. 1607; PUBL. 1613)

[Several Gentlemen, sitting on Stools upon the Stage. The Citizen (George), his Wife (Nell), and Rafe, below the stage, among the audience.]

[Enter Prologue, a person who comes out to give a preface or introduction to the play]

Prologue: From all that's near the Court, from all that's great
Within the compass of the City-walls,
We now have brought our scene.

Enter Citizen [mounting to the stage]

George: Hold your peace, good-man boy.

Prologue: What do you mean, sir?

George: That you have no good meaning. This seven years there hath been plays
at this house, I have observed it, you continually sneer at citizens; and now you
call your play? *The London Merchant.* Down with your title, boy! Down with
your title!

Prologue: Are you a citizen of the noble City?

George: I am.

Prologue: And a free-man, no longer under apprenticeship?

George: Yea, and a grocer.

Prologue: So, Grocer, then by your sweet favor, we intend no abuse to the City.

George: No sir, yes sir; if you were not resolved to play [tricks], what need you study
for new subjects, purposely to abuse your betters? Why could not you be
contented, as well as others, with plays glorifying the City of London and
members of the Citizenry?

Prologue: You seem to be an understanding man: what would you have us do, sir?

George: Why, present something notably in honor of the commons of the City
(London freemen, who are not aristocratic or royal).

Prologue [speaking sarcastically]: Why, what do you say to *The Life and Death of
Fat Drake*, or the *Repairing of Fleet- privies* and sewers?

George: I do not like that, but I will have a citizen, and he shall be of my own trade.

Prologue: Oh, you should have told us your mind a month ago; our play is ready to
begin now.

George: 'Tis all one for that; I will have a grocer, and he shall do admirable things.

Prologue: What will you have him do?

George: Marry, I will have him —

Nell (his wife, who is still below the stage): Husband, husband!

Rafe (also below): Peace, mistress!

Nell: Hold thy peace, Rafe; I know what I do, I warrant thee. Husband, husband!

George: What sayest thou, honey?

Nell: Let him kill a lion with a pestle, husband! Let him kill a lion with a pestle!

George: So he shall; I'll have him kill a lion with a pestle.

Nell: Husband, shall I come up, husband?

George: Aye, cunny. Rafe, help your mistress this way. Pray, gentlemen, make her a
little room. I pray you, sir, lend me your hand to help up my wife: I thank you, sir. So.

[Nell comes on the stage]

Nell: By your leave, gentlemen all, I'm something troublesome; I'm a stranger here;
I was never at one of these plays, as they say, before; but I should have seen *Jane
Shore* once, and my husband hath promised me any time this twelve-month to
take me to the *Bold Beauchamps*, but in truth he did not. I pray you bear with me.

George: Boy, let my wife and I have a couple of stools, and then begin; and let the
grocer do unusual and rarely accomplished feats.

Prologue: But, sir, we have never a boy to play him; every one hath a part already.

Nell: Husband, husband! for God's sake, let Rafe play him! Beshrew me if I do not
think he will go beyond them all.

George: Well remembered, wife. Come up, Rafe. I'll tell you, gentlemen, let them but lend him a suit of apparel, and necessaries, and by Gad, if any of the other actors come near to surpassing him, I'll be hanged.

[Rafe comes on the stage.]

Nell: I pray you, youth, let him have a suit of apparel. I'll be sworn, gentlemen, my husband tells you true: he will act you sometimes at our house, that all the neighbors cry out on him: he will fetch you up a spirited part so in the garret, that we are all as feared, I warrant you, that we quake again. We'll scare our children with him; if they be never so unruly, do but cry, Rafe comes, Rafe comes, to them, and they'll be as quiet as lambs. Hold up thy head, Rafe: show the gentlemen what thou canst do. Speak a huffing (loud bombastic) part; I warrant you the gentlemen will accept of it.

George: Do, Rafe, do.

Rafe [reciting almost entirely Hotspur's speech from Shakespeare's I Henry IV *(1.3.101 ff.)]:* By heaven, me thinks it were an easy leap.
To pluck bright honor from the pale-faced moon,
Or dive into the bottom of the sea,
Where never fathom line touches any ground,
And pluck up drowned honor from the lake of hell.

George: How say you, gentlemen? Is it not as I told you?

Nell: Nay, gentlemen, he hath played (amateur theater) before, my husband says, *Musidorus* before the officers of our Company.

George: Aye, and he should have played Jeronimo with a shoemaker, for a wager.

Prologue: He shall have a suit of apparel, if he will go in.

George: In, Rafe! In, Rafe! And make the grocers look good, if thou lovest me.

[Exit Rafe]

Nell: I warrant our Rafe will look finely when he's dressed.

Prologue: But what will you have it called?

George: *The Grocer's Honor.*

Prologue [sarcastically]: I think *The Knight of the Burning Pestle* were better.

Nell: I'll be sworn, husband, that's as good a name as can be.

George: Let it be so. Begin, begin! My wife and I will sit down.

Prologue: I pray you do.

George: What stately music do have you? You have oboes?

Prologue: Oboes? No.

George: No? I'm a thief if my mind did not give me so. Rafe plays a stately part, and he must needs have oboes. I'll be at the charge of them my self, rather then we'll be without them.

Prologue: So you are like to be.

George: Why, and so I will be: there's two shillings; let's have the town musicians of Southwark, they are as rare fellows as any are in England; and that will fetch them all over the water with vengeance, as if they were mad.

Prologue: You shall have them. Will you sit down then?

George: Come, wife.

Nell: Sit you merry all, gentlemen; I'm bold to sit amongst you, for my ease.

[Citizen and Wife sit down.]

Prologue: From all that's near the Court, from all that's great
Within the compass of the City-walls,
We now have brought our scene. Fly far from hence
All attacks and ridicule of individual persons, all immodest phrases,
Whatever may but show like vicious:
For wicked mirth never true pleasure brings,
But honest minds are pleased with honest things.
Thus much for that we do: but for Rafe's part—
You must answer for your self.
George: Take you no care for Rafe; he'll discharge himself, I warrant you.

[Exit Prologue.]

Wife: In faith, gentlemen, I'll give my word for Rafe.

AEMILIA LANYER (1569–1649)

Lanyer is the author of the first volume of original poetry to be published by an Englishwoman. The daughter of Italian Jewish musicians in the Tudor courts, Lanyer spent time in the households of Susan Bertie, Countess of Kent, and Margaret Russell, Countess of Cumberland. She was also the mistress to Elizabeth I's Lord Chamberlain, Henry Cary, Lord Hunsdon, but when she became pregnant, she was married to Alfonso Lanyer, a captain in the navy and also a court musician. *Salve Deus* includes numerous dedications to prominent royal and aristocratic women in the court of James I, a lengthy central poem depicting the crucifixion of Christ from women's points of view, and an appended country house poem—the first of this genre to be published in English. Within the narrative detailing Christ's passion, the narrator turns her attention to Pilate's wife, who presents an impassioned apology (or defense) of Eve in light of the atrocities perpetrated in the name of male authority. Lanyer's volume of poetry makes a sweeping and serious bid for the patronage needed to place her back in the court circles she inhabited with Hunsdon and the others. (*Salve Deus, Rex Judaeorum*, London: Valentine Simmes, 1611.)

DOCUMENT: "EVE'S APOLOGIE," FROM *SALVE DEUS, REX JUDAEORUM*

Now Pontius Pilate is to judge the Cause
Of faultlesse Jesus, who before him stands;
Who neither hath offended Prince, nor Lawes,
Although he now be brought in woefull bands:
O noble Governour, make thou yet a pause,
Doe not in innocent blood imbrue thy hands;
    But heare the words of thy most worthy wife,
    Who sends to thee, to beg her Saviours life.
Let barb'rous crueltie farre depart from thee,
And in true Justice take afflictions part;

Open thine eyes, that thou the truth mai'st see,
Doe not the thing that goes against thy heart,
Condemne not him that must thy Saviour be;
But view his holy Life, his good desert.
    Let not us Women glory in Mens fall,
    Who had power given to over-rule us all.
Till now your indiscretion sets us free,
And makes our former fault much lesse appeare;
Our Mother Eve, who tasted of the Tree,
Giving to Adam what shee held most deare,
Was simply good, and had no powre to see,
The after-comming harme did not appeare:
    The subtile Serpent that our Sex betraide,
    Before our fall so sure a plot had laide.
That undiscerning Ignorance perceav'd
No guile, or craft that was by him intended;
For had she knowne, of what we were bereav'd,
To his request she had not condiscended.
But she (poore soule) by cunning was deceav'd,
No hurt therein her harmelesse Heart intended:
    For she alleadg'd Gods word, which he denies,
    That they should die, but even as Gods, be wise.
But surely Adam can not be excusde,
Her fault though great, yet hee was most too blame;
What Weaknesse offerd, Strength might have refusde,
Being Lord of all, the greater was his shame:
Although the Serpents craft had her abusde,
Gods holy word ought all his actions frame,
    For he was Lord and King of all the earth,
    Before poore Eve had either life or breath.

Who being fram'd by Gods eternall hand,
The perfect'st man that ever breath'd on earth;
And from Gods mouth receiv'd that strait command,
The breach whereof he knew was present death:
Yea having powre to rule both Sea and Land,
Yet with one Apple wonne to loose that breath
    Which God had breathed in his beauteous face,
    Bringing us all in danger and disgrace.
And then to lay the fault on Patience backe,
That we (poore women) must endure it all;
We know right well he did discretion lacke,
Beeing not perswaded thereunto at all;
If Eve did erre, it was for knowledge sake,
The fruit beeing faire perswaded him to fall:
    No subtill Serpents falshood did betray him,
    If he would eate it, who had powre to stay him?
Not Eve, whose fault was onely too much love,
Which made her give this present to her Deare,

That what shee tasted, he likewise might prove,
Whereby his knowledge might become more cleare;
He never sought her weakenesse to reprove,
With those sharpe words, which he of God did heare:
    Yet Men will boast of Knowledge, which he tooke
    From Eves faire hand, as from a learned Booke.
If any Evill did in her remaine,
Beeing made of him, he was the ground of all;
If one of many Worlds could lay a staine
Upon our Sexe, and worke so great a fall
To wretched Man, by Satans subtill traine;
What will so fowle a fault amongst you all?
    Her weakenesse did the Serpents words obay;
    But you in malice Gods deare Sonne betray.
Whom, if unjustly you condemne to die,
Her sinne was small, to what you doe commit;
All mortall sinnes that doe for vengeance crie,
Are not to be compared unto it:
If many worlds would altogether trie,
By all their sinnes the wrath of God to get;
    This sinne of yours, surmounts them all as farre
    As doth the Sunne, another little starre.
Then let us have our Libertie againe,
And challendge to your selves no Sov'raigntie;
You came not in the world without our paine,
Make that a barre against your crueltie;
Your fault beeing greater, why should you disdaine
Our beeing your equals, free from tyranny?
    If one weake woman simply did offend,
    This sinne of yours, hath no excuse, nor end.
To which (poore soules) we never gave consent,
Witnesse thy wife (O Pilate) speakes for all;
Who did but dreame, and yet a message sent,
That thou should'st have nothing to doe at all
With that just man; which, if thy heart relent,
Why wilt thou be a reprobate with Saul?
    To seeke the death of him that is so good,
    For thy soules health to shed his dearest blood.

ELIZABETH CARY (1585–1639)

After she had been with him for more than twenty-five years of marriage and borne him eleven children, Cary's husband abandoned her when her conversion to Catholicism was made public in 1626, refusing her any contact with her children and leaving her destitute despite repeated royal orders that he provide maintenance. While most, if not all, of Cary's work was written before her separation, the theme of obedience and tyranny are central to *The Tragedy of Mariam, the Fair Queen of Jewry* (1613). By falsely making his people believe he has been executed abroad, Herod tests the loyalty of a number of characters in the play—most notably that of his wife. Although Mariam is faithful in terms of her body, her mind is less constant in terms of loving her husband, who has killed many of her relatives in order to attain his position on the throne. The Chorus's distinction between the outward actions of obedience and an obedience of the mind is one that Mariam must grapple with throughout the play. When the Chorus claims that "in a wife it is no worse to find / A common body, than a common mind," they are playing on the multiple meanings of "common," which means simultaneously "low-class" but also "held in common by a group." Thus, a "common woman" was a term for a prostitute (a woman held or "owned" in common by many men), suggesting that a wife whose mind was not entirely devoted to her lord and husband was no better than a whore, regardless of whether or not she has been unfaithful with another person. The Chorus is also working from an essential assumption about woman's status as *femme covert*. The practical implications of the notion that a married couple become "one" person—and that person is the husband who "covers" his wife—was a situation faced by many married couples, both literary and real, throughout the early modern period. A woman who claims her thoughts and her person as her own, according the Chorus, "usurps upon" her husband's right to sovereignty over her. While a question posed by the play concerns whether Mariam is guilty of a kind of petty treason, the play's answer is difficult to discern. Interestingly, while Mariam is executed at the end of the play, her sister-in-law, Salome, who engages in adulterous affairs, arranges the deaths of her husband, and advocates for divorce, is one of the few characters not dead at the end of the play. *The Tragedy of Mariam* is a closet drama, meant to be given a private dramatic reading but not performed onstage. The more private and elite nature of closet drama, which centers on lengthy discourses to explore political or philosophical questions, was also deemed more suited to aristocratic female writers. In addition to *Mariam*, Cary also wrote a dramatic prose history of King Edward II (*Specimens of British Poetesses: Selected and Chronologically Arranged*. Ed. Alexander Dyce. London: T. Rodd, 1825. 28–31.)

DOCUMENT: *CHORUS FROM ACT 3 OF THE TRAGEDY OF MARIAM, THE FAIR QUEEN OF JEWRY* (1613)

Chorus: 'Tis not enough for one that is a wife
To keep her spotless from an act of ill;
But from suspicion she should free her life,
And bare herself of power as well as will.
'Tis not so glorious for her to be free,
As by her own self restrained to be.
When she hath spacious ground to walk upon,
Why on the ridge should she desire to go?
It is no glory to forbear alone
Those things that may her honor overthrow:
But 'tis thankworthy, if she will not take
All lawful liberties for honor's sake.

That wife her hand against her fame doth rear,
That more than to her lord alone will give
A private word to any second ear;
[For to speak alone with a man not her husband puts her reputation at stake]
And though she may with reputation live,
Yet though most chaste, she doth her glory blot,
And wounds her honor, though she kills it not.
When to their husbands they themselves do bind,
Do they not wholly give themselves away?
Or give they but their body, not their mind,
Reserving that, though best, for others' prey?
No, sure, their thoughts no more can be their own,
And therefore should to none but her husband alone be known.
Then she usurps upon her husband's right,
That seeks to be by public language graced;
And though her thoughts reflect with purest light
Her mind, if not peculiar [or belonging to only one person], is not chaste.
For in a wife it is no worse to find
A common body, than a common mind.
And every mind, though free from thought of ill,
That out of glory seeks a worth to show,
When anyone's ears except their husband's they fill,
Doth in a sort her pureness overthrow.
Now Mariam had (but that to this she bent)
Been free from fear, as well as innocent.

THOMAS OVERBURY (1581–1613)

An English poet and essayist, Overbury was a courtier to James I and friend to Robert Carr. Overbury strenuously objected when Carr embarked upon an affair with Frances Howard, Lady Essex, the married daughter of a wealthy family. By this time, Carr had become a royal favorite of James I, and eventually the Lady Essex's marriage was annulled to enable to the pair to marry. When Overbury continued to object, he was imprisoned in the tower where he was soon poisoned, a crime to which Frances Howard admitted guilt but Robert Carr did not. "The Wife" (1614) is believed to have been written in order to convince Carr of the error of his infatuation with the adulterous Lady Essex. Overbury's portrait conforms to a number of conventional notions about women: He believes women to be physiologically cooler (which, among other things, made them more phlegmatic, less intellectual, and caused their reproductive organs to be on the inside rather than "popped outside" like men's). While Overbury presents the coverture of marriage ("she is he") as the ultimate destiny for a "good woman," such a woman "finds" a husband without "seeking" one, a sentiment echoed by other writers such as Juan Luis Vives. Once married, a "good wife" becomes her husband's best piece of personal property ("man's best moveable"). Following Overbury's murder, his portraits of women were published numerous times, singly as well as included in the many anthologies of Overbury's "characters" which appeared throughout the seventeenth century (*The Miscellaneous Works in Prose and Verse of Sir Thomas Overbury, now First Collected*. Ed. with notes by Edward F. Rimbault, London: Reeves and Turner, 1890. 47, 72–73).

DOCUMENT: "A GOOD WOMAN" (1614)

A good woman is a comfort, like a man. She lacks of him nothing but heat. Thence is her sweetness of disposition, which meets his stoutness more pleasantly; so wool meets iron easier than iron, and turns resisting into embracing. Her greatest learning is religion, and her thoughts are on her own sex, or on men, without casting the difference. Dishonesty never comes nearer than her ears, and then wonder stops it out, and saves virtue the labor. She leaves the neat youth telling his luscious tales, and puts back the serving man's putting forward with a frown: yet her kindness is free enough to be seen; for it hath no guilt about it: and her mirth is clear, that you may look through it, into virtue, but not beyond. She hath not behavior at a certain, but makes it to her occasion. She hath so much knowledge as to love it, and if she have it not at home, she will fetch it; for this sometimes in a pleasant discontent she dares chide her sex, though she use it never the worse, she is much within, and frames outward things to her mind, not her mind to them. She wears good clothes, but never better; for she finds no degree beyond decency. She hath a content of her own, and so seeks not a husband , but finds him. She is indeed most, but not much to description, for she is direct and one, and hath not the variety of ill. Now she is given fresh and alive to a husband, and she doth nothing more than love him, for she takes him to that purpose. So his good becomes the business of her actions, and she doth her self kindness upon him. After his, her chiefest virtue is a good husband. For she is he.

DOCUMENT: "CHARACTER OF A GOOD WIFE" (1614)

Is a man's best moveable, a twig or branch engrafted to the [husband's] stock, bringing forth sweet fruit [or heirs]; one that to her husband is more than friend, less than a trouble; an equal with him in the yoke. Calamities and troubles she shares alike, nothing pleases her that doth not him. She is relative in all; and he without her, but half himself. She is his absent hands, eyes, ears and mouth; his present and absent all. She frames her nature unto his howsoever: the hyacinth follows not the sun more willingly. Stubbornness and obstinacy are herbs that grow not in her garden. She leaves tattling to the gossips of the town, and is more seen than heard. Her household is her charge; her care makes her seldom non-resident. Her pride is but to be cleanly, and her thrift not to be prodigal. By her discretion she hath children, not naughty wantons; a husband without her is a misery in man's apparel; none but she hath an aged husband, to whom she is both a staff and a chair. To conclude, she is both wise and religious, which makes her all this.

RACHEL SPEGHT (1597–AFTER 1630)

The daughter of a London clergyman, Speght was nineteen years old when she became the first to respond in print to the misogynist pamphlet published under the pseudonym, Thomas Tell-Truth, whom Speght exposed as court fencing master, Joseph Swetnam. Swetnam's pamphlet claimed to be "an arraignment" (a formal charging or legal indictment) of women. A number of other writers, most probably writing pseudonymously like Swetnam, also responded in defense of women; Speght not only was the first to respond, but she did so under her own name. Although Speght clearly is capable of wit, which is demonstrated in both the epistles or letters addressed to her readers and to Swetnam, she also took the task of her defense seriously. She saw herself as a divinely inspired "David" to Swetnam's devilish "Goliath." Speght titles A *Muzzle for Melastomus* "an Apologetical Answer," meaning (as was the common use of the term) a formal defense against being wronged rather than an expression of contrition for a fault. In A *Muzzle for Melastomus*, Speght uses a thorough knowledge of scripture, secular history, and a keen use of logic to provide a point-by-point refutation of the arguments made in Swetnam's work. Swetnam claimed his work was a "bear-baiting," a popular "entertainment" in which trained dogs are set on a bear chained or otherwise confined in a pit. Speght picked apart the analogy, pointing out that if women were the bear, then Swetnam was the dog. She develops the point further by linking Swetnam to certain cynical philosophers. Not only were they known for their contemptuousness, churlishness, and disposition to find faults in others, etymologically the word "cynic" is related to the word meaning "dog-like." In 1621 Speght published *Mortalities Memorandum, with a Dreame Prefix'd*, a verse mediation on mortality and an endorsement of female education, which she dedicated to her godmother. (A *Muzzle for Melastomus, The Cynical Baiter of, and foul-mouthed Barker against Eve's Sex. Or an Apologetical Answer to that Irreligious and Illiterate Pamphlet made by Joseph Swetnam, and by him Intitled, The Arraignment of Women.* London: Nicholas Okes, 1617. A2r–B3v).

DOCUMENT: "TO ALL VIRTUOUS LADIES HONORABLE OR WORSHIPFUL, AND TO ALL OTHER OF EVE'S SEX FEARING GOD, AND LOVING THEIR JUST REPUTATION, GRACE AND PEACE THROUGH CHRIST, TO ETERNAL GLORY," FROM *A MUZZLE FOR MELASTOMUS* (1617)

It was the simile of that wise and learned North African rhetorician, Lactantius, that if fire, though but with a small spark kindled, be not at the first quenched, it may work great mischief and damage: So likewise may the scandals and defamations of the malevolent in time prove pernicious, if they be not nipped in the head at their first appearance. The consideration of this (right Honorable and Worshipful Ladies) hath incited me (though young, and the unworthiest of thousands) to encounter with a furious enemy to our sex, lest if his unjust imputations should continue without answer, he might insult and account himself a victor; and by such a conceit deal, as Historiographers report the viper to doe, who in the Winter time doth vomit forth her poison, and in the spring time sucketh the same up again, which becommeth twice as deadly as the former: And this our pestiferous enemy, by thinking to provide a more deadly poison for women, then already he hath foamed forth, may evaporate, by an addition unto his former illiterate Pamphlet (intituled *The Arraignment of Women*) a more contagious slander than he hath already done, and indeed hath threatened to do. Secondly, if it should have had free passage without any answer at all (seeing that *tacere* is, *quasi consentire*, or "to be silent is equivalent to consenting") the vulgar ignorant might have believed his Diabolical infamies to be infallible truths, not to be infringed; whereas now they may plainly perceive them to be but the scum of Heathenish brains, or a building raised without a foundation (at least from sacred Scripture) which the wind of Gods truth must needs cast down to the ground. A third reason why I have adventured to fling this stone at vaunting Goliath is, to comfort the minds of all Eve's sex, both rich and poor, learned and unlearned, with this Antidote, that if the fear of God reside in their hearts, in spite of all adversaries, they are highly esteemed and accounted of in the eyes of their gracious Redeemer, so that they need not fear the darts of envy or slander: For shame and disgrace (saith Aristotle) is the end of them that shoot such poisoned shafts. Worthy therefore of imitation is that example of the stoic philosopher Seneca, who when he was told that a certain man did exclaim and rail against him, made this mild answer; Some dogs bark more upon custom than from any natural inclination to be wicked; and some speak evil of others, not that the defamed deserve it, but because through custom and corruption of their hearts they cannot speak well of any. This I allege as a paradigmatical pattern for all women, noble & ignoble to follow, that they be not enflamed with choler against this our enraged adversary, but patiently consider of him according to the portraiture which he hath drawn of himself, his Writings being the very emblem of a monster.

This my brief Apology [or defense] (Right Honorable and Worshipful) did I enterprise, not as thinking my self more fit then others to undertake such a task, but as one, who not perceiving any of our Sex to enter the catalogues of soldiers heading to battle with this our grand enemy among men, I being fearless, because armed with the truth, which though often blamed, yet can never be shamed, and the Word of Gods Spirit, together with the example of virtues Pupils for a Shield, did no whit dread to combat with our said malevolent adversary. And if in so doing I shall be censured by the judicious to have the victory, and shall have given content unto the wronged, I have both hit the mark whereat I aimed, and obtained that prize which I desired. But if the Greek critic Zoilus shall adjudge me presumptuous in Dedicating this my written pledge unto personages of so high rank; both because of my insufficiency in literature and tenderness in years: I thus Apologize for my self; that seeing the Baiter of Women hath opened his mouth against noble as well as ignoble, against the rich as well as the poor; therefore meet it is that they should be joint spectators of this encounter: And withal in regard of my imperfection both in learning and age, I need so much the more to impetrate patronage from some of power to shield me from the biting censure and ridicule those who oftentimes setteth a rankling tooth into the sides of truth. Wherefore

I . . . have presumed to shelter my self under the wings of you (Honorable personages) against the persecuting heat of this firey and furious Dragon; desiring that you would be pleased, not to look so much *ad opus* ("at the work"), as *ad animum* ("at the spirit and intention"): And so not doubting of the favorable acceptance and censure of all virtuously affected, I rest Your Honors and Worships Humbly at commandment. Rachel Speght.

DOCUMENT: "NOT UNTO THE TRUEST IDIOT THAT EVER SET PEN TO PAPER, BUT TO THE CYNICALL BAYTER OF WOMEN, OR METAMORPHOSED MISOGYNIST, JOSEPH SWETNAM," FROM *A MUZZLE FOR MELASTOMUS* (1617)

From standing water, which soon putrefies, can no good fish be expected; for it produces no other creatures but those that are venomous or noisome, as snakes, adders, and such like. Similarly, no better stream can we look, should issue from your idle corrupt brain, than that whereto the rough of your fury (to use your own words) hath moved you to open the sluice. In which excrement of your roaring cogitations you have used such irregularities touching concordance, and observed so disordered a method, as I doubt not to tell you, that a very Rudimental Scholar would have quite put you down in both. You appear herein not unlike that Painter, who seriously endeavoring to portray Cupids Bow, forgot the String: for you being greedy to botch up your mingle mangle invective against Women, have not therein observed, in many places, so much as Grammar sense. But the emptiest Barrel makes the loudest sound; and so we will account of you.

Many propositions have you framed, which (as you think) make much against Women, but if one would make a Logical assumption, the conclusion would be flat against your own Sex. Your dealing wants so much discretion, that I doubt whether to bestow so good a name as the Dunce upon you: but my youth bids me keep within my bounds; and therefore I only say unto you, that your corrupt Heart and railing Tongue, hath made you a fit scribe for the Devil.

In that you have termed your virulent foam, the Bear-baiting of Women, you have plainly displayed your own disposition to be Cynical, in that there appears no other Dog or Bull to bait them but your self. Good had it been for you to have put on that Muzzle, which Saint James would have all Christians to "Speak not evil one of another": and then had you not seemed so like the Serpent Porphyrus, as now you do; which, though full of deadly poison, yet being toothless, hurteth none so much as himself. For you having gone beyond the limits not of Humanity alone, of Christianity, have done greater harm unto your own soul, than unto women, as may plainly appear. First, in dishonoring of God by palpable blasphemy, wresting and perverting every place of Scripture, that you have alleged; which by the testimony of Saint Peter, is to the destruction of them that so do. Secondly, it appears by your disparaging of, and opprobrious speeches against that excellent work of Gods hands, which in his great love he perfected for the comfort of man. Thirdly, and lastly, by this your hodge-podge of heathenish Sentences, Similes, and Examples, you have set forth your self in your right colors, unto the view of the world: and I doubt not but the Judicious will account of you according to your demerit: As for the Vulgar sort, which have no more learning then you have showed in your Book, it is likely they will applaud you for your pains.

As for your Bug-bear or advice unto Women, that whatsoever they do think of your Work, they should conceal it, lest in finding fault, they betray their galled backs to the world; in which you allude to that Proverb, "Rub a galled horse, and he will kick": Unto it I answer by way of Apology, that though every galled horse, being touched, doth kick; yet every one that kicks, is not galled: so that you might as well have said, that because burnt folks dread the fire, therefore none fear fire but those that are burnt, as made that illiterate conclusion which you have absurdly inferred.

In your Title Page, you arraign none but lewd, idle, perverse and unfaithful women, but in the Sequel (through defect of memory as it seemeth) forgetting that you had made a distinction of good from bad, condemning all in general, you advise men to beware of, and not to match with any of these six sorts of women, viz. Good and Bad, Fair and Foul, Rich and Poor: But this doctrine of Devils [forbidding marriage, which is not divine law (I Tim. 4:3)] Saint Paul, foreseeing would be broached in the latter times, gives warning of.

There also you promise a Commendation of wise, virtuous, and honest women, when as in the subsequent, the worst words, and filthiest Epithets that you can devise, you bestow on them in general, excepting no sort of Women. Herein may you be likened unto a man, which upon the door of a scurvy house sets this Superscription, "Here is a very fair house to be rented": whereas the door being opened, it is no better than a dog-hole and dark dungeon.

Further, if your own words be true, that you wrote with your hand, but not with your heart, then you are an hypocrite in Print: but it is rather to be thought that your Pen was the betrayer of the abundance of your mind, and that this was but a little mortar to daub up again the wall, which you intended to break down.

The revenge of your railing Work we leave to God, who hath appropriated vengeance unto himself, whose Pen-man hath included Railers in the Catalogue of them, that shall not inherit Gods Kingdome, and your self unto the mercy of that just Judge, who is able to save and to destroy.

Your undeserved friend, Rachel Speght.

HORATIO BUSINO (FL. 1617–1621)

A Roman Catholic priest, Busino served as chaplain to Piero Contarini, the Venetian Ambassador to England during the early seventeenth century. As part of a Venetian embassy, Busino travelled to England between 1617 and 1618, where his diary entries and official dispatches to Venice record numerous details about London excitement. He attended a number of civic entertainments, court masques, and plays in theaters during his stay. During one visit to the theater, he was approached by an "elegant dame." Busino's description of the woman never makes explicit her status, but his response to her suggests that he distinguishes her form the "respectable . . . ladies," perhaps imagining her as a prostitute or at least a woman of loose sexual morals. It is also quite possible, given this is a trick played on Busino, the "elegant dame" may have been a beautiful boy player. Anti-theatrical polemicists included such scenarios in their arguments for closing the theaters. ("Chaplain to the Venetian Ambassador during his trip to England in 1617–18." The Quarterly Review 102 (1857): 398–437, 416.)

DOCUMENT: FROM *A DISPATCH TO VENICE BY HORATIO BUSINO,* CHAPLAIN TO THE VENETIAN AMBASSADOR (1617)

These theatres are frequented by a number of respectable and handsome ladies, who come freely and seat themselves among the men without the slightest hesitation. On the evening in question his Excellency and the Secretary were pleased to play me a trick by placing me amongst a bevy of young women. Scarcely was I seated ere a very elegant dame, but in a mask, came and placed herself beside me. She asked me for my address both in French and English; and, on my turning a deaf ear, she determined to honor me by showing me some fine diamonds on her fingers, repeatedly taking off no fewer than three gloves, which were worn one over the other. This lady's bodice was of yellow satin richly embroidered, her petticoat of gold tissue with stripes, her robe of red velvet with a raised pile, lined with yellow muslin with broad stripes of pure gold. She wore an apron of point lace of various patterns: her head-tire was highly perfumed, and the collar of white satin beneath the delicately-wrought ruff struck me as extremely pretty.

MARY WROTH (1587–1651)

Wroth came from the famously literary Sidney family, which included her father, Robert, and her aunt, Mary Sidney Herbert, and her uncle Philip. In 1621 Wroth published a long prose romance, *The Countess of Montgomery's Urania,* to which were appended a sequence of sonnets entitled *Pamphilia to Amphilanthus* ("all-loving" to "lover-of-two"). Her work also includes a number of songs, two of which are reproduced here. Wroth's writing was especially influenced by the highly esteemed work of her aunt and especially her uncle, whose sonnet sequence *Astrophil and Stella* (star-lover and star) and prose romance *The Arcadia* are particularly significant works from the Renaissance. Both *The Urania* and *Pamphilia to Amphilanthus* explore such themes relating to love as constancy and inconstancy, pain and delight, and whether or not one has control over one's own will while in love. (*Specimens of British Poetesses: Selected and Chronologically Arranged.* Ed. Alexander Dyce. London: T. Rodd, 1825. 40–42.)

DOCUMENT: "SONG," FROM *THE COUNTESS OF MONTGOMERY'S URANIA*

Who can blame me, if I love?
Since Love before the world did move:

When I loved not, I despaired,
Scarce for handsomeness I cared;

Since so much I am refined,
As new framed of state and mind,
Who can blame me if I love,
Since Love before the world did move?

Some in truth of Love beguiled,
Have him blind and childish styled;
But let none in these persist,
Since so judging, judgment mist.
Who can blame me?

Love in chaos did appear:
When nothing was, yet he seemed clear:
Nor when light could be descried,
To his crown a light was tied.
Who can blame me?

Love is truth, and doth delight,
Whereas Honor shines most bright:
Reason's self doth Love approve,
Which makes us ourselves to love.
Who can blame me?

Could I my past time begin,
I would not commit such sin,
To live an hour, and not to love;
Since Love makes us perfect prove.
Who can blame me?

DOCUMENT: "SONG," FROM *PAMPHILIA TO AMPHILANTHUS*

Love, a child, is ever crying;
Please him, and he straight is flying;
Give him, he the more is craving,
Never satisfied with having.

His desires have no measure;
Endless folly is his treasure;
What he promiseth he breaketh;
Trust not one word that he speaketh.

He vows nothing but false matter;
And to cozen you will flatter;
Let him gain the hand, he'll leave you,
And still glory to deceive you.

He will triumph in your wailing;
And yet cause be of your failing:

These his virtues are, and slighter
Are his gifts, his favors lighter.

Feathers are as firm in staying;
Wolves no fiercer in their preying :
As a child then, leave him crying;
Nor seek him so given to flying.

ELIZABETH JOCELINE (1596–1622)

The child of parents who separated (divorce not being possible at the time), Joceline was raised by her grandfather, a bishop who believed in educating girls, providing her with training in languages, history, and other liberal arts. Fearing she would die in childbirth, and thus not be able to direct the rearing of her child firsthand, Joceline composed this small treatise as an educational legacy for her unborn child of unknown sex. Her fears were not without warrant, and she died nine days after the birth of her only child, a daughter. Contrary to her own educational experiences, Joceline was not a keen advocate for extensive education for girls. Her *Mother's Legacy*, although unfinished at the time of her death, was published posthumously in 1625 (*The Mother's Legacy to her Unborn Child by Elizabeth Joceline* [1625]. *Blackwood's Edinburgh Magazine* 71 [1852]: 491–497).

DOCUMENT: FROM *THE MOTHER'S LEGACY TO HER UNBORN CHILD*

If it be a daughter . . . I desire her bringing up may bee learning the Bible, as my sisters doe, good houswifery, writing, and good workes: other learning a woman needs not: though I admire it in those whom God hath blest with discretion, yet I desired not much in my owne, having seene that sometimes women have greater portions of learning, than wisdome, which is of no better use to them than a main saile to a flye-boat [or small skiff], which runs it under water. But where learning and wisdome meet in a vertuous disposed woman, she is the fittest closet for all goodnesse. Shee is like a well-ballanced ship that may beare all her saile. She is, Indeed, I should but shame my selfe, if I should goe about to praise her more.

But, my deare, though she have all this in her, she will hardly make a poore mans wife: Yet I leave it to thy will. If thou desirest a learned daughter, I pray God give her a wise and religious heart, that she may use it to his glory, thy comfort, and her owne salvation.

But howsoever thou disposest of her education, I pray thee labour by all meanes to teach her true humility, though I much desire it may be as humble if it be a son as a daughter; yet in a daughter I more feare that vice; Pride being now rather accounted a vertue in our sex worthy praise, than a vice fit for reproofe.

RICHARD BRATHWAITE (1588–1673)

The second son of a country gentleman (and therefore not the primary inheritor of the estate), Brathwaite was a poet, playwright, and pamphleteer, including a popular pair of conduct books for English gentlemen and gentlewomen. Following the popular reception of *The English Gentleman* in 1630, Brathwaite followed up with a companion piece, *The English Gentlewoman Drawn Out to the Full Body, Expressing What Habiliments [Apparel] Do Best Attire Her, What Ornaments Do Best Adorn her, What Complements Do Best Accomplish Her* (1631). His conduct book is aimed at promoting gentility, refinement, and of course chastity among elite women. The selection included here focuses on maintaining a stillness of both body and mind, even while remaining busy and undistracted by the lures of the world. Brathwaite also encourages gentlewomen to emulate Odysseus's wife, Penelope, who remained faithful even when her husband failed to return from war after twenty years. During the period of her husband's absence, Penelope staved off potential suitors by claiming she first needed to finish weaving her tapestry, a never-ending task because each night she secretly undid the day's work (Richard Brathwaite, *The English Gentlewoman*, London: 1631. 48–49).

DOCUMENT: "BEHAVIOR," FROM *THE ENGLISH GENTLEWOMAN* (1631)

You are taught to enter your chambers and be still. Still, and yet stirring still. Still from the clamors and turbulent insults of the world, still from the mutinous motions and innovations of the flesh, but never still from warring, wrestling, bickering, and battling with the leader of those treacherous associates, tyrannous assassins. Oh, should you consider what troops of furious and implacable enemies are ever laying in ambush for you; how many soul-tempting Sirens are warbling notes of ruin to delude you. . . . Make then your chamber your private theater, wherein you may act some devout scene to God's honor. Be still from the world but stirring towards God. Meditation, let it be your companion. . . . Let not a minute be misspent, lest security become your attendant. Be it in the exercise of your Needlework or any other manual employment: attempt that labor with some sweet meditation to God's honor. Choose rather with Penelope to weave and unweave, than to give Idleness the least leave: Wanton Wooers are time-wasters. They make you idolize yourselves, and consequently hazard the state of your souls. . . . Be you in your Chambers or private Closets; be you retired from the eyes of men; think how the eyes of God are on you. Do not say, the walls encompass me, darkness over-shadows me, the Curtain of night secures me: These be the words of an Adulteress. Therefore do nothing privately, which you would not do publicly. There is no retirement from the eyes of God. . . .

CHARLES II (1630–1685)

Upon the restoration of the monarchy with Charles II in 1660, the English theaters were reopened after having been closed since 1649. On January 15, 1662, and then later, on April 25, 1662, King Charles II signed patents authorizing the respective theater companies of William Davenant and Thomas Killigrew. The patents individually grant Davenant and Killigrew permission to procure or build playhouses and to offer a range of entertainments, including plays. Killigrew took on the repertory company of the King's Men, while Davenant took the company of the Duke of York's Players. Although the two were rivals, the royal warrants eliminated any other competition, providing the two men with exclusive rights to London theater. As part of the patents, Charles also authorized the performance on stage of women actors. Although no law has been discovered previously barring women from the stage, custom seems to have worked with the force of law— hence the need for a license permitting their appearance on stage. Apparently, the potential scandal of women publicly exposing themselves to voyeuristic audiences, rather than the homoerotic potential of males playing the roles of women, seems to have been viewed by the monarchy as the lesser of two evils. The patents are roughly similar, and therefore only the pertinent section from one is reproduced here. ("Two Patents." A New History of the English Stage. Vol. 1. Ed. Percy Hetherington Fitzgerald. London: Tinsley Brothers, 1882. 72–86.)

DOCUMENT: FROM THE 1662 ROYAL PATENT TO WILLIAM DAVENANT

And forasmuch as many plays formerly acted do contain several profane, obscene, and scurrilous passages, and the women parts therein have been acted by men in the habits of women, at which some have taken offence; for the pre-venting of these abuses for the future we do strictly charge, command, and enjoin that from henceforth no new play shall be acted by either of the said companies containing any passages offensive to piety and good manners, nor any old or revived play containing any such offensive passages as aforesaid, until the same shall be corrected and purged by the said masters or governors of the said respective companies from all such offensive and scandalous passages as aforesaid. And we do likewise permit and give leave that all the women's parts to be acted in either of the said two companies from this time to come may be performed by women, so long as these recreations, which by reason of the abuses aforesaid were scandalous and offensive, may by such reformation be esteemed not only harmless delights, but useful and instructive representations of human life, by such of our good subjects as shall resort to see the same.

THOMAS JORDAN (1612?–1685)

Jordan was an actor, poet, pamphleteer, and staunch supporter of Charles II. His collection includes numerous pro-royalist poems, depictions of various aristocrats and nobility, as well as prologues and epilogues for productions of plays in theaters that had recently been reopened following the restoration of Charles II in 1660. In addition to prologues for a number of Shakespeare's plays, Jordan wrote pieces for the first woman to act the role of Desdemona on a public English stage. Although the actor's name has been lost to the certainties of history, the actor may have been Margaret Hughes and Anne Marshall, both players in Thomas Killigrew's King's Company who are known to have taken this role. The prologue and epilogue address many of the concerns and arguments against women acting in public theater. It also alludes to recent political events to generate some of the speech's metaphors. In the analogy made between those who sit in the theater's most prestigious seats (in the "pit") and the judges who sat in the Star Chamber court (which was abolished in 1641 because of its link to tyranny and was commonly used as a metaphor of abusive authority), the speech calls into question the audience's right to make judgments on the play. Barebones, mentioned in the final line, alludes to the radical dissenter and preacher. A member of the Parliament during Cromwell's reign, Barebones, whose given name was Praise-God, was a vehemently outspoken opponent of the restoration of Charles II.

(A *Royal Arbor of Loyal Poesie* (1664). *Illustrations of Old English Literature*. Vol. 3. Ed. John Payne Collier. London: published privately, 1866. 24–25.)

DOCUMENT: A PROLOGUE, TO INTRODUCE THE FIRST WOMAN THAT CAME TO ACT ON THE STAGE IN THE TRAGEDY CALL'D *THE MOOR OF VENICE*

I come, unknown to any of the rest,
To tell you news: I saw the Lady dressed.
The Woman plays today: mistake me not;
No man in gown, or [serving-boy] Page in petty-coat;
A Woman to my knowledge, yet I can't
(If I should die) make affidavit on't.
Do you not twitter, Gentlemen? I know
You will be censuring; do't fairly though.
Tis possible a virtuous woman may
Abhor all sorts of looseness, and yet play,
Play on the stage, where all eyes are upon her.
Shall we count that a crime France calls an honour?
In other kingdoms husbands safely trust'um,
The difference lies only in the custom;
And let it be our custom, I advise:
I'm sure this Custom is better than [cutting it off],
And may procure us custom: hearts of flint
Will melt in passion when a woman's in't.
    But, Gentlemen, you that as judges sit
In the Star-Chamber of the house, the pit,
Have modest thoughts of her: pray, do not run
To give her visits when the Play is done.
With Dam me, your most humble servant, Lady.
She knows these things as well as you, it may be:
Not a bit there, dear Gallants; she doth know
Her own deserts, and your temptations too.
    But to the point. In this reforming age
We have intents to civilize the Stage.
Our women are defective, and so sized,
You 'd think they were some of the Guard disguised;
For (to speak truth) men act, that are between
Forty and fifty, wenches of fifteen;

With bone so large, and nerve so incompliant,
When you call Desdemona, enter Giant.
We shall purge every thing that is unclean,
Lascivious, scurrilous, impious or obscene;
And when we've put all things in this fair way,
Barebones himself may come to see a Play.

DOCUMENT: EPILOGUE [TO THE FIRST PERFORMANCE OF DESDEMONA BY AN ACTRESS]

And how d'ye like her? Come, what is 't ye drive at?
She's the same thing in public and in private;
As far from being what you call a Whore,
As Desdemona injur'd by the Moor.
Then, he that censures her in such a case
Hath a soul blacker then Othello's face.
   But, Ladies, what think you? for, if you tax
Her freedom with dishonour to your sex,
She means to act: no more, and this shall be
No other Play but her own Tragedy:
She will submit to none but your commands,
And take Commission only from your hands [i.e., your applause].

GLOSSARY

Amazons: Mythic tribe of warrior women. The image of the Amazon warrior queen was also linked to Elizabeth I as a way of signifying her power.

Annulment: The act of legally declaring a marriage as invalid from the start as a result of fraud (e.g., bigamy); consanguinity or degree of kinship (as in the case of Henry VIII's "divorce" from Catherine of Aragon); inability to produce children; or other canonical or legal impediments. Annulment rendered the marriage as if it had never taken place. Unlike **divorce**, an annulment was the only form of marital dissolution that permitted the parties to enter into a subsequent marriage. However, it also rendered any children from the annulled marriage illegitimate (as in the case of Mary and Elizabeth Tudor).

Aristocracy: Privileged ruling class whose power derived from inheritance of land and titles. Below the nobility, the aristocracy ranked above the **common people**, including the **middling sort**, and the **gentry**.

Banns of marriage: Public announcement made in church that a couple intends to marry. The Banns were read over a period of three Sundays prior to the actual wedding ceremony, providing an opportunity for anyone knowing of impediments (e.g., fraud or consanguinity) to the marriage to make their objection.

Bed trick: Theatrical plot device in which (typically) a man is tricked into believing he is having sex with one woman, but another woman is substituted without his knowledge. Shakespeare uses this device in *All's Well that Ends Well* and *Measure for Measure*. In both cases, the man is an unwilling husband who is tricked into having sex with his own wife, thus consummating their marriage.

Blason (also spelled blazon): Poetic device in which a poet praises a woman by presenting an inventory of the parts of her body, comparing each body part with a treasure or other metaphor of value. The blason is used in the biblical Song of Songs and Shakespeare's Sonnet 130, as well as at various moments in Shakespeare's plays, in the poems of John Donne, and in the poems of Aemilia Lanyer, to name a few.

Breeches part: Character played by a woman and involving the wearing of pants, or breeches.

Carting: Shaming ritual, like **charivari** and **skimmington**, in which a person not conforming to social mores was carried in a cart throughout the town, subjecting the offending person to public humiliation and ridicule.

Charivari: A shaming ritual akin to **skimmington** and **carting** used by neighbors as a kind of vigilante law to curb social deviance, especially the transgression of gendered or sexual mores. In response to households whose domestic violence disturbed the neighborhood peace—especially households in which wives dominated, abused, or beat their husbands, or were otherwise considered **shrews** or **scolds**—community members would parade through the streets making "rough music" with pots and pans and shouting in order to shame the offending neighbors into reforming their behavior. Because of its supposedly festive aura, charivari was believed capable of diffusing social tensions and serving as a means of reintegrating the offender back into the community.

Childbed: The bed in which a child is born; the state of a woman in labor.

Churching: The traditions and ceremonies of thanksgiving and purification connected to a woman's first attendance in church after giving birth, typically forty days after **confinement**.

Clandestine marriage: A marriage made secretly, without the reading of the Banns or the authorization of the parents or guardians. In the absence of witnesses, women in particular could find themselves in a precarious position if the man denied the marriage after deceiving them into consummating the marriage. Romeo and Juliet, Othello and Desdemona, and Fenton and Anne Page enter into clandestine marriages.

Closet drama: Typically an elite genre of drama written for private reading among a privileged coterie of writers and patrons, rather than for staged performance on a public stage. Closet dramas are typically tragedies in the tradition of the Greek playwright Seneca, and they involve characters debating philosophical, moral, or religious questions.

Commoners or common people: The majority of the population, as distinct from the nobility, **aristocracy**, and the **gentry**. The common people included everyone from the destitute through the **middling sort** of free citizens and the **yeomanry**, some of whom held positions of power in local governments and sometimes seats in parliament.

Companionate marriage: Marriage as a source of companionship, deriving from God's creation of Eve following his observation that "It is not good that the man should be alone" (Genesis 3.18).

Confinement: The period of a pregnant woman's being in **childbed** leading up to, during, and following the delivery of a child.

Cuckold: A term of derision for a man whose wife is unfaithful to him. Men who are cuckolds are often claimed figuratively to have horns.

Cucking stool: Instrument of torture consisting of a chair mounted at the end of long wooden beam and mounted to a large cart with a fulcrum allowing the chair, containing a person, to be dunked into a river, lake, or pond. Used to punish women convicted of being a **scold** or a witch. Also known as a **ducking stool** or **dunking stool**.

Degree: A person's relative position in the social hierarchy; the rank or class of a person.

Divorce a mensa et thoro: Literally, separation from bed and board, a legal separation in which the parties maintained separate households. Unlike in **annulment**, a divorced couple technically remained married in the eyes of the law and the church, and could not therefore remarry until the death of their spouse. Also unlike in an **annulment**, the children under divorce retained their legitimacy.

Dowry: The money and other property a wife brings to her husband upon her marriage; also called a **marriage portion**.

Ducking stool: See **cucking stool**.

Dunking stool: See **cucking stool**.

Elizabethan: Period during the reign of Elizabeth I from 1558 to 1603, and during which the first half of Shakespeare's career occurred.

Entailment: A legally set pattern by which property (lands, titles, and estates) is inherited by a series of predetermined recipients (e.g., eldest sons), so that an individual owner in the line of succession cannot bequeath the property to another person of his or her choice.

Equality in marriage: Not as in our time, when such a phrase would denote an equality of power between the two partners; rather, a similarity (equality) in age, class status, nationality, and religion.

Estate: Term used to designate a person's status, standing, degree of rank, or position in the world.

Femme covert: A woman whose legal status is under the cover or protection of a man; a married woman.

Femme sole: A single or widowed woman whose legal status is not covered by a man; a married woman whose legal status permits her to engage independently in business transactions, legal matters, or to work in a trade on her own, without her husband.

Gentry: Social status above the **middling sort** of the citizenry and yeomanry, but at the lower ranks of the **aristocracy**—typically small landowners with non-hereditary titles, such as knight (sir).

Gossips: Literally, god's siblings. A pregnant woman's female friends who are invited to be present at a birth; some of them may serve as godparents to the newborn. Conversely, the term also refers to trivial friendships among (often amoral) women.

Handfasting: A betrothal or public agreement to be married in the future; also can mean a **clandestine marriage**, made privately; sometimes can also mean a probationary form of marriage.

Housewife: The woman (usually the wife, but not always) who manages the affairs of a household.

Housewifery: The management of household affairs, including the production or procurement of food (including farming, preserving, and cooking), clothing (including spinning, weaving, and sewing), and other goods needed by the members of the household, as well as the overseeing of the servants and workers needed. Depending on her rank and the number of servants in her household, a housewife may personally participate in some, most, few, or none of these activities.

Jacobean: Period during the reign of James I (James VI of Scotland) from 1603 to 1625, during which the latter half of Shakespeare's career occurred.

Jointure: Property, land, or other wealth set aside for the maintenance of a wife in the event that she is widowed.

Lying in: The period of private confinement during which a woman gives birth; the state of being in **childbed**.

Maid: A young woman (usually unmarried) who is still a virgin; can also refer to a sexually inexperienced man. Also used with a defining word as prefix, as in chambermaid or lady's maid. While such "maids" may not necessarily be virgins, their sexual reputations needed to be untainted.

Marriage portion: The money and other property a wife brings to her husband upon her marriage; also called a **dowry**.

Middling sort: People of moderate means or of the middle class, but without titles.

Misogamy: Hatred or contempt for marriage.

Misogyny: Hatred or contempt for women as a group.

Patriarchy: Literally, rule by the father or patriarch; in England, the idea of the patriarch was used both literally and metaphorically to indicate a system of government by men. Thus some men were also under the control of men of higher rank, with the monarch as the supreme head beneath only God.

Petty (petit) treason: The murder of someone to whom the murderer owes loyalty and obedience, as a wife of her husband or a servant of his or her master. Although such convictions were rare, a wife found guilty of petty treason was delivered the same punishment as a traitor (often burning alive), while a husband convicted of murdering his wife was delivered the punishment of a murderer (typically hanging). The infidelities of Anne Boleyn and Catherine Howard resulted in convictions of treason (to place an illegitimate child on the throne is to usurp the rightful heir), and they were delivered the more noble punishment of beheading.

Primogeniture: System of inheritance in which the eldest son succeeded to titles and inherited the entire estate to the exclusion of any remaining younger siblings.

Querelle des femmes: Literally, "argument about women." A debate about the nature and value of women, beginning in the fifteenth century and continuing throughout the centuries, with some writers defaming women, some defending them, and others taking both sides as a rhetorical exercise in debate.

Romance: A genre term typically referring to a tale written in verse or prose that details the exploits of a chivalric hero, such as a knight or other adventurer, who lived long ago and far away. Philip Sidney and Mary Wroth wrote prose romances, while Margaret Tyler translated a Spanish romance into English. With respect to Shakespeare, the term includes such plays as *Cymbeline*, *The Winter's Tale*, and *The Tempest*.

Scold: Term used both colloquially and legally for a loud and argumentative woman whose speech disrupted the peace. While neighbors often dealt with scolds by means of **charivari** or **carting**, being a scold was also a legal crime. A woman brought to court and convicted could face such punishments as a fine but also the public humiliation of the public stocks, the **scold's bridle or brank,** or the **cucking stool.** Although rarely prosecuted in more modern times, the crime of being a scold was not officially removed from British law books until the mid-twentieth century.

Scold's brank, scold's bridle: Instrument of torture, sometimes similar to those used for horses and other livestock and sometimes a metal cage put over the head, used on a woman deemed a **scold.** The device prevented the woman from speaking by forcing her tongue down with a metal plate (a brank) inserted into her mouth. Women forced to wear the bridle or brank also were typically paraded through town.

Service: The condition of being a servant to a particular master or mistress (e.g., to be in service to the Countess of Cumberland).

Shrew: A boisterous, argumentative, ungovernable woman; a **scold.**

Skimmington: Carnivalesque shaming ritual, like **charivari** and **carting.** Community members stage a procession in which one of them impersonates a neighbor whose wife is a shrew or has **cuckolded** him. The ritual was used to enforce conformity to community social mores, especially that husbands should control their wives. The word seems to be connected to skimming ladles, as the impersonator typically wielded one during the procession.

Stuart: English rule by the Stuart family from 1603 to 1714, beginning with James I.

Sumptuary laws: Laws regulating, based on sex and **degree** or **estate,** who could wear what types and styles of clothing; fabrics; hosiery; feathers; and jewels; as well as ruffs at the neck or sleeves (none, single, or double); hats; and other accessories, such as daggers, swords, and rapiers. Conformity to sumptuary laws was a means of making obviously apparent a person's rank and privilege. However, such laws were difficult to enforce.

Tetralogy: A collection containing four separate works or volumes. Scholars often divide eight of Shakespeare's history plays into two tetralogies, or sets of four plays. The first tetralogy, written earlier, includes the three parts of *Henry VI* and *Richard III*; the second tetralogy includes *Richard II*, the two parts of *Henry IV*, and *Henry V*.

Tudor: English rule by the Tudor family from 1485 to 1603, beginning with Henry VII and ending with Elizabeth I.

Virago: Strong, manly, and warlike woman.

Waiting: The activity of someone who serves in attendance upon a superior, as in a lady-in-waiting.

Yeomanry: Group of free **commoners** (hence untitled) who own some land but cultivate or farm it themselves, rather than leasing it out to the labor of others; of respectable standing, but under the rank of the **gentry**.

BIBLIOGRAPHY

CULTURAL AND HISTORICAL BACKGROUND

Print Sources

Amussen, Susan Dwyer. *An Ordered Society: Gender and Class in Early Modern England*. New York: Columbia UP, 1994.

Bennet, Judith. *Ale, Beer, and Brewsters in England: Women's Work in a Changing World, 1300–1600*. New York: Oxford UP, 1996.

Boose, Lynda. "Scolding Brides and Bridling Scolds: Taming the Woman's Unruly Member." *Shakespeare Quarterly* 42 (1991): 179–213.

By Brown, Meg Lota, and Kari Boyd McBride. *Women's Roles in the Renaissance*. Westport, CT: Greenwood, 2005.

Bruster, Douglas. "Female-Female Eroticism and the Early Modern Stage." *Renaissance Drama* n.s. 24 (1993): 1–32.

Clark, Alice. *Working Life of Women in the Seventeenth Century*. 3rd ed. London: Routledge, 1992.

Davis, Natalie Zemon. "Women on Top: Symbolic Sexual Inversion and Political Disorder in Early Modern Europe." *Feminism and Renaissance Studies*. Ed. Lorna Hutson. Oxford: Oxford UP, 1999. 156–185.

Dolan, Frances. *Dangerous Familiars: Representations of Domestic Crime in England 1550–1700*. Ithaca: Cornell UP, 1994.

Duncan-Jones, Katherine. *Ungentle Shakespeare: Scenes from his Life*. London: Arden, 2001.

Elliott, Vivien. "Single Women in the London Marriage Market: Age, Status and Mobility, 1598–1619." R.B. Outhwaite, ed. *Marriage and Society: Studies in the Social History of Marriage*. New York: St. Martin's, 1982. 81–100.

Erickson, Amy Louise. *Women and Property in Early Modern England*. London: Routledge, 1993.

Ezell, Margaret. *Writing Women's Literary History*. Baltimore: Johns Hopkins UP, 1993.

Fildes, Valerie. *Breasts, Bottles, and Babies: A History of Infant Feeding*. Edinburgh: Edinburgh UP, 1986.

Findlay, Alison. *A Feminist Perspective on Renaissance Drama*. Oxford: Blackwell, 1999.

Frye, Susan. *Elizabeth I: The Competition for Representation*. Oxford: Oxford UP, 1993.

Greer, Germaine. *Shakespeare's Wife*. New York: Harper, 2008.

Hall, Kim F. *Things of Darkness: Economies of Race and Gender in Early Modern England*. Ithaca: Cornell UP, 1995.

Hannay, Margaret, ed. *Silent but for the Word: Tudor Women as Patrons, Translators, and Writers of Religious Works*. Kent: Kent State UP, 1985.

Henderson, Katherine U., and Barbara F. McManus, eds. *Half Humankind: Contexts and Texts of the Controversy about Women in England, 1540–1640*. Urbana: U of Illinois P, 1985.

Hendricks, Margo, and Patricia A. Parker, eds. *Women, "Race," and Writing in the Early Modern Period*. London: Routledge, 1994.

Hooper, Wilfred. "The Tudor Sumptuary Laws." *English Historical Review* 30 (1915): 433–449.

Howard, Jean. *The Stage and Social Struggle in Early Modern England*. London: Routledge, 1994.

Jed, Stephanie. *Chaste Thinking: The Rape of Lucretia and the Birth of Humanism*. Bloomington: Indiana UP, 1989.

Jordan, Constance. *Renaissance Feminism: Literary Texts and Political Models*. Ithaca: Cornell UP, 1990.

Jones, Ann Rosalind, and Peter Stallybrass. *Renaissance Clothing and the Materials of Memory*. Cambridge: Cambridge UP, 2000.

Kelly-Gadol, Joan. "Did Women Have a Renaissance?" *Women, History, and Theory: The Essays of Joan Kelly*. Chicago: U of Chicago P, 1984. 19–50.

Klein, Joan Larsen. *Daughters, Wives and Widows: Writings by Men about Women and Marriage in England, 1500–1640*. Urbana: U of Illinois P, 1992.

Laqueur, Thomas. *Making Sex: Body and Gender from the Greeks to Freud*. Cambridge, MA: Harvard UP, 1992.

Levin, Carole. *The Heart and Stomach of a King: Elizabeth I and the Politics of Sex and Power*. Philadelphia: U of Pennsylvania P, 1994.

Loomba, Ania. *Gender, Race, Renaissance Drama*. Manchester: Manchester UP, 1989.

Maclean, Ian. *The Renaissance Notion of Woman*. Cambridge: Cambridge UP, 1983.

Mendelson, Sara, and Patricia Crawford. *Women in Early Modern England 1550–1720*. Oxford: Clarendon, 1998.

Miller, Naomi J., and Naomi Yavneh, eds. *Maternal Measures: Figuring Caregiving in the Early Modern Period*. Aldershot: Ashgate, 2000.

Orlin, Lena. *Private Matters and Public Culture in Post-Reformation England*. Ithaca: Cornell UP, 1994.

Pacheco, Anita, ed. *A Companion to Early Modern Women's Writing*. Oxford: Blackwell, 2002.

Paster, Gail Kern. *The Body Embarrassed: Drama and the Disciplines of Shame in Early Modern England*. Ithaca: Cornell UP, 1993.

Peters, Christine. *Women in Early Modern Britain, 1450–1640*. Houndsmills: Palgrave Macmillan, 2004.

Rubin, Gayle. "The Traffic in Women: Notes on the 'Political Economy' of Sex." *Towards an Anthropology of Women*. Reina Reiter, ed. New York: Monthly Review, 157–210.

Smith, Hilda, ed. *Women Writers and the Early Modern British Political Tradition*. Cambridge: Cambridge UP, 1998.

Stallybrass, Peter. "Patriarchal Territories: The Body Enclosed." *Rewriting the Renaissance: The Discourses of Sexual Difference in Early Modern Europe*. Maureen Quilligan and Nancy J. Vickers, eds. Chicago: U of Chicago P, 1986. 123–142.

Stone, Lawrence. *The Family, Sex, and Marriage in England, 1500–1800*. New York: Harper, 1986.

Tileny, Edmund. *The Flower of Friendship: A Renaissance Dialogue Contesting Marriage*. Edited with an introduction, Valerie Wayne. Ithaca: Cornell UP, 1994.

Walker, Julia, ed. *Dissing Elizabeth: Negative Representations of Gloriana*. Durham: Duke UP, 1998.

Woodbridge, Linda. *Women and the English Renaissance: Literature and the Nature of Womankind, 1540–1640*. Urbana: U of Illinois P, 1984.

Wrightson, Keith. *English Society, 1580–1680*. London: Routledge, 1982.

TEXTS BY FEMALE WRITERS CONTEMPORARY WITH SHAKESPEARE

Askew, Anne. *The Examinations of Anne Askew*. Ed. Elaine V. Beilin. Oxford: Oxford UP, 1996.

Cary, Elizabeth. *The Tragedy of Mariam*. Ed. Barry Weller and Margaret Ferguson. Berkeley: U of California P, 1994.

Cavendish, Margaret. *The Blazing World and Other Writings*. Ed. Kate Lilley. New York: Penguin Classics, 1994.

Cerasano, Susan, and Marion Wynne-Davies. *Renaissance Drama by Women: Texts and Documents*. London: Routledge, 1996.

Clarke, Danielle, ed. *Isabella Whitney, Mary Sidney, and Aemelia Lanyer: Renaissance Women Poets*. New York: Penguin Classics, 2000.

Clifford, Anne. *The Diaries of Lady Anne Clifford*. Ed. D. J. H. Clifford. Wolfeforo Falls, NH: Alan Sutton, 1992.

Lanyer, Aemilia. *The Poems of Aemilia Lanyer: Salve Deus Rex Judaeorum*. Ed. Susanne Woods. Oxford: Oxford UP, 1993.

Martin, Randall, ed. *Women Writers in Renaissance England*. New York: Longman, 1997.

Speght, Rachel. *The Polemics and Poems of Rachel Speght*. Ed. Barbara Kiefer Lewalski. Oxford: Oxford UP, 1996.

Stuart, Arabella. *The Letters of Lady Arbella Stuart*. Ed. Sara Jayne Steen. Oxford: Oxford UP, 1994.

Travitsky, Betty, ed. *The Paradise of Women: Writings by Englishwomen of the Renaissance*. New York: Columbia U, 1989.

Wroth, Mary. *The Poems of Lady Mary Wroth*. Ed. Josephine A. Roberts. Baton Rouge: Louisiana State UP, 1992.

SHAKESPEARE'S PLAYS AND POEMS

Bibliographical

Kolin, Philip C. *Shakespeare and Feminist Criticism: Annotated Bibliography and Commentary*. New York: Garland, 1991.

Kujoory, Parvin. *Shakespeare and Minorities: An Annotated Bibliography, 1970–2000*. London: Scarecrow, 2001.

Multigenre works

Adelman, Janet. *Suffocating Mothers: Fantasies of Maternal Origin in Shakespeare's Plays, Hamlet to the Tempest*. New York: Routledge, 1991.

Bamber, Linda. *Comic Men, Tragic Women: A Study of Gender and Genre in Shakespeare*. Stanford: Stanford UP, 1982.

Barker, Deborah E. and Ivo Kamps, eds. *Shakespeare and Gender: A History*. London: Verso, 1995.

Belsey, Catherine. *Shakespeare and the Loss of Eden: The Construction of Family Values in Early Modern Culture*. New Brunswick, NJ: Rutgers UP, 1999.

Callaghan, Dympna, ed. *A Feminist Companion to Shakespeare*. Oxford: Blackwell, 2000.

Chedgzoy, Kate, ed. *Shakespeare, Feminism and Gender*. New York: Palgrave, 2001.

Dash, Irene. *Wooing, Wedding, and Power: Women in Shakespeare's Plays*. New York: Columbia UP, 1981.

Dusinberre, Juliet. *Shakespeare and the Nature of Women*. 3rd ed. London: Palgrave MacMillan, 2003.

Erickson, Peter. *Rewriting Shakespeare, Rewriting Ourselves*. Los Angeles: U of California P, 1991.

Gangi, Mario di. "Queering the Shakespearean Family." *Shakespeare Quarterly* 47.3 (1996): 269–290.

Jardine, Lisa. *Still Harping on Daughters*. New York: Columbia UP, 1989.

Kahn, Coppélia. *Man's Estate: Masculine Identity in Shakespeare*. Berkeley: U of California P, 1981.

———. *Roman Shakespeare: Warriors, Wounds, and Women*. New York: Routledge, 1997.

Lenz, Carolyn, and Gayle Greene and Carol Neely, eds. *The Woman's Part: Feminist Criticism of Shakespeare*. Urbana: U of Illinois P, 1983.

Neely, Carol Thomas. *Distracted Subjects: Madness and Gender in Shakespeare and Early Modern Culture*. Ithaca: Cornell UP, 2004.

Newman, Karen. *Fashioning Femininity and English Renaissance Drama*. Chicago: U of Illinois P, 1991.

Novy, Marianne, ed. *Cross-cultural Performances: Differences in Women's Re-visions of Shakespeare*. Urbana: U of Illinois P, 1993.

———. *Women's Re-visions of Shakespeare: On the Responses of Dickinson, Woolf, Rich, H.D., George Eliot, and Others*. Urbana: U of Illinois P, 1990.

Roberts, Jeanne Addison. *The Shakespearean Wild: Geography, Genus, and Gender*. Lincoln: U of Nebraska P, 1994.

Thompson, Ann, and Sasha Roberts, eds. *Women Reading Shakespeare, 1660–1900: An Anthology of Criticism*. Manchester: Manchester UP, 1997.

Traub, Valerie. *Desire and Anxiety: Circulations of Sexuality in Shakespearean Drama*. London: Routledge, 1992.

Wayne, Valerie, ed. *The Matter of Difference: Materialist Feminist Criticism of Shakespeare*. Ithaca: Cornell UP, 1991.

SPECIFIC PLAYS AND/OR GENRES

Histories

Desens, Marliss C. "Cutting Women Down to Size in the Olivier and Loncraine Films of *Richard III*." *Shakespeare Performed: Essays in Honor of R. A. Foakes*. Grace Ioppolo, ed. Newark: U of Delaware P, 2000. 260–272.

Holderness, Graham. "'A Woman's War': Feminist Reading of Richard II." *Shakespeare Left and Right*. Ivo Kamps, ed. New York: Routledge, 1991. 167–183.

Howard, Jean, and Phyllis Rackin. *Engendering a Nation: A Feminist Account of Shakespeare's English Histories*. London: Routledge, 1997.

Kim, Hwa-Seon. "Witches, Transvestites, and Dangerous Female Bodies: A Feminist Reading of Joan of Arc in *1 Henry VI*. *Feminist Studies in English Literature* 6.2 (1998): 37–59.

Levin, Carole. "'Murder Not Then the Fruit within My Womb': Shakespeare's Joan, Foxe's Guernsey Martyr, and Women Pleading Pregnancy in Early Modern English History and Culture." *Quidditas: Journal of the Rocky Mountain Medieval and Renaissance Association* 20 (1999): 75–93.

Lowe, Veronica. "'These Women Are Shrewd Tempters with Their Tongues': Women, Speech, and Power in Shakespeare's First Tetralogy." *Southeast Asian Review of English* 37 (1998): 74–92.

Maguire, Laurie E. "'Household Kates': Chez Petruchio, Percy, and Plantagenet." *Gloriana's Face: Women, Public and Private, in the English Renaissance.* S. P. Cerasano and Marion Wynne-Davies, eds. Detroit: Wayne State UP, 1992. 129–165.

Rackin, Phyllis. "Women's Roles in the Elizabethan History Plays." *Cambridge Companion to Shakespeare's History Plays.* Michael Hattaway, ed. Cambridge: Cambridge UP; 2002. 71–85.

Comedies

Aspinall, Dana E., ed. *The Taming of the Shrew: Critical Essays.* New York: Routledge, 2002.

Barker, Simon, ed. *Shakespeare's Problem Plays: Contemporary Critical Essays.* New York: Palgrave, 2005.

Calvo, Clara. "In Defence of Celia: Discourse Analysis and Women's Discourse in *As You Like It*." *Essays and Studies* 47 (1994): 91–115.

Cotton, Nancy. "Castrating (W)itches: Impotence and Magic in *The Merry Wives of Windsor*." *Shakespeare Quarterly* 38.3 (198): 321–326.

Coyle, Martin, ed. *The Merchant of Venice: Contemporary Critical Essays.* New York: Palgrave, 1998.

Desmet, Christy. "Disfiguring Women with Masculine Tropes: A Rhetorical Reading of *A Midsummer Night's Dream*." *A Midsummer Night's Dream: Critical Essays.* Dorothea Kehler, ed. New York: Garland, 1998. 299–329.

Dolan, Frances, ed. *The Taming of the Shrew: Texts and Contexts.* New York: St. Martin's, 1996.

Dowd, Michelle M. "Labours of Love: Women, Marriage, and Service in *Twelfth Night* and *The Compleat Servant-Maid*." *Shakespeare and the Bonds of Service.* Michael Neill, ed. Aldershot: Ashgate, 2005. 103–126.

Gay, Penny. *As She Likes it: Shakespeare's Unruly Women.* New York: Routledge, 1994.

Hall, Kim F. "Guess Who's Coming to Dinner? Colonization and Miscegenation in *The Merchant of Venice*." *Renaissance Drama* 23 (1992): 87–111.

Jones, Ann Rosalind. "Revenge Comedy: Writing, Law, and the Punishing Heroine in *Twelfth Night*, *The Merry Wives of Windsor*, and *Swetnam the Woman-Hater*. *Shakespearean Power and Punishment.* Gillian Murray Kendall, ed. Madison, NJ: Fairleigh Dickinson UP, 1998. 23–38.

Kaplan, M. Lindsay. "Jessica's Mother: Medieval Constructions of Jewish Race and Gender in *The Merchant of Venice*." *Shakespeare Quarterly* 58.1 (2007): 1–30.

Londré, Felicia Hardison, ed. *Love's Labour's Lost: Critical Essays.* New York: Routledge, 2001.

Tomarken, Edward, ed. *As You Like It from 1600 to the Present: Critical Essays.* New York: Garland Publishing, 1997.

Tvordi, Jessica. "Female Alliance and the Construction of Homoeroticism in *As You Like It* and *Twelfth Night.*" *Maids and Mistresses, Cousins and Queens: Women's Alliances in Early Modern England.* Susan Frye, et al., ed. New York: Oxford UP, 1999. 114–130.

Wynne-Davies, Marion, ed. *Much Ado about Nothing and The Taming of the Shrew.* Basingstoke: Palgrave, 2001.

Tragedies

Berry, Philippa. *Shakespeare's Feminine Endings: Disfiguring Death in the Tragedies.* London: Routledge, 1999.

Brown, Elizabeth A. "'Companion Me with My Mistress': Cleopatra, Elizabeth I, and Their Waiting Women." *Maids and Mistresses, Cousins and Queens: Women's Alliances in Early Modern England.* Susan Frye, et al., eds. New York: Oxford UP, 1999. 131–145.

Callaghan, Dympna. *Woman and Gender in Renaissance Tragedy: A Study of King Lear, Othello, The Duchess of Malfi and The White Devil.* Atlantic Highlands: Humanities, 1989.

Coyle, Martin, ed. *Hamlet: Contemporary Critical Essays.* New York: Palgrave, 1992.

Daileader, Celia R. *Racism, Misogyny, and the Othello Myth: Inter-racial Couples from Shakespeare to Spike Lee.* Cambridge: Cambridge UP, 2005.

Garner, Shirley Nelson, and Madelon Sprengnether, eds. *Shakespearean Tragedy and Gender.* Bloomington: Indiana UP, 1996.

Gruber, Elizabeth. "Insurgent Flesh: Epistemology and Violence in *Othello* and *Mariam.*" *Women's Studies: An Interdisciplinary Journal* 32.4 (2003): 393–410.

Halio, Jay L., ed. *Shakespeare's Romeo and Juliet: Texts, Contexts, and Interpretations.* Newark, DE: U of Delaware P, 1995.

Hamer, Mary. *Signs of Cleopatra: History, Politics, Representation.* New York: Routledge, 1992.

McBride, Kari Boyd, ed. *Domestic Arrangements in Early Modern England.* Pittsburgh, PA: Duquesne UP, 2002.

Mullaney, Steven. "Mourning and Misogyny: *Hamlet, The Revenger's Tragedy,* and the Final Progress of Elizabeth I, 1600–1607." *Centuries' Ends, Narrative Means.* R. Newman, ed. Stanford, CA: Stanford UP, 1996. 238–260.

Newman, Karen. "'And wash the Ethiop white': Femininity and the Monstrous in *Othello.*" *Shakespeare Reproduced.* Eds. Jean Howard and Marion F. O'Connor. New York: Methuen, 1987. 141–162.

Orlin, Lena Cowen, ed. *Othello: Contemporary Critical Essays.* New York: Palgrave, 2004.

Parker, Patricia. "*Othello* and *Hamlet*: Dilation, Spying, and the 'Secret Place' of Woman." *Shakespeare Reread: The Texts in New Contexts*. Russ McDonald, ed. Ithaca: Cornell UP, 1994. 105–146.

Romanska, Magda. "Ontology and Eroticism: Two Bodies of Ophelia." *Women's Studies* 34 (2005): 485–513.

Rowe, Katherine. "The Politics of Sleepwalking: American Lady Macbeths." *Shakespeare Survey* 57 (2004): 126–136.

Seidel, Monika. "Room for Asta: Gender Roles and Melodrama in Asta Nielsen's Filmic Version of *Hamlet* (1920)." *Film/Literature Quarterly* 33.3 (2002): 208–216.

Showalter, Elaine. "Representing Ophelia: Women, Madness, and the Responsibilities of Feminist Criticism." *Shakespeare and the Question of Theory*. Patricia Parker and Geoffrey Hartman, eds. New York: Methuen, 1985. 77–94.

White, R. S. *Romeo and Juliet: Contemporary Critical Essays*. New York: Palgrave, 2001.

Woodbridge, Linda, and Sharon Beehler, eds. *Women, Violence, and English Renaissance Literature: Essays Honoring Paul Jorgensen*. Tempe, AZ: Arizona Center for Medieval and Renaissance Studies, 2003.

Romances

Adelman, Janet. "Masculine Authority and the Maternal Body: The Return to Origins in *Cymbeline*." *Shakespeare: The Last Plays*. Kiernan Ryan, ed. London: Longman, 1999. 107–133.

Erickson, Peter B. "Patriarchal Structures in *The Winter's Tale*." *PMLA: Publications of the Modern Language Association of America* 97.5 (1982): 819–829.

Johnson, Jeffrey. "'Which 'Longs to Women of All Fashion': Churching and Shakespeare's *The Winter's Tale*." *Early Theatre* 7.2 (2004): 75–85.

Kalpin, Kathleen. "Framing Wifely Advice in Thomas Heywood's *A Curtaine Lecture* and Shakespeare's *The Winter's Tale*." *SEL: Studies in English Literature, 1500–1900* 48.1 (2008): 131–146.

Kehler, Dorothea. "Teaching the Slandered Women of *Cymbeline* and *The Winter's Tale*." *Approaches to Teaching Shakespeare's The Tempest and Other Late Romances*. Maurice Hunt, ed. New York: Modern Language Association of America, 1992. 80–86.

Mazzola, Elizabeth. "'Slippery Wives' and Other Missing Persons: Disappearing Acts in *The Winter's Tale*." *Women's Studies: An Interdisciplinary Journal* 24 (1995): 219–227.

Murphy, Patrick M., ed. *The Tempest: Critical Essays*. New York: Routledge, 2001.

Van Elk, Martine. "'Our Praises Are Our Wages': Courtly Exchange, Social Mobility, and Female Speech in *The Winter's Tale*." *Philological Quarterly* 79.4 (2000): 429–457.

Vanita, Ruth. "Mariological Memory in *The Winter's Tale* and *Henry VIII*." *SEL: Studies in English Literature, 1500–1900* 40.2 (2000): 311–337.

Wayne, Valerie. "The Woman's Parts of *Cymbeline*." *Staged Properties in Early Modern English Drama*. Jonathan Gil Harris and Natasha Korda eds. Cambridge: Cambridge UP, 2002. 288–315.

Sonnets and Poems

Belsey, Catherine. "Tarquin Dispossessed: Expropriation and Consent in *The Rape of* Lucrece." *Shakespeare Quarterly* 52.3 (2001): 315–335.

Berry, Philippa. "Woman, Language, and History in *The Rape of Lucrece*." *Shakespeare Survey* 44 (1991): 33–39.

Callaghan, Dympna. *Shakespeare's Sonnets*. Oxford: Blackwell, 2007.

Duncan-Jones, Katherine. "Much Ado with Red and White: The Earliest Readers of Shakespeare's *Venus and Adonis* (1593)." *Review of English Studies* 44 (1993): 479–501.

Feinberg, Nona. "Erasing the Dark Lady: Sonnet 138 in the Sequence." *Assays: Critical Approaches to Medieval and Renaissance Texts* 4 (1987): 97–108.

Grazia, Margreta de. "The Scandal of Shakespeare's Sonnets." *Shakespeare Survey* 46 (1994): 35–49.

Greenstadt, Amy. "'Read It in Me': The Author's Will in *Lucrece*." *Shakespeare Quarterly* 57.1 (2006): 45–70.

Hall, Michael "Lewd but Familiar Eyes: The Narrative Tradition of Rape and Shakespeare's *The Rape of Lucrece*." *Women, Violence, and English Renaissance Literature: Essays Honoring Paul Jorgensen*. Eds. Linda Woodbridge and Sharon Beehler. Tempe, AZ: Arizona Center for Medieval and Renaissance Studies, 2003. 51–72.

Kahn, Coppelia. "The Rape in Shakespeare's *Lucrece*" *Shakespeare Studies* 9: (1976): 45–72.

Kolin, Philip C., ed. *Venus and Adonis: Critical Essays*. New York: Garland; 1997.

MacDonald, Joyce Green. "Speech, Silence, and History in *The Rape of Lucrece*." *Shakespeare Studies* 22 (1994): 77–103.

Roberts, Josephine A. "'Thou Maist Have Thy Will': The Sonnets of Shakespeare and His Stepsisters." *Shakespeare Quarterly* 47.4 (1996): 407–423.

Staub, Susan C. "'My Throbbing Heart Shall Rock You Day and Night': Shakespeare's Venus, Elizabeth, and Early Modern Constructions of Motherhood." *The Literary Mother: Essays on Representations of Maternity and Child Care*. Susan C. Staub, ed. Jefferson, NC: McFarland, 2007. 15–32.

Traub, Valerie. "Sex without Issue: Sodomy, Reproduction, and Signification in Shakespeare's Sonnets." *Shakespeare's Sonnets: Critical Essays*. Ed. James Schiffer. New York: Garland, 2000. 431–452.

Vickers, Nancy. "'The Blazon of Sweet Beauty's Best': Shakespeare's *Lucrece*." Patricia Parker and Geoffrey Hartman, eds. *Shakespeare and the Question of Theory*. London: Methuen, 1985. 95–116.

ELECTRONIC RESOURCES

The Brown University Women Writers Project and *Renaissance Women Online*. http://www.wwp.brown.edu.

The Complete Works of William Shakespeare. Massachusetts Institute of Technology. http://shakespeare.mit.edu.

Early Modern Resources. Sharon Howard. http://www.earlymodernweb.org .uk/emr.

Emory Women Writers Resource Project. http://chaucer.library.emory.edu/wwrp.

Folger Shakespeare Library. http://www.folger.edu.

In Her Own Words: Elizabeth I Onstage and Online. Brown University. http://www .wwp.brown.edu/about/rich/QEIindex.html.

Internet Shakespeare Editions. University of Victoria. http://internetshakespeare .uvic.ca/index.html.

Life in Elizabethan England. Maggie Pierce Secara. http://elizabethan.org.

Luminarium. Anniina Jokinen. http://www.luminarium.org/lumina.htm.

Mr. William Shakespeare and the Internet. Palomar College. http://daphne.palomar .edu/shakespeare.

The National Portrait Gallery. http://www.npg.org.uk.

The Orlando Project. University of Alberta. http://www.ualberta.ca/orlando.

Oxford English Dictionary. Oxford University Press. http://www.oed.com.

The Perdita Project. Nottingham Trent University. http://human.ntu.ac.uk/research/ perdita.

Shakespeare's Globe. http://www.shakespeares-globe.org.

Touchstone. British Library. http://www.touchstone.bham.ac.uk.

Tudor History. Lara Eakins. http://www.tudorhistory.org.

INDEX

About the Author

Theresa D. Kemp is Professor of English and women's studies at the University of Wisconsin, Eau Claire. Her articles on early modern British women's writings have appeared in *Literature Compass*, *Clio*, and *Renaissance Quarterly*. Since 1989 she has been a member of the Editorial Collective for *Feminist Teacher* (University of Illinois Press).